International Nuclear Export Controls and Non-Proliferation

This book examines the evolution of international nuclear non-proliferation trade controls over time.

The book argues that the international nuclear export controls have developed in a sub-optimal way as a result of a non-proliferation collective action problem. This has resulted in competition among suppliers, owing to the absence of an overarching effective system of control. While efforts have been undertaken to address this collective action problem and strengthen controls over time, these measures have been inherently limited, it is argued here, because of the same structural factors and vested interests that led to the creation of the problem in the first place. This study examines international controls from the beginning of the nuclear age and early efforts to control the atom, up to more recent times and the challenge posed by Iranian and North Korean nuclear ambitions. Drawing on a rich body of original archival research and interviews, the book demonstrates that the collective action problem has restrained cooperation in preventing nuclear proliferation and that gaps persist in the international nuclear trade control regime.

This book will be of much interest to students of nuclear proliferation and arms control, security studies, and International Relations.

Ian J. Stewart is Executive Director of the James Martin Center for Nonproliferation Studies in Washington DC, USA.

Routledge Global Security Studies

Series Editors: Aaron Karp and Regina Karp

Global Security Studies emphasizes broad forces reshaping global security and the dilemmas facing decision-makers the world over. The series stresses issues relevant in many countries and regions, accessible to broad professional and academic audiences as well as to students, and enduring through explicit theoretical foundations.

Renegotiating the Nuclear Order
A Sociological Approach
Tarja Cronberg

The Treaty Prohibiting Nuclear Weapons
How it was Achieved and Why it Matters
Alexander Kmentt

The Nuclear Terrorism Threat
An Organisational Approach
Brecht Volders

The International Atomic Energy Agency's Six Decades
Historical Reflections, Current Challenges and Future Prospects
Edited by Joseph F. Pilat

Russia and the World in the Putin Era
From Theory to Reality in Russian Global Strategy
Edited by Roger E. Kanet and Dina Moulioukov

International Nuclear Export Controls and Non-Proliferation
The Collective Action Problem
Ian J. Stewart

For more information about this series, please visit: www.routledge.com/Routledge-Global-Security-Studies/book-series/RGSS

International Nuclear Export Controls and Non-Proliferation

The Collective Action Problem

Ian J. Stewart

Routledge
Taylor & Francis Group
LONDON AND NEW YORK

First published 2022
by Routledge
2 Park Square, Milton Park, Abingdon, Oxon OX14 4RN

and by Routledge
605 Third Avenue, New York, NY 10158

Routledge is an imprint of the Taylor & Francis Group, an informa business

British Library Cataloguing-in-Publication Data
A catalogue record for this book is available from the British Library

Library of Congress Cataloging-in-Publication Data
A catalog record has been requested for this book

ISBN: 978-1-032-04687-7 (hbk)
ISBN: 978-1-032-04688-4 (pbk)
ISBN: 978-1-003-19426-2 (ebk)

DOI: 10.4324/9781003194262

Typeset in Times New Roman
by Newgen Publishing UK

Contents

Acknowledgements

This book is a culmination of more than seven years of part-time effort. I would thus like to thank a number of individuals and organisations for their support over an extended period of time. Principally, I would like to express my sincere gratitude to Professor Wyn Bowen for his supervision during my PhD studies which formed the basis of this book. I would also like to recognise and thank colleagues at King's College London, former colleagues in the British government, and colleagues in the non-proliferation practitioner community more generally for their encouragement and support. I would like to thank the individuals who agreed to be interviewed for this research, including, in particular, Dr Jonathan Brewer, whose support has been invaluable.

Finally, and perhaps most importantly, I would like to recognise and thank Anna Sliwon-Stewart for her patience and support despite the countless lost evenings and weekends caused by my pursuit of this research.

Abbreviations

ABACC	Agency for Accounting and Control of Nuclear Materials
ACDA	Arms Control and Disarmament Association
AEC	Atomic Energy Commission (US unless otherwise specified)
AP	Additional Protocol
BoG	Board of Governors
CAP	Collective Action Problem
CDT	Combined Development Trust
CENTO	The Central Treaty Organisation
CIRUS	Canada India Research Reactor
CPC	Combined Policy Committee
CSA	Comprehensive Safeguards Agreement
DIQ	Design Information Questionnaire
DPRK	Democratic People's Republic of Korea (North Korea)
ENDC	Ten National Disarmament Commission (later expended to the Eighteen Nation Committee on Disarmament)
EURATOM	European Atomic Energy Community
FMCT	Fissile Material Cut-Off Treaty
GC	General Conference
HEU	Highly Enriched Uranium
IAEA	International Atomic Energy Agency
INFCIRC	Information Circular (a formal document of the IAEA)
JCPOA	Joint Comprehensive Plan of Action
JPOA	Joint Plan of Action
KANUPP	Karachi Nuclear Power Plant
KG	Kilogram
LEU	Low Enriched Uranium
MLF	Multilateral Nuclear Force
MTCR	Missile Technology Control Regime
MW	Megawatt
NAM	Non-Aligned Movement
NATO	North Atlantic Treaty Organisation
NNPA	Nuclear Non-Proliferation Act
NNWS	Non-Nuclear Weapons States

NPT	Nuclear Non-Proliferation Treaty
NSC	National Security Council
NSG	Nuclear Suppliers Group
NWS	Nuclear Weapons States
P5	Permanent Five (members of the Security Council)
PINSTECH	Pakistan Institute of Nuclear Science and Technology
PSI	Proliferation Security Initiative
UF6	Uranium hexafluoride
UN	United Nations
UNAEC	United Nations Atomic Energy Commission
UNGA	United Nations General Assembly
UNMOVIC	United Nations Monitoring, Verification and Inspection Commission
UNSC	United Nations Security Council
UNSCOM	UN Special Commission
UNSCR	United Nations Security Council Resolution
UO_2	Uranium dioxide
WMD	Weapons of Mass Destruction
WSG	Western Suppliers Group

Archive Abbreviations

BNA	British National Archive
CA	Churchill Archive
DDEPL	Dwight D. Eisenhower Presidential Library
GRFPL	Gerald R. Ford Presidential Library
HSTPL	Harry S. Truman Presidential Library
JCPL	Jimmy Carter Presidential Library
JFKPL	John F. Kennedy Presidential Library
LAC	Library and Archives Canada
RNPL	Richard Nixon Presidential Library
RRPL	Ronald Reagan Presidential Library
USNARA	United States National Achieve and Records Administration

1 Introduction

International nuclear export controls and non-proliferation, and the collective action problem

> Development of atomic energy for peaceful purposes and the development of atomic energy for bombs are in much of their course interchangeable and interdependent ... and as such that ... the only assurance that a conversion to destructive purposes would not be made would be the pledged word and the good faith of the nation itself ... fear of such surprise violation of pledged word will surely break down any confidence in the pledged word of rival countries developing atomic energy if the treaty obligations and good faith of the nations are the only assurance upon which to rely.
>
> Acheson–Lilienthal Report 1946[1]

Introduction

This book examines how and why opportunities have been seized and lost in the context of enhancing international nuclear non-proliferation trade controls over time. It examines the nature of the evolving nuclear proliferation challenge, drawing in part on previously un-utilised primary source archival material and interviews, and provides original insights into how and why international controls did not evolve in a more optimal fashion during key periods from the beginning of the nuclear age, and early efforts to control the atom, to more recent times and the challenge posed by the Iranian and the North Korean nuclear ambitions.

Understanding how the proliferation challenge has evolved and how international collaborative trade control efforts have developed in response is of fundamental importance because the risks of nuclear war and the spread of nuclear weapons have been at the heart of international affairs since the Second World War. Political leaders, senior military officials, and populations at large have concerned themselves with the question of nuclear proliferation and efforts to prevent it because of a generally held assumption that further proliferation increases the risk of a nuclear use.[2]

Given the population's fear of nuclear weapons over the period of study, it might be expected that there would be a general, albeit perhaps not continuous, consensus among the great powers that nuclear proliferation is undesirable and international efforts should be undertaken to prevent it. Indeed, many

DOI: 10.4324/9781003194262-1

schemes have been conceptualised and pursued with this objective. Many states – including, principally, the US – have invested substantial political and economic capital in the pursuit of non-proliferation objectives. During the Cold War, the Superpowers did find common ground in relation to non-proliferation issues, negotiating a Nuclear Non-Proliferation Treaty (NPT) that restrained both party's ability to transfer nuclear weapons to allies as part of a broader effort to achieve non-proliferation goals. Despite this general consensus on the principle of non-proliferation and the impetus provided by numerous nuclear proliferation 'shocks' to the system over time, it has routinely proven difficult and often impossible to reach a consensus on the adoption of an effective non-proliferation trade controls. This has been true even since the late 1960s when the US, the Soviet Union, and the UK agreed to forgo transfers of nuclear weapons capabilities to allied nations. The result has been the incremental adoption of limited and imperfect international nuclear non-proliferation trade controls. Indeed, despite gradual iterative improvements to the system of international non-proliferation trade controls, known gaps or flaws in the system of controls have remained following each proliferation 'shock' and are reflected in the non-proliferation architecture as it exists today.

In the last two decades alone, the failure of international controls has been at the heart of many of the 'threats to international peace and security' referred to the UN Security Council (UNSC), including proliferation challenges in Iraq, Iran, North Korea, and Libya. Indeed, so important has this challenge become that the UNSC is now 'seized upon' the issue of nuclear proliferation, meaning that it is one of the subjects on which several UNSC meetings take place each year independent of any active cases of proliferation that might be on its agenda. At the time of this writing, the UNSC was seized upon two specific cases – Iran and North Korea. In 2004, the Security Council had also adopted a wide-ranging resolution that remains in effect – UNSCR 1540 – which requires all states to take action to prevent non-state actor involvement in proliferation. Such is the scale of the problem related to international non-proliferation trade controls more broadly that leading analysts have commented:

> Of the roughly two dozen countries that have pursued or obtained nuclear weapons during the last fifty years, almost all of them depend critically on foreign supplies. These nations have sought complete nuclear facilities, subcomponents of facilities, nuclear materials classified know-how, and manufacturing capabilities to make key nuclear components themselves.[3]

This book seeks to get at the heart of understanding why international nuclear non-proliferation trade controls have evolved in a sub-optimal way. Drawing on the original archive materials and research interviews, the book sheds light on why this issue has persisted over the last seven decades. Specifically, it addresses the question of why have nuclear non-proliferation trade controls evolved in a sub-optimal fashion since the dawn of the nuclear age despite a general consensus among the great powers that nuclear proliferation is something to be avoided?

The term 'sub-optimal' requires some definition. The term as used here is intended to convey instances in which, when one or more options or approaches for control were foreseen, the less effective option was enacted. Thus, this is not a definitive concept that is fixed over time; it must be understood in the context of the major decision points in which non-proliferation controls were shaped. However, while this definition is meant to be understood in relative terms, it is also true in absolute terms. At various points, including after the Second World War and during the negotiation of the NPT, the elements that were foreseen to be an effective system of control were set out but not adopted. As such, while this book principally concerns itself with the question of why controls evolved in a sub-optimal way at certain key junctures, the analysis that follows also speaks to the broader question of why the overall system of non-proliferation controls that exists today is not optimal in preventing proliferation.

This question is of immense importance. International nuclear trade controls are at the heart of a non-proliferation regime but continue to be imperfect in design and implementation. Every proliferation episode since Second World War has been characterised by the state in question accessing materials, equipment or technology from international suppliers. It is quite possible that more states will seek nuclear weapons in the decades ahead. The inherent flaws in the international nuclear trade control regime continue to exist to this day. This has a direct impact on limiting the scope and effectiveness of controls on the nuclear programmes of countries such as Saudi Arabia, a country which may well exploit nuclear cooperation in pursuit of a nuclear weapons program.[4] By understanding those factors that have affected the evolution of international trade controls to date, it may be possible to address the current limitations.

Relevance of this book to existing literature

The evolution of international nuclear non-proliferation trade controls has been subject to increasing academic interest in recent years. Prior to this, the academic literature on such controls was sparse and generally focused on specific proliferation episodes and specific export control regimes or developments. Despite the wealth of academic literature relevant to the topic of nuclear proliferation as a whole, it has largely failed to address questions related to how and why international nuclear non-proliferation trade controls have evolved as they have. This gap may be a result of a tacit belief among many in the academic community that non-proliferation trade controls do not affect demand. Indeed, there is some evidence to support this assertion. R. Scott Kemp, one of the few scholars to grapple with the question of whether non-proliferation trade controls are effective, wrote a piece in the *International Security* titled

'The Nonproliferation Emperor Has No Clothes', a title chosen in an attempt to suggest that it is widely known but not recognised that non-proliferation trade controls have been ineffective.[5] To support his assertion, Kemp presents a *prima facie* case as to why supply-side non-proliferation trade controls have not, and indeed could not have, been effective since the advent of the gas centrifuge for enriching uranium.[6,7] The crux of his argument is that gas centrifuges can be manufactured using materials and technology that are not subject to control. The episodes examined in this book will demonstrate that despite Kemp's argument that such controls cannot be effective, the controls have frequently resulted in specific transfers being stopped when assurances were not in place regarding the end use. Further, the chapters that follow demonstrate that the existence of controls has changed how states proliferate. The problem with controls is not that they are inevitably ineffective but that they have evolved and been implemented in an *ad hoc* and limited way. It will be shown that opportunities for an overarching effective system of control were missed for reasons that will be explained but which fundamentally relate to the existence of the non-proliferation Collective Action Problem (CAP). Additionally, even if Kemp's argument is true, the observation of Fuhrmann that states do in fact seek external assistance and technology when considering a nuclear weapons programme is sufficient basis to warrant investigation of how controls impact upon these efforts.[8] Further, as Bowen asserts with regards to ballistic missiles, it is clear that where a state lacks the indigenous capability to produce all items required for a programme and the necessary technical and industrial base, it must import both for the programme to proceed.[9]

In recent years, efforts have begun to be made to explore the reasons for the evolution of international nuclear trade controls. Key literature in this regard includes the work of Kroening and Fuhrmann. Fuhrmann, for example, sought to understand the drivers for states to conclude nuclear cooperation agreements, which he argued were good proxies for overall nuclear cooperation. Based on a quantitative approach, he concludes that the primary driver for such cooperation was to gain influence over allies and enemies of enemies. He finds more evidence for this than for economic drivers being key determinates for the provision of nuclear assistance. However, Fuhrmann's work focuses on understanding why nuclear cooperation took place rather than on understanding why controls evolved as they did. While these two areas are related, it is argued that Fuhrmann's book misses an important piece of the puzzle. More effective controls would have lessened concern about the type of atomic assistance Fuhrmann describes. Similarly, Kroening sought to understand the motivations of states in providing what was described as 'sensitive' nuclear assistance, which he described as nuclear-weapons-related assistance, weapons usable fissile material, and enrichment and reprocessing capabilities. Kroening identifies a key differentiator, which is whether the state is a power projecting state or not. If a state is power projecting, he argues, it will more likely be averse to proliferation as the spread of nuclear weapons would constrain the exporting state's ability to project power. There are also limitations to Kroening's work that limit its relevance to this book. In particular, Kroening does not directly account for the utility of international safeguards in his assessment of the proliferation risks of sensitive nuclear assistance and nuclear smuggling networks, which have been important in many state proliferation networks. Furthermore, many forms of atomic assistance, including the transfer of nuclear reactors, fall outside of his definition of sensitive nuclear assistance. It will be argued in this book that coordination and competition among reactor suppliers have been important factors in the evolution of controls, so the exclusion of these from Kroening's work limits its relevance to the present study.

Overall, therefore, while the contributions of Kroening and Fuhrmann are valuable, they do not directly speak to the question of why international nuclear trade controls evolved in a sub-optimal way. Instead, their focus is on understanding state decision making regarding different types of atomic assistance. While important, both works thus miss an important element of the puzzle. To some extent, national decision making on the provision of nuclear assistance must be informed by an assumption about whether other states would provide the assistance if one state did not. Thus, in examining the evolution of non-proliferation controls through the lens of the CAP, this book can provide a specific complement to the work of Kroening and Fuhrmann. Important contributions have also been made by scholars such as Knopf, who led a group of specialist scholars in studying what factors drove states to cooperate in non-proliferation. Knopf noted that levels of cooperation are not consistent with the more limited level of cooperation that would be expected from international relations[10] The study did address non-proliferation trade controls as a case study but did not offer detailed insights on the factors leading states to cooperate or otherwise in the evolution of non-proliferation trade controls over time.

More recently, Jason Enia has directly examined the Nuclear Suppliers Group (NSG) through the lens of political economy.[11] That work had a more restricted scope than this book in that it only focused on the NSG and did not draw on contemporary sources. However, the work effectively demonstrates the value of examining trade control regimes through the lens of political economy, which has common routes with the collective action theory used as the basis of the framework used in this book.[12]

Through applying a quantitative approach, Stinnett *et al.* recognised that "combating proliferation through export control has many characteristics of a collective action problem" and that the benefits and costs of fighting proliferation are not evenly shared. They examined data on 30 states to gain insight into the question of whether compliance with international obligations is driven more by state interest and enforcement or by state capacity. Interestingly, it was argued that state capacity is the primary barrier to implementation of international commitments such as export controls and it is more important than external pressure *vis-à-vis* improving implementation of controls.[13]

There is a substantial body of literature in which the case study approach has been used to examine the evolution of non-proliferation trade controls. This work, while impressive in volume, has generally been tied to specific proliferation episodes. Specific proliferation episodes are often extensively studied in order to both understand the nature of the specific programme and identify lessons for preventing future proliferation cases. There is a great deal of academic literature on how the nuclear programmes of the US, UK, Canada, China, India, Pakistan, Iraq, Iran, Libya, and North Korea evolved, all of which was examined during the course of this research.[14] Significant attention has also been given to the actions of A.Q. Khan, the notorious serial proliferator who proliferated nuclear technology first to Pakistan, then to Iran, Libya, South Africa, and North Korea, as well as offered nuclear technology to half a dozen more countries.[15] To the extent this body of literature is relevant to the research question, its limitations are that it tends to focus on the gaps in supply-side controls as identified in the specific cases, rather than seeking to address how these gaps developed and how they could have been addressed at a more systemic level.

There is a broad interest in specific non-proliferation tools, such as the individual export control regimes, the role and effectiveness of UN sanctions, the effectiveness of UNSCR 1540, and the utility of International Atomic Energy Agency (IAEA) safeguards. This literature often focuses on how to make a specific measure more effective by, for example, identifying gaps and limitations, increasing membership or adherence and encouraging and supporting implementation. Recent literature on the NSG, for example, has focused primarily upon issues related to membership rather than broader strategic issues of nonproliferation.[16] In addition to the work on the main export control measures, some of the literature has explored the implementation of trade controls in particular countries,[17] export controls on certain specific technologies (particularly enrichment and reprocessing),[18] the status and outlook of specific international export control regimes[19] and on the limitations of financial measures in preventing proliferation.[20] The literature has also sought to provide insight into the perspectives of specific countries in relation to non-proliferation controls, such as India in relation to the NSG.[21] As mentioned, other literature in this category has examined the origins of specific initiatives and treaties, including the Atoms for Peace initiative and the NPT. This includes the work of Mohamed Shaker in exploring the evolution of the NPT from 1959 to 1979 and the work of Mara Drogan on the Atoms for Peace initiative.[22] Again, however, this element of the literature largely fails to address how the gaps came to be or to analyse the gaps holistically from the perspective of the effectiveness of the overall non-proliferation regime.

The literature examining resolution 1540 has identified the factors that are likely to lead states to implement the resolution's requirements and has gauged the level of implementation across several topics, such as export controls, transshipment controls, licensing, and enforcement.[23] This literature has examined why 1540 implementation is lacking in certain regions.

However, this work has failed to address the question of what 'full implementation' of resolution 1540 – as called for in the address of the President of the Security Council on 7 May 2014 – would mean in practice or the full origins of the resolution.[24]

There is also a growing body of work that takes the opposite perspective, seeking to explain not as to why states enact controls but instead why it is that states enter into sensitive nuclear assistance agreements.[25] Nicholas Miller, for example, finds support for the argument that it is predominately inward-facing states that are likely to proliferate as these states tend to be better positioned to weather the pressure of the international community to comply.[26] However, his work does not explain how it is that the non-proliferation regime has acted to curtail the interests of other states in acquiring nuclear weapons, only that these interests appear to have been resolved.

This examination of the existing literature relevant to international nuclear trade control highlights that there is currently an insufficient understanding of the evolution of these controls. In particular, it is not apparent from the existing literature why opportunities to improve non-proliferation trade controls have often been missed at key moments despite political impetus and numerous 'shocks' to the system. Moreover, there has been no systematic examination of the non-proliferation problem through the lens of the CAP. This book seeks to address this gap by providing insights into why opportunities to strengthen non-proliferation trade controls have been either seized or lost at key points since the beginning of the nuclear age. The next section lays out the methodology that was developed to do this.

Research approach

The book examines the following central research question: why have nuclear non-proliferation trade controls evolved in a sub-optimal fashion since the dawn of the nuclear age despite a general consensus among the great powers that nuclear proliferation is something to be avoided?

To address this question, a loose conceptual framework was developed by drawing in part on the academic literature that examines CAPs. The framework, which is outlined in the following, is used to aid the examination of the time-based episodes that follow. Examination of each episode generates knowledge and insight into the factors that best explain progress, or the lack of it, in developing international non-proliferation trade controls during specific periods. The chronological development of the episodes also provides insights into the development of these controls over the broader time span.

Inherent to the central research question is an assumption about the evolution of international non-proliferation trade controls: that controls have evolved in a sub-optimal way. It is important to note that there were reasons to believe this assumption was valid at the outset of the research. Indeed, that controls have evolved in a sub-optimal way has been noted – explicitly or implicitly – in much of the existing literature related to every proliferation episode and period. Examples from the early nuclear age include: Finch's 'Exporting Danger: History of the Canadian Nuclear Energy Export Programme'[27]; Leonard Spector's work aptly highlights the issues seen in the 1980s[28] and David Albright's work highlights the issues seen in the 1990s and 2000s.[29] Even a cursory examination of the narrative around the development of controls over time supports these assumptions, including Ian Anthony's work on 'reforming nuclear export controls'.[30]

Conceptual framework

To aid the examination of the evolution of non-proliferation controls over time, this research used a loose framework developed for this purpose. It draws in part on literature addressing CAPs. CAPs are widely studied phenomena in the economic and public goods spheres, such as in relation to environmental management. A CAP can be characterised as a situation in which it might be in the interest of all actors to forgo a short-term benefit in pursuit of a higher-value collective benefit, but where the structure of incentives and information sharing make cooperation less likely.

As Ostrom has argued about CAPs, sometimes actors can select 'strategies based on a calculus that maximizes short-term benefits to self',[31] rather than on considerations of long-term collective benefit. Academics have on occasion described non-proliferation in general and export controls in particular as a CAPs, although no academic literature to date has expressly examined the coordination of trade controls as a CAP.[32]

There is an expansive literature on CAPs focusing on how such problems have been overcome, or otherwise, in a wide variety of contexts related to 'the commons' (i.e., environmental and resource issues). This started with founding work by Olsen in the 1970s, who demonstrated, using economic tools, that there are situations in which rational, self-interested actors will opt to pursue less than ideal outcomes because of problems of cooperation in a group.[33] Olsen's work effectively initiated the development of collective action theory, which has developed substantially since. Olsen's early work identified various factors likely to be important in overcoming CAPs, including the size of the group involved (with smaller groups being more effective) and the existence of coercive influence, or some other special device, to encourage cooperation. Olsen also found that to overcome CAPs, incentives that are separate from the good being sought are necessary.[34]

The ideas put forward by Olsen have been widely studied and broadly challenged over the decades. Despite this, studies continue to find that the factors Olsen identified are present in circumstances where CAPs have been overcome.[35] One problem with the literature on collective action is that a comprehensive theory of collective action has not yet emerged. This is despite hundreds of studies being conducted, including quantitative analyses, to identify the most relevant generic factors.[36] Indeed, over 30 factors have been identified as being potentially relevant across various studies.[37]

In recent years scholars, including principally Ostrom, have sought to consolidate the factors that appear most important, in part by drawing upon the results of quantitative studies. One of Ostrom's papers, while not going as far as to present a complete theory of collective action, presented a loose model through which CAPs can be examined.[38] This work revisited the earlier work of Olsen and it forms a partial foundation for the loose framework adopted in this book. It is important to note that this project is not seeking to make a contribution to theory in this area. Rather, the research framework utilises some of the generic factors highlighted in this literature and then supplements them in other ways, all of which is outlined in the following.

In identifying sets of factors relevant to the ability of actors to overcome CAPs, Ostrom begins with highlighting structural factors, which she argues should not affect the outcome if one assumes that actors take decisions based upon the rational actor model.[39] For this book, the following structural factors were judged to be relevant:

- the number of participants involved: a large number of participants is expected to reduce the probability of achieving any form of collective action;
- whether benefits are subtractive or fully shared: In the non-proliferation context, this would relate to how benefits and consequences of nuclear assistance and proliferation are distributed;
- the heterogeneity of participants: heterogeneity could mean many things, but key factors recognised in the literature relate to the power and influence distribution within the group. It could be anticipated that homogeneity of participants could increase the likelihood of cooperation because of an alignment of interests among participants. At the same time, however, homogeneity of assets, information and payoffs could negatively affect cooperation by making distribution of benefits more difficult;[40]
- the existence of face-to-face communications: in practice where actors can discuss non-compliance the likelihood of cooperation increases;
    - information about past actions: positive interactions might serve to increase trust among actors while negative interactions might serve to reduce it;
    - how actors are linked: are actors interconnected and is there inter-reliability which might serve to increase cooperation and trust; and
    - whether individuals can enter and exit the game voluntarily.[41]

Ostrom also reflected on how decisions are made and considered that decisions can also be based upon heuristics and informed by norms. Heuristics she defines as 'rules of thumb', which can be learned over time. Ostrom further highlights what she calls 'core relationships', which she believes guide the decision making of individual actors in the bounded rationality in which decisions are actually taken. In such bounded rationality, decisions might have to be made quickly and with imperfect information. These core relationships are built upon and are influenced by reputation, trust, reciprocity, levels of cooperation and net benefit. In the bounded rationality of decision making, as Ostrom argues, these factors are decided upon through norms and heuristics.[42]

Ostrom's argument that 'core' factors are significant in the context of collective action is important in the context of the research question. As was highlighted, much of the existing literature about the evolution of non-proliferation trade controls focuses on structural factors, such as the power relations between states and the distribution of benefits. Applying this loose research framework will thus provide an additional level of analysis to understanding the problem of preventing nuclear proliferation currently unconsidered in the literature.

While a part of the originality of this book is that it examines the issue of international nuclear trade controls through the lens of collective action, there are evidently a host of other factors that should be considered when examining the evolution of controls. For example, it is necessary to keep in mind that nuclear technologies could also have had a substantial impact on the evolution of international nuclear non-proliferation trade controls over the study period. Kemp has argued that the emergence of centrifuge enrichment technology might have fundamentally changed the nature of non-proliferation.[43] Additionally, and unlike in the domestic sphere in which CAPs are most often studied, it is argued that there are three 'imperatives' that have come to define the political and technical discussions around nuclear technology since the 1940s. These imperatives are commonly described today as the 'three pillars' of the NPT. However, the 'three pillars' are a relatively recent construct as these imperatives predate the Treaty.[44]

- The use of atomic energy for either peaceful or military purposes or both.
- Nuclear disarmament.
- Nuclear non-proliferation, including associated normative factors.

Since the dawn of the nuclear age, political and popular interest in these three imperatives, or factors, has been significant and must be weaved into the analysis, recognising, of course, that the relative importance of each of these three factors is subjective and has changed over time.

Table 1.1 draws together these factors as propositions to form a loose conceptual framework. This framework is then utilised in the case study chapters to help shed light on the central research question. Within the framework, a set of sub-questions is then derived from the propositions to aid in interrogating the five case studies. This allows for the identification not only of a case study or period-specific conclusions regarding the sub-optimal evolution of international nuclear trade controls but also for drawing broader conclusions from across the cases.[45]

This book draws heavily on archival sources and, to the author's knowledge, is the first study to attempt to comprehensively examine available archival sources related to the evolution of international nuclear non-proliferation

Table 1.1 Research Framework

Type	*Proposition*	*Illustrative sub-questions*
Structural	The number and type of actors involved in nuclear-related trade will affect the ability of states to cooperate on nuclear trade controls. Specifically, more actors of different types will make cooperation less likely.	Does the number and type of actors involved influence the evolution of international non-proliferation trade controls?
	The heterogeneity of participants will influence the ability of states to cooperate.	Does heterogeneity amongst key participating actors influence the evolution of international non-proliferation trade controls?
	The issue of whether benefits are subtractive or fully shared will affect the extent to which states are willing to cooperate. Specifically, states will be more likely to pursue subtractive rather than shared benefits when taking decisions about restricting supply or allowing transactions.	Do benefits – both shared and subtractive (e.g., profit) – influence the evolution of international non-proliferation trade controls?
	The ability for face-to-face communications to take place will positively affect the ability of states to cooperate on non-proliferation trade controls.	Do forums or other communications channels for participating actors influence the evolution of international non-proliferation trade controls?
	Information about past actions will positively influence the willingness of states to implement non-proliferation trade controls.	To what extent does past positive or negative interaction between participating actors influence the evolution of international non-proliferation trade controls? What role does reputation, trust, reciprocity, levels of cooperation and net benefit play?
	How actors are linked will affect the willingness of states to cooperate.	Does the way in which actors are linked – politically, economically and strategically – influence the evolution of international non-proliferation trade controls?
Core	The existence of non-proliferation norms will positively influence the willingness of states to cooperate on non-proliferation trade controls.	Does a nuclear non-proliferation norm influence the evolution of international non-proliferation trade controls?

(*continued*)

Table 1.1 Cont.

Type	*Proposition*	*Illustrative sub-questions*
	The existence of trust will positively influence the willingness of states to cooperate on non-proliferation trade controls.	How has the level of trust and cooperation among states affected the evolution of non-proliferation trade controls?
Other	Technological change, including proliferation 'shocks', will negatively affect the evolution of non-proliferation trade controls.	How do technological change and proliferation 'shocks' influence the evolution of international non-proliferation trade controls?
	Civil and military uses of atomic energy will impede the evolution of controls.	How do perceptions of civil and military uses of atomic energy amongst participating actors influence the evolution of international non-proliferation trade controls?
Imperatives	The non-proliferation imperative will drive the evolution of controls.	How do perceptions of non-proliferation commitments and norms amongst participating actors influence the evolution of international non-proliferation trade controls?
	The Disarmament imperative will drive the evolution of controls.	How do perceptions of nuclear disarmament amongst participating actors influence the evolution of international trade non-proliferation trade controls?

trade controls over time. In the course of this research, the author visited the UK, the US, the Canadian national archives and the Presidential libraries of every US President from Truman to Reagan. Hundreds of thousands of pages were digitised for later review during the course of these visits. There are certain gaps and biases in the material collected for this project. For example, most of the archival material reviewed for this project was from the perspective of the US or the UK. While these countries played a vital role in the evolution of international nuclear trade controls, this does also mean that the views of other important states, such as France, the Soviet Union, India, and Pakistan are examined primarily as they were understood to the UK and US. Further archival work in any of these countries could provide additional insight into the argument presented in this book. The archival material was also complemented with a small number of interviews, particularly to cover the period from around 1990, after which archival material ceased being available. It is worth noting that, in the UK at least, archival material should have been available after this date, given that the '30-year rule' is being changed to a '20-year rule' with the corresponding release of two years of material per year. However, it transpired that for the relevant records-set, the UK Foreign and Commonwealth Office was behind on its target and had thus not yet begun to implement the 20-year rule changes. There will thus be more archival material available in the future for the period after 1990.

The chapters of this book are structured around a number of 'episodes' which evolve in a roughly chronological way. These episodes are forms of case study that examine the evolution of controls in each period. However, a number of these episodes also include specific programmatic case studies, including in relation to the nuclear programmes of India and Pakistan.

- The episode examined in Chapter 2 relates to the immediate post-WW2 period in which there was an effort to achieve 'international control' of atomic energy. The purpose of this chapter is somewhat different from the subsequent chapters, as no international system of control was agreed upon in this period. The chapter thus examines the system of control that was contemplated in this period and the reasons that it was not introduced.
- The episode examined in Chapter 3 focuses on the concept and implementation of the Atoms for Peace initiative, including civil nuclear assistance that took place in this period. The case study examined in this period relates to the so-called Indian Peaceful Nuclear Explosion (PNE).
- The episode examined in Chapter 4 relates to the evolution of non-proliferation trade controls in the 1964–1980 period, particularly in relation to US strategy. It focuses on US efforts to coordinate non-proliferation controls following the Chinese nuclear test in 1964 and the Indian test in 1974, particularly by examining the policies of successive US administrations.
- The episode examined in Chapter 5 relates to the evolution of non-proliferation trade controls after the cold war. The chapter focuses on the evolution of international nuclear trade controls following the discovery of Iraq's secret nuclear programme in the early 1990s.
- The episode examined in Chapter 6 relates to the adoption of UNSCRs after 2004 as a means to universalise controls. This chapter focuses on the evolution of international trade controls following the discovery of the A.Q. Khan proliferation network. The proliferation case studies examined in this chapter include those of Iraq and Iran.

These five main episodes were selected because initial research indicated that it was during these periods that the most substantial evolution in international nuclear non-proliferation trade controls took place. To inform the analysis in each case study, the evolution of specific nuclear programmes is examined in order to provide insights into how controls were being applied during each period. In the Atoms for Peace case study, for example, it was natural to include an exploration of India's nuclear programme and its so-called PNE. The PNE marked a culmination of the Atoms for Peace era, although it came after the non-proliferation regime had moved on for other countries, including those that had become party to the NPT. The PNE can be seen to mark the end of the era. In the period related to the formation of the non-proliferation regime in the 1970s, it was natural to include an exploration of Pakistan because international concern that it might seek nuclear weapons was a significant driver for the developments in international controls that took place. Chapter 5 focuses on the Iraq proliferation episode as it was the discovery of this programme that prompted an updating of trade controls in the 1990s. Chapter 6 focuses on the A.Q. Khan proliferation network and the programmes of its customers because it was the discovery of this network that led to the adoption of UNSCR 1540 in 2004.

Other programmes could have been explored in the case studies. Instead of examining the interaction between the evolution of India's nuclear programme and non-proliferation trade controls, it may have been possible to examine the evolution of the nuclear programme of Israel beyond its acquisition of a French-supplied reactor. Instead of the Pakistan programme, it may have been possible to examine the South African programme. Instead of examining the interaction between non-proliferation trade controls and the evolution of the Iranian nuclear programme, it may have been possible to examine the North Korean programme. However, in all of these alternative cases, the programmes had a less significant impact on the evolution of non-proliferation trade controls. Moreover, in the case of countries, such as Israel and the DPRK, the level of secrecy surrounding these programmes limited the feasibility of accessing data to provide original analysis.

Book structure and summary of findings

The book is organised into seven chapters, a bibliography, and annexes. This introduction (Chapter 1) introduces the research problem and sets out the research method. It locates the research in existing literature and provides an overview of the book. The chapter sets out the research design, including the framework for examining the case studies, which are also outlined. The introduction summarises the overall findings of the research.

Chapter 2 examines early considerations around international control of atomic energy. This includes an examination of the transition from war time to peace time controls on atomic energy, cooperation between the war-time allies (UK, US, and Canada), and efforts led by the US to establish an effective system of international control for atomic energy as set out in the Acheson–Lilienthal Report of 1946, the Baruch plan and ultimately considered by the UN Atomic Energy Commission. The primary purpose is to set out the factors that influenced efforts to control atomic energy after the Second World War and why the envisioned system of international control of atomic energy was not adopted. It is concluded that the primary and specific reason this early initiative failed was the unwillingness of the Soviet Union to accept what the US (and other Western powers) considered to be the essential elements of an effective system of control, which included international control of atomic energy. More generally, however, the failure must be seen in the context of the evolving Cold War environment within which the Soviet Union was behind in the production of nuclear weapons. In applying the research framework, it is concluded that both structural and core factors (i.e., mistrust and a lack of a non-proliferation norm in the period) aligned to discourage cooperation on nuclear non-proliferation trade controls in this period.

Chapter 3 examines the Atoms for Peace period. Of particular interest here is the question of why the initiative proceeded without an effective system of control and why only limited item-specific safeguards were adopted instead of broader comprehensive safeguards?[46] The chapter begins by exploring the nature of the Atoms for Peace initiative, including its purpose and scope. A focus of this examination of the nature of the non-proliferation controls associated with the Atoms for Peace initiative and why these had a limited scope. Drawing on materials from a variety of archives, it explores the negotiation of the safeguards arrangements that became associated with the initiative. The decision of France to transfer a reactor and reprocessing capability to Israel is examined, as is how the controls affected India's nuclear programme.

The key finding in this chapter is that nuclear cooperation during the period was driven almost entirely by geostrategic factors. The Atoms for Peace initiative proceeded despite the knowledge of US officials that the control system associated with the initiative was not sufficient to prevent the further proliferation of nuclear weapons. President Eisenhower initially wanted, and then felt pressured, to implement the initiative for wider diplomatic purposes in the context of the Cold War. To some extent, there was also a selfless desire for nuclear technology to be used to the benefit of mankind even though a disarmament plan could not be reached. Commercial and economic factors were largely secondary considerations during this period and primarily concerned the supply of uranium.

There are few signs that non-proliferation objectives featured prominently in national priorities in this period, and no systematic means of control nor a non-proliferation norm existed. This problem was compounded by the fact that states interested in acquiring nuclear weapons, such as India, were participants in the forums that sought to devise controls. In the absence of controls, and with the introduction of competition in supply, a nuclear proliferation trade control CAP emerged that would shape the periods that followed. It was in this context that India acquired a reactor from Canada without safeguards.

In applying the research framework, it is found that so-called core factors, such as a lack of trust among key parties, affected cooperation between the Superpowers in this period. Additionally, the non-proliferation norm – to the extent such a thing existed – was limited to the non-misuse of supplied technology (i.e., peaceful uses). The chapter shows that the effect of this was limited, however, as at least some countries entered into nuclear supply agreements despite knowing of the weapons interest of recipients. The French transfer of a reactor to Israel comes primarily to mind in this respect.

Chapter 4 examines the evolution of non-proliferation trade controls following the first Chinese nuclear explosion in 1964 to Pakistan's announcement in the mid-1980s that it had enriched uranium to over 90%. The chapter is loosely structured around the different approaches taken by the Nixon, Ford, Carter, and Reagan administrations to the problem of non-proliferation in general and to the nuclear programme of Pakistan in particular.

The controls adopted in this period were insufficient to counter known proliferation risks. This was a result of multiple factors, including the legacy of the Atoms for Peace initiative. It is argued that controls associated with the NPT were insufficient despite a strong desire among all countries to ensure that the NPT had no 'loopholes', and increasing cooperation between the Superpowers, which had come to recognise that further proliferation was not in either of their interest.

The primary reason that trade controls were not advanced further during this period, despite cooperation between the Superpowers, is that the vested interests of other states involved in the negotiations – notably states within the European Atomic Energy Community (Euratom) and India – worked against this. These states exercised their influence to prevent the development of a more rigorous system of technology control because of a concern that this would have negatively affected their own nuclear programmes. A more rigorous system – which might have included 'international control' – would only have been feasible if it had been associated with steps towards disarmament and would thus have affected the self-interest of these states. In effect, therefore, geostrategic factors continued to be the principal barrier to the adoption of effective technology controls. Nevertheless, nuclear technology holders had learned lessons from the Atoms for Peace era and would largely agree to forego nuclear cooperation that directly aided other countries to acquire nuclear weapons.

The chapter argues that the purpose of the London suppliers meeting – later called the NSG – was to bridge gaps in the non-proliferation regime that had been formalised with the adoption of the NPT by preventing a 'race to the bottom' regarding safeguards as a condition of nuclear supply between suppliers. In particular, the purpose of the suppliers' meetings was to seek common ground on nuclear exports between countries that had signed the NPT, such as the US, and countries that had not, such as France. It is shown that domestic political factors in the US, which had been championing the adoption of stronger international non-proliferation trade controls, resulted in Washington overly focusing on the risks of plutonium reprocessing at the expense of the spread of enrichment capabilities. European states also restricted the intrusiveness of IAEA safeguards in order to gain a favourable settlement between the IAEA and Euratom on the issue of safeguards in which the IAEA recognised the existing Euratom measures. This problem was compounded by growing commercial interests associated with nuclear supply and the lack of progress on disarmament. Interestingly, there are few signs that geostrategic rivalries between the US and the USSR frustrated non-proliferation efforts at this time, although the geostrategic rivalry between India and China doubtless drove the former's desire to keep open its own nuclear options.

The problem was further exacerbated by the differing approaches of each US presidential administration over this period. While each administration would, to some extent, build upon the frameworks devised by its predecessor, each sought to embark on a different and often incompatible approach to non-proliferation policy, which undermined the development of international trade controls as a means to address the CAP. The reasons for this are complex and encompass domestic political and technological factors. Ultimately, the interplay between them meant that the non-proliferation regime was not well placed to respond to the nuclear proliferation activities of Pakistan and then later to Iraq and the A.Q. Khan network.

In examining this episode through the research framework, it is shown that structural factors aligned to allow for limited cooperation in this period but overcoming core factors proved difficult, which meant that states would only agree not to assist others in acquiring nuclear weapons. Even when this geostrategic interest in non-proliferation was recognised, developing trust-based relationships proved difficult allowing for only slow and incremental progress. As in the Atoms for Peace era, non-proliferation ultimately proved to be a secondary geostrategic objective for the US, which was primarily focused on Cold War competition, thus explaining the US position on Pakistan, for example. Beginning with the Carter administration and expanding with the Reagan administration, the US would place greater priority on securing Pakistan's support for actions in Afghanistan in the context of containing Soviet expansionism than on non-proliferation measures. For example, by continuing to certify that Pakistan was not developing nuclear weapons, the Reagan Administration, in particular, sought to ensure that aid to the Mujahideen could continue to flow via Pakistan.

Chapter 5 examines the evolution of non-proliferation trade controls after the end of the Cold War in the particular context of the discovery of Iraq's clandestine nuclear programme. The chapter begins by examining the elements of Iraq's clandestine nuclear programme both before and after the destruction of the Osiraq reactor in 1981. It examines in particular how the programme continued through overt and later covert transfers from the international marketplace. It is shown that Iraq maintained a complex clandestine network to acquire goods from overseas and that western governments, in particular, appear to have turned a blind eye to Iraq's activity as a result of a perceived need to keep Iraq on the side in the broader context of the cold war. Iraq's pursuit of enrichment technology is examined in some depth to highlight the limitations of controls that existed in this period. The chapter then proceeds by examining the international response to revelations about Iraq. This includes an examination of the improvements in international trade controls, particularly through the reconstitution of the NSG, the creation of an NSG dual-use regime and the adoption of the IAEA's additional protocol. A particular focus is given to the evolving German approach to export controls which it is shown resulted from diplomatic embarrassment and therefore relates to the evolving non-proliferation trade control norm. It is shown that the evolving national approach of countries, such as the US, France, and Germany set the scene for the NSG to address issues left unaddressed in the NSG meetings from the 1970s, including the adoption of full-scope safeguards as a condition of supply.

The main argument here is that the Iraq episode prompted an improvement of international trade controls, but the improvements were too limited in scope to address the proliferation risks of nuclear-related trade more generally. There were multiple reasons for this. First, at a high level, the nature of the international nuclear trade control scene created in the earlier periods meant that it was still for each state to make its own decisions with regards to nuclear supply: the CAP remained and no overarching governance framework had been agreed other than the NPT which did not restrict cooperation among NPT parties. Additionally, with technological advancement and spread, more and more of these states were capable of nuclear supply. These factors together meant that while there was progress in improving both the scope and geographical coverage of controls in this period, this was down more to implementation of *ad hoc* and voluntary measures rather than universal measures and treaties.

Indeed, it is shown that there are a number of practical and political reasons that *ad hoc* and voluntary measures were favoured over universal and treaty-based measures. Principal among these was the priority assigned to securing the future of the NPT: Securing agreement for an indefinite extension of the NPT was given priority over other nuclear non-proliferation initiatives, including in relation to trade control issues. The result was that enhanced controls were enacted on an *ad hoc* basis, often by like-minded countries rather than in a universal fashion.

Chapter 6 examines the role and limitations of UNSCR 1540 in universalising non-proliferation trade controls. The main argument presented in this chapter is that while 1540 created a universal requirement for national non-proliferation trade controls, the resolution could not overcome other barriers to effective implementation of non-proliferation trade controls, including geopolitics and domestic politics.

The chapter begins with an exploration of the revelations that emerged about the A.Q. Khan network, which led to the adoption of the resolution. This included an examination of the main elements of the network, including its broad geographical scope and its activities in countries with weak non-proliferation controls, and the role of the network in supplying Iran, Libya and to a lesser extent North Korea. It is shown that the network had a global character in that it procured goods from western countries and involved manufacturing hubs in countries, such as Malaysia and the UAE, which did not have export controls at the time.

The chapter then examines the response to the discovery of the A.Q. Khan network. This includes principally the adoption of UNSCR 1540 in 2004. However, this is framed in the context of broader efforts by the George W. Bush administration to work with like-minded and *ad hoc* groups of countries to improve controls post-Iraq. It is argued that UNSCR provided a mechanism to pursue universalisation of non-proliferation controls while continuing the trend of working with small numbers of principal partners including, in the case of resolution 1540, the permanent members of the Security Council. The views of other states on this approach to universalising non-proliferation controls – principally India and China – are also examined.

The chapter further examines two episodes following the adoption of UNSCR 1540 to understand the nature of the non-proliferation regime after the adoption of the resolution. These relate to the NSG's exemption for India and the adoption of UN sanctions on Iran and the DPRK. Examination of these episodes highlight that while there is general support for non-proliferation trade control measures, this support is often overtaken by geo-political factors specific to each case.

With India, for example, the US pursued an exemption to the requirement of full-scope safeguards as a condition of supply largely to secure India as a geopolitical and trading partner and to leverage India in balancing China from a geostrategic perspective. In the case of Iran, both Russia and China worked to limit the scope of sanctions to allow for bilateral cooperation on strategically important topics. Overall, the chapter argues that although controls were 'universalised' as a result of the discovery of the A.Q. Khan network, geopolitics and other vested interests continued to limit the effectiveness of controls.

Chapter 7 presents the overall findings of the research. It examines the relevance of each proposition from the research framework in turn and addresses the research question. It summarises the factors involved in the outcomes of several key development points in the evolution of international nuclear trade controls. The relevance of the factors highlighted in the conceptual framework is considered in turn.

The overall finding of the book, as presented in Chapter 7, is that nuclear non-proliferation trade controls have evolved in a structurally flawed fashion since the inception of international concern over proliferation primarily because of the geostrategic interests of the Cold War Superpowers. This was a direct and foreseeable result of the decision by President Eisenhower to move forward with the Atoms for Peace initiative without an effective system of trade control based on short term US self-interest in the context of the Cold War. In implementing the Atoms for Peace initiative, the US explicitly accepted that nuclear proliferation was inevitable but pressed ahead because of the value that supplying atomic energy to other states held for diplomatic purposes. In so doing, these states created the conditions from which a CAP emerged notably because these and other states began to compete against one another to supply technology in the absence of adequate safeguarding provisions.

Consensus on arresting proliferation grew following the Chinese and then the Indian nuclear tests in 1964 and 1974, respectively. While the consensus developed in the 1960s around non-proliferation being a benefit worth pursuing, it did not prove possible to erase the legacy of the Atoms for Peace initiative, which had been institutionalised through the IAEA. Indeed, initiatives to bolster trade controls were limited in scope and iterative in nature. There were several reasons for this. First, there was a reluctance, even an unwillingness, of key states to agree to measures that would restrict their own nuclear programmes. This included states as diverse as India and the Euratom states. States were more willing to agree on measures to constrain the nuclear programmes of others. Second, despite the fact that non-proliferation was in the interests of both the US and Soviet Union, the distrust that existed between the US and Soviet blocs had a limiting effect. This was gradually overcome through dialogue between the two aided by face-to-face meetings of US and Soviet technical experts. Third, the growing number of actors involved – boosted the policies of Atoms for Peace – created challenges. The growing number of actors limited progress in numerous ways, including by establishing a need for additional core relationships to be developed between more countries, and which required the passage of more time for confidence in reciprocity to be established. The growing number of participants also introduced more actors that had vested interests in pursuing different benefits to that of non-proliferation. Principal among these vested interests were states interested in acquiring nuclear weapons. While commercial interests were also important, governments were usually willing to prevent transfers when it was clear they would directly aid a weapons programme and where there was a legal means to do so. Ultimately, it is argued that the proliferation episodes in Pakistan, Iraq, Iran and elsewhere were a direct result of the failure to overcome the underlying structural problems that existed from the Atoms for Peace era onwards.

Since the end of the Cold War, in response to several proliferation-related episodes, efforts have been made by like-minded states, often within the UNSC, to address the legacy of the Cold War and the gaps in nuclear trade controls. This accounts for the adoption of the Additional Protocol, the creation of a new nuclear suppliers regime in the 1990s and the adoption of UNSCR 1540. Nonetheless, the book shows that it continues to be in the self-interest of some states to oppose broader trade controls even though it is recognised and accepted that a stronger non-proliferation regime would be in the collective interest of most states. It is argued that a fully effective non-proliferation regime would need to include structural changes, perhaps along the lines pursued by the UN Atomic Energy Commission. However, the research for this book suggests this highly unlikely in the absence of progress on disarmament. In the absence of this, non-proliferation trade controls will likely continue to be traded off by states against other geostrategic interests, as infamously happened with the US–India deal, for example.

Notes

1 '*A report on the International Control of Atomic Energy*' (the "Acheson-Lilienthal report"), 16 March 1946.
2 On this debate, see for example: Sagan, S., and Waltz, K., *The spread of nuclear weapons: A debate renewed,* W.W. Norton & Company, Inc., 2003.
3 Albright, D., Brannan, P., and Scheel Stricker, A., 'Detecting and disrupting illicit nuclear trade after A.Q. Khan', *The Washington Quarterly*, April 2010. doi: https://doi.org/10.1080/0163660l003673857.
4 At the time of writing, Saudi Arabia has pursued nuclear cooperation while resisting reneging on the so-called small quantities protocol, which limits the scope of IAEA safeguards. In parallel, the country's leadership have said on several occasions that Saudi Arabia will seek nuclear weapons if Iran does. While the Saudi case is not examined in this book, the underlying questions of why countries such as Saudi Arabia can engage in nuclear cooperation without sufficient controls is at the heart of this book.
5 This refers to a fairytale based upon a story by Hans Christian Andersen entitled "The Emperor's New Clothes", in which the emperor is tricked into buying an 'invisible garment' that cannot be seen by those who are unfit for their positions, stupid, or incompetent. The emperor proudly wears these invisible clothes, with those around him compelled to act as though they can see the garments to show that they are worthy. Applied to supply-side controls, this fairytale implies that everyone should know that the controls do not work, but that they are also afraid to state this. R. Scott Kemp. "The Nonproliferation Emperor Has No Clothes: The Gas Centrifuge, Supply-Side Controls, and the Future of Nuclear Proliferation". *International Security,* vol. 38, no. 4, Spring 2014, pp. 39–78. doi: www.mitpressjournals.org/doi/full/10.1162/ISEC_a_00159.
6 Kemp, R.S., 'Centrifuges: A new era for nuclear proliferation', H. Solkolski (ed.), *Nuclear nonproliferation: Moving beyond pretense.* Nonproliferation Policy Education Center, July 2012.
7 Kemp, R.S., 'The Nonproliferation Emperor Has No Clothes: The Gas Centrifuge, Supply-Side Controls, and the Future of Nuclear Proliferation'. *International Security* vol. 38, no. 4, Spring 2014, pp. 39–78. doi: www.mitpressjournals.org/doi/full/10.1162/ISEC_a_00159.
8 Fuhrmann, M., 'Taking a Walk on the Supply Side: The Determinants of Civilian Nuclear Cooperation', *Journal of Conflict Resolution*, vol. 53, no. 2, 1 April 2009, pp. 181–208. doi: https://doi.org/10.1177/0022002708330288.
9 Bowen, W., *The politics of ballistic missile non-proliferation*, Southampton Studies in International Policy, 2000, p. 19. doi: 10.1057/9780333982280.
10 Knopf, J.W., *International cooperation on WMD non-proliferation*, University of Georgia Press, 2016. www.jstor.org/stable/j.ctt189ts81.
11 Enia, J., "Greasing the wheels of the nuclear nonproliferation regime: The political economy of nuclear suppliers group rules", *Journal of Peace and Nuclear Disarmament*, vol. 3, no. 2, 2020.

12 Enia's article was published after the research for this manuscript had been drafted. Use of the political economy lens would have been a valid alternative to the research approach to this book and would likely have allowed similar conclusions to be reached.

13 Stinnett, D.M., Early, B.R., Horne, C., and Karreth, J., 'Complying by denying: Explaining why states develop nonproliferation export controls'. *International Studies Perspectives*, vol. 12, 2011, pp. 308–326. doi: 10.1111/j.1528-3585.2011.00436.x.

14 On the UK, see Arnold, L., and M. Smith. *Britain, Australia and the bomb: The nuclear tests and their aftermath*, Palgrave Macmillan UK, 2006. ProQuest Ebook Central, https://ebookcentral.proquest.com/lib/kcl/detail.action?docID=293459. doi: 10.1057/9780230627338,

On Canada, see Bothwell, R., *Nucleus: The history of Atomic Energy Canada Limited*, University of Toronto Press, 1988.

On Israel, Cohen, A. *Israel and the bomb*, Columbia University Press, 2005. ProQuest Ebook Central, https://ebookcentral.proquest.com/lib/kcl/detail.action?docID=909169.

On China, Lewis, J., and Litai, X., *China builds the bomb*, Stanford University Press, 1988. On India, see Perkovich, G., *India's nuclear bomb: The impact on global proliferation*, University of California Press, February 2002.

On Pakistan, Khan, F., *Eating grass: The making of the Pakistani bomb*, Stanford Security Studies, 7 November 2012; Malik, Z., *Dr A.Q. Khan and the Islamic bomb*, Hurmat Publication Ltd, 1992; Rehman, S.U., 'Long road to Chagai', September 1999; Weissman, S., and Krosney, H., *The Islamic bomb*, Times Books, 1981.

On Libya, Bowen, W. Libya and nuclear proliferation: stepping back from the brink, Adelphi Paper 380, The International Institute for Strategic Studies, 2006; Braut-Hegghammer, M., *Unclear Physics: Why Iraq and Libya failed to build nuclear weapons*, Cornell University Press, 2016.

On Iran and North Korea, see: Shen D., 'Can sanctions stop proliferation?', *The Washington Quarterly*, vol. 31, no. 3, 2008, pp. 89–100, doi: 10.1162/wash.2008.31.3.89. Mousavian, S.H., *Iran and the United States*, Bloomsbury Academic Press, 2014; Albright, D., *Peddling peril: How the secret nuclear trade arms America's enemies*, Free Press, 2012.

On Iraq, see Lopez, G., and Cortright, D., 'Containing Iraq: Sanctions worked', Foreign Affairs, vol. 83, no. 4, July–August, 2004, pp. 90–103. On Pakistan, see 'Alpha in depth: Pakistan's strategic nuclear and missile industries: A baseline study for non-proliferation efforts', Project Alpha, King's College London. 3 November 2016. Available online at: http://projectalpha.eu/research-opens-a-window-into-pakistans-nuclear-weapons-programme/ (Accessed 27 November 2016).

15 For example, Corera, G., *Shopping for bombs: nuclear proliferation, global insecurity, and the rise and fall of the A.Q. Khan network*. OUP USA, 1 October 2009.

16 See for example, Hibbs, M., 'The future of the nuclear suppliers group', Carnegie Endowment for International Peace, 2011.

17 See for example, Bulkeley, J.C., 'Making the system work: Chinese export control reform', *The Nonproliferation Review*. Spring, 2004, and Nayan, R. and Stewart, I., 'Export controls and India', *CSSS Occasional Paper Series*, no. 1, King's College London, 2013.

18 See for example, McGoldrick, F., 'Limiting transfers of enrichment and reprocessing technology: Issues, constraints, options'. Report for Belfer Center for Science and International Affairs, Harvard Kennedy School, May 2011.

19 See for example, Bowen, W., 'The MTCR and EU expansion', *Non-proliferation Review*, vol. 5, no. 3, 1998.
20 Ouagrham-Gormley, S.B., 'Banking on non-proliferation', *Non-proliferation Review*. vol. 19, no. 2, 2012. doi: https://doi.org/10.1080/10736700.2012.690963.
21 Joshi, Y., 'Between principles and pragmatism: India and the nuclear non-proliferation regime in the post-PNE era, 1974–1980', *The International History Review*, pp. 1–21 | Published online: 02 January 2018. doi: https://doi.org/10.1080/07075332.2017.1417322.
22 Shaker, M.I., *The nuclear non-proliferation treaty: Origin and implementation – 1959–1979*. Oceana Publications Inc, 1980; Drogan, M., 'The nuclear imperative: Atoms for peace and the development of U.S. policy on exporting nuclear power, 1953–1955'. *Diplomatic history*, vol. 40, no. 5. November 2016.
23 Ibid., Stinnet *et al.*
24 Statement by the President of the Security Council, 7 May 2014, UN, New York. Some literature has now begun to examine the history of UNSCR 1540, including work initiated by the author. See for example, Salisbury, D., Stewart, I., and Viski, A. "Preventing the proliferation of WMDs, measuring the success of UN Security Council resolution 1540", Palgrave Pivot, 2018. doi: 10.1007/978-3-319-72203-0.
25 Kroenig, M., 'Importing the bomb: Sensitive nuclear assistance and nuclear proliferation', *Journal of Conflict Resolution,* vol. 53, 1 April 2009, pp. 161–180. www.jstor.org/stable/20684580.
26 Miller, N.L., 'The secret success of non-proliferation sanctions', *International Organisation*, 9 September 2014. www.jstor.org/stable/43283283.
27 Finch, R., *Exporting danger: History of the Canadian Nuclear Energy Export Programme*, Black Rose Books, 1986.
28 Spector L.S., and Smith, J.R., *Nuclear ambitions: Spread of nuclear weapons, 1989–90*, Westview Press Inc. 17 September 1990.
29 Albright, '*Peddling peril*'.
30 Anthony, I., Reforming Nuclear Export Controls: the future of the Nuclear Suppliers Group, SIPRI Research Report No. 22, 2007.
31 Ostrom, E., 'Analysing Collective Action', International Association of Agricultural Economists, 2010. doi: https://doi.org/10.1111/j.1574-0862.2010.00497.x.
32 See for example, Jones, S., 'The multilateral export control regimes: informality begets collaboration' in Knopf, J.W. (ed.), *International cooperation on WMD non-proliferation*, University of Georgia Press, 2016. www.jstor.org/stable/j.ctt189ts81.
33 Olsen, M., *The logic of collective action*, Harvard University Press, 1965 and 1971. www.jstor.org/stable/j.ctvjsf3ts.
34 Ibid.
35 Ostrom, E., 'Analysing collective action'.
36 Ostrom, E., 'Collective action and the evolution of social norms', *The Journal of Economic Perspectives*, vol. 14, no. 3, Summer, 2000, pp. 137–158. 10.1257/jep.14.3.137.
37 Agrawal, A., 'Common resources and institutional sustainability' In Ostrom, E., Dietz, T., Dolˇsak, N., Stern, P.C., Stonich, S., Weber, E. (Eds.), *The Drama of the Commons*, National Research Council, Committee on the Human Dimensions of Global Change. National Academies Press, Washington DC, pp. 41–85, 2002.
38 Ostrom, E., 'Analysing collective action'.
39 The rational actor model assumes that the actor will always act in their own best interest.
40 Ibid.

41 This final point is less relevant in the context of the book as states largely cannot opt not to engage in the international system. The closest relevant example during the period of interest is perhaps China during its 'cultural revolution'. However, it was during that period that China pursued nuclear weapons and provided assistance to Pakistan. This factor is thus not taken forward in the book.

42 Norms are values "that the individual attaches to an internal valuation – positive of negative to taking a particular type of action", ibid.

43 Kemp, R.S., 'The nonproliferation emperor has no clothes: The gas centrifuge, supply-side controls, and the future of nuclear proliferation'. *International Security,* vol. 38, no. 4, Spring 2014, pp. 39–78. doi: www.mitpressjournals.org/doi/full/10.1162/ISEC_a_00159.

44 See for example, Mukhatzhanova, G., and Potter, W., Nuclear politics and the non-aligned movement, Adelphi Series, vol. 2011, Edition 427, 15 February 2012.

45 This proposition approach to case study analysis was informed by an approach taken by Jeffery Knopf in an edited volume examining cooperation in the WMD non-proliferation sphere. See Knopf, J.W., *International Cooperation on WMD non-proliferation,* University of Georgia Press, 2016. www.jstor.org/stable/j.ctt189ts81.

46 Adoption of broader safeguards would have required recipient states to commit not to acquire nuclear weapons, whereas the more limited safeguards that were adopted simply meant that states could not use supplied materials in nuclear weapons production.

Bibliography

Acheson–Lilienthal Report. A report on the international control of atomic energy (Acheson–Lilienthal Report), 16 March 1946.

Agrawal, A. Common resources and institutional sustainability. In Ostrom, E., Dietz, T., Dolˇsak, N., Stern, P.C., Stonich, S., & Weber, E. (Eds.), *The drama of the commons, national research council, committee on the human dimensions of global change.* National Academies Press. pp. 41–85. 2002.

Albright, D. *Peddling peril: How the secret nuclear trade arms America's enemies,* Free Press, 2012.

Albright, D., Brannan, P., & Scheel Stricker, A. Detecting and disrupting illicit nuclear trade after A.Q. Khan. *The Washington Quarterly*, April 2010. doi: https://doi.org/10.1080/0163660100367385 7.Alpha in depth: Pakistan's strategic nuclear and missile industries: A baseline study for non-proliferation efforts, *Project Alpha*, King's College London. 3 November 2016. Available online at: http://projectalpha.eu/research-opens-a-window-into-pakistans-nuclear-weapons-programme/ (Accessed 27 November 2016).

Anthony, I. *Reforming nuclear export controls: The future of the nuclear suppliers group.* SIPRI Research Report No. 22, 2007. Available online at: www.sipri.org/publications/2007/reforming-nuclear-export-controls-future-nuclear-suppliers-group. ISBN: 978-0-19-929085-7

Arnold, L., & Smith, M. *Britain, Australia and the bomb: The nuclear tests and their aftermath,* Palgrave Macmillan UK, 2006. ProQuest Ebook Central. Available online at: https://ebookcentral.proquest.com/lib/kcl/detail.action?docID=293459. doi: 10.1057/9780230627338.

Bothwell, R. *Nucleus: The history of Atomic Energy Canada Limited*, University of Toronto Press, 1988.

Bowen, W. The MTCR and EU expansion. *The Non-Proliferation Review*, vol. 5, no. 3, 1998, pp. 84–88.

Bowen, W. *The politics of ballistic missile non-proliferation*. Southampton Studies in International Policy, 2000. doi: 10.1057/9780333982280.

Bowen, W. *Libya and nuclear proliferation: Stepping back from the brink*, Adelphi Paper 380, The International Institute for Strategic Studies, 2006.

Braut-Hegghammer, M. *Unclear Physics: Why Iraq and Libya failed to build nuclear weapons*, Cornell University Press, 2016.

Bulkeley, J.C. Making the system work: Chinese export control reform. *The Non-Proliferation Review*, vol. 11, no. 1, Spring 2004, pp. 145–169.

Cohen, A. *Israel and the bomb*, Columbia University Press, 2005. ProQuest Ebook Central. doi: https://ebookcentral.proquest.com/lib/kcl/detail.action?docID=909169.

Corera, G. Shopping for bombs: Nuclear proliferation, global insecurity, and the rise and fall of the A.Q. Khan network. *OUP USA*, 1 October 2009.

Drogan, M. The nuclear imperative: Atoms for peace and the development of U.S. policy on exporting nuclear power, 1953–1955. *Diplomatic History*, vol. 40, no. 5, November 2016, pp. 948–974.

Enia, J. Greasing the wheels of the nuclear nonproliferation regime: The political economy of nuclear suppliers group rules. *Journal of Peace and Nuclear Disarmament*, vol. 3, no. 2. 2020. doi: https://doi.org/10.1080/25751654.2020.1856553.

Finch, R. *Exporting danger: History of the Canadian nuclear energy export programme*, Black Rose Books, 1986.

Fuhrmann, M. Taking a walk on the supply side: The determinants of civilian nuclear cooperation. *Journal of Conflict Resolution*, vol. 53, no. 2, 1 April 2009, pp. 181–208. doi: https://doi.org/10.1177/0022002708330288.

Hibbs, M. The future of the nuclear suppliers group. *Carnegie Endowment for International Peace*, 2011. Available online at: http://carnegieendowment.org/files/future_nsg.pdf (Accessed 2 September 2017).

Jones, S. The multilateral export control regimes: Informality begets collaboration. In Knopf, J.W. (Ed.), *International cooperation on WMD non-proliferation*. University of Georgia Press. pp. 23–46. 2016. www.jstor.org/stable/j.ctt189ts81.

Joshi, Y. Between principles and pragmatism: India and the nuclear non-proliferation regime in the post-PNE era, 1974–1980. *International History Review* vol. 40, no. 5, 2018, pp. 1073–1093. Published online: 02 January 2018. doi: https://doi.org/10.1080/07075332.2017.1417322.

Kemp, R.S. Centrifuges: A new era for nuclear proliferation. In H. Solkolski (ed.), *Nuclear nonproliferation: Moving beyond pretense.* Nonproliferation Policy Education Center. pp. 227–262. July 2012.

Kemp, R.S. The nonproliferation emperor has no clothes: The gas centrifuge, supply-side controls, and the future of nuclear proliferation. *International Security* vol. 38, no. 4, Spring 2014, pp. 39–78. doi: www.mitpressjournals.org/doi/full/10.1162/ISEC_a_00159.

Khan, F. *Eating grass: The making of the Pakistani bomb*, Stanford Security Studies, 7 November 2012.

Knopf, J.W. International cooperation on WMD non-proliferation, University of Georgia Press, 2016. www.jstor.org/stable/j.ctt189ts81.

Kroenig, M. Importing the bomb: Sensitive nuclear assistance and nuclear proliferation. *Journal of Conflict Resolution*, vol. 53, 1 April 2009, pp. 161–180. www.jstor.org/stable/20684580.

Lewis, J., & Litai, X. *China builds the bomb*, Stanford University Press, 1988 Paper 380, The International Institute for Strategic Studies, 2006.
Lopez, G., & Cortright, D. Containing Iraq: Sanctions worked. *Foreign Affairs*, vol. 83, no. 4, July–August 2004, pp. 90–103.
Malik, Z. *Dr A.Q. Khan and the Islamic bomb*, Hurmat Publication Ltd, 1992.
McGoldrick, F. *Limiting transfers of enrichment and reprocessing technology: Issues, constraints, options*. Cambridge, MA: Report for Belfer Center for Science and International Affairs, Harvard Kennedy School, May 2011.
Miller, N.L. The secret success of non-proliferation sanctions. *International Organisation*, 9 September 2014. www.jstor.org/stable/43283283.
Mousavian, S.H. *Iran and the United States*, Bloomsbury Academic Press, 2014.
Mukhatzhanova, G., & Potter, W. *Nuclear politics and the non-aligned movement*. Adelphi Series. vol. 2011, Edition 427, 15 February 2012.
Nayan, R., & Stewart, I. Export controls and India. *CSSS Occasional Paper Series*, no. 1, King's College London, 2013.
Ostrom, E. Collective action and the evolution of social norms. *Journal of Economic Perspectives*, vol. 14, no. 3, Summer, 2000, pp. 137–158. doi: 10.1257/jep.14.3.137.
Ostrom, E. Analysing collective action. *International Association of Agricultural Economists*, vol. 41, no. 1, 2010, pp. 155–166. doi: https://doi.org/10.1111/j.1574-0862.2010.00497.x.
Ouagrham-Gormley, S.B. Banking on nonproliferation. *The Non-Proliferation Review*, vol. 19, no. 2, 2012, pp. 241–265.
Perkovich, G. *India's nuclear bomb: The impact on global proliferation*, University of California Press, February 2002.
Rehman, S.U., *Long road to Chagai*. September 1999.
Salisbury, D., Stewart, I., & Viski, A. *Preventing the proliferation of WMDs, measuring the success of UN Security Council resolution 1540*. Palgrave Pivot, 2018. doi: 10.1007/978-3-319-72203-0.
Shaker, M.I. *The nuclear non-proliferation treaty: Origin and implementation – 1959–1979*. vol. 1–3. Oceana Publications Inc., 1980.
Shen, D. Can sanctions stop proliferation? *The Washington Quarterly,* vol. 31, no. 3, 2008, pp. 89–100, doi: 10.1162/wash.2008.31.3.89.
Spector L.S., & Smith, J.R. *Nuclear ambitions: Spread of nuclear weapons, 1989–90*. Westview Press, Inc. 17 September 1990.
Stinnett, D.M., Early, B.R., Horne, C., & Karreth, J. Complying by denying: Explaining why states develop nonproliferation export controls. *International Studies Perspectives*, vol. 12, 2011, pp. 308–326. doi:10.1111/j.1528-3585.2011.00436.x.
UN GA 1/46, Establishment of a commission to deal with the problem of raised by the discovery of atomic energy, *UN General Assembly Resolution*, 24 January 1946. Available online at: https://digitallibrary.un.org/record/671200?ln=en
Weissman, S., & Krosney, H. *The Islamic bomb*. Times Books, 1981.

2 The missed opportunity?

Effective control of atomic energy

Atomic weapons went from black-board theory to deployable military capability over the course of a few short years during the Second World War. This compressed development period during a time of war meant there was little time for discussion about the exploitation or sharing of atomic energy for peaceful purposes. Instead, the US and the UK – the principal wartime allies – agreed to address the question of civil uses of atomic energy and control after the war.[1] At the end of the war, a discussion began in earnest about the use and control of atomic energy, particularly in the US. Various options were considered in Washington, including, on one extreme, sharing nuclear technology with the Soviet Union, and on the other seeking to maintain a US monopoly on the technology.[2] Perhaps the option that received the most attention was that of developing an "effective system of international control" of atomic energy so that it could be exploited for peaceful uses while also ensuring that it could not be exploited for military uses. This idea to effectively combine a plan for nuclear disarmament with a global system to ensure non-proliferation led to the creation of a UN Atomic Energy Commission (UNAEC) and several years of detailed negotiations through this mechanism.[3]

A key argument presented in this chapter is that the US viewed nuclear weapons spread as inevitable in the post-1945 period, a view that was solidified following the Soviet Union's first nuclear test in 1949. It was for this reason that the US sought to negotiate an international system of control for atomic energy that would also result in nuclear disarmament: only through the elimination of existing nuclear weapons could demand for nuclear weapons be eliminated. While the US appears to have begun negotiations in good faith, the discussions were overtaken by the emerging Cold War environment. As such, by the time of the Soviet Union's first nuclear test, Moscow likely had also reached the conclusion that disarmament was not achievable in the developing Cold War context because nuclear weapons provided a tool to balance with the US. By the end of the 1940s, neither side thought disarmament and non-proliferation were achievable, and the negotiations collapsed as a result. Nonetheless, despite the fact that agreement was not reached on 'international control' of atomic energy, this period did give birth to concepts for control subsequently built upon in the decades that followed. Moreover,

DOI: 10.4324/9781003194262-2

the interaction of domestic political and geo-strategic issues during the period shaped what came later.

Given the fact that no system of control was ultimately agreed upon in this period, the chapter differs somewhat from the chapters that follow. In relation to the overall question examined in this book, the potential 'optimal' system of control in this period is taken as the system of international control proposed to the UNAEC. The collective action framework is used to gain insight into what drove and hindered the development of controls in this period. However, given that no controls were agreed in the end, an important secondary purpose of this chapter is to provide necessary contextual background for the later episode-specific chapters. This is important as the system of control envisioned by the UNAEC was in some ways more ambitious than those that were envisioned in the periods that followed. An implicit third purpose of this chapter is to demonstrate the utility of the research framework in examining such episodes.

The chapter starts by setting out developments related to the control of nuclear technology after the Second World War and examining the strategies for control that were considered. Then, the chapter examines the post-war debate on atomic energy at both the domestic US and international levels as embodied in the UNAEC. The key factors relevant to the evolution of controls during this period are then identified.

Harnessing the atom

Before examining the factors that influenced the development of controls in the period 1945–1953, it is useful to summarise the war-time controls put in place on nuclear technologies by western powers and how the transition from war to peace time controls occurred. While the aim is not to present a history of the Manhattan Project, it is helpful nevertheless to highlight specific issues that became central to shaping the nature of the controls adopted on nuclear technology after the war.[4]

The Manhattan Project should not be viewed, of course, as a purely US programme but an allied effort. The US initiated the Manhattan Project at the urging of European scientists, most notably Albert Einstein, Leo Szilard, and Alexander Sachs.[5] The programme also had British and Canadian engineers, and scientists embedded for much of its duration. In 1943, the US took steps to limit any cooperation that could not be used for military purposes during the war. A personal appeal by Prime Minister Winston Churchill to President Harry Truman resulted in full cooperation being restored based on an agreement between the US and UK that post-war controls would be mutually agreed.[6,7] This led to the formation of the "Combined Policy Committee" (CPC) involving the US, UK, and Canada, the purpose of which was to coordinate efforts to ensure their access to uranium. This body would become important in shaping nuclear cooperation over the course of the following decade.[8] Under the CPC, a Combined Development Trust (CDT) was created on 15 June 1944, with the purpose to "Acquire and undertake the treatment and disposal of uranium and thorium materials".[9] While intended primarily to serve the nuclear needs of the CPC countries, which were largely dependent on imported uranium, success with this objective was also intended to limit other countries' access to uranium or thorium for their own nuclear programmes.[10] Given that nuclear weapons could not be produced without uranium, controlling uranium ore become a top geostrategic priority for the US, UK, and Canada.

During the Second World War, some consideration was given to the question of how to manage atomic energy after the war. In an exchange of letters with the US in 1942, for example, UK officials wrote that, "Utilisation of nuclear energy, whether as a military weapon or industrial purpose, will require a special and powerful system of control".[11] The so-called Hyde Park agreement of September 1944 reached between Churchill and Roosevelt can be understood as a measure to satisfy the US that the UK could not exploit atomic energy for commercial purposes without its agreement. The Hyde Park agreement thus allowed for the "full cooperation between the US and the British government in developing Tube Alloys for military and commercial purposes following the defeat of Japan unless and until terminated by joint agreement".[12]

During the war, the US also believed that it and its closest allies held nearly all of the know-how related to nuclear technologies. The substantial investment necessary for the US in particular to achieve this monopoly would lead some US Cabinet members, including for example, the Secretary of Agriculture, to believe that it might be possible for the US to maintain this monopoly.[13] Moreover, the know-how associated with atomic energy was held by the Manhattan engineering district as a wartime military project rather than in commercial hands. This had the effect of making it easier to keep the knowledge associated with the programme secret while also preventing the emergence of commercial vested interests in the earliest days of the nuclear age.

Apart from the factors outlined earlier, there were few guiding principles or agreements that shaped post-war controls on the uses of atomic energy. In fact, there were signs that US policymakers in the Truman Administration and Congress did not feel bound to some of the agreements reached with US allies during the war – and the Hyde Park agreement in particular – with Arnold and Smith suggesting this was, in part, because no one in the US administration knew about the agreement given the need for war-time secrecy.[14] Indeed, nuclear policymaking in this period was undertaken by a small number of individuals and in secret. Consequently, ideas did not always receive the additional and wider consideration that could have resulted in the identification of issues and problems.

Wartime to peacetime

The use of atomic weapons against Japan in July 1945 marked the true beginning of the atomic age. The powerful demonstration of the destructiveness of atomic weapons and their contribution to ending the Second World War prompted a debate about the future role of atomic energy. This debate took place in various national and international forums, including the soon-to-be-established United Nations (UN), where the first-ever General Assembly resolution focused on the topic. However, the real starting point for the debate was in the US, which had pioneered the development and application of atomic energy. In order to inform this debate and the public discourse about atomic weapons, a report written by American physicist Henry Smyth titled, "Atomic Energy for Military Purposes" was released on 12 August 1945, shortly after the atomic bombing of Japan.[15] The report was commissioned by Major General Leslie R. Groves, Jr., who had overseen the Manhattan Project with the purpose of setting out to the extent possible, given secrecy requirements, what had been achieved by the project. The report was designed to inform US policymakers, allies, potential enemies and the public at large about the significance of this new type of weapon.

The debate on the future of atomic energy was also taken up by the US Cabinet. President Truman dedicated the 21 September 1945 meeting of his cabinet to this question and its minutes highlight the diverse options considered.[16] It is apparent from the President's remarks to his cabinet that the question of the future of atomic energy was entirely open. He pondered, for example, whether the US should 'give the secret' of nuclear weapons to the USSR or whether the US could maintain a monopoly on nuclear know-how. He sought the views of his cabinet both at the meeting and via written submission afterwards.[17]

Unencumbered by the commercial and other vested interests that had yet to emerge around atomic energy – largely because of the need for secrecy which necessitated state ownership – the views submitted were diverse. Secretary Stimson, the Secretary of State for War, opened the discussion by stating that the US did "not have a secret to give away – the secret will give away itself".[18] Others argued that the advanced scientific and technical capacities of the US were unique and other states could not be expected to develop nuclear weapons. This view was rebutted by the influential Vannevar Bush – the US chair of the CPC – who stated that Russia could "get to about the place we are now in five years provided they devote a very large part of their scientific and industrial effort to it".[19] He, therefore, favoured "giving Russia everything [the US] had as regards the principles of atomic energy".[20] Dean Acheson, Secretary of State, "saw no alternative except to give full information to the Russians".[21] The Secretary of the Navy and the Secretary of the Interior pondered whether the US could hold nuclear weapons in trusteeship for the UN. The Secretary of Agriculture expressed doubt about the ability of Russia to produce nuclear weapons within five years. He stated that Russia could acquire knowledge but not the "know how" necessary for nuclear weapons. The Secretary of Commerce supported, whereas the Attorney General and the Secretary of the Treasury were against, sharing nuclear knowledge with

Russia. The Joint Chiefs of Staff expressed support for UN discussions on international control.[22]

The majority of the views expressed were in support of the idea that the US could not keep the atomic secret for long. However, it is apparent from the cabinet minutes that there was no consensus among cabinet members at the meeting or afterward. Indeed, President Truman pursued a third way following the cabinet meeting. Instead of seeking to maintain the US monopoly or giving the technology away, he sought international support for an ambitious initiative to verifiably eliminate nuclear weapons while also allowing for the peaceful uses of nuclear technology. The principles of this initiative were set out in a statement from the leaders of the US, UK, and Canada – the three main war-time nuclear allies – on 15 November 1945, which is reproduced at Annex 1 of this book, and then endorsed at a meeting with the Soviet leadership the same month. UN General Assembly resolution 1/46 (the first ever) endorsed the principles of the plan and created the UNAEC.[23]

The plan involved the development of an 'effective system of control' for atomic energy. The US government commissioned a report – which became known as the Acheson–Lilienthal report – in order to inform the UN process about what such a system of control might involve.

In parallel to the international effort to devise an effective system of control for atomic energy, the US Congress acted to restrict access to nuclear know-how and technology. The McMahon Act of 1946 forbade US persons from helping any other country acquire nuclear weapons technology.[24] The intention of US legislators was to maintain the US monopoly on nuclear technology, at least until an international agreement was reached on its regulation.[25] The McMahon Act could thus have been temporary in nature if international control had been agreed.

This act restricted cooperation with all foreign nationals on nuclear issues, including with Canada and the UK. There are signs that Congress did not appreciate at the time the full contribution of the UK to the Manhattan Project when it adopted the act.[26] The move also spurred efforts in the UK to drive forward with its own programme to produce nuclear weapons.[27] In limiting international cooperation and preventing industry involvement in shaping the future of atomic energy, the act had a significant effect on the future evolution of the atomic age. Adoption of the act was a clear and early demonstration of the important role that domestic politics would play in shaping matters related to the international control of atomic energy.

By introducing the act, Senator Brien McMahon of the Democratic Party also sought to keep atomic technology in the hands of the state rather than corporations.[28] It was this drive that led to the creation of the US Atomic Energy Commission (USAEC) with the authority to "develop, control, and supervise the use and application of atomic energy" in the US.[29] As such, atomic technology in the aftermath of Second World War was deliberately kept out of the hands of US commercial enterprise, with the President going as far as federalising land containing deposits of thorium and uranium.[30] It is worth pointing out that at this time, before nuclear power had been commercialised, there was no real commercial lobby for the atomic energy industry outside of government.

Significantly, the bill that emerged from Congress prohibited international cooperation on all aspects of atomic energy and so went against the 1943 Quebec agreement between Churchill and Truman, under which both the US and the UK agreed to share nuclear technology.

International control of atomic energy

Following the US cabinet meeting of 21 September 1945, the US raised the issue of post-war controls on atomic energy with the CPC partners that November. The CPC meeting resulted in a seminal statement issued by the leaders of the US, the UK, and Canada. This statement contained the first expression of many of the elements that would define the nuclear age. A central element of the text was the notion of international control. Moscow agreed to enter into negotiations on devising a system of control and the UNAEC, a body of the UN tasked with devising a system of international control for atomic energy.[31]

From the perspective of the CPC states, the objectives of the discussions were to outlaw the "national production and use of atomic weapons" and to create an agency for its enforcement.[32] This would be achieved by ensuring that, "the manufacture, possession, and use of atomic weapons by all nationals and by all persons under their jurisdiction should be forbidden". Existing stocks of nuclear weapons were also to be disposed of and nuclear technology was to be used for peaceful purposes.[33]

This was evidently an ambitious agenda and one that would be challenging to fulfil. Nuclear weapons were, after all, the most powerful weapons ever invented, which made them attractive for states to possess and possibly use. In the early nuclear age, there was no expectation or norm related to the non-use of nuclear weapons. Indeed, in the context of the emerging Cold War of the late 1940s, it is perhaps unsurprising that the Western and Soviet Blocs would enter discussions with little trust of one another.

The US position at the UNAEC would ultimately be based largely on a report commissioned for the purpose – the Acheson–Lilienthal report. This report was based on deliberations by a panel of expert scientists from across the US nuclear enterprise designated to examine the question of how to control atomic energy. The group's task was to "seek by all reasonable means to bring about international arrangements to prevent the use of atomic energy for destructive purposes and to promote the use of it for the benefit of society".[34] The report, like the UNAEC, thus started from the premise that atomic energy would be made available for peaceful purposes if an effective system of control could be established.

The authors of the report focused on the question of what an 'effective system of control' for atomic energy might look like. They expressly recognised that the "development of atomic energy for peaceful purposes and the development of atomic energy for bombs are in much of their course interchangeable and interdependent", and as such,

> the only assurance that a conversion to destructive purposes would not be made would be the pledged word and the good faith of the nation itself ... fear of such surprise violation of pledged word will surely break down any confidence in the pledged word of rival countries developing atomic energy if the treaty obligations and good faith of the nations are the only assurance upon which to rely.[35]

In short, the authors concluded that commitments made by states were not enough, so a system of international control of national "intrinsically dangerous" fuel cycle facilities would be required.[36,37] The authors also recommended that an international agency be established with the role of taking ownership of these facilities with the and responsibility for "the construction and operation of production plants, and the conduct of research in explosives".[38] Non-dangerous activities were to be left in national hands.

Significantly, the group also concluded that a system of inspection – which is ultimately what was pursued in relation to the Atoms for Peace initiative – could not counter the risks of a breakdown of trust among states. As a result, the authors stated that they did not foresee a need for large-scale inspections by the agency.[39] In the decades that followed, the IAEA would come to rely on inspections as its primary investigative means but, as predicted, there was often a lack of trust in these modalities, as evidenced for example by Israel's destruction of Iraq's Osiraq reactor in 1981 as examined in Chapter 5.

While the report was forward leaning, in retrospect, the underlying concept had limitations and flaws. For example, the authors assumed that fissile material would be scarce and could thus be easily brought under international ownership. This proved not to be the case. At the time, nuclear reactors existed only for the purpose of producing fissile material for use in nuclear weapons programmes. The authors foresaw a need to develop higher temperature reactors for use in power generation, but no practical experience of operating such reactors was available to inform the authors' recommendations.[40] As a result of these limitations in the report, the recommendations would ultimately have proven to be unworkable in practice. Nonetheless, the report can certainly be considered a "best effort" at the time to devise an original solution to the competing challenges of controlling atomic energy for military purposes, while also making it available for peaceful uses. Perhaps for this reason, the report's recommendations would ultimately form the basis of the discussions at the UNAEC, despite the fact that the US lead negotiator, Bernard Baruch, would seek an alternative solution to become known as the Baruch Plan.

The Baruch plan

President Truman appointed Bernard Baruch in 1946, a wealthy and successful confidant and friend who had been closely involved in leading aspects of the US war effort, to the role of US representative of the UNAEC. Baruch initially rejected the Acheson–Lilienthal report, conducting instead his own review of the problem of controlling atomic energy.[41] However, he ultimately identified no better system than that which had been recommended in the Acheson–Lilienthal report and so incorporated that system into his proposal to the UNAEC. His proposal did, therefore, include the idea of setting up an authority to exercise international control of so-called dangerous nuclear activities as a prerequisite to nuclear disarmament. However, he did include new provisions related to enforcement that had not been contained in the largely organisationally focused Acheson–Lilienthal report. This additional idea would remove the veto of the permanent members of the UN Security Council in relation to nuclear matters in order to avoid a situation in which a veto-wielding power could prevent or frustrate international inspection and enforcement action. This would require the veto-welding permanent members of the Security Council to give up substantial sovereignty to an international organisation but perhaps was considered feasible given that the UN was new and the veto-wielding powers were newly established in the UNSC.

Baruch appears to have recognised that cheating on the implementation of the plan for international control of atomic energy would be destabilising and could result in an arms race. He also believed that the untested UN Security Council could not be relied upon to respond to such cheating if the cheating party was a veto-wielding permanent member. It was these factors that framed his amendments. Baruch submitted this plan to the UNAEC on 14 June 1946.[42]

UN Atomic Energy Commission

The mandate of the UNAEC was to make specific proposals for:[43]

1 extending between all nations the exchange of basic scientific information for peaceful ends;
2 control of atomic energy to the extent necessary to ensure its use only for peaceful purposes;
3 the elimination from national armaments of atomic weapons and all other major weapons adaptable to mass destruction; and
4 effective safeguards by way of inspection and other means to protect complying States against the hazards of violations and evasions.

Reviewing this negotiating record, it is apparent that the principal stumbling block that was discussed was one of the modalities. The Soviet Union took the view that it would be necessary to simultaneously advance two conventions. The first would relate to a prohibition of atomic weapons. The second to the establishment, in connection with prohibition, of an international control system.[44] The negotiating record also shows that this was to be an "effective" system covering a country's "entire nuclear industry".[45] There was nonetheless disagreement over a fundamental point regarding international ownership. The Soviet Union argued that, "international management and operation were equivalent to international control; and that neither international ownership nor international management and operation was essential to control".[46] The Soviets also linked this to sovereignty issues arguing that, "the powers suggested in the Statement of Principles would permit the international agency to interfere in the internal economy of individual states".[47] The other sponsoring powers believed that management and ownership were essential to control.[48] In practice, Russia's reluctance to agree to inspections was doubtless also a result of a concern that such inspections could be used to collect information on Russia's conventional military capabilities. It was for these reasons that the Soviet Union rejected Baruch's proposal.

While it was not expressed as such in the negotiation, it appears that Moscow's practical concern was that a system of control would be introduced to prevent more states from acquiring nuclear weapons but without also resulting in the US eliminating its existing arsenal.

In the absence of an agreement between the US and the USSR, other states attempted to broker an agreement. India proposed an alternative after the first Soviet nuclear test of August 1949.[49] A Soviet draft resolution in October contained, according to the US, nothing new.[50] Nonetheless, by this point, it was becoming apparent that no agreement would be possible based on the proposals put forward at the time.

As a result of the inability of the main powers to reach common ground, the UNAEC reported on 19 July 1949 its inability to continue to work. Baruch would later put the issue to a vote of the UNAEC in the knowledge that the US resolution would not be supported by Moscow in order to demonstrate to other powers what he considered to be the unreasonableness of the Soviet position.[51] The post-war effort to establish international control had thus failed primarily as a result of the rising tension and growing distrust between the US and Soviet Union.

Nuclear trade controls from 1945 to 1953

The failure of the UNAEC to reach an agreement left the provisions of the McMahon Act in effect. Nonetheless, outside of the discussions about international control of atomic energy, some nuclear cooperation and national nuclear advancement did take place. The nature of this cooperation would have a substantial impact on the future of international non-proliferation efforts, particularly after the failure of the UNAEC and is thus important to examine.

Cooperation between the US, the UK, and Canada

Nuclear cooperation between the US, the UK, and Canada tailed off at the end of the Second World War as the debate began over how to manage atomic energy in the post-war period.[52]

The McMahon act was envisioned as a temporary measure until international control was agreed upon. Nonetheless, the act restricted cooperation with all foreign nationals on nuclear issues, including those from Canada and the UK, two of the key countries that had participated in the Manhattan Project. It also went against the Quebec agreement of 1943. The actions of Congress in adopting the Act interfered with the cooperation that had developed with the UK and Canada, both of which were frustrated by the disruption in cooperation. However, the US also suffered as a result of the Act because it was through the consent and cooperation of the UK and Canada that the US was sourcing much of the uranium required for its own nuclear programme. Lack of access to uranium became a vital issue for the US and, by December 1947, US officials realised that its uranium allocation was insufficient to meet the programme's plutonium production targets, with the result that facilities would have to be shuttered unless an increased allocation was secured.[53]

As a result, the US reconvened a meeting of the CPC, which had paused as a result of the McMahon Act to enable the US to work with its wartime allies in addressing its material shortfall.[54] Cooperation between the US, UK, and Canada was then taken forward under the auspices of a new agreement, the *modus vivendi* of 7 January 1948.[55] The *modus vivendi* tasked the CPC with three activities: "allocating raw materials in accordance with such principles as may be determined from time to time by the Committee"; "considering the general questions arising with respect to cooperation among the three governments"; and "supervis[ing] the operations and policies of the Combined Development Agency (CDA)".[56] After this meeting, the CDA secured access to uranium from South Africa and Portugal for the first time, although supplies from the Belgian Congo began to reduce.[57] The US thus sought to take forward cooperation to the maximum extent possible under the act in order to satisfy its own programme needs. An indirect benefit of this policy was that less uranium would be available for the Soviet Union or other countries should they embark on a nuclear programme, although this would be undercut by 1952 when it became known that natural uranium was more readily accessible than previously believed. By October 1952, the CDA had come to realise that the "usable sources of uranium which were available throughout the world were much larger than formerly believed".[58]

The decision to negotiate a *modus vivendi* is an interesting one. *Modus vivendi* is "executive agreements which are temporary or provisional in character", and which fall within the US President's power to enact.[59] As a result, they have the same binding effect under international law as other international agreements but are considered temporary or provisional in nature, meaning that Congressional approval (and even public disclosure) was unnecessary. In effect, the US executive was acting on its own to resume cooperation with allies in partial defiance of the law adopted by Congress. The reason for doing so appears to have been the narrow strategic interest of the US in obtaining access to fissile material for its weapons programme. However, US officials also recognised that cooperation with the UK could have implications for the effort to negotiate international control of atomic energy. In particular, US officials feared that providing assistance to the UK nuclear weapons programme would make achieving international control less likely. This was likely why the agreement was secret and temporary in nature: if the UNAEC had been successful, the scope of cooperation would have to be revisited along with the US atomic energy act of 1946.

Nine areas of technical cooperation were taken forward despite the McMahon Act, including "fundamental properties of reactor materials".[60] It is notable that one member of the US CPC delegation dissented in a vote on this cooperation. After the meeting, Lewis Strauss, then a Commissioner on the USAEC, stated that he was concerned to learn that the UK was pursuing plutonium production and wrote to the US atomic energy commissioners seeking their support in asking for a Presidential decision to be made regarding nuclear cooperation with the UK.[61] Strauss was concerned that the UK was pursuing nuclear weapons and that US officials were cooperating with the UK to support aspects of its programme.

> Once the manufacture of plutonium in quantity is out of our hands, security is also out of our hands and beyond our control forever. Even if it should become our national policy to help Great Britain to arm herself with atomic weapons, that can be done demonstrably with much greater economy and far less hazard by other means, at the proper time.[62]

The other commissioners failed to support Strauss, finding that technical cooperation with the UK in the field of "fundamental properties of reactor materials" was "clearly in the interests of the national security of the United States".[63] In effect, Strauss had made the case that the US should not assist other states in pursuing nuclear weapons but was overruled first by the USAEC and then by CPC-related officials in other government departments.[64]

When Strauss then raised the question of whether the US participants appreciated that the UK would use material acquired by the CPC for the production of plutonium for weapons use, Vannevar Bush – the official responsible for the CDT – expressed surprise that the question had arisen at all: the US had known even during WWII that the UK was interested in acquiring nuclear weapons.[65]

Despite the McMahon Act, the programmes of the UK and Canada advanced. Canada, for example, completed and then commercialised the NRX reactor, thus creating a market for radioisotopes. The flux characteristics of Canadian reactors were unique at the time. The US thus requested that

Canada test US materials in the reactor but without telling the Canadians what the materials were because of the McMahon Act's restrictions.[66]

Cooperation with other countries

The failure of the UNAEC and the resumption of US nuclear cooperation with the UK in the knowledge that the fruits of this could be put to military ends raised broader questions about nuclear cooperation with other states. These questions were not fully addressed by the Truman administration after the failure of the UNAEC in 1949. This resulted in a somewhat inconsistent approach to civil nuclear cooperation. On the one hand, there was a concern that a country such as France could take the lead in terms of promoting civil nuclear cooperation if the US did not act, but there was no move to lift the restrictions contained in the McMahon Act.[67] At the same time, there was a recognition that an arrangement may need to be reached with countries such as Belgium and South Africa, which were supplying uranium to the CDT, should these countries wish to pursue the use of atomic energy. Finally, the McMahon Act was still in effect meaning that cooperation could not take place in any event without amendment to US domestic law. The US policy on nuclear assistance was, therefore, one of contradictions and confusion by the end of the Truman administration.

Chapter findings and conclusions

In the immediate aftermath of the Second World War, a debate began over how best to control atomic energy. The debate was centred in the US as the leading atomic power at the time. The debate was generally open in nature and no options appear to have been off the table. The US settled on pursuing the idea of international control of atomic energy. This would involve the internationalisation of the nuclear fuel cycle to bringing about nuclear disarmament to ensure non-proliferation. This was clearly a significant and ambitious plan.

The purpose of this chapter was to examine the system of control that was contemplated in this period and to gain insight into why it was not introduced. This chapter differs from the chapters that follow in that agreement was not reached on the adoption of coordinated international controls in this period. Nonetheless, the examination of controls in this period provides useful insight and background to the question of why controls in later periods evolved in a sub-optimal way. In this context, this concluding section of this chapter will briefly highlight insights gleaned through the research framework and will draw broader findings from efforts to agree on controls in the post-war period.

Insights from the research framework

The immediate post-war period saw a rewriting of the international landscape. The defeat of Germany and Japan meant that the pre-war power dynamics had fundamentally shifted. The invention and possession of nuclear weapons by one country, which anyway was perhaps the sole power in the period, created a new impetus to the international landscape.

The US put forward an ambitious proposal for the international control of atomic energy and instigated the creation of the UNAEC to negotiate its implementation. For the purpose of examining the overall research of this book, this conceived system of control can be considered the optimal system considered in this period.

In examining the factors that drove and hindered the development of controls in this period, this concluding section will draw on the CAP research framework. The framework includes propositions related to the following factors: structural factors such as the number of actors, how actors are linked; and whether benefits are subtractive or fully shared; core factors such as whether trust and norms existed; imperatives including around the uses of atomic energy, non-proliferation, and disarmament; and technological factors. Each of these propositions is examined in turn.

Structural factors

- Number and type of actors: Even in the early nuclear age where non-military uses of atomic energy were nascent, this was evidently an important factor. In the US, the administration and Congress had subtly different priorities. Additionally, a number of key state's including Canada, the UK, and the Soviet Union, each had their own priorities. These divergent priorities hindered the development of controls, despite the fact that the number of states holding nuclear technology was small and private sector actors had not yet entered the scene.
- Heterogeneity of participants: Even though the number of actors involved was relatively limited, the strategic rivalry between the US and the Soviet Union was a key barrier to the introduction of effective control. It was this point that prevented the implementation of the ambitious system of control being considered by the UNAEC.
- Whether benefits are subtractive or fully shared: The mutual benefit of nuclear disarmament and international control was recognised in this period and sought by both the US and Soviet Union. There was tension between a pursuit of these and nuclear armament in the context of the emerging Cold War. Other benefits, such as commercial interests, were not yet significant.
- Information on past action was largely irrelevant in this period. The Second World War resulted in a realignment of the global order and the emergence of atomic weapons. This added a new dynamic that had not existed prior to this point and made information on past action largely irrelevant.
- How actors are linked: The power structure which emerged with the Cold War provided the key linkages in this period. The UN provided space for

talks, but the emerging Cold War disrupted the cooperation that could have emerged under UN auspices.

Core factors

Non-proliferation norm: There was no non-proliferation norm in this period. Had the UNAEC negotiations been successful, such a norm may have emerged. However, in the absence of this, there are signs that key states such as the US accepted proliferation as inevitable.

Trust: The absence of trust between the US and Soviet Union was a key factor in the failure of the UNAEC to reach an agreement on international control of atomic energy. While the Soviet Union articulated its concern as being about a sequencing issue – that is, whether control and inspection could be brought about at the same time, the reality is that it was mistrust in the context of the emerging Cold War that drove Soviet thinking. This mistrust drove suspicion about sequencing and promoted hesitation at the idea of allowing intrusive inspection.

Imperatives

- Uses of atomic energy: In this period, the imperative of uses of atomic energy was nascent. While atomic weapons had been produced, the potential for atomic energy to produce vast quantities of electrical power had not yet been realised. Given this formative stage of atomic energy development, the imperative was established and less important than in the subsequent periods.
- Disarmament: The creation of the UNAEC is a clear indicator that prominence was placed on the possibility of eliminating nuclear weapons in the immediate post-war period. There are no signs that states were not sincere in entering into the UNAEC process. However, it became clear that no agreement could be reached between the US and the Soviet Union on the question of disarmament in this period, not least because of growing mistrust in the context of the emerging Cold War.
- Non-proliferation: This imperative appears to have been less prominent for much of this period. Immediately after the Second World War, there are signs that key states, including the US, thought non-proliferation was not feasible. There was then a concerted effort to buy up uranium supplies which would also have the effect of restraining proliferation. However, by 1949 when the Soviet Union tested its first nuclear weapon, it was evident that this approach would not prevent proliferation.

Technology

Technology factors: Uranium availability was not well understood in this period nor was the nuclear fuel cycle. For example, the action of

> the CPC in buying up foreign uranium indicates that the CPC countries thought uranium deposits were more scarce than they proved to be. As a result, it seems unlikely that the UNAEC could anyway have devised an effective system of control. Additionally, the only reactor technology that had been developed was designed for military purposes. The result was that the assumptions on which the concept of international control of atomic energy was based were flawed.

From this brief application of the collective action framework, it is apparent that structural factors, including principally intensified US/Soviet rivalry, prevented controls from being adopted in this period. This is true despite the fact that the number of actors was limited and the uses of atomic energy imperative were nascent. These structural factors could not be overcome by core factors as there was also a lack of trust and an absence of a non-proliferation norm in this period.

Broader findings

The concept of international control of atomic energy was an ambitious one. There are a few signs that this policy was pursued disingenuously by the US. The US would come to believe that the Soviet Union was not serious about pursuing international control of atomic energy, although it is not possible to say with certainty which factors drove Moscow's reluctance to agree to the US proposal beyond its stated position. Nonetheless, the mistrust inherent in the emerging Cold War environment was certainly a key factor in preventing efforts to bring about international control of atomic energy at this time.

In the absence of an agreement, the default US policy was to prevent the sharing of atomic energy. This was enshrined through the McMahon Act, which was intended to be temporary in nature and which forbade US persons from helping other countries to acquire nuclear weapons. With the failure of the UNAEC to reach an agreement, however, this temporary US policy became enduring in the absence of a substantial new initiative. The act also locked commercial entities out of atomic energy development in the US at this stage.

Overall, therefore, it was a combination of mistrust between the US and Soviet Union and structural factors inherent in the Cold War, which prevented cooperation on non-proliferation and trade controls in this period. Other factors such as the number of states 'principally involved' appear to have been secondary to the structural and trust issues discussed earlier. Given these dynamics, it would have perhaps been surprising if an agreement had been reached on international control of atomic energy in the 1940s.

Notes

1 Anderson to Bush, 5 August 1942, NARA, RG59 Box 56, USNARA.
2 Minutes of a US Cabinet Meeting on the Atomic Bomb, 21 September 1945, President's Secretary's Files Containers 134–139, HSTPL.

3 Full text of Baruch's statement is reproduced in Annex 3.
4 For a more detailed examination of the Manhattan Project, see Rhodes, R, *Making of the Atomic Bomb.*
5 Wallace to Sachs, 10 August 1945. President's Secretary's Files, Box 174, HSTPL.
6 In 1942, when it became apparent that a military-useful explosion could be produced by means of nuclear technology, the US re-evaluated cooperation with the UK and Canada, with it being decided that cooperation could continue with the British and Canadians only "in order to further the prosecution of the war in which both are engaged". Bush to President, 15 December 1942 RG59 Box 56, USNARA.
7 Cooperation did reduce for a time as a result of the US decisions. However, at the meeting between Roosevelt and Churchill to discuss the matter on 26 May 1943, it was agreed that the exchange of information in Tube Alloys (the UK code name for Atomic Weapons) should be resumed in full and the enterprise should be considered a joint one, to which both countries should contribute their best endeavours. Churchill to Anderson, 26 May 1943. CA. CHAR 20/128/53.
8 Churchill to Anderson, 20 August 1943, CA. CHAR 20/129/33.
9 Modus Vivendi, 7 January 1948.
10 See for example, Steury, D.R., "How the CIA missed Stalin's Bomb: Dissecting soviet Analysis, 1946–1950", *Studies in Intelligence Studies.* vol. 49, no 1. doi: https://doi.org/10.1177/1354066119859925.
11 Anderson to Bush, 5 August 1942. RG59 Box 56. USNARA.
12 Churchill to Hopkins, 27 February 1943. CHAR 20/107/37-39, WCA.
13 Minutes of the Cabinet meeting on the atomic bomb, 21 September 1945. President's Secretary's Files, Box 174 HSTPL.
14 Arnold, L., and M. Smith. *Britain, Australia and the bomb: The nuclear tests and their aftermath*, Palgrave Macmillan UK, 2006. ProQuest Ebook Central, https://ebookcentral.proquest.com/lib/kcl/detail.action?docID=293459. p. 6. doi: 10.1057/9780230627338.
15 Smyth, H., DW., *Atomic energy for military purposes* (The Smyth Report), The Official Report on the Development of the Atomic Bomb Under the Auspices of the United States Government.
16 Minutes of the Cabinet meeting on the atomic bomb, 21 September 1945. President's Secretary's Files, Box 174 HSTPL.
17 Ibid.
18 Ibid.
19 Ibid.
20 Ibid.
21 Ibid.
22 Chief of staff of the joint chiefs of staff to the President, 23 October 1945. Papers of Harry S. Truman, President's Secretary's Files, Box 174, HSTPL.
23 UN General Assembly Resolution 1/46. United Nations, New York, 1946.
24 Atomic Energy Act of 1946, Public Law 585, 79th Congress.
25 Testimony of Mr. Barnard to Joint Committee on Atomic Energy, US Senate, 1947.
26 See for example, Smith, *Disarming Diplomat*, p. 82.
27 Arnold and Smith note the reasons for the UK seeking nuclear weapons as including 'status' and a desire not to be reliant on the US for nuclear weapons. Arnold, L., and M. Smith. *Britain, Australia and the bomb: The nuclear tests and their aftermath*, Palgrave Macmillan UK, 2006. ProQuest Ebook Central,

https://ebookcentral.proquest.com/lib/kcl/detail.action?docID=293459. p. 5. doi: 10.1057/9780230627338.

28 McMahon presented the case for preventing private exploitation of atomic energy because of the negative impact that it would have on other energy sectors, such as coal, oil and gas. In his speech covering the introduction of the act, McMahon stated, "Obviously, then, atomic energy must not be turned loose to fall into private hands for unlimited private exploitation and gain". Press Release, 15 November 1945l OF 692: Atomic Power, Atomic Energy. Student Research File: "The Quest for the peaceful atom: The Baruch plan and the Atomic Energy Act of 1946", HSTPL. The US government also took ownership of land containing Uranium. Withdrawing and reserving for the use of the United States lands containing radio-active mineral substances, Executive Order, 13 September 1945, HSTPL (3188).

29 Press Release, 15 November 1945l OF 692: Atomic Power, Atomic Energy. Student Research File: 'The Quest for the peaceful atom: The Baruch plan and the Atomic Energy Act of 1946', HSTPL.

30 Executive Order 9701, "Providing for the reservation of rights to fissionable materials in lands owned by the United States", Executive Orders, HSTPL.

31 Goldschmidt, B., The origins of the International Atomic Energy Agency, *IAEA Bulletin*.

32 General Assembly fourth session Item 23 on the agenda. A/1050. 1 "International Control of Atomic Energy: Statement by the representatives of Canada, China, France, the United Kingdom and the United States of America on the consultations of the six permanent members of the Atomic Energy Commission", RG59, Box 15 (25 October 1949).

33 Ibid.

34 *A report on the International Control of Atomic Energy* (the 'Acheson-Lilienthal report'), 16 March 1946.

35 Ibid.

36 The report separated nuclear fuel cycle activities into those that were inherently dangerous, such as reprocessing, and those that were not. Interestingly, reactors were included in the category of dangerous activities.

37 Intrinsically dangerous was defined by the authors in the first instance as activities that offered

> "a solution either in the actual fact of its physical installation, or by subtle alterations thereof, to one of the three major problems of making atomic weapons: I. The provision of raw materials, II. The production in suitable quality and quantity of the fissionable materials plutonium and U 235, and III. The use of these materials for the making of atomic weapons.

This definition was to be re-examined by the Agency.

38 Ibid.

39 'The Acheson-Lilienthal & Baruch Plans, 1946', Office of the Historian, US Department of State.

40 Higher temperature reactors would be needed for power production compared to the reactors used during the Second World War for plutonium production.

41 Ibid.

42 Text of Baruch's Statement, Annex 3.

43 UNGA Resolution 1/46, United Nations, 1946.

44 General Assembly fourth session Item 23 on the agenda. A/1050. 1 "International Control of Atomic Energy: Statement by the representatives of Canada, China, France, the United Kingdom and the United States of America on the consultations of the six permanent members of the Atomic Energy Commission". RG59, Box 15. (25 October 1949).
45 Ibid.
46 Ibid.
47 Ibid.
48 The sponsoring powers were Australia, Belgium, Canada, France, South Africa, United Kingdom and the United States. Forland, A. "Negotiating supranational rules: The Genesis of the International Energy Agency Safeguards System", Dr Art Thesis, University of Bergen, 1997.
49 Memorandum of address given by Sir B.N. Rau at a reception for the Indian Delegation by the India League of America on October 9 at the Biltmore Hotel, New York City, 10 October 1949, RG59 box 15. US NARA.
50 "Atomic energy", memorandum of meeting between President Conant, Dr. Oppenheimer, General Groves, Dr. Bacher, General Nichols, General Farrel, Mr. Barnard, and Dr. Vance, 10 March 1949, RG55 box 15. USNARA.
51 'Atomic Energy Commission', International Organization, vol. 1, no. 1, February 1947, pp. 99–102. University of Wisconsin Press. www.jstor.org/stable/2703521.
52 Prime Minister to President, 7 June 1946, HSTPL, President's Secretary's Files, Box 175.
53 'Technical Cooperation', 6 January 1949. RG59 Box 56 USNARA.
54 'Introductory Remarks at Meeting of CPC', December 1947. RG59, Box 55. USNARA.
55 Letter from Harry S. Truman, 14 November 1945. RG59 Box 56 USNARA.
56 Modus Vivendi, 7 January 1948.
57 'Memorandum to the chairman, Combined Policy Committee', 28 July 1948. RG59 Box 56 USNARA.
58 Memorandum for Mr. Gordon Arneson, American Secretary Combined Policy Committee subject 'Proposed military inspection of chief uranium mining areas of the world', 6 October 1962. RG59 Box 55, USNARA.
59 "Nature and Scope of Modi Vivendi", CPC Minute, 18 December 1947. RG59 Box 55, USNARA.
60 The nine areas were "declassifiable subject matter", "health and safety", "radioactive and stable isotopes", "nuclear and extra nuclear properties of all elements", "detection of distant nuclear explosion", "extraction chemistry", "design of natural uranium power reactors", and "research experience with low-power reactors". "Technical Cooperation", 6 January 1949. RG59 Box 56. USNARA.
61 Strauss to Commissioners, 15 July 1948. RG59 Box 56. USNARA Lilienthal to Hickenlooper, 30 July 1948. RG59 Box 56. USNARA.
62 Letter of Lewis Strauss to the atomic energy commissioners attached to Letter to Senator Hickenlooper from David Lilienthal, Chairman [the atomic energy commission] 30 June 1948, RG59, Box 56. USNARA.
63 Memorandum from Robert P. Bacher, Summer T. Pike, W.W. Waymack, and David E. Lilitenthal, 23 July 1948. RG59 Box 56 USNARA.
64 Ibid.
65 'British Plutonium Production', 12 August 1948. RG 59 Box 55 USNARA.

66 Bothwell, R., *Nucleus: The history of Atomic Energy Canada Limited*, University of Toronto Press, 1988, p. 184.

67 A report to the President by the special committee of the National Security Council on the Atomic Energy Policy with respect to United Kingdom and Canada, 2 March 1949, President's Secretary's Files, Box 175, HSTPL.

Bibliography

A report on the International Control of Atomic Energy (the 'Acheson-Lilienthal report'), 16 March 1946.

A report to the President by the special committee of the National Security Council on the Atomic Energy Policy with respect to United Kingdom and Canada, 2 March 1949, President's Secretary's Files, Box 175, HSTPL.

Anderson to Bush, 5 August 1942. NARA, RG59, Box 56. USNARA.

Arnold, L., & Smith, M. *Britain, Australia and the bomb: The nuclear tests and their aftermath*, Palgrave Macmillan UK, 2006. ProQuest Ebook Central, https://ebookcentral.proquest.com/lib/kcl/detail.action?docID=293459. p. 6. doi: 10.1057/9780230627338.

"Atomic energy", Memorandum of meeting between President Conant, Dr. Oppenheimer, General Groves, Dr. Bacher, General Nichols, General Farrel, Mr. Barnard, and Dr. Vance, 10 March 1949. RG55, box 15. USNARA.

'Atomic Energy Commission', *International Organization*, vol. 1, no. 1, February 1947, pp. 99–102. University of Wisconsin Press. www.jstor.org/stable/2703521.

Atomic energy act of 1946, Public Law 585, 79th Congress.

Bothwell, R. *Nucleus: The history of atomic energy Canada limited*, University of Toronto Press, 1988, p. 184.

'British Plutonium Production', 12 August 1948. RG59, Box 55. USNARA.

Bush to President, 15 December 1942. RG59, Box 56. USNARA.

Churchill to Anderson, 26 May 1943. CA. CHAR 20/128/53.

Churchill to Anderson, 20 August 1943. CA. CHAR 20/129/33.

Churchill to Hopkins, 27 February 1943. CHAR 20/107/37-39, WCA.

Chief of staff of the joint chiefs of staff to the President, 23 October 1945. Papers of Harry S. Truman, President's Secretary's Files, Box 174, HSTPL.

Executive Order 9701, "Providing for the reservation of rights to fissionable materials in lands owned by the United States", Executive Orders, HSTPL.

Forland, A. *Negotiating supranational rules: The genesis of the international energy agency safeguards system*, Dr Art Thesis, University of Bergen, 1997.

General Assembly fourth session Item 23 on the agenda. A/1050. 1 "International Control of Atomic Energy: Statement by the representatives of Canada, China, France, the United Kingdom and the United States of America on the consultations of the six permanent members of the Atomic Energy Commission", RG59, Box 15 (25 October 1949).

Goldschmidt, B. The origins of the International Atomic Energy Agency, *IAEA Bulletin*, vol. 19, no. 4, August 1977, pp. 12–19. Available online at: www.iaea.org/publications/magazines/bulletin/19-4/origins-international-atomic-energy-agency.

'Introductory Remarks at Meeting of CPC', December 1947. RG59, Box 55. USNARA.

Letter from Harry S. Truman, 14 November 1945. RG59, Box 56. USNARA.

Letter of Lewis Strauss to the atomic energy commissioners attached to Letter to Senator Hickenlooper from David Lilienthal, Chairman (the atomic energy commission) 30 June 1948. RG59, Box 56. USNARA.

Minutes of a US Cabinet Meeting on the Atomic Bomb, 21 September 1945, President's Secretary's Files Containers, 134–139, HSTPL.

Memorandum from Robert P. Bacher, Summer T. Pike, W.W. Waymack, and David E. Lilitenthal, 23 July 1948. RG59, Box 56. USNARA.

Memorandum of address given by Sir B.N. Rau at a reception for the Indian Delegation by the India League of America on October 9 at the Biltmore Hotel, New York City, 10 October 1949, RG59 box 15. USNARA.

Memorandum for Mr. Gordon Arneson, American Secretary Combined Policy Committee subject 'Proposed military inspection of chief uranium mining areas of the world', 6 October 1962. RG59, Box 55. USNARA.

Modus Vivendi, 7 January 1948.

"Nature and Scope of Modi Vivendi", *CPC Minute*, 18 December 1947. RG59, Box 55. USNARA.

Prime Minister to President, 7 June 1946, HSTPL, President's Secretary's Files, Box 175.

President's Secretary's Files, Box 174, HSTPL.

Rhodes, R. *Making of the atomic bomb*, Simon & Schuster, 1 August 1985.

Smith, G. *Disarming diplomat: The memoirs of ambassador Gerard C. Smith. Arms control negotiator*, Madison books, 1996.

Smyth, H. D.W. *Atomic energy for military purposes (The Smyth report)*, The Official Report on the Development of the Atomic Bomb Under the Auspices of the United States Government.

Steury, D.R. How the CIA missed Stalin's Bomb: Dissecting soviet analysis, 1946–1950. *Studies in Intelligence Studies*, vol. 49. no. 1, 2005. Available online at: www.cia.gov/static/cf745b3d96a35d42228add593f41887d/CIA-Missed-Stalins-Bomb.pdf. doi: https://doi.org/10.1177/1354066119859925.

Strauss to Commissioners, 15 July 1948. RG59, Box 56. USNARA Lilienthal to Hickenlooper, 30 July 1948. RG59, Box 56. USNARA.

Student Research File: "The Quest for the peaceful atom: The Baruch plan and the Atomic Energy Act of 1946", HSTPL.

'Technical Cooperation', 6 January 1949. RG59, Box 56. USNARA.

Testimony of Mr. Barnard to Joint Committee on Atomic Energy, US Senate, 1947.

UNGA Resolution 1/46, United Nations, 1946.

Wallace to Sachs, 10 August 1945. President's Secretary's Files, Box 174, HSTPL.

'The Acheson-Lilienthal & Baruch Plans, 1946', Office of the Historian, US Department of State.

UN General Assembly Resolution 1/46. United Nations, New York, 1946.

3 Atoms, sometimes for peace

The emergence of the non-proliferation collective action problem

The failure of the UNAEC to reach an agreement on a plan for international control of atomic energy, and the haphazard approach to nuclear cooperation that followed at the end of the Truman administration, set the scene for a new approach during the administration of President Eisenhower.

Eisenhower[1] took office in January 1953, at a time when the US and Soviet Union were engaged in a military build-up as a result of the ideological differences that divided them during the Cold War. In effect, the Eisenhower administration disassociated the pursuit of peaceful uses of atomic energy and the pursuit of nuclear disarmament. The rationale for this approach was to maximise the contribution that atomic energy would play in waging the Cold War, not only in terms of military power but also by means of diplomatic and economic leverage. But in launching the "Atoms for Peace" initiative absent the 'effective system of control' envisioned by the UNAEC, the Eisenhower administration implicitly – and at one key juncture explicitly – recognised that the spread of nuclear weapons could result from such an approach. The initiative proceeded because of the US geostrategic imperative but in the absence of any real means to prevent misuse of transfers.

The purpose of examining this episode is to understand why nuclear non-proliferation trade controls evolved in a sub-optimal fashion, from the Atoms for Peace speech in 1953 to just before China's nuclear test in 1964. The chapter also examines the Indian PNE episode from Canada's decision to supply a reactor in 1955 to the PNE in 1974 as this episode demonstrates the limitations of Atoms for Peace with regards to international trade controls. The chapter begins by examining the context within which the Atoms for Peace speech was conceived and delivered. This includes a consideration of the geopolitical and domestic political context that faced President Eisenhower during his first year in office, when it was felt there must be 'candor' with the American people over the dangers posed by the nuclear-armed Soviet Union, particularly after the Moscow's hydrogen bomb test on 2 August 1953.[2] The chapter then examines the factors that explain why the Atoms for Peace initiative lacked an effective system of control as had been proposed in the 1940s. It is argued that the decision to pursue Atoms for Peace in the absence of an agreement on disarmament, and in the context of growing competition for

DOI: 10.4324/9781003194262-3

nuclear exports, meant that not only was it inevitable, but it was accepted by the US government that an 'effective system of control' could and would not be implemented. To demonstrate the long-term consequences of this failure to establish such controls, consideration is then given to the implications of the Atoms for Peace initiative for proliferation. For illustrative purposes, these implications are specifically examined in the context of the progress made by India with its nuclear programme from the 1950s up to and including its PNE in 1974.

The chapter argues that non-proliferation controls evolved in a sub-optimal way in this period. By this, it is meant that the Atoms for Peace initiative proceeded without any meaningful system of control. It will specifically be shown that no system of control was designed as part of the Atoms for Peace initiative. Despite this, President Eisenhower took a deliberate decision to proceed with the initiative in 1954 when the risks of the initiative became clear for fear that the US might lose ground to the Soviet Union if the US did not proceed with implementation. As a result, it is argued that the Atoms for Peace initiative introduced structural flaws into the non-proliferation regime which, in turn, would result in the emergence of a non-proliferation CAP. The following chapters will argue that this CAP introduced by the Atoms for Peace initiative has persisted to the present day and undermine efforts to prevent nuclear proliferation. The principal reason for this was geostrategic, with Eisenhower seeing nuclear cooperation as a way to influence strategically important states during the early Cold War. The core factors of trust and reputation were directly challenged by these structural factors and prevented cooperation on non-proliferation trade control issues.

Nevertheless, some cooperation on non-proliferation measures was achieved in this period, particularly among western states and at the IAEA in relation to the Agency's Statute and Safeguards. Progress here was achieved despite the distrust that existed between the US and USSR, and despite the fact that a non-proliferation norm did not exist at this time. Cooperation was limited to two main forums: cooperation over limited safeguards to be associated with technical assistance provided through the IAEA; and cooperation among western suppliers. In both cases, the scope of this cooperation was limited to the extent that it did not impede the actions of key states. This limited cooperation was achieved in part because face-to-face meetings among a small number of countries and in particular the US and Soviet Union involved in these initiatives allowed some degree of trust to be established, and because failure to cooperate would have been against the strategic interest of both states.

The scope of the controls developed in this period was limited by the influence of vested interests, with countries like India seeking to keep their nuclear weapons options open. In part, this was because India effectively played supplier states off against one another to secure a reactor with the minimum possible safeguards. This challenge was compounded by the fact that the nuclear technology of the time was inherently proliferation-relevant.

Eisenhower and peaceful uses of atomic energy

President Eisenhower had taken office in January 1953 in the context of worsening relations with the Soviet Union. The deteriorating situation was marked by the Korean war, the East Berlin uprising of 1953, and the news in August 1953 that the Soviet Union had tested a thermonuclear weapon. As a response, the Eisenhower administration took up where the Truman administration had left off, investing considerably in the development of military capabilities that could counter the Soviet threat. This included greatly expanding defence spending on the US nuclear arsenal.

Candor and atoms for peace

Such was the level of defence investment being considered in 1953 that the administration felt it necessary to alert the US population to the dangers posed by the Soviet Union in order to justify the spending. Starting in July 1953, administration staff began to prepare drafts of a speech – codenamed "Candor" – to "inform the public of the realities of the 'age of peril'".[3] Eisenhower directed the National Security Council (NSC) through NSC paper 151 to prepare the speech.[4] The need for candor was predicated on a belief that the US public needed to be informed about the "steady growth of the Soviet economy and the corollary fact that the rate of its growth is much more rapid than that of the United States and the NATO allies".[5]

The concept of candor built on two assumptions: that the total potential of the US must be leveraged against the "total menace it faces"; and that the "public will accept this discipline only if it acquires a true awareness of the basic facts concerning the world [in which they lived]".[6] It was hoped this would result in an 'enlightened behaviour' among the population at large.[7] Writing to National Security Advisor General Cutler, another Whitehouse official, James M. Lambie, who was Special Assistant to the President and Assistant Staff Secretary coordinating public information programmes, wrote that "a general policy of candor presumes an end to which it is a means" and that, "a policy of candor arises from an appreciation that a way must be found somehow, short of war, to energise the people".[8] In effect, therefore, candor was about mobilising the US population for the Cold War.

Drafts of the speech were entitled "security of the republic in the atomic age".[9] Such was the importance that the administration placed on the speech that the administration contracted Gallop to conduct polls on the drafts.[10] Nonetheless, as CD Jackson – who served as an advisor to the President on psychological warfare – noted, there were "many drafts of 'candor', none of them satisfactory because they either told too much or too little and were uniformly dull".[11] He was also mindful of the importance of having an optimistic component to the speech:

> As you [President Eisenhower] said yourself, the speech must contain more than just "attack" and "retaliation", which is what a speech dealing only with the Bomb and continental defense would be. It must besides contain a tremendous lift for the world - for the hopes of men everywhere.[12]

As a result of this debate, there was a moratorium on the project "pending a new idea".[13] It was after the President had been invited to speak at the United Nations that the 'atomic pool' idea emerged.[14] Indeed, it broke the impasse, with Lewis Strauss of the USAEC, and close confidant of the President, "grabbing the idea".[15]

Eisenhower's determination to include an optimistic component endured. It was in this context that he is credited with developing the idea for an 'atomic bank' in which the US and USSR would make available fissile material for peaceful purposes in third countries. The President discussed the idea with Strauss and General Cutler, but there are no indications that an interagency review of the idea was undertaken. It seems that, with the exception of Strauss, the other atomic energy commissioners were not consulted. Strauss held a uniquely influential position in the US government on atomic matters during the Eisenhower period, despite, as Gerald Smith dismissively put it in his memoir, "having a business background and little scientific training".[16] Smith went on to state that he believed, "Strauss was in good part responsible for this presidential ignorance" on atomic matters, a problem compounded by the fact that another senior nuclear adviser, Robert Oppenheimer – who had headed Los Alamos during the Manhattan Project – had his security clearance suspended in 1953 and revoked in 1954.[17] In all of the archive materials related to the speech and accessed for this project, there is no record of the proposal being subjected to analysis or assessment based on potential proliferation risks. When asked by the British Prime Minister whether there might be certain dangers in the US offering to help other countries to possess atomic reactors, President Eisenhower replied that he had not thought there was much danger but would have the matter examined.[18]

It was recognised within the administration, perhaps even hoped, that the speech could put the Soviet Union in a difficult position.[19] Either the Soviet Union could contribute to the international bank of fissile material, in which case less Soviet material would be available for its own nuclear weapons production programme, or it would not, in which case Washington would win a significant propaganda and diplomatic advantage with allied and non-aligned states.[20] The speech was seen therefore as an essential element of the Cold War and was supported by the Joint Chiefs of Staff, the USAEC and the Department of State. In considering this possibility, the administration recognised from the outset that it might prove necessary to move forward with the initiative without the participation of the Soviet Union. It was also recognised that the Atoms for Peace concept marked a departure from the US promotion of the Baruch plan for international control of atomic energy. This was the essence of the President's proposal: it could be undertaken "without the irritations and mutual suspicions incident to any attempt to set up a completely acceptable system of worldwide inspection and control".[21] The Baruch plan had linked international inspection and control with disarmament, with the implications that peaceful uses could go ahead only in the context of disarmament. The Atoms for Peace concept, however, would disassociate (peaceful) uses from disarmament.

The speech and the international response

President Eisenhower delivered his Atoms for Peace speech at the UN General Assembly on 8 December 1953. The speech was broadcast live and, in order to maximise its propaganda value, the US Information Agency arranged for it to be widely rebroadcast around the world, with extensive polling by Gallup to evaluate the impact of the speech. The international response to the speech was positive. Overall, it is clear that the US mission to the United Nations sent back to Washington the comments of many of the foreign diplomats that attended.[22] Evidently, the promise of access to atomic energy for peaceful purposes was attractive to countries around the world. In addition to a general sense of positivity resulting from the speech, the responses of most states related to their own self-interest. The UK hoped the speech would allow for a relaxation of the restrictions on military cooperation with the US on nuclear matters. However, both the UK and the Soviet Union would also raise concerns about the implications of the announcement for proliferation.[23]

The Soviet Union had, as the Eisenhower administration had hoped, been placed in a difficult position. There were signs that the Soviet Union was concerned about the initiative as it did not wish to pass on nuclear materials to other countries, but it also recognised that failing to contribute to the fuel bank would leave the US with a major propaganda victory and could allow the US to strengthen diplomatic ties with a host of non-aligned states. It was perhaps for this reason that the Soviet Union would ultimately agree to participate in the Atoms for Peace initiative. However, Moscow's immediate response to the US proposal was to question its wisdom on the grounds that it would result in the spread of fissile material, which could be used to manufacture nuclear weapons by additional countries.[24]

The Soviet Union also continued to pursue initiatives related to disarmament.[25] It remains unclear whether the Soviet Union's pursuit of these proposals was sincere or whether the policies were pursued for propaganda purposes alone. However, while the Soviet Union would eventually respond positively to a US invitation to participate in the Atoms for Peace initiative in isolation from disarmament, Moscow continued to press for effective safeguards over the years that followed, with one major exception noted in the following. This may imply that the Soviet Union's concern about proliferation was sincerer than its proposals concerning disarmament, even though

Moscow would by the early 1960s be opposed to safeguards on bilateral nuclear cooperation as further explored in the following.

Atoms for peace versus disarmament

The Soviet Union did not, immediately at least, respond positively to the invitation to participate in the programme and this left the US with a dilemma. In late 1954, almost a year after the speech, there was growing concern in the Eisenhower administration that the US had not followed through on its grand offer. This viewpoint was put forward, in particular, by Governor Stassen, who was responsible for US negotiations on disarmament.[26] There was also a concern that if the US did not move forward with the initiative but the USSR did, the Soviets could leverage the very diplomatic influence that Washington had sought in formulating the initiative. At the same time, discussions on disarmament continued, with the Soviet Union taking the diplomatic advantage by proposing new initiatives. Soviet disarmament proposals were put forward through the Disarmament Commission, which was established under UN auspices following the failure of the UNAEC.[27]

An important Whitehouse meeting was held on 16 January 1954, including Eisenhower and his key advisers to discuss how to proceed to discuss these issues and decide how to follow-through on the Atoms for Peace speech. The questions to be discussed were how to respond to Soviet initiatives on disarmament and whether to move forward with the Atoms for Peace initiative. At the meeting, the President made clear that he would be willing to reach an agreement with the Soviet Union if it resulted in the verifiable elimination of nuclear threat to the US – that is, disarmament. In part, his rationale was that the superior US industrial capacity could be the decisive factor in any conventional war.[28] In January 1954, he also made clear that, in his view, "in the present state of world affairs it is impossible that any effective agreement toward this end could be worked out which would provide the necessary safeguards".[29]

Eisenhower's cabinet debated a new Soviet disarmament proposal in October 1955, soon after the UK had proposed the creation of an international panel to devise methods for detecting the production of fissile material. The Soviet disarmament proposal appeared intended to break the impasse and included both concessions and novel proposals for this purpose.[30] The Chatham House publication, *The World Today* described this proposal as follows.[31]

> On 10 May [1955], Mr. Malik introduced comprehensive new Soviet proposals 'on the reduction of armaments, the prohibition of atomic weapons, and the elimination of the threat of a new war'. These were set out in three draft resolutions to be adopted by the General Assembly – the first, a declaration on the relaxation of international tension and the ending of the 'cold war'; the second, outlining an international disarmament treaty; and the third, outlining the principles of international control.

The proposed declaration covered a wide field of important East-West problems and included the following recommendations:

(a) the elimination of war propaganda;
(b) the occupation forces in Germany, with the temporary exception of strictly limited contingents, should be withdrawn to their national frontiers, and limited local police forces should be formed in both parts of Germany;
(c) the five great Powers should liquidate their foreign military bases;
(d) assistance in the peaceful uses of atomic energy should be rendered by the atomic countries to others, free of any demands of a political or military nature;
(e) discrimination in international trade should be eliminated; and
(f) international cultural relations should be extended. Implementation of these measures, the declaration stated, would help to create confidence between States and facilitate the execution of a broad disarmament programme with the necessary international control.

The ambition of the Soviet proposal evidently raises questions about Moscow's sincerity. However, US scepticism of the proposal appears to have been even more fundamental. Admiral Radford, the chief of the Joint Chiefs of Staff, stated that while he had believed in the 1940s that a ban on nuclear weapons was possible, he no longer did.[32] Secretary Dulles was concerned about a recent UK proposal to create a panel with the task of devising ways to detect the production of fissile material as the US had "invoked in recent years the inability to devise any sure scientific means of detecting the production of fissionable materials as the chief reason why [the US could] no longer agree to the reduction or banning of nuclear weapons".[33] Another suggestion concerned a matter about which the Secretary of State had already expressed great concern.[34]

> If things were allowed simply to drift along as they were now doing, it was inevitable that other nations than the three now possessing them would in due course learn how to make and stockpile atomic weapons. The problem was how to prevent this development and the President's Special Committee had been studying the problem.[35]

Governor Stassen responded that he was "strongly against either the President or the Secretary of State getting up and saying publicly that nuclear weapons should not be banned".[36] Secretary Wilson, Secretary of Defense, confirmed that Admiral Radford's view reflected that of NATO.[37] In short, therefore, the US had given up on disarmament as a practical proposition and, while this was justified on technical grounds, Washington was not willing to admit to this position publicly.

Even though the US had given up on complete disarmament as an immediate goal, it still saw value in exploring disarmament themes that matched US interests. America's priorities in the disarmament discussions were fourfold: to prevent proliferation to fourth powers (after the US, USSR, and UK); to reduce the likelihood of a surprise attack by the Soviet Union; to begin to open up the Soviet Union to inspection; and to achieve "cautious steps designed to achieve a limited initial disarmament agreement". The 'fourth power problem' was considered primarily in the context of France and Germany, and it has assumed that Germany would seek nuclear weapons after France, which was thought already to have made the decision to fabricate nuclear weapons.[38] The Soviet Union appears to have been concerned about this prospect too, which helps to explain why Moscow was willing to consider opening its facilitates to inspection and to abandon its demands for an immediate agreement to outlaw all nuclear weapons. The discussions at this point were limited in scope, however, with the Soviet Union not insisting that the US abandon its nuclear weapons or its overseas bases in the UK.[39]

An NSC meeting on 10 February 1955 also discussed concerns raised by the "technical folks" about the wisdom of going ahead with a programme of supplying atomic energy overseas (i.e. Atoms for Peace). The President stated that,

> before he had made any of his speeches on Atoms for Peace, he had insisted on the most painstaking check by the technicians on every line he had written, precisely to avoid any suggestion of false optimism as noted above.[40]

It should be noted there appears to be no evidence that any other person beyond Strauss at the USAEC was consulted prior to the speech. The President went on to say that,

> when you stop to consider the gravity of the present world situation, you would have to conclude that it was worth sticking out your neck a bit if we can achieve our great objectives as set for in the nuclear power program.[41]

On how to proceed, Secretary Dulles argued that,

> of course it was hard for a layman to combat the technical arguments against the practicality of going ahead with a programme for nuclear power abroad. On the other hand, it would be altogether disastrous from the point of view of foreign policy if we should at this point give up the "Atoms for Peace" program.[42]

The President reflected that:

> If in point of fact the speeches had got ahead of our performance, this might be a useful spur for the US to keep its development of nuclear power abreast of its words on the subject. He dreaded to think of the results if the Soviets should get ahead of us in this area.[43]

In effect, therefore, President Eisenhower decided to proceed with the initiative despite his understanding of the risks associated with it. Not proceeding was seen to be disadvantageous from a public relations and diplomatic perspective. The US also opted to proceed with Atoms for Peace while believing that disarmament was not achievable and did therefore in isolation from broader disarmament initiatives. In this respect, the US put narrow political and diplomatic interests ahead of collective security because it had come to believe that cooperation with Moscow on disarmament was not feasible. As noted earlier, the Soviet Union was evidently concerned about the proliferation risks of President Eisenhower's initiative, so further face-to-face meetings and greater trust between Soviet and American officials might have resulted in these risks being addressed at the outset. However, the bilateral dynamic did not allow for this because of their geostrategic competition and mistrust of one another, which prevented open discussion of such matters. Instead, Washington forged ahead with the implementation of a flawed initiative from a non-proliferation standpoint.

Implementation of the initiative

Implementation of the Atoms for Peace initiative would be a complex undertaking, requiring actions at the US national level as well as international negotiations to set up a new international agency. In seeking to understand the purpose and implications of the Atoms for Peace initiative and the impact of the evolution of trade controls, it is worth exploring each in turn.

US national implementation

Implementation of the Atoms for Peace initiative would require the Atomic Energy Act (the McMahon Act) to be repealed or changed. The Act classified much of the information related to atomic energy that would have to be shared if the initiative was to be enacted internationally. It expressly forbade US persons from helping other nations to develop nuclear energy. The Act also shaped and constrained how atomic energy was exploited in the US, with commercial entities excluded from exploiting atomic energy.

Draft US atomic legislation adopted in 1954 allowed the President to negotiate civil nuclear cooperation agreements with third countries.[44] It enabled:

1 industrial participation in the atomic energy programme, particularly as to the development of atomic power, by licences of the atomic energy commission;
2 a means of cooperation with our allies in the atomic energy field, under adequate security safeguards (but not in relation to the design and fabrication of nuclear weapons); and
3 a means by which the President can implement an international atomic pool plan under adequate security safeguards.

In seeking support for the initiative, Secretary Dulles testified that the initiative was in the national interest. He also noted that there was the potential for the US to lose its near-monopoly on the possible provision of nuclear assistance as other nuclear supplier states emerged:

> Other countries are making progress in atomic power technology. There is a growing tendency for certain raw materials supplying nations which are not industrially well advanced, to turn to such other countries for nuclear power information because they have been disappointed by our inability to give them significant help. It is clear to me that if this trend continues, the interest of the United States will be seriously affected. There is no need here to emphasize how important it is for us to stay ahead of the USSR in providing knowledge of how to put atomic energy to peaceful uses.[45]

The US would nonetheless seek to maintain influence over recipient states. This was achieved in part by the inclusion of section 123 in the Atomic Energy Act, which would require recipient states to conclude nuclear cooperation agreements with the US in order to access US nuclear technology.[46] This provision remains in effect to this day and requires Congressional approval of all nuclear cooperation agreements between the US and other countries. This measure gives Congress some influence over nuclear programmes in countries that wish to benefit from cooperation with the US. As Chapter 4 demonstrates, for example, this provision had an influential effect on China's nuclear programme in the 1990s.

Declassification and military cooperation

In order to realise the Atoms for Peace concept, it would be necessary for those countries that held nuclear know-how to share it with other countries. In practice, it was the US, the UK, and Canada that had the majority of the nuclear know-how available in the early 1950s, so it was these states that would have on implementation. However, the *modus vivendi* between the three countries required that atomic information be subject to classification and not passed on to third countries. It was thus necessary for the three countries to agree with rules on declassification in order for the initiative to move forward. The UK, in particular, resented the fact that nuclear cooperation had been restrained with the US, however, and approached the question of implementation of the Atoms for Peace initiative with the objective of restoring military cooperation with the US. The Eisenhower administration had implicitly accepted that disarmament would not be achieved in the near term when it launched the Atoms for Peace initiative, so the perceived need for restraint in military-related cooperation with the UK for fear of undermining disarmament negotiations was reduced. Eisenhower was thus sympathetic to the British request for a resumption in full cooperation and sought to include military cooperation with the UK and Canada in changes to US domestic legislation. This culminated in the Mutual Defence Agreement of 1958, which allowed for full cooperation between the US and the UK on military nuclear matters, including in relation to the exchange of technology and material.[47] The Eisenhower administration would also champion a similar amendment to allow nuclear sharing with NATO countries.

Commercial involvement

Another notable aspect of the amended Atomic Energy Act was that it allowed for the involvement of private enterprise in the use of atomic energy in the US. As noted before, this had been ruled out in the 1940s in part because of the concern that a free market in atomic energy would undermine the viability of the existing energy industry. The move was supported by pro-nuclear lobbyists, including those who sought to profit from atomic energy use, such as Westinghouse, which would later opt to pass any profit from the first reactor it constructed to the USAEC.[48] Another reason for the move was to ensure that the US would not lose its leadership in the nuclear field – that is, a first mover's advantage in the supply of atomic energy to third countries. Indeed, there was nothing stopping other countries from allowing their industries to sell reactors overseas.[49]

The Atomic Energy Act of 1954 thus was both a response to the lobbying of nuclear interests and a facilitator of US international influence by allowing commercial exploitation of atomic energy. Given the earlier argument that the US did not believe non-proliferation was possible, and the desire of the Eisenhower administration to see the Atoms for Peace initiative as a diplomatic instrument of the Cold War, the question of what controls would be agreed upon concerning the need to compete against Moscow technology thus became key. Indeed, the introduction of commercial interests would also have an important impact in the years that followed by driving the creation of an international market for atomic technology. At the same time, however, officials in the State Department pointed out that the decision by the US to give away research reactors would 'prejudice' these commercial interests.[50]

The Atomic Energy Act thus set the scene for the international implementation of the Atoms for Peace Initiative and began to set the conditions under which US cooperation with other countries would take place. There were many other factors that affected international implementation beyond US national law, however, and these are considered in the following.

International implementation

The alternation of US domestic law was a vital prerequisite to the implementation of the Atoms for Peace initiative, but it was only a first step and one which was as much about the US domestic nuclear landscape as it was about the international landscape. It was also necessary to create an international agency with its related system of safeguards; to agree with other states how material and funding for the initiative would be provided; to negotiate bilateral nuclear cooperation agreements with other countries; and, ultimately, realise the construction of reactors in third countries.

Bilateral nuclear cooperation

When the Soviet Union did not opt immediately to participate in the Atoms for Peace initiative, the US and other nuclear supply-capable western states decided to press forward with the initiative on a bilateral basis before the IAEA's statute and related safeguards had been agreed. As noted, there were few states that were capable of nuclear supply at this point and these included the three war-time allies (the US, UK, and Canada) and the producers of uranium, principally the Belgian Congo and South Africa. In practice, the UK does not appear to have provided substantial nuclear assistance to other states during the Atoms for Peace era, with the exception of Iraq, focusing resources instead on its own nuclear weapons programme. The main assistance undertaken by Canada related to the provision of technology to India, which is explored separately in the following. This section thus focuses on the bilateral assistance provided by the US, given its prominence during the period.

The Eisenhower administration was keen to cooperate with strategically important countries such as Turkey.[51] Turkey was an important target in the context of the US policy of containing the Soviet Union, which Eisenhower had continued from the Truman administration. On 11 June 1955, President Eisenhower announced that the US would pay one-half of the cost of a research reactor in any free nation and provide technological assistance to recipient nations.[52,53] By 1958, the annual appropriation of Atoms for Peace was US $4 million, and 17 grants had been made at US $350,000 each.[54] This equates to approximately $3 million per reactor at 2016 prices.[55]

American cooperation generally took place on a bilateral basis rather than through the IAEA. There were a number of reasons for this: it was a number of years before the IAEA was established, although it might have been possible to establish the Agency more quickly if greater priority had been assigned to the task. Perhaps the main reason, therefore, was that supplier states preferred to offer bilateral assistance rather than assistance through the IAEA so that it could be exploited for maximum diplomatic leverage. For the US then, bilateral nuclear assistance because an important tool to maximise its influence with key states in the context of the Cold War.

An important consideration relates to the nature of the reactors that were being supplied by the US. At one Cabinet meeting in February 1956, Admiral Strauss felt compelled to defend himself against 'soft impeachment' on the grounds that the AEC had failed to develop a small research reactor (10,000 kW range) for sale overseas as required by the Atomic Energy Act of 1954.[56,57] The President said that he could "not comprehend the difference, in view of all the companies which Admiral Strauss had said were planning to develop and construct small output power reactors". Strauss also "denied the position advanced by Governor Stassen" that the real problem was that there had been a gap of over a year without action to develop a reactor by the AEC. Strauss went on to say that, "in his opinion there was nothing 'magic' about a power reactor in the 10,000-kilowatt range", and "he again wondered about the competence of those behind this judgment on the necessity for a power reactor of this precise range".[58] In practice, a small specially-designed research reactor would be less suited to the production of plutonium. In the absence of such a reactor type, the standard reactor type to be exported was based upon the designs prepared by the war-time allies for their own nuclear programmes, which tended to be well suited to plutonium production. It appears, therefore, that the lead administration officials, who were not nuclear technology experts, simply did not understand the implications of the initiative. This conclusion is supported by the reaction of Dulles to the concern expressed by Vyacheslav Moloto, the Soviet Foreign Minister, in reaction to the initiative's announcement.[154] Dulles was evidently concerned when the Soviet Union told him about the proliferation risks of the initiative.[59]

Beyond administration officials, however, others in the US had concerns and took action concerning the proliferation risks, including the USAEC and the Joint Commission for Atomic Energy in Congress.[60] A condition of the 1954 Atomic Energy Act was that material supplied under civil agreements for cooperation contain "a guarantee by the other party that material supplied will not be used for any military purpose". The US also required safeguards to "make possible the detection of a diversion of materials" for bilateral agreements other than those with the UK and Canada.[61] Under such agreements, the US would have the right to suspend future deliveries or assistance if a violation occurred. In relation to the supply of uranium, the US would also have a right to require the return of the material.

International implementation and the International Atomic Energy Agency

In his Atoms for Peace speech, President Eisenhower had announced his intention to create an international agency to promote the peaceful uses of atomic energy. The agency was envisioned as one route through which states could gain access to nuclear assistance, with the other primary route being bilateral assistance from other states. He also announced that the US would give the agency a donation of an amount of fissile material in support of the projects that it implemented.[62]

It would appear that the decision to create an international agency, instead of offering assistance only on a bilateral basis, was central to the credibility of the US claim that it was making atomic energy available for the good of all mankind. Without such an agency, decisions regarding to which countries the US (and other nuclear-capable states) would give assistance would inevitably be influenced by bilateral relations and geopolitics. The creation of the agency was thus essential if the US was to maximise the propaganda and diplomatic value of the Atoms for Peace speech.[63]

There were, however, difficult issues to be addressed to allow the creation of an IAEA. These included the question of Soviet participation and the need for safeguards. These issues shaped the international implementation of the Atoms for Peace initiative and would play out over the years that followed. These are explored in turn.

Soviet participation

As mentioned, the initial Soviet reaction to the Atoms for Peace speech was negative. The Soviet Union privately criticised the US for spreading fissile material around the world.[64] This appears to have been a sincere criticism as Moscow would later make important contributions to the development of the IAEA's safeguards system. In its public statements, the USSR also tried to link the implementation of Atoms for Peace to new disarmament initiatives, but as noted, the Eisenhower administration opted to proceed with its initiative in isolation from disarmament efforts.[65,66]

The US believed that Soviet criticism of the initiative, and its efforts to link the proposal to disarmament, were driven by the Soviet strategic interest rather than genuine concern about the nature of the initiative. While the Soviet Union's position may have been genuine on both accounts, Moscow's arguments likely also masked broader Soviet concerns about the initiative, particularly in relation to the potential diplomatic value of the programme in the context of the Cold War.

Based upon the Soviet Union's reluctance to participate in the fissile material pooling idea, the US initially 'shelved' the atomic pool proposal and proceeded with bilateral cooperation.[67] However, the US did not give up on the idea of involving the Soviet Union in the programme and continued to communicate with Moscow through diplomatic channels. Sensing an opportunity when the Soviet Union's opposition to the atomic pool idea seemed to waiver during an exchange on the Soviet disarmament initiative, the US again invited Moscow to participate in the initiative. Moscow responded that, while it was desirable that both move forward together, it was prepared to discuss the creation of an atomic energy agency but was concerned about proliferation risks.[154]

In response to Soviet concerns, the US suggested to Moscow a meeting of experts to explore what methods of control could be devised. In doing so, the US sought to establish whether Soviet concerns about the risks were genuine and the real reason for its reluctance to participate or whether other factors were at play.[68] The conclusion of this experts meeting, from the UK's perspective at least, was that, "although fairly effective controls on assistance given by the agency [could] be devised based upon a system of auditing with inspection, any extension to prevent the manufacture of weapons raised difficult political problems".[69] These political problems were recognised as being related to national prestige in recipient countries and the risk that the three nuclear weapons states would be pressured to enact such controls on their own programmes and facilities.[70] Following the meeting, the Soviet Union agreed to participate in the IAEA. However, the Soviet Union, for its part, opted to delay overall agreement on safeguards for bilateral nuclear cooperation until after the IAEA's statute was concluded. Moscow also insisted that IAEA safeguards be negotiated after the IAEA statute had been negotiated. This meant that the safeguards provisions in the statute could only really be considered as a placeholder.[71] The net result was that, in 1958, the Soviet Union did agree to donate 50 kg of ^{235}U to the IAEA to complement the US donation.[72]

Negotiating the IAEA's statute

The drafting of the statute of the IAEA took place in an iterative format involving a growing number of states over a number of years. The first discussions on the statute took place in early 1954 between eight states (the sponsoring powers), including the US, the UK, Canada, France, Portugal, Belgium, Australia, and South Africa. The 1954 UN General Assembly adopted a resolution proposed by this group. By the 1955 General Assembly, the draft prepared by the group of eight had been circulated to all members of the UN – a total of 84 states at that point – but considerable concerns emerged about aspects of the draft.[73] The General Assembly, therefore, decided that the group of eight should be expanded to 12 with the inclusion of additional states, including Brazil, Czechoslovakia, India, and the Soviet Union, in order to address concerns about representativeness, particularly with regard to what was then often known as the developing world, and to make the process of drafting the statute more representative of the international political environment. This expanded group met in early 1956 to agree on a revised statute. It unanimously agreed on a draft statute on 18 April that was put forward to a UN conference on the statute in October 1956.[74]

In February 1956, a key meeting had taken place between the UK, the US, and Canada with the objective of arriving at a common position on the question of safeguards ahead of a 12-power meeting later that month. At the tripartite meeting, the positions of the three countries were set out before a common position was agreed.[75] The UK's aim was to "prevent for as long as possible the manufacture of nuclear weapons of all types by countries other than the US, USSR and UK".[76] In this context, the UK favoured the inclusion of controls "over assistance given to a country by the IAEA" as well as "the application of controls to assistance given under a bilateral agreement with a member country of the agency".[77] With this in mind, the UK proposed that a provision be included in the IAEA statute that allowed for bilateral assistance to be subjected to agency control. The UK believed that the incentive of accessing assistance would be an inducement for states to accept controls but that this inducement would decline over time as states indigenised capabilities. The UK considered it desirable to require states obtaining assistance to forgo nuclear weapons and that assistance should cease should a state break this undertaking. Importantly, however, the UK believed that such a requirement would not be practical, not least because of 'national prestige' in recipient states. This could only be overcome, in the UK's view, if such controls were broadly implemented. However, such broad implementation could not be reached as the UK, the US, and the USSR would not subject their own facilities to control, at least not without a broader disarmament plan.[78]

The US position on control was not dissimilar to that of the UK.[79] Its position was that a system of control was a necessary prerequisite to the granting of US materials to the agency. However, the conceptual starting point of the US position may have been different from the UK. The US had attempted to introduce a so-called "standstill" clause into the agency's statute that would see states forgo nuclear weapons for a period of five years (a provision that would not meet with broad support).[80] In his opening statement to the statute conference, Lewis Strauss representing the US stated that:

> We well understand that much of the military danger of the atom lies beyond the reach of controls – and indeed beyond the reach of the agency itself. We know that there is nothing in the draft statute to prevent states from building nuclear weapons with their own resources. But the fact that the agency will not be able to solve the whole immense world problem of nuclear weapons control does not exempt us from the duty to do all we can to provide safeguards for the agency's own operation.[81]

The US had thus accepted that nuclear proliferation could not be prevented but that nuclear cooperation should continue nonetheless, albeit with provisions to prevent the misuse of assistance. In adopting the statute, all other states participating in the IAEA also implicitly accepted this consequence. This evidently calls into question the concept of 'Atoms for Peace', which was adopted as the slogan of the IAEA.

The Canadian position was quite different. The starting point for the Canadians was the argument that a moratorium on weapons production was a disarmament question rather than a question for the agency, whose purpose was to promote the peaceful uses of atomic energy. Based upon this logic, "a country's weapons program was not the agency's business and Agency's controls should be limited to safeguarding against diversion of assistance given for peaceful purposes".[82] The culmination of the Canadian position was that there should be no expectation that states would not give assistance to other states which were working to acquire nuclear weapons. Indeed, the Canadian representative stated that,

> Canada herself would reserve the right to make nuclear weapons and would not expect a country with which she concluded a bilateral agreement to give up that right. If a country asked for her help with a military programme she would consider the request on its merits as with any other request for arms.[83]

This position was likely informed by Canada's desire to maintain room for manoeuvre regarding its transfer of reactors and fuel to India, transfers under discussion at this time and which Canada was keen to undertake in order to ensure that a Canadian-origin reactor under construction in India had an operable first fuel load, thus confirming Canada as a credible nuclear exporter.

Despite the substantially different positions of the three, a common position was reached based on Washington's minimum position, which included agency-based controls and the inclusion of a provision that would enable bilateral assistance to be subjected to Agency control. It was this position that was taken into the meeting of the 12 later in the month.[84]

It was not only the principal Western states that were scheming to obtain the best possible outcome from the statute conference. By March of 1956, the Australian government representative had taken a leading role in creating a 'producer's bloc' including countries such as South Africa, whose interests related primarily to membership of the board of governors.[85] The Indian position was also important as India felt that it represented all African and Asian countries. India thus sought to champion the under-developed nations that could benefit from nuclear technology. Indian officials voiced the view during talks related to the creation of the IAEA that,

> It is not feasible to ensure security by controlling the production and sale of natural uranium, since, as was established at the Geneva Atomic Conference, natural uranium is very widely dispersed, and many nations are in a position to produce their own. A surrender of the right to produce natural uranium does not seem feasible or consistent with the principles of the agency with regards to equality of states and protection of sovereignty.[86]

The result of the Indian position would be to seek to minimise the safeguards requirements. From this examination, it is apparent that the 12-power process saw the emergence of substantial vested interests with international atomic cooperation and trade. Vested interest could have had a substantial negative effect on the IAEA statute. However, the sponsoring powers of the Statute negotiations also set up the rules of procedure such that it would be difficult for states to introduce amendments to the draft statute. This scheme apparently annoyed the representatives of other states, with the UK feeling that it actually resulted in more amendments being proposed. Perhaps partly in protest at the rules, more than 30 amendments were submitted. Nonetheless, diplomatic manoeuvres and the rules of procedure (including voting rules) ensured that few were adopted.[87]

The focus of many of the amendments were the safeguards clauses. For example, Poland, with the support of India and in line with South Africa's interests, put forward an amendment that would have substantially weakened safeguards by excluding 'source materials' from Agency control and inspection and denying the agency the 'right of pursuit' of separated materials.[88] The Soviet Union did not seriously campaign for this amendment, however, which weakened the likelihood of its adoption. Nonetheless, under pressure to reach an agreement before the appearance of President Eisenhower, the UK felt that the US delegation was willing to accept a position that was below the minimum of what was considered for the system to be effective.[89] The Polish amendment was eventually voted down in part through a non-substantive compromise brokered by the UK, then minor amendments of the text were accepted to placate the Soviet Bloc. The statute was ultimately approved by the statute conference on 23 October 1956 and came into effect on 29 July 1957.[90]

Negotiation of the safeguards resolution

Adoption of the IAEA's Statute did not bring an end to the negotiations over the safeguards that would be associated with nuclear assistance. Indeed, as noted earlier, the US had agreed to a Russian request to return to the subject of bilateral safeguards after the conclusion of the statute. Furthermore, a discussion would be required on the technicalities of safeguards related to the supply of equipment subjected to agency control.

There was also a sense of impending crisis unless common ground could be reached on safeguards.[91] Rumours were circulating unsafeguarded bilateral transfers, including with regards to exports to India. Such rumours risked undermining the effectiveness of the safeguards system.[92] It was this concern that resulted in a US initiative to hold a meeting of countries with the capability to supply nuclear fuel in 1961 – dubbed the Western Suppliers Group (WSG) – while the IAEA safeguards system was being devised.[93] However, the primary forum where this was discussed was the IAEA. The starting point for the discussions was the IAEA statute and specifically Article XII.[94] As discussed earlier, this had a relatively limited scope. Additionally, as Sterling Cole, the Director General of the IAEA stated, the role of the IAEA would be limited to safeguarding only "direct" atomic assistance between states, and not "indirect" where the state could use acquired expertise to develop a parallel indigenous nuclear capability beyond the scope of controls.[95] The agency had thus aligned to the view expressed by Lewis Struss in his remarks to the statute conference as quoted earlier. Nonetheless, it is valuable in the context of the research question to explore the machinations of each negotiating period in turn.

Discussion at the IAEA on the safeguards agreement was dominated by a small group of states, which included a Western bloc, the Soviet bloc and other countries. India and the Soviet Union took firm positions against the imposition of intrusive safeguards. The Indian position was consistent with the line that it had taken during the statute negotiations. Specifically, India's officials argued that safeguards would be acceptable only if they were applied to all countries and thus facilities and material equally, which would in effect require disarmament:

> India is willing to exert every effort to assist the evolution of a system to prevent the diversion of fissionable materials to military purposes, provided such a system takes into account certain basic considerations. For example, it must be consistent with the honour and dignity of every nation to which it is made applicable. Secondly, it must be uniformly implemented if it is to have any significant value. Thirdly, it must take into account, the fact that atomic energy has been an absolute necessity for the peaceful development and prosperity of several countries, and that fissionable material is, so to be the life blood of the future economy of States. It is, therefore, the responsibility of nations to cooperate in arrangements for the most rapid exchange of technical knowledge and material required to put the Atom to its most beneficial use. The Government of India has given the most careful consideration to the system of safeguards, which has been under consideration in the International Atomic Energy Agency and has come to the conclusion that it satisfies none of the three criteria articulated in [this] paragraph.[96]

It was not only India that had objections to the proposed safeguards provisions. The Soviet position does not appear to have been in keeping with its earlier support for, and even promotion of, safeguards and thus requires exploration. One reason for the less conducive Soviet position was that it was separately proposing new disarmament and test ban measures.[97] Moscow was also at this time providing nuclear assistance to China, its then communist ally, which included assistance directly relevant to the acquisition of nuclear weapons. This was likely another reason the Soviet's resisted intrusive safeguards, although Moscow would reduce its nuclear cooperation with China around the time the resolution was adopted (as examined in Chapter 4).[98]

These factors interacted to produce limited safeguards provisions that only covered declared facilities and transfers. Despite this limited scope, certain enforcement methods were built in. For example, if the recipient state did not comply with safeguards requirements, the IAEA Board of Governors could refer the matter to the Security Council or the UN General Assembly and/or suspend future cooperation with the country. In 1960, the then chairman of the USAEC wrote to the President, noting that he believed, "in aggregate, the guarantees, the exercise of the safeguards rights, and the moral censure that would follow the detection of any diversion, constitute an effective deterrent against diversion".[99]

Ultimately, the IAEA Board of Governors adopted a safeguards resolution by a majority vote, with six states voting against. The final text states:

> Agency safeguards will be applied to facilities and to materials in facilities in accordance with agreements entered into by the Agency with the State or States concerned. The application of such safeguards shall be as specified in the agreements and may extend, as appropriate, to the following:[100]

(a) The Agency shall examine the design and approve it only from the viewpoint of assuring that it will not further any military purpose and that it will permit effective application of Agency safeguards;
(b) The State shall maintain a system of records as agreed with the Agency of the material and facilities to which Agency safeguards are to be applied;
(c) The State shall submit to the Agency routine and special reports on the facilities and the materials under safeguards; and
(d) The State shall permit inspections by the Agency to account for material to which Agency safeguards are applied and to detect diversion.

These safeguards would prove to be very limited in scope and applied only to materials and facilities specifically placed under safeguards.

Western suppliers group

In addition to pursuing negotiations within the framework of the IAEA, the US convened a meeting of the so-called "western suppliers" in June 1961 with a view to agreeing on a common position of safeguards, including with regards to bilateral nuclear transfers. The perceived advantage of this forum, as opposed to the IAEA, was that it excluded the Soviet Union and India – the two principal countries opposed to the conclusion of more effective IAEA safeguards. The first item on the agenda of the group was to consider a "common front on bilateral Safeguards in relation to bilateral transfers for peaceful use of source and special fissionable materials, production facilities and equipment".[101] The meeting was limited to only the US, the UK, France, Belgium, South Africa, Australia, and Canada.[102] However, the US position paper recognised that other states, notably Germany and Japan, would soon enter the market and these countries must "soon be brought into any common front".[103] To achieve this, the US proposed that, "a meeting including those suppliers might be held and would also afford an opportunity to resolve any matters not settled at the June [1961] meeting".[104]

The importance of a common front was clear. During the meeting, Canada stated, "if there was no general uniformity in bilateral safeguards practices, the Canadian government would naturally have to reconsider its position".[105] Another country stated that "an understanding of the course other suppliers will follow is essential if there are to be safeguards on peaceful nuclear assistance which are meaningful and yet do not interfere with the development of peaceful nuclear commerce".[106] The WSG could help to address this issue by providing a mechanism to counter the rumours that were circulating. In this context, it one topic discussed at the WSG was the possibility of the IAEA being used as a "central repository of international transfers for peaceful purposes of uranium and other items subject to safeguards".[107] The UK was against this idea but instead favoured sharing information among

WSG participants.[108] Canada and the US subsequently began to share information with the IAEA, but there was no agreement among all to do so. South Africa later lamented that it was willing to share information if all states agreed to do so, per its own earlier proposal, but in the absence of sharing by everyone, it was not prepared to do this.[109]

A second central purpose of the forum was to reach an agreement on what type of transfers would require safeguards. The US pushed for "entire facilities, significant specialised nuclear equipment, or materials having a potential direct military end use", but not "normal items of commerce for non-nuclear applications or minor components of any kind" – that is, 'dual-use items' as they would become known in the years that followed and the control of which is discussed in later chapters.[110] The South African representative "opined undue emphasis had been placed on the source material as compared to equipment"[111] and that,

> eventually, South Africa would like to look forward to a completely free market in source materials ... as safeguards on source material would not really deter any country from becoming a nuclear power if that country seriously desired to become one.[112]

The US position paper for the WSG stated that, "commercial pressures" were responsible for the opposition to the US position.[113] The US position paper noted that South Africa generally supported the US approach, whereas the UK wanted to export a uranium metal preparation plant to India and Australia had expressed concern over market instability in industries affected by safeguards.[114] The US thus feared "commercial pressures" were responsible for opposition to the US the proposals for a common front on safeguards.[115]

The group discussed applying safeguards to non-nuclear materials such as zirconium and heavy water. However, the UK, at least, resisted controlling zirconium for fear that the US would impose safeguards on exports of zirconium to the UK's submarine programme as a result.[116] It is unlikely that the UK would be unable to acquire zirconium as a result of the WSG process. Nonetheless, it is clear in this instance that the UK was putting its own perceived strategic interest ahead of even the possibility that international trade controls would affect its own strategic programme.

While there was recognition of the need for a common front, and the discussions informed the positions of states in the IAEA discussions, the group did not reach a consensus on the major issues at hand. For example, the French representative stated that there had been no change in the French position, which was to consider each situation on a "case-by-case" basis as had been its practice since May 1959. France was also "not prepared at this time to enter into commitments regarding uniform practice".[117] The French reluctance was a result of several factors, including its commercial interests in maximising nuclear exports and its strategic reasons for resisting US influence.[118] Given that agreement could not be reached even among a smaller group of states, the outlook for broader controls on bilateral cooperation was bleak at this time.

French–Israeli cooperation

An important aside in the 1950s relates to Franco-Israeli nuclear cooperation, which culminated in the transfer of a plutonium production reactor and reprocessing capability to Israel. Secrecy in both France and Israel surrounding past transfers continues to the present day and questions remain about the deal. According to Avner Cohen, the relationship was initiated because of the French desire to obtain access to a new heavy water enrichment technology originating in Israel, as well as a technique for optimising uranium extraction from phosphate ore, and a desire on Israel's part to obtain French assistance in constructing a nuclear reactor.[119] The sale of Israeli technology to France in 1954 opened the door for Israeli scientists to be trained on reactor physics in France. A relationship between Israel and France had thus been forged by the time Eisenhower gave his Atoms for Peace speech, after which the US offered Israel a research reactor. Cohen notes that by the time of the Suez crisis in 1956, France was ready to seek assistance from Israel in securing the canal, assistance that Israel would be willing possibly to provide in the hope that it could lead to the transfer of a reactor used for weapons production.[120] Cohen notes that it was at the point of the Soviet ultimatum for Israel to withdraw in 1956 that the plan for French nuclear cooperation with Israel – including the transfer of a plutonium production reactor and plutonium separation plant – was agreed upon.[121] The Suez crisis thus illustrated to both France and Israel the importance of not being subject to either Superpower's influence, something that could best be countered through possession of nuclear weapons. At a key juncture in 1957, Israel signed an agreement with France that the reactor would be used only for 'scientific research', for example, but no safeguards were included on the transfer and French officials clearly knew of Israel's true intentions.[122]

France's decision to resist common ground on nuclear supply provisions, and to supply a weapons-suited reactor to Israel, raises an important question in the context of the research framework. There are signs that France's immediate decision over nuclear supply were reactionary to an immediate strategic need and were intended to cement relations with an emerging strategic partner. In this way, the decision is not so different from the Soviet Union's decision to provide assistance to China in the 1950s or even Canada's decision to supply a reactor to India around the same time. The decision must also be understood in the context of broader French foreign policy that was expressly non-aligned (i.e., de Gaullean) in nature. While the French position is understandable in this context, the failure to align controls in this period evidently left open proliferation pathways that could be, and were later, exploited.

The failure of atoms for peace and India's peaceful nuclear explosion

As the previous sections demonstrated, the Atoms for Peace initiative was primarily conceived to fulfil the geostrategic interests of the US, and Washington pushed ahead even after it became apparent that a broader system of international control on atomic energy could not be established. In the absence of this broader system, the controls to be associated with transfers under the Atoms for Peace initiative varied considerably throughout the 1950s and 1960s. Even after the IAEA adopted a safeguards resolution requiring safeguards on transfers that could be of "direct" support to a country's nuclear programme, states could still opt to utilise bilateral safeguards arrangements rather than the IAEA system. In this respect, the WSG was largely unsuccessful in bringing about a common front on trade controls among nuclear suppliers. Nuclear cooperation under Atoms for Peace was thus generally subject to poor control. In the context of the research question, it is important to understand how the promise of peaceful uses of atomic energy played out in practice. India is an excellent example in this respect, given that international nuclear cooperation with India began relatively soon after the initiative was launched, and its programme was shaped by the developing safeguards. As Perkovich argues, India's nuclear programme was inherently 'dual-interest' from its inception.[123] Despite this, India was able to acquire international assistance for its nuclear programme, and indirectly for its PNE, largely because of the inadequacy of the controls established during the period covered in this chapter.

Atoms for peace and India

As a strategically important non-aligned state, India was exactly the type of country the Eisenhower administration wanted to influence when it conceived Atoms for Peace. However, India's independent status and membership of the British Commonwealth had implications for how the US could cooperate with India. Indeed, India itself was hesitant to become beholden to the Atoms for Peace programme.[124] While western states did train Indian engineers and scientists, the primary mechanism for implementation of the Atoms for Peace initiative in the mid-1950s was the "Colombo Plan for Cooperative Economic Development in South and Southeast Asia", which included several commonwealth countries, including Australia, Canada, India, Pakistan, New Zealand, Sri Lanka, and the UK.[125]

The idea of providing a reactor to India under this initiative was credited to Nick Cavell, the Canadian administrator of the Colombo plan and, apparently in the absence of consulting India itself.[126] India's leading nuclear voice, Homi Bhabha, founding director of India's Atomic Energy Establishment Trombay, had studied at the Cavendish Laboratory in the UK and was a friend of W.B. Lewis, a central character in the Canadian nuclear programme.[127] Through the Colombo Plan, an offer was made by Canada to supply India with a research reactor identical to one that had been constructed in Canada, the NRX. This reactor was one of the highest neutron flux reactors in the world at the time.[128] It was thus recognised that the reactor was "specifically suited for making engineering studies and research on reactor materials which can be tested under the conditions of high neutron intensity", and "the research and development facilities of the reactor would enable advanced engineering experiments to be performed in connection with the design of future power reactors".[129] As a result, the same characteristics that made the reactor suited to these research purposes also made it suitable for the production of plutonium for use in nuclear explosive devices. Indeed, one paper estimates that CANDU-type reactors, which are based on NRX technology, produce twice the amount of plutonium for a given unit of energy compared to Light Water Reactors.[130]

Under the agreement, Canada was to provide India with the "reactor itself and the steel rotunda to surround it", whereas Indian contractors would build the foundations and basement of the reactor.[131] The agreement allowed for the possibility of obtaining fuel from Canada, but the intended option was for the fuel to be produced in India.[132] Canada communicated this offer to India just before the conference on peaceful uses of atomic energy in 1953.[133] The original idea does not appear to have been motivated by shorter-term commercial interests, at least not on behalf of the Atomic Energy Corporation of Canada Limited (AECL), which is said to have had "no single view" of the initiative.[134] The initiative was motivated primarily by Canada's geostrategic interest in strengthening its relationship with the newly independent India.[135] The transfer would, however, establish Canada as a key supplier of nuclear technology, which promised to be of future commercial benefit. It is in this context that Undersecretary Jules Leger wrote that Canada must not 'lag behind' other suppliers in 1955.[136]

Despite being provided with the reactor at no cost, India took a firm stand over the conditions of supply for the reactor known as CIRUS. Drawing upon their discussion with India over the supply of CIRUS to inform the discussions over the statute of the IAEA, for example, Canadian officials noted in 1956 that India would not accept fuel on a loan basis, would not give an undertaking to return irradiated rods to Canada for processing, and insisted on reserving the right to provide the uranium from Indian sources and to manufacture the rods themselves.[137,138] Canada was content to assist with this effort and, in 1958, authorised the export of certain materials, including 2,240 lbs of calcium granules for use in fuel manufacture for which Canada was one of the few possible commercial suppliers[139] Canada continued to press India to utilise Canadian-supplied fuel in CIRUS or at least to use Canadian material for the first powered run of the reactor so that issues of fuel quality would not affect its commissioning.[140] Canada's interest here was twofold: first, Canadian officials were worried Indian fuel was not good enough. Second, Canada was worried that any problems in commissioning the reactor could damage its credentials as a nuclear supplier. Indeed, Canadian officials commented that, "we would have no insurance against serious failures of fuel elements during the start-up period" if Indian fuel was used.[141] Officials at AECL also believed that sales of Canadian fuel would provide a longer-term income stream, although it is not clear that shorter-term commercial factors weighed significantly on decision making.[142]

India was opposed to the inclusion of safeguards on supplied equipment and material, although the common position of the suppliers following the WSG meeting in 1959 was generally to require safeguards on supplied materials. India eventually asked whether Canada could supply uranium for the CIRUS reactor. Canada's policy was to require safeguards on the sale of uranium, but there was no common standard defining what this meant at the time. Canadian officials, therefore, considered whether India could "self-inspect and report" on the fuel and whether Canada could buy back any excess plutonium produced in the reactor.[143]

India's resistance to safeguards was likely based on several factors. Certainly, India had principled objections to the concept of accepting inspections on its facilities without all other countries doing likewise. In parallel, however, India was also keeping its options open to acquire nuclear weapons if a decision was taken to do so. This was acknowledged in various western capitals as the following quote from 1962 shows:

> According to Martin [of the Service des Factes: Atomic energy], the French have other evidence as well that the Indians are not losing sight of militarily significant research in the course of their civil atomic programme. With at least the tacit approval of the highest echelon of government, the Indian atomic energy authorities are proceeding in a manner similar to that of France in the late forties with a view to reaching in a couple of years the French position of 1953–54 at which point a decision to "go for the bomb" could, if desired, be given practical application.[144]

India, at this point, had also constructed an indigenous, modestly-sized reprocessing plant based in part upon designs provided by a US contractor with a view to become capable of separating plutonium from irradiated uranium.[145] The plant was capable of handling 20 tons of spent fuel per year.[146] India was interested in reprocessing for several reasons, which included reprocessing CIRUS fuel and developing novel fuel cycles to utilise its vast thorium reserves.[147] However, the plant could also be used to produce material for nuclear weapons. India was also able to obtain 10 tons of uranium from Canada without safeguards save for a peaceful uses clause and an agreement that the fuel would not be re-exported.[148] India is further believed to have received 35 tons of uranium from Spain without safeguards around 1962.[149]

In parallel, India pursued the indigenisation of other production capabilities, including heavy water, by importing a 14-ton facility from West Germany as well as a uranium metal production facility and a graphite production facility around 1961.[150] India also concluded nuclear cooperation agreements with other states, including with the Soviet Union, in 1961.[151]

At the time India's 1956–1961 five-year plan was adopted, India only had the CIRUS reactor and two smaller reactors. One was a 1 MW pool-type research reactor that utilised enriched uranium. The second was a 100-watt zero energy reactor. Both were located at Trombay and were not usable for plutonium production because of the design, fuel and level of flux.[152] To meet the aspirations of the five-year plan, therefore, it would be necessary to substantially increase India's nuclear infrastructure and to do so with outside assistance. India thus sought to negotiate the sale of other reactors, including a light-water reactor from the US to be located at Tarapur and the supply of a CANDU type reactor from Canada. The negotiations between Canada and India over the supply of a power reactor are particularly insightful. Canada had already provided India with the CIRUS research reactor without safeguards. This reactor was subsequently used to produce plutonium for India's PNE.[153] India could thus argue that safeguards on the power reactor would not constrain its nuclear options as it already had the capability to produce nuclear explosions. The actual deal for the CANDU reactor was even more complex because India wanted to domestically construct the power reactor based on the Canadian design. India argued that safeguards were irrelevant because it could simply build an indigenous copy of the reactor without safeguards being applicable. The detailed consideration of the Canadian position is worthy of further examination.[154]

> On balance, it appears that the long-term disadvantages resulting from the abandonment of Canada's safeguards requirements cannot be justified by the short-term advantage, especially in view of the probable United States reaction. Whether Canadian insistence on safeguards will result in loss of the opportunity to conclude the agreement depends largely on whether the safeguards requirements can be made sufficiently palatable to India while still maintaining the general safeguards principle and certain key requirements. Working in Canada's favour is the fact that India has shown great interest in the Canadian design, especially because it used natural uranium fuel which is widely available and which India has more recently begun to develop from her own resources. Working against Canada is, of course, India's strong opposition to safeguards and the loss of face she would suffer if she retreated. Although it is difficult to conceive of any compromise that would be easily acceptable to both sides, some adjustment of Canada's position might be possible. For example, provision could be made for a review of safeguards provisions after five or ten years in the light of possible changed circumstances.
>
> No such minor concessions are likely to overcome India's strong emotional reaction to a system that, in her eyes, brands her as a second-class nation compared with the U.S., the U.K., Canada and the six Euratom

> countries. The best hope of success may therefore lie in finding a formula that puts Canada and India on an equal footing, as evidenced by the admission that India might accept IAEA safeguards if the United States required all other aid-receiving countries to accept them. For example, Canada could propose to admit Indian inspectors freely to nuclear installations in Canada in return for the same rights in India. In its most appealing form this proposal could cover all nuclear reactors in both countries, making the relationship entirely reciprocal. In this fashion Canada and India could set an example and could lead the world in encouraging the application of nuclear science and technology to peaceful purposes. An agreed formula now between our two countries could well pave the way for similar agreements among other countries and could make a significant contribution to the development of nuclear energy for peaceful purposes throughout the world.

A limited variation of this formulation was eventually taken forward, with the RAPS reactor in India and the Douglas point reactor in Canada made subject to IAEA safeguards.[155] The IAEA had not yet agreed safeguards provisions for power reactors at this point and states could still sign bilateral (as opposed to IAEA) safeguards.

India's strategy was to play states off against each another in an effort to minimise the safeguards conditions. There were some signs that India's strategy bore fruit: the UK, for example, issued an aide memoire that proposed to limit safeguards to so-called 'first generation' fuel (and not to reprocessed materials).[156] The limited safeguards agreed with Canada were neither an optimal or worst-case outcome: the common position of the western suppliers bore fruit in part because Canada was concerned about the US reaction.

For the Tarapur reactor, the US agreed to supply a light water reactor with fuel for a period of 30 years. This was made subject to bilateral safeguards with US officials stating:

> … it has been possible to achieve a mutually satisfactory arrangement without either governments giving up its basic position regarding the attachment of safeguards to equipment, since the Tarapur station will be operated only on enriched uranium supplied by the United States or on plutonium produced therefrom; the United States would guarantee the supply of enriched uranium for the period of the agreement.[157]

The Indians told the Canadians they had accepted safeguards on the deposition of the fuel on the US-supplied reactor because the fuel for the reactor was enriched and would be supplied by the US in its entirety for the whole life of the reactor.[158] The US-India agreement over Tarapur did allow for the possibility of placing the safeguards responsibilities with the IAEA once IAEA safeguards on large power reactors had been agreed.[159]

Regarding the CANDU reactor, and under pressure from both the UK and the US, Canadian officials asked the two countries to review the safeguards agreement. US and British officials heavily criticised it on several grounds, including in relation to provisions of access, the lack of continuous inspection, that safeguards should apply to subsequent generations of material, that more specific peaceful use conditions should be included, and that the fuel from other sources would not be subject to safeguards.[160] Canadian officials were also mindful of the possibility that India could construct an indigenous duplicate of a CANDU-like reactor. The Canadian policy did not require full-scope safeguards as a condition of supply, however, and Canada was willing to provide a safeguarded reactor in the knowledge that India could indigenously construct unsafeguarded clones of it.[161]

From this examination of the safeguards to be attached to the sale of the CANDU reactor, it is apparent that Canadian officials understood and accepted the limitations of the agreement vis-a-vis preventing India's future production of nuclear weapons. This raises the question of why Canada went ahead with the transfer? Indeed, questions must also be asked about the US sale which, even though subject to more complete safeguards, would still aid the nuclear programme of a country with an interest in nuclear weapons.

The position taken by Canada in the discussions of controls is relevant to addressing these questions. As noted earlier, Canada had said that it would reserve the right to assist other countries in acquiring nuclear weapons on a case-by-case basis. The end result was that Canadian officials opted to sell the reactor with a minimum level of safeguards in pursuit of commercial and bilateral interests.

By the time of China's nuclear test in 1964, India had a limited nuclear capability, including the ability to produce plutonium in CIRUS, which could then be separated. Weaponising nuclear material was still out of the reach of India, however, as the country only had a modest fissile material production capability, had not conducted relevant nuclear explosive testing, and had no means to deliver nuclear warheads. Substantial and sustained financial investment would have been required to pursue nuclear weapons. Perkovich also argues that Indian officials saw no immediate security threat from China that required them to immediately embark on a weapons programme.

The peaceful nuclear explosion and its aftermath

Indian scientists quietly began to work on a nuclear explosive device in the late 1960s. It is unclear to what extent these actions were expressly endorsed by the country's political leadership at the time, which put off the question of acquiring or testing nuclear weapons.[162] Successive leaders subscribed to the Nehru view of nuclear weapons, which was that they should be eliminated.[163] Some in India's political establishment did believe that India should acquire nuclear weapons, however, and this view was increasingly expressed by Indian political parties. For example, Bhumita Chakma notes:[164]

> Notwithstanding Shastri's 'no policy change' stance, various political parties (including a majority of the All India Congress Committee members), the Indian media, many influential public opinion-makers and a majority of the Indian polity reacted sharply, demanding the manufacturing of nuclear weapons by India. Jana Sangh, at a working committee meeting on 4 December 1964, resolved that the party ' ... considers it imperative that an all out effort be made to build up an independent nuclear deterrent ... and urges the government of India to revise its stands accordingly'. The Praja Socialist Party (PSP), in a similar fashion, demanded immediate manufacturing of Indian bombs.

The idea to conduct a PNE was thus a clever way to square several competing imperatives as peaceful nuclear explosions had long been theorised as a potentially viable approach to large scale civil engineering projects. India could thus conduct a nuclear explosion while claiming its purpose was 'peaceful' in nature.[165]

Cooperation with India, including the construction of the above-mentioned reactors, continued into the 1970s. In the early part of the decade, it became known that India was considering a PNE. The US and Canada wrote to India, making clear they would view this as not in keeping with the peaceful uses requirements of the CIRUS reactor agreement. However, India held with the line that the explosion was peaceful in nature. On 18 May 1974, India conducted its PNE, testing a plutonium-based implosion device approximately 100 feet below the earth's surface to ostensibly learn lessons related to the future application of peaceful nuclear explosions. The explosion itself was codenamed 'smiling Buddha'.[166] The test demonstrated that India could acquire nuclear weapons if it decided to do so, although evidently, further work would be required to deploy nuclear explosives for military purposes.

It is possible to surmise that by conducting a PNE, India sought to maintain its moral position on the NPT, which is explored further in the following, and to increase its nuclear capability in response to the Chinese weapons test of 1964, all while making the case the conditions associated with nuclear supply had not been violated.[167] Indeed, then Prime Minister Indira Gandhi defended the explosion by stating that Canadian-supplied materials had not been used in the test, which was 'peaceful' in nature.[168] While the test utilised uranium outside of safeguards, it had been irradiated to produce plutonium in the CIRUS reactor without India violating any specific commitment. The Indian government maintained that it was exercising its legitimate nuclear rights in conducting the PNE and that it had not violated supply agreements with the US and Canada. The test did, however, cause substantial international concern and prompted Pakistan to accelerate its own nuclear weapons efforts. It may also have increased China's willingness to provide nuclear assistance to Pakistan, something addressed in Chapter 4.

A number of conclusions can be drawn from this exploration of the Indian case. First, both Canada and the US were willing to agree on contracts to supply India with nuclear capabilities during the 1950s even before a system of control had been devised, and with no expectation that India could be made to forego nuclear weapons in the absence of a broader agreement on disarmament. Second, while the coverage and coordination of safeguards improved over the course of the 1960s, particularly after the creation of the IAEA, there was no expectation that the safeguards devised would prevent India from acquiring nuclear weapons. Instead, their purpose was to ensure that only supplied materials and equipment were not misused. India also had some success in pitting suppliers against one another in order to minimise its safeguards obligations.

Findings and conclusions: atoms for peace and the collective action problem

In the last chapter, it was demonstrated that the failure of the UN Atomic Energy Commission to reach an agreement on international control of atomic energy resulted in no framework through which international cooperation could take place outside of weapons-related interests. This chapter has examined how the Atoms for Peace initiative came about and created a framework for such cooperation despite the absence of an effective system of control.

The purpose of this concluding section of this chapter is to summarise the insights from examining the evolution of controls in this period by drawing on the CAP framework. It then presents broader conclusions about the Atoms for Peace initiative and its relevance to the core argument of this book.

Findings

The loose research framework highlights core and structural factors, imperatives and technological factors. Findings from examining these factors in this period are presented in turn.

Structural factors

- Face-to-face communications: Given the context of the Cold War, bilateral face-to-face communications were limited in this period, in particular between the US and the USSR, but when such discussions occurred, they were key in achieving mutual understanding about proliferation risks and the need for trade controls. A meeting between the US, the UK, and Canada also helped to thrash out a common position on safeguards requirements for nuclear sales. For large group meetings such as the statute negotiations, tactics were more important than face-to-face meetings in securing agreements. For example, the Superpowers were able to cooperate to establish rules of procedures that minimized the likelihood of amendments being adopted.

- Information on past actions: This was largely irrelevant given that the atomic age was still in its infancy and given that the world order was being reshaped in the context of the Cold War. Nonetheless, the existence of rumours about possible transfers outside of Safeguards could have undermined cooperation on controls had concentrated effort not taken place to encourage information sharing and dialogue between key nuclear suppliers.
- How actors are linked: As mentioned earlier, the primary linkages (or lack thereof) in this period were based on a triangular relationship between the western states, the Soviet bloc and third countries. These linkages were significant and the competition for influence drove the provision of atomic assistance without effective control. The second set of links – between nuclear haves and have nots – were also significant. The effect of these linkages was to drive forward the transfer of atomic energy capabilities absent an effective system of control.

Core factors

- Core factors: Core factors worked hand-in-hand with the structural factors set out earlier to prevent cooperation on nuclear trade controls. It was the difficult relationship between the Superpowers that primarily led to competition in this period, although this difficult relationship was itself driven by structural factors. There was no trust between the US and the USSR, which led the US to be sceptical of Moscow's concerns about the proliferation risks related to the Atoms for Peace initiative, for example. As a result, Western and Communist blocs were directly influenced by their mistrust of one another rather than issues of potential agreement such as non-proliferation. This mistrust was gradually overcome in relation to non-proliferation, but only between the two Superpowers. A non-proliferation norm did not emerge in the period before the mid-1960s, primarily because key states did not believe non-proliferation was practical without disarmament, which again was directly influenced by the difficult nature of relations between the two blocs.

Technology: Technological factors were secondary but still important in this period. The main proven reactor technology in the period was highly suited to plutonium production as a result of the way that atomic energy was developed during the Second World War. The US, Canada and the Soviet Union would all sell or transfer such reactors to other states, and the USAEC also failed to develop a small power research reactor for export as required under the Atomic Energy Act. As a result, the technologies transferred during this period were not often suited to plutonium production.[169]

Imperatives: The imperatives of non-proliferation, disarmament and peaceful uses were out of alignment as a result of the Cold War dynamics. The US and the Soviet Union opted to proceed with promoting the peaceful use of atomic energy without effective non-proliferation trade controls. This was in the belief that non-proliferation was not an achievable goal without agreement on disarmament, which was also considered to be impractical.

Overall, in examining this period through the lens of the CAP framework, it is clear that structural factors were pivotal in shaping nuclear cooperation over nuclear trade control in this period, particularly because of the developing dynamics of the Cold War. The period was initially marked by competition between the US and the USSR, and this continued throughout the period. Nonetheless, both states would eventually find sufficient ground to cooperate to ensure IAEA-supplied atomic assistance could not directly be misused for weapons purposes.

However, it is also notable that in launching the Atoms for Peace initiative, the US created a situation in which the number of actors involved in atomic energy grew rapidly. The Atomic Energy Act, for example, allowed private sector involvement for the first time and opened up atomic energy to countries for whom it was not previously viable.

This broadening of the number of actors, in turn, also increased the range of interests being pursued. The deliberate inclusion of diverse states in the IAEA statute negotiations highlights that there was not complete homogeneity. Cooperation among the Superpowers partly overcame the potentially negative effect the inclusion of non-aligned states might have had, particularly in relation to the IAEA statute discussions. These discussions took place in a climate of mistrust, but face-to-face discussions between parties, such as the technical meeting with the Soviets to discuss safeguards and the meeting between the US, UK, and Canada to devise a consolidated position ahead of the Statue discussions, were instrumental in agreeing a coordinated position.

Broader conclusions

The Atoms for Peace initiative was a clear outcome of the structural factors that had come to define international politics in the context of the early Cold War period. It arose out of a perceived US need to justify expanded military spending and to win over allies and non-aligned states.

While it might be expected that it would be the interests of all states to cooperate to make international controls effective during this period, in practice, a variety of factors stood in the way of such cooperation. At the structural level, the fact that the two Superpowers were ultimately supportive of the initiative, despite initial Soviet hesitation, doubtless encouraged cooperation. However, because these controls would not apply to the US or the Soviet Union, this made countries like India resistant to the measures.

Ultimately, in announcing the Atoms for Peace initiative, President Eisenhower clearly believed that atomic energy could benefit mankind and sought to ensure that it could do so. Importantly, he also saw a role for the initiative in assisting the US in its political-strategic struggle with the Soviet Union. A less hostile relationship could have eased the way for nuclear disarmament to take place, but this was at best only a secondary goal for both states. Despite the proliferation risk associated with the initiative coming to light in 1954, the US opted to press ahead because there was little prospect of reaching an agreement on disarmament, and Washington feared the loss of face if it did not proceed. It can be concluded, then, that in pursuing the initiative, Washington accepted that the proliferation of nuclear weapons could not be stopped.

From this starting point, it was perhaps inevitable that the statute of the IAEA, and then the safeguards to be associated with the implementation of the initiative, were not designed to prevent states from acquiring nuclear weapons. Instead, they were designed to ensure that direct assistance was not granted through the agency to weapons programmes in partner states with international trade controls also being aligned to this limited objective. It was also perhaps inevitable that some states would take advantage of the Atoms for Peace initiative to indirectly assist their own nuclear weapons programmes. The India case demonstrates that this did indeed happen in practice: India was able to acquire facilities and materials despite the fact that supplier states were aware of the strong possibility that India could seek to acquire nuclear weapons. India, for its part, was able to play supplier states off against one another to minimize its own obligations in relation to safeguards. It did so partly because it wished to keep its nuclear weapons options open.

It can therefore be concluded that the Atoms for Peace initiative was devised in the geostrategic context of the Cold War and created a situation in which states could advance capabilities towards acquiring nuclear weapons because inadequate trade control requirements were placed on nuclear technology and material transfers for civil use. This may well be the main legacy of the Atoms for Peace initiative because it had a direct impact on efforts to prevent further states from acquiring nuclear weapons after the Indian test. Indeed, it was in this context that future proliferation episodes transpired and which subsequently prompted the US to lead efforts to coordinate nuclear supplier controls. In order to examine these dynamics, Chapter 4 examines how the NPT emerged, how this affected trade controls and why it was the treaty was not 'loophole free'. Chapter 4 also examines the emergence of a nuclear suppliers regime and the practical effects of these emergent controls on Pakistan's nuclear programme in the period up to 1990.

Notes

1 The 'executive branch officials chiefly concerned' would later describe the situation when Eisenhower entered office as "a disarmament stalemate and an atomic arms race". "Weapons Tests and Peaceful Uses of the Atom", Ann Whitman files, Administration Series, Box 4, DDEPL.

2 The 1953 test was actually a 'boosted' design rather than a thermonuclear bomb as conventionally defined. However, this technical distinction was lost in the narrative that followed the Soviet test codenamed Joe 4.

3 Project Candor, 22 July 1953, Ann Whitman files, Administration Series, Box 12 DDEPL (5251).
4 NSC 151, *Foreign Relations of the United States*, 1952–1954, vol. II, part 2.
5 'Report to the President by the President's Committee on International Information Activities', 30 June 1953. *Foreign Relations of the United States*, 1952–1954· National Security Affairs, vol. II, part 2.
6 'Rationale of Candor or underlying philosophy', Memorandum for General Cutler, (5048) and Project "Candor" (Lamb Presentation), Memorandum to Governor Adams (5055), Ann Whitman files, Confidential File Subject Series, Box 12, DDEPL.
7 'Memorandum on a public information program in support of operation candor', Ann Whitman files, Confidential File Subject Series, Box 12 DDEPL (5064).
8 Letter from James M. Lambie to General Cutler, 23 July 1959 (5048) Ann Whitman files, Confidential File Subject Series, Eisenhower Library, Box 12 DDEPL.
9 'Safety of the republic', 9, 9, 1953, Ann Whitman files, Administration Series, Box 12 DDEPL.
10 Letter to Mr. Janes H Lambie Jr., 23 July 1953, Ann Whitman files, Administration Series, Box 12 DDEPL.
11 As read in Ira Chernus, *Eisenhower's Atoms for Peace*, Texas A&M University: College Station, p. 68.
12 Memorandum to the President, by the Special Assistant to the President (Jackson), "Briefing memo for Saturday's 'Candor' breakfast" 2 October 1953. *Foreign Relations of the United States*, 1952–1954, vol. II, Part 2, National Security Affairs, Document 111.
13 'Chronology – Candor Wheaties', 30 September 1954. Ann Whitman files, Administration Series, Box 4, DDEPL (A75-22).
14 'Draft of Presidential Speech Before General Assembly Of the United States' (6 December 1953), minutes of meeting on Presidential speech dated 16 January 1954. Ann Whitman files, Confidential File Subject Series, Box 12, DDEPL (5131, 5136).
15 Untitled letter from C.D. Jackson to Lewis Strauss, 25 September 1954. Ann Whitman files, Administration Series, Box 4, DDEPL (A75-22) (4578).
16 Ibid., Smith, *Disarming Diplomat*, p. 27.
17 Unlocking the Mysteries of the J. Robert Oppenheimer Transcript, Department of Energy, 3 October 2014.
18 Ibid., Smith, *Disarming Diplomat*.
19 For example, Admiral Strauss stated that "the idea behind the President's speech was that even limited contributions from the several stockpiles would improve international relations, and if the USSR rejected the proposal, the US would have won a psychological victory". Untitled meeting on disarmament, 16 January 1954, Ann Whitman files, Administration Series, Box 12 (5136). DDEPL.
20 The question was posed

> Suppose the United States and the Soviets were each to turn over to the United Nations, for peaceful use, X kilograms of fissionable material. The amount X could be fixed at a figure which we could handle from our stockpile, but which would be difficult for the Soviets to match.

Strauss observed that it would not be possible to say how much material would put the Russians in a difficult position. It should be noted that the US did not know how much fissile material the Soviet Union had access to at this point, however. "Memorandum for the President from Lewis Strauss, 17 September 1953" and "Memorandum for Admiral Strauss and Mr. C.D. Jackson from Robert Cutler", Ann Whitman files, Administration Series, Box 4 (A75-22). DDEPL (4601, 4604).

21 "Remarks prepared by Lewis L. Strauss, Chairman of the United States Atomic Energy Commission For Delivery to the Los Angeles World Affairs Council. Monday, April 19, 1954", Ann Whitman files, Administration Series, Box 4, DDEPL (A75-22) (4196).

22 Washburn, A., "US Information Agency", *World Affairs*, vol. 119, no. 4, Winter, 1956, pp. pp. 101–103. www.jstor.org/stable/20669305.

23 "International Atomic Energy Agency, brief for 12 power meeting, safeguarding of assistance given by the International Atomic Energy Agency", FO371/123086, BNA (UK 361).

24 See footnote 59.

25 The Chatham House publication, the World Today, noted that "For its part, the Soviet Union in the Disarmament Commission adhered to its previous proposals. It called for the prohibition of atomic and other weapons of mass destruction, but with the new proviso that effective international control was to 'be instituted simultaneously' therewith, and repeated its call for a one-third reduction in the armaments of the great Powers within one year. The U.S.S.R. would not, however, give any elaboration or details of the precise working of its proposals". 'Disarmament: Proposals and Negotiations, 1946–1955', Chatham House, The World Today, vol. 11, no. 8, August 1955, pp. 334–348. www.jstor.org/stable/20669305.

26 Discussion at the 261st Meeting of the National Security Council, Thursday, 13 October 1955, Ann Whitman files, Administration Series, Box 7, DDEPL (4909).

27 'Disarmament: Proposals and Negotiations, 1946–1955', Chatham House, *The World Today*, vol. 11, no. 8, August 1955, pp. 334–348. www.jstor.org/stable/20669305.

28 "Summary of meeting in the White House, 16 January 1954", Ann Whitman files, Confidential File Subject Series, Box 12, DDEPL (5266).

29 Ibid.

30 Ibid., Chatham House, 'Disarmament'.

31 Ibid.

32 Ibid., "Summary of meeting in the White House, 16 January 1954".

33 Ibid.

34 Ibid.

35 Discussion at 261st Meeting of the National Security Council, Thursday, 13 October 1955, Ann Whitman Files, NSC Series, Box 7, DDEPL (4906).

36 Ibid.

37 Ibid.

38 Discussion at the 32th Meeting of the National Security Council, 24 May 1957, Ann Whitman Files, NSC Series, Box 8, DDEPL(4983).

39 Ibid.

40 Discussion at the 236th Meeting of the National Security Council, Thursday, February 1955. Letter to the President. 29 July 1955. Ann Whitman files, Administration Series, Box 6, DDEPL(4860). *Foreign Relations of the United States*, 1955–1957, Regulation of Armaments; Atomic Energy; vol. XX.

41 Ibid.

42 Ibid.
43 Ibid.
44 Press Statement from the Office of the Joint Committee on Atomic Energy, 30 June 1954.
45 Statement of John Foster Dulles Before the Joint Committee on Atomic Energy in support of Atomic Energy Act Amendment, 3 June 1954.
46 Atomic Energy Act, 1954, Section 123.
47 'Agreement between the Government of the United States of America and the Government of the United Kingdom of Great Britain and Northern Ireland for Cooperation on the uses of Atomic Energy for Mutual Defense Purposes', 3 July 1958.
48 Letter from Lewis Strauss to the President of the United States dated 16 October 1954. Administration Series box 4, DDEPL (4167).
49 Letter from Commissioner Thomas Murray to the President of the United States, 1 May 1953. Administration Series box 4, DDEPL (4247).
50 Ibid., Smith, *Disarming Diplomat*, p. 38.
51 Twelfth Meeting of the Interagency Nuclear coordinating committee (draft), 14 February 1957. RG59 Box 298 USNARA.
52 Letter from Strauss to CD, 11 June 1956, GWDNSA.
53 The US shipped five kg of HEU fuel to Turkey in 1961. See Department of Energy, "Highly enriched uranium: striking a balance. A historical report on the United States Highly Enriched Uranium Production, Acquisition and Utilisation Activities from 1945 through September 30, 1996", January 2001. Freedom of information act response to the Federation of American Scientists. Available online at: https://fas.org/sgp/othergov/doe/heu/striking.pdf (Accessed 21 December 2021).
54 Letter to the President. 29 July 1955. Ann Whitman files, Administration Series, Box 4, DDEPL (4558).
55 Calculated using usinflationcalculator.com (Accessed 27 December 2016)
56 This term was not defined. In the context of its use, it can be taken to mean a sustained criticism of the competence of Strauss to deliver on atomic energy initiatives. From this episode and the broader primary source material examined in the course of this project, it is apparent both that Strauss played an important role in shaping the atomic age – in part because he had the ear and support of President Eisenhower, and that the atomic age would have played out differently if Strauss had not held this role. Strauss shoulders a good deal of responsibility for the creation of the atoms for peace initiative without an associated effective system of control.
57 Discussion at the 348th Meeting of the National Security Council, 12 December 1957, Ann Whitman files, Administration Series, Box 4 (A75-22). DDEPL.
58 Discussion at the 276th Meeting of the National Security Council, 9 February 1956. Ann Whitman files, Administration Series, Box 7, DDEPL (4917).
59 Gerard Smith recounts that in response to the announcement, the Russian Foreign Minister asked Secretary of State Dulles "what in the world Americans thought they were doing proposing to spread weapon-grade nuclear materials around the world. Dulles seemed incredulous and asked 'that's not true, is it?'" Smith confirmed it was so and was tasked by Dulles with drafting a response to the Soviets that would state that ways "can be devised to safeguard against diversion of materials from electric power producing reactors". Ibid., *Disarming Diplomat.*

60 The Atomic Energy Commission in considering implementation of the initiative, highlighted, for example, that … "The Commission wishes to point out that the transfer of U-235 abroad and subsequent production of fissionable material power reactors increased the possibility of the development of weapon potential by those who receive our assistance. However, in connection with distributions of U-235 either through the International Agency or under agreements for cooperating the Commission will require, as a minimum, assurance and guaranties against diversion to other than peaceful uses, appropriate record keeping and accounting procedure, and access for purposes of audit and observation of compliance. In the case of material distributed under bilateral or multi-lateral arrangements, the Commission will require that irradiated fuel elements be reprocessed in ABC facilities or in facilities designated by the AEG. In addition, the percentage of U-235 in the uranium to be made available, except as specifically authorized by the Commission, will not exceed twenty percent". Strauss to President, 20 February 1956, Ann Whitman files, Administration Series, Box 4, DDEPL (4360).

61 Letter to the President. 29 July 1955. Ann Whitman files, Administration Series, Box 4, DDEPL (4561).

62 Address by Mr. Dwight D. Eisenhower, President of the United States of America, to the 470th Plenary Meeting of the United Nations General Assembly, Tuesday, 8 December 1953, 2:45 p.m. As reproduced on the website of the International Atomic Energy Agency.

63 Gerard Smith stated in his memoir that it was Rockefeller who led the administration's efforts to utilise the initiative for propaganda purposes. Ibid., Smith, *Disarming Diplomat*, p. 38.

64 See footnote 59.

65 In 1954, Baruch re-pitched his plan for disarmament to Strauss to be relayed to the President. His view that atomic weapons becoming cheaper and that disarmament more difficult as more possess. Strauss forwarded to President but without full support, saying that he didn't think weapons were as accessible to small nations. Also cited problems of inspection and control. Ann Whitman files, Administration Series, Box 4, DDEPL.

66 In 10 May 1955, the 'USSR made a disarmament proposal which included, without provision of safeguards, as one of the first measures of its execution: the reduction of arms and the prohibition of atomic weapons, states possessing atomic and hydrogen bombs shall pledge themselves to discontinue tests of these weapons', Memorandum: Disarmament Negotiations (8 pages, undated). Ann Whitman files, Administration Series, Box 4, DDEPL (4277).

67 Memorandum by the Consultant to the Secretary of State for Atomic Energy Affairs (Smith) to the Secretary of State, 1 November 1954, Atomic Energy files, lot 57 D 688, "IAEA Policies". *Foreign Relations of the United States*, 1952–1954, volume II, part 2, National Security Affairs, document 272.

68 Memorandum for the President. Subject: Progress on international atomic energy agency, Ann Whitman files, Administration Series, Box 4, DDEPL (4363).

69 "International Atomic Energy Agency, brief for 12 power meeting, safeguarding of assistance given by the International Atomic Energy Agency", FO371/123086, BNA (UK 364).

70 Ibid.

71 Memorandum handed to U.S. Chargé d. Affaires in Moscow by M. Zorin, 18 July 1955 expressing willingness to participate in negotiations towards an Atomic

Energy Agency and proposing a preliminary meeting of exports to consider the problem of safeguarding the peaceful uses of atomic energy.

72 Letter from the chairman of the atomic energy commission to the President, 18 June 1958. Ann Whitman files, Administration Series, Box 4, DDEPL (4519).

73 Brief, International Atomic Energy Agency, 27 February 1956. FO371/123078, BNA (UK 292).

74 US Statement, Verbatim Record of the Third Plenary Meeting held on 24 September 1956, Conference on the Statute of the International Atomic Energy Agency, 24 September 1956. FO371/123092, BNA (UK 78).

75 "International Atomic Energy Agency, brief for 12 power meeting, safeguarding of assistance given by the International Atomic Energy Agency", FO371/123086, BNA (UK 365).

76 Ibid.

77 Ibid.

78 Ibid.

79 Ibid.

80 Certain points made in a meeting in Mr. Hall's Office in February 10 at which an AEC tentative re-draft of the statute was circulated, 10 February 1956. FO 371/ 123077: Working party on President Eisenhower's Plan, BNA (UK 435).

81 'Welcome Remarks, Lewis Strauss, 'Verbatim Record of the First Plenary Meeting Held on Thursday, 20 September 1956 at 2:45 P.M'. United Nations, New York.

82 "International Atomic Energy Agency, brief for 12 power meeting, safeguarding of assistance given by the International Atomic Energy Agency", FO371/123086, BNA (UK 369).

83 Ibid.

84 Ibid.

85 Working Group on the Proposed International Atomic Energy Agency, From Washington to Foreign Office, 2 March 1956, FO371/123083. BNA (353).

86 Statement of FRG, Verbatim Record of the Third Plenary Meeting held on 24 September 1956, Conference on the Statute of the International Atomic Energy Agency, 24 September 1956. FO371/123092, BNA.

87 Verbatim Record of the Third Plenary Meeting held on 24 September 1956, Conference on the Statute of the International Atomic Energy Agency, 24 September 1956. FO371/123092, BNA.

88 FCO, Report on the Conference on the Statute of the International Atomic Energy Agency – New York – 20 September–26 October 1956, FCO371/123088, BNA.

89 In fact, the UK noted that

> as the conference drew on, it became apparent that there was open conflict within the United States delegation between the representatives of the State Department and the Atomic Energy Commission: the former anxious to make some accommodation, the latter doctrine to a point which was quite out of keeping with the general feeling of the conference and political realities. This development produced a fresh set of problems since the United States delegation now appeared willing to go so far in order to meet the Indians as to run a serious risk of giving the Agency an unworkable system of controls. As the conference drew towards its close the United States delegation began to show signs of panic lest the Statute was not completed in time to enable President Eisenhower to make his planned appearance on October 26. It was then left mainly to the United Kingdom delegation to perform the ungrateful task of holding the Americans in Check.

FCO, Report on the Conference on the Statute of the International Atomic Energy Agency – New York – 20 September–26 October 1956, FCO371/ 123088, BNA.

90 'About the IAEA Statute', Website of the International Atomic Energy Agency.

91 Canadian officials noted in 1959 during a discussion with the Indian High Commissioner to Canada that:

> with the rapid spread of nuclear technology, the problem of safeguards had become more than ever acute. The Canadian view was that unless the question were dealt with soon, the problem of control of weapons might get completely out of hand.
>
> 14003-J2-3 (volume 1) (134) LAC

92 "Atomic Safeguards: Proposed Indian Nuclear Power Station" RG134 Box 96, USNARA.

93 Australia, Belgium, Canada, France, Republic of South Africa, United Kingdom, and the United States.

94 Statute of the International Atomic Energy Agency. Available online at: www.iaea.org/about/statute (Accessed 27 November 2020).

95 'Agency Safeguards to US Reactors', 21 November 1961, Atomic Energy – International Atomic Energy Agency – Material – supply of materials and safeguards against diversion, 14001-9-8 (volume 9) (3204) LAC.

96 'Statement of Homi Bhabha to the Conference on the Statute of the International Atomic Energy Agency. Verbatim Record of the Fourteenth Meeting of the Main Conference held on Monday 15 October 1956. IAEA/CS/OR.28 15 October 1956.

97 The Soviet delegate stated that

> Before the safeguards Item was actually discussed in the Board, the Soviet delegation moved that it be delated from the agenda for the present series of meetings. They and those who supported their motion argued that there was no need for haste, that any agreement on the cessation of nuclear tests would alter the whole context in which the safeguards document had been evolved, and that there would be no difficulty in handling requests for Agency assistance, to the extent that they involved safeguards, on the same *ad-hoc* basis on which such requests had been handled in the past. More specifically, they held that the Secretarial had been at fault in not providing the Board with an analytical document on the basis of which the views expressed in the General Conference could be adequately taken into account.

Ibid.

98 Zhihua, S., and Yafeng, X., 'Between Aid and Restriction: Changing Soviet Policies toward China's Nuclear Weapons Program: 1954–1960', Wilson Centre.

99 Note, this should not be mistaken with "Comprehensive Safeguard Agreements" as agreed in the 1990s.

100 INFCIRC/26, 30 March 1961.

101 'Agenda for Westerns Suppliers Meeting, Paris, June 12, 1961', 'The US Position Book: Western Suppliers Meeting, Paris, June 12 1961', RG59 Box 112, USNARA.

102 Ibid.

103 Ibid.

104 Ibid.

105 Atomic Energy – 'Western Suppliers Meeting, Paris, June 12–13, 1961', International Atomic Energy Agency – Supply of Materials and safeguards against diversion, 14001-9-8 (volume 9) (3204) LAC.
106 "Agenda for Westerns Suppliers Meeting, Paris, June 12, 1961", "The US Position Book: Western Suppliers Meeting, Paris, June 12 1961", RG59 Box 112, General Records of the Department of State, USNARA.
107 Atomic Energy – "Western Suppliers Meeting, Paris, June 12–13, 1961", International Atomic Energy Agency – Supply of Materials and safeguards against diversion, 14001-9-8 (volume 9) (3204) LAC.
108 Summary Minutes of Tripartite (Canada, UK, USA) Suppliers meeting held in Washington 18 and 19 May 1965. 5/26/1964. AB46/659, Safeguards: Proposed Agreement Among "western Suppliers" of nuclear plant and material. BNA.
109 "Record of a meeting of the nuclear suppliers group held in the U.S. Embassy, London, June 22–23, 1965". AB46/659, Safeguards: Proposed Agreement Among "western Suppliers" of nuclear plant and material. BNA.
110 Ibid.
111 Ibid.
112 Ibid.
113 Ibid.
114 Ibid.
115 Ibid.
116 Letter from AA Pritchard to J.D. Fraser Esq, Ministry of Technology "Zirconium", 21 October 1965, AB48/659, BNA.
117 Ibid.
118 Muller, H., 'Falling into line? France and the NPT', Programme for promoting nuclear non-proliferation, Occasional Paper No 6, Centre for International Policy Studies, Department of Politics, University of Southampton May 1990.
119 Cohen, A., *Israel and the bomb*, Columbia University Press, 2005. ProQuest Ebook Central, https://ebookcentral.proquest.com/lib/kcl/detail.action?docID=909169. pp. 42–43. www.jstor.org/stable/10.7312/cohe10482.
120 Ibid., p. 59.
121 Ibid., p. 60.
122 Ibid., p. 62.
123 Ibid., Perkovich, *India's Nuclear Bomb.*
124 Ibid., p. 26.
125 Ibid., Overview of the Colombo Plan.
126 Bothwell, R. *Nucleus: The History of Atomic Energy of Canada Limited*, University of Toronto Press, p. 352.
127 Ibid.
128 "Meeting to Discuss Atonic Energy and the Colombo Plan", Atomic Energy in Other Countries – General: India, Peaceful Uses of. 14003-J2-3 251, LAC.
129 Ibid.
130 P.G. Boczar, 11 - CANDU nuclear reactor designs, operation and fuel cycle, In Woodhead Publishing Series in Energy, edited by Ian Crossland, Woodhead Publishing, 2012, p. 278–299, *Nuclear Fuel Cycle Science and Engineering,* ISBN 9780857090737, doi: https://doi.org/10.1533/9780857096388.3.278
131 "Canada – India Atomic reactor", Atomic Energy in Other Countries – General: India, Peaceful Uses of. 14003-J2-3 241, LAC.

132 Untitled meeting record involving, E.C. Allardice, H.N. Sethan, N.R. Prasad (DAE) and R.F. Wright, F. Gilbert, and D.J. Wallace (AECL), 9 September 1959, Other Countries General – India – Cooperation with Canada – 14003-J2-3 (51), LAC.
133 Bothwell, R. *Nucleus: The History of Atomic Energy of Canada Limited,* University of Toronto Press. p. 354.
134 Ibid., p. 354.
135 Ibid., p. 356.
136 As read in Bothwell *Nucleus: The History of Atomic Energy Canada Limited,* p. 353.
137 Telegram from Secretary of State for external affairs Canada, head of post, permanent mission, New York, 3 February 1956, Atomic Energy: Safeguards against diversion, file 14001-2-6, volume one, LAC (8501).
138 India had found substantial quantities of thorium and some sources of uranium during surveys in 1957). Report appearing on page 27 of "Nucleonics of July 1957: Priority for Indian U-plant" Atomic Energy in Other Countries – General: India, Peaceful Uses of. 14003-J2-3 203, LAC.
139 "Export of Nuclear Materials to India", June 58. Atomic Energy in Other Countries – General: India, Peaceful Uses of. 14003-J2-3 127, LAC.
140 "CIR Agreement-Safeguards", Atomic Energy in Other Countries – General: India, Peaceful Uses of. 14003-J2-3 134, LAC.
141 Ibid.
142 "Re supply of fuel Elements for Canada-India Reactor", 3 October 1957, 14003-J2-3 11, LAC.
143 "Aide Memoire", 30 September 1959. Atomic Energy in Other Countries – General: India, Peaceful Uses of. 14003-J2-3 10, LAC; "CIR Agreements: Safeguards", 29 September 1959, Atomic Energy in Other Countries – General: India, Peaceful Uses of. 14003-J2-3 11, LAC.
144 "India and possible nuclear weapons research programme", 17 August 1962, 14003-J2-1, LAC.
145 Ibid., Perkovich, *India's Nuclear Bomb,* p. 28.
146 Rajagopalan, R., and Mishra, A., *Nuclear South Asia: Keywords and Concepts,* Routledge India, 2014. doi: https://doi.org/10.1080/01495933.2017.1338485.
147 Thorium is a naturally-occurring element found in abundance in India which is fertile. This means that it can be turned into a fissile material through neutron bombardment.
148 Untitled meeting record involving, E.C. Allardice, H.N. Sethan, N.R. Prasad (DAE) and R.F. Wright, F. Gilbert, and D.J. Wallace (AECL), 9 September, 1959, Other Countries General – India – Cooperation with Canada – 14003-J2-3 (51), LAC.
149 Telegram "Uranium for India", 14403-J2-1, Atomic Energy in Other Countries – General: India, Peaceful Uses of 337, 14003-J2-3 251, LAC.
150 "Intelligence Brief: Indian Atomic Energy", 1 June 1961, Atomic Energy in Other Countries – General: India, Peaceful Uses of. 14003-J2-3 (347), LAC.
151 Ibid., Perkovich, *India's Nuclear Bomb*, p. 42.
152 Ibid.
153 Ibid., Perkovich, *India's Nuclear Bomb*, p. 186.
154 Memorandum To Ministers: Canadian-designed Nuclear Power Station for India, 7 May 1963. RG59, vol. 5629, File no. 14003-J2-3, vol. 6, LAC.

155 N11378: "International Atomic Energy Agency, Canada and India Agreement relating to safeguards provisions". Signed at Vienna on 30 September 1971. Available online at: https://treaties.un.org/doc/publication/unts/volume%20798/volume-798-i-11378-english.pdf later incorporated into INFCIRC/211: "The text of a safeguards agreement between the Agency, Canada and India", 6 November 1974.
156 'Indian Attitude on Safeguards: UK Proposals', 22 April 1961, RG134 (1053).
157 'Department of State: for the Press: United States Indian Negotiations on Nuclear Power Stations at Tarapur, India' (1963), Atomic Energy in Other Countries – General: India, Peaceful Uses of, LCA.
158 Candu reactor safeguards, 17 July 1963, 14003-J2-3-40 (3663, 3742), LAC.
159 Safeguards for Indian reactor, 3 July 1963, 14003-I2-3-40 (3663), LAC.
160 Candu reactor safeguards: memorandum to ministers, department of external affairs, 21 October 1963, Atomic Energy: India Cooperation With Canada, File No 14033-J2-3, LAC (3975).
161 Atomic Energy Advisory Panel meeting, 25 July 1963, 14003-J2-3-40 (3663), Canadian National Archives (3724).
162 Ibid., 142.
163 Ibid.
164 Toward Pokhran II: Explaining India's Nuclearisation Process, *Modern Asian Studies,* vol. 39, no. 1, 2005, pp. 189–236. C 2005 Cambridge University Press. doi: 10.1017/S0026749X04001416.
165 Ibid.
166 "Indian Nuclear Test", Cable from American Embassy New Delhi to Secretary of State, 18 May 1974, folder NSSM-156 [2 of 2], Box H-192, National Security Council Institution ("H") files, RNPL.
167 The Treaty on the Non-Proliferation of Nuclear Weapons (NPT) was negotiated in the 1960s and came into effect in 1970. India has not become a party to the treaty.
168 Telegram from Delhi entitled "Indian Nuclear Explosion", Candu Reactor General 252-2-1, LAC.
169 By proliferation resistant, it is meant that the reactors being exported were well suited to use in nuclear weapons programmes.

Bibliography

14003-J2-1, LAC.

14003-J2-3, LAC.

'About the IAEA Statute', Website of the International Atomic Energy Agency.

Address by Mr. Dwight D. Eisenhower, President of the United States of America, to the 470th Plenary Meeting of the United Nations General Assembly, Tuesday, 8 December 1953, 2:45 p.m. As reproduced on the website of the International Atomic Energy Agency.

'Agency Safeguards to US Reactors', 21 November 1961, Atomic Energy – International Atomic Energy Agency – Material – supply of materials and safeguards against diversion, 14001-9-8 (vol. 9) (3204) LAC.

"Agenda for Westerns Suppliers Meeting, Paris, June 12, 1961", "The US Position Book: Western Suppliers Meeting, Paris, June 12 1961", RG59 Box 112, General Records of the Department of State, USNARA.

'Agenda for Westerns Suppliers Meeting, Paris, June 12, 1961', 'The US Position Book: Western Suppliers Meeting, Paris, June 12 1961', RG59 Box 112, USNARA.

'Agreement between the Government of the United States of America and the Government of the United Kingdom of Great Britain and Northern Ireland for Cooperation on the uses of Atomic Energy for Mutual Defense Purposes', 3 July 1958.

Ann Whitman files, Administration Series, Box 4, DDEPL.

Atomic Energy Advisory Panel meeting, 25 July 1963, 14003-J2-3-40 (3663), Canadian National Archives (3724).

Atomic Energy Act, 1954, Section 123.

"Atomic Safeguards: Proposed Indian Nuclear Power Station" RG134 Box 96, USNARA.

Boczar, P.G. 11 – CANDU nuclear reactor designs, operation and fuel cycle, In *Woodhead Publishing Series in Energy*, edited by Ian Crossland, Woodhead Publishing, 2012, pp. 278–299, Nuclear Fuel Cycle Science and Engineering, ISBN: 9780857090737, doi: https://doi.org/10.1533/9780857096388.3.278.

Bothwell, R. *Nucleus: The history of atomic energy of Canada limited*, University of Toronto Press. p. 352.

Brief, International Atomic Energy Agency, 27 February 1956. FO371/123078, BNA (UK 292).

"Canada – India Atomic reactor", Atomic Energy in Other Countries – General: India, Peaceful Uses of. 14003-J2-3 241, LAC.

Candu reactor safeguards, 17 July 1963, 14003-J2-3-40 (3663, 3742), LAC.

Candu reactor safeguards: Memorandum to ministers, department of external affairs, 21 October 1963, Atomic Energy: India Cooperation With Canada, File No 14033-J2-3, LAC (3975).

Certain points made in a meeting in Mr. Hall's Office in February 10 at which an AEC tentative re-draft of the statute was circulated, 10 February 1956. FO 371/123077: Working party on President Eisenhower's Plan, BNA (UK 435).

"CIR Agreement-Safeguards", Atomic Energy in Other Countries – General: India, Peaceful Uses of. 14003-J2-3 134, LAC.

Chernus, I. *Eisenhower's atoms for peace*, Texas A&M University: College Station.

'Chronology – Candor Wheaties', 30 September 1954. Ann Whitman files, Administration Series, Box 4, DDEPL (A75-22).

Cohen, A. *Israel and the bomb*, Columbia University Press, 2005. ProQuest Ebook Central, https://ebookcentral.proquest.com/lib/kcl/detail.action?docID=909169. pp. 42–43. www.jstor.org/stable/10.7312/cohe10482.

'Department of State: for the Press: United States Indian Negotiations on Nuclear Power Stations at Tarapur, India' (1963), Atomic Energy in Other Countries – General: India, Peaceful Uses of, LCA.

'Disarmament: Proposals and Negotiations, 1946–1955', Chatham House, The World Today, vol. 11, no. 8, August 1955, pp. 334–348. www.jstor.org/stable/20669305.

Discussion at the 261st Meeting of the National Security Council, Thursday, 13 October 1955, Ann Whitman files, Administration Series, Box 7, DDEPL (4909).

Discussion at the 236th Meeting of the National Security Council, Thursday, February 1955. Letter to the President. 29 July 1955. Ann Whitman files, Administration Series, Box 6, DDEPL (4860). Foreign Relations of the United States, 1955–1957, Regulation of Armaments; Atomic Energy; vol. XX.

Discussion at the 276th Meeting of the National Security Council, 9 February 1956. Ann Whitman files, Administration Series, Box 7, DDEPL (4917).

Discussion at the 348th Meeting of the National Security Council, 12 December 1957, Ann Whitman files, Administration Series, Box 4 (A75-22). DDEPL.

Discussion at the 32th Meeting of the National Security Council, 24 May 1957, Ann Whitman Files, NSC Series, Box 8, DDEPL (4983).

'Draft of Presidential Speech Before General Assembly of the United States' (6 December 1953), minutes of meeting on Presidential speech dated 16 January 1954. Ann Whitman files, Confidential File Subject Series, Box 12, DDEPL (5131, 5136).

FCO, Report on the Conference on the Statute of the International Atomic Energy Agency – New York – 20 September–26 October 1956, FCO371/123088, BNA.

Freedom of information act response to the Federation of American Scientists. Available online at: https://fas.org/sgp/othergov/doe/heu/striking.pdf (Accessed 21 December 2021).

INFCIRC/26, 30 March 1961.

'Indian Attitude on Safeguards: UK Proposals', 22 April 1961, RG134 (1053).

"Indian Nuclear Test", Cable from American Embassy New Delhi to Secretary of State, 18 May 1974, folder NSSM-156 [2 of 2], Box H-192, National Security Council Institution ("H") files, RNPL.

"Intelligence Brief: Indian Atomic Energy", 1 June 1961, Atomic Energy in Other Countries – General: India, Peaceful Uses of. 14003-J2-3 (347), LAC.

"International Atomic Energy Agency, brief for 12 power meeting, safeguarding of assistance given by the International Atomic Energy Agency", FO371/123086, BNA (UK 361).

Letter from AA Pritchard to J.D. Fraser Esq, Ministry of Technology "Zirconium", 21 October 1965, AB48/659, BNA.

Letter from Commissioner Thomas Murray to the President of the United States, 1 May 1953. Administration Series box 4, DDEPL (4247).

Letter from James M. Lambie to General Cutler, 23 July 1959 (5048) Ann Whitman files, Confidential File Subject Series, Eisenhower Library, Box 12 DDEPL.

Letter from Lewis Strauss to the President of the United States dated 16th October 1954. Administration Series box 4, DDEPL (4167).

Letter from Strauss to CD, 11 June 1956, GWDNSA.

Letter from the chairman of the atomic energy commission to the President, 18 June 1958. Ann Whitman files, Administration Series, Box 4, DDEPL (4519).

Letter to the President. 29 July 1955. Ann Whitman files, Administration Series, Box 4, DDEPL (4558).

'Memorandum on a public information program in support of operation candor', Ann Whitman files, Confidential File Subject Series, Box 12 DDEPL (5064).

"Meeting to Discuss Atonic Energy and the Colombo Plan", Atomic Energy in Other Countries – General: India, Peaceful Uses of. 14003-J2-3 251, LAC.

Memo, Articles XIII and XVIII of safeguards for Candu Reactor, 14 August 1963, 14003-J2-3-40 (3663, 3668), LAC.

Memorandum by the Consultant to the Secretary of State for Atomic Energy Affairs (Smith) to the Secretary of State, 1 November 1954, Atomic Energy files, lot 57 D

688, "IAEA Policies". Foreign Relations of the United States, 1952–1954, vol. II, part 2, National Security Affairs, document 272.
Memorandum for the President. Subject: Progress on international atomic energy agency, Ann Whitman files, Administration Series, Box 4, DDEPL (4363).
Memorandum to Ministers: Canadian-designed Nuclear Power Station for India, 7 May 1963. RG59, vol. 5629, File no 14003-J2-3, vol. 6, LAC.
Memorandum to the President, by the Special Assistant to the President (Jackson), "Briefing memo for Saturday's 'Candor' breakfast" 2 October 1953. Foreign Relations of the United States, 1952–1954. vol. II, Part 2, National Security Affairs, Document 111.
"Memorandum for the President from Lewis Strauss, 17 September 1953" and "Memorandum for Admiral Strauss and Mr. C.D. Jackson from Robert Cutler", Ann Whitman files, Administration Series, Box 4 (A75-22). DDEPL (4601, 4604).
Memorandum handed to U.S. Chargé d. Affaires in Moscow by M. Zorin, 18 July 1955 expressing willingness to participate in negotiations towards an Atomic Energy Agency and proposing a preliminary meeting of exports to consider the problem of safeguarding the peaceful uses of atomic energy.
Muller, H. 'Falling into line? France and the NPT', Programme for promoting nuclear non-proliferation, Occasional Paper No 6, Centre for International Policy Studies, Department of Politics, University of Southampton, May 1990.
N11378: "International Atomic Energy Agency, Canada and India Agreement relating to safeguards provisions". Signed at Vienna on 30 September 1971. Available online at: https://treaties.un.org/doc/publication/unts/volume%20798/volume-798-i-11378-english.pdf later incorporated into INFCIRC/211: "The text of a safeguards agreement between the Agency, Canada and India", 6 November 1974.
NSC 151, Foreign Relations of the United States, 1952–1954, vol. II, part 2.
'Rationale of Candor or underlying philosophy', Memorandum for General Cutler, (5048) and Project "Candor" (Lamb Presentation), Memorandum to Governor Adams (5055), Ann Whitman files, Confidential File Subject Series, Box 12, DDEPL.
Perkovich, G. *India's nuclear bomb: The impact on global proliferation*, University of California Press, February 2002.
Press Statement from the Office of the Joint Committee on Atomic Energy, 30 June 1954.
Rajagopalan, R., & Mishra, A. *Nuclear South Asia: Keywords and concepts*, Routledge India, 2014. doi: https://doi.org/10.1080/01495933.2017.1338485.
"Record of a meeting of the nuclear suppliers group held in the U.S. Embassy, London, June 22–23, 1965". AB46/659, Safeguards: Proposed Agreement Among "western Suppliers" of nuclear plant and material. BNA.
'Report to the President by the President's Committee on International Information Activities', June 30, 1953. Foreign Relations of the United States, 1952–1954, National Security Affairs, vol. II, part 2.
"Re supply of fuel Elements for Canada-India Reactor", October 3, 1957, 14003-J2-3 11, LAC.
"Remarks prepared by Lewis L. Strauss, Chairman of the United States Atomic Energy Commission for Delivery to the Los Angeles World Affairs Council. Monday, April 19, 1954", Ann Whitman files, Administration Series, Box 4, DDEPL (A75-22) (4196).

'Safety of the republic', 9, 9, 1953, Ann Whitman files, Administration Series, Box 12 DDEPL.

Safeguards for Indian reactor, 3 July 1963, 14003-I2-3-40 (3663), LAC.

Smith, G. *Disarming Diplomat: The memoirs of Ambassador Gerard C. Smith, Arms Control Negotiator*, Madison books, 1996.

Statement of FRG, Verbatim Record of the Third Plenary Meeting held on 24 September 1956, Conference on the Statute of the International Atomic Energy Agency, 24 September 1956. FO371/123092, BNA.

Statement of John Foster Dulles Before the Joint Committee on Atomic Energy in support of Atomic Energy Act Amendment, 3 June 1954.

'Statement of Homi Bhabha to the Conference on the Statute of the International Atomic Energy Agency. Verbatim Record of the Fourteenth Meeting of the Main Conference held on Monday 15 October 1956'. IAEA/CS/OR.28, 15 October 1956.

Statute of the International Atomic Energy Agency. Available online at: www.iaea.org/about/statute (Accessed 27 November 2020).

Strauss to President, 20 February 1956, Ann Whitman files, Administration Series, Box 4, DDEPL (4360).

"Summary of meeting in the White House, 16 January 1954", Ann Whitman files, Confidential File Subject Series, Box 12, DDEPL (5266).

Summary Minutes of Tripartite (Canada, UK, USA) Suppliers meeting held in Washington 18 and 19 May 1965. 5/26/1964. AB46/659, Safeguards: Proposed Agreement Among "western Suppliers" of nuclear plant and material. BNA.

Telegram from Delhi entitled "Indian Nuclear Explosion", Candu Reactor General 252-2-1, LAC.

Telegram from Secretary of State for external affairs Canada, head of post, permanent mission, New York, 3 February 1956, Atomic Energy: Safeguards against diversion, file 14001-2-6, vol. 1, LAC (8501).

Telegram "Uranium for India", 14403-J2-1, Atomic Energy in Other Countries – General: India, Peaceful Uses of 337, 14003-J2-3 251, LAC.

Toward Pokhran II: Explaining India's nuclearisation process, *Modern Asian Studies* vol. 39, no. 1, 2005, pp. 189–236. C 2005 Cambridge University Press. doi: 10.1017/S0026749X04001416.

Twelfth Meeting of the Interagency Nuclear coordinating committee (draft), 14 February 1957. RG59 Box 298 USNARA.

US Statement, Verbatim Record of the Third Plenary Meeting held on 24 September 1956, Conference on the Statute of the International Atomic Energy Agency, 24 September 1956. FO371/123092, BNA (UK 78).

Unlocking the Mysteries of the J. Robert Oppenheimer Transcript, Department of Energy, 3 October 2014.

Untitled meeting record involving, E.C. Allardice, H.N. Sethan, N.R. Prasad (DAE) and R.F. Wright, F. Gilbert, and D.J. Wallace (AECL), 9 September 1959, Other Countries General – India – Cooperation with Canada – 14003-J2-3 (51), LAC.

Untitled meeting on disarmament, 16 January 1954, Ann Whitman files, Administration Series, Box 12 (5136). DDEPL.

Untitled letter from C.D. Jackson to Lewis Strauss, 25 September 1954. Ann Whitman files, Administration Series, Box 4, DDEPL (A75-22) (4578).

Verbatim Record of the Third Plenary Meeting held on 24 September 1956, Conference on the Statute of the International Atomic Energy Agency, 24 September 1956. FO371/123092, BNA.

Washburn, A. US Information Agency, *World Affairs*, vol. 119, no. 4, Winter, 1956, pp. 101–103. www.jstor.org/stable/20669305.

'Welcome Remarks, Lewis Strauss, 'Verbatim Record of the First Plenary Meeting Held on Thursday, 20 September 1956 at 2:45 P.M'. United Nations, New York.

Working Group on the Proposed International Atomic Energy Agency, From Washington to Foreign Office, 2 March 1956, FO371/123083. BNA (353).

Zhihua, S., & Yafeng, X. *Between aid and restriction: Changing Soviet policies toward China's nuclear weapons program: 1954–1960*, Wilson Centre, 2012.

4 Strategies that failed?

US non-proliferation strategy from 1964 to 1980

China's first nuclear test in 1964 and India's PNE of 1974 brought vividly to attention the risks associated with nuclear cooperation and trade in the Atoms for Peace era. Following the Chinese test, the US began to view efforts to prevent the spread of nuclear weapons as a central foreign policy objective and sought Soviet support for a 'non-spread' treaty, which ultimately culminated in the finalisation of the Nuclear Non-Proliferation Treaty (NPT) text in 1968. International efforts were intensified again following India's PNE, which prompted the US to pursue coordination among nuclear suppliers of export conditions on transfers to countries outside of the NPT.

Despite the significant investment of American political and diplomatic capital in the non-proliferation issue during this period, the development of international trade controls was limited, and a variety of countries succeeded in advancing their nuclear weapons ambitions as a result. Perhaps the most notable of these was Pakistan, which in the 1970s and 1980s sought to develop a complete nuclear fuel cycle including uranium enrichment. The programmes of several other countries, including India and Iraq, also advanced. The question therefore arises: why was US leadership in international non-proliferation efforts, including trade controls, not more successful during this period, despite the growing emphasis placed by Washington on preventing nuclear spread?

The purpose of this chapter is to examine the nature of the international nuclear trade controls adopted between 1964 and 1980 and why, ultimately, these measures were of limited success in preventing nuclear proliferation. In particular, in the context of the overall research question of the book, the chapter examines why the controls that were adopted were suboptimal. In the context of this chapter, suboptimal means why the NPT was not 'loophole-free', as had been discussed, and why the NSG did not adopt full-scope safeguards as a condition of supply or controls on dual-use technologies, as was also discussed in this period.

It is argued that the lack of progress on disarmament, combined with the impact of vested interests and geopolitical factors, slowed the adoption of international controls, while the emergence of risks associated with gas centrifuge technology for uranium enrichment were inadequately recognised

DOI: 10.4324/9781003194262-4

or addressed, partly because a greater focus was given to the problem of reprocessing for US policymakers by domestic political reasons. Consequently, the imperative of the peaceful uses of atomic energy prevailed and the US-led efforts of the 1970s to strengthen controls were insufficient in overcoming the inherent proliferation risks associated with the Atoms for Peace initiative. There are a number of reasons why US leadership on non-proliferation in the 1970s did not achieve more success, including structural factors such as the number of actors involved and their associated vested interests. Indeed, the US was itself willing to go only as far as other states in restraining nuclear transfers. Moreover, the situation was compounded by successive US administrations and Congress placing different emphases on different approaches to non-proliferation. Ultimately, this undermined and restricted continuity in cooperation among nuclear supplier states, including through the newly formed Nuclear Suppliers Group (NSG).

The chapter begins by exploring the response of the US and the USSR to the first Chinese nuclear test in 1964. This includes a brief exploration of the assistance provided by the Soviet Union to China in the late 1950s and early 1960s, drawing largely on secondary sources, including the work of John Wilson Lewis and Xue Litai.[1]

This is followed by an examination of the work of the US Gilpatric Commission, the recommendations of which can be considered as the first statement of what a US non-proliferation strategy might look like. The chapter then examines the negotiation and entry into force of the NPT, which was negotiated largely by the US and the USSR after the Chinese nuclear test and which entered into force in 1970.

The chapter next examines the response to India's PNE, with a particular focus on US leadership in developing a non-proliferation strategy. It is shown that the US invested substantial political and diplomatic capital in its pursuit of a non-proliferation strategy and had some success in coordinating common rules among nuclear suppliers and overcoming vested interests such as commercial interests in exporting reprocessing capability notably through the NSG. However, the success of this strategy was ultimately limited by a number of factors, including US domestic politics and bureaucratic constraints, which saw the NSG prematurely terminate its activities. Moreover, international control efforts could not keep pace with the availability of enrichment technology and related materials.

An examination of the Pakistan proliferation episode from 1974 to 1985 is included to illustrate these limitations and the ineffectiveness of the US non-proliferation strategy in constraining the nuclear weapons programme of several countries.

The main argument in this chapter is that, while US non-proliferation strategy during this period went some way towards addressing the problems created by the Atoms for Peace initiative, it was too limited and too slow to prevent nuclear proliferation in those states intent on acquiring nuclear weapons during the 1970s and 1980s. This was largely a result of the collective action problem and the vested interests that had emerged as a result of the way the Atoms for Peace initiative was implemented. This problem was compounded by the emergence of a new enrichment process based on the gas centrifuge.

Towards a Nuclear Non-proliferation Treaty

There was a growing sense of nuclear danger in the 1950s.[2] This was not only a result of concerns about the possibility of nuclear war between the Superpowers. It was also based on concerns about the health effects of atmospheric testing of nuclear weapons, which caused public health concerns, particularly after the testing of megaton thermonuclear weapons and the onwards proliferation of nuclear weapons.[3] The sense of danger was exacerbated by the tense geopolitical situation and the war in Korea, in particular when the US openly contemplated using nuclear weapons against Chinese forces to end the Korean war.[4] It was in this context that China approached the USSR for nuclear assistance in 1954.[5] The USSR agreed to provide civil and non-civil nuclear assistance to its then ally, apparently in part to access Chinese uranium for its own strategic programme. The Hungarian uprising of 1954 provided a motivation for Moscow to solidify its influence in communist states. As such, China was said to have 'seized' the opportunity to make its proposal to the USSR.[6] The cooperation involved training Chinese scientists and the provision of information, data, and equipment.

It was this international concern that would lead to efforts in the UN General Assembly (UNGA) to conclude a so-called non-spread treaty, an effort that gathered momentum after the first Chinese nuclear test explosion in 1964. The main steps toward the adoption of a non-proliferation treaty started with the adoption of two resolutions proposed by the Irish government at the UNGA in 1958 and 1961. These resolutions were part of a series of annual proposals, although it was perhaps the 1961 resolution that was more pivotal and is generally known as the 'Irish resolution'.[7] These resolutions sought to pave the way for talks on disarmament, which helps to explain why the resolutions did not gain broad support from the Western and Soviet camps. Two imperatives drove Ireland to pursue this course:

> The first was the slowness with which negotiations towards general disarmament were proceeding. The second was that failure to halt the spread of nuclear weapons during the long period of negotiations on general disarmament was likely to make those negotiations abortive.[8]

Based upon these imperatives, Irish officials put forward a plan that nuclear weapons states should undertake not to transfer nuclear weapons to other states because other non-weapons states might fear such transfers and be driven to pursue nuclear weapons.[9] Many states were hesitant about the approach without it being linked to disarmament. For example, in relation to the Irish resolution of 1958, Canadian officials argued that the transfer of nuclear weapons should not be prohibited completely, "until appropriate disarmament measures had been agreed upon".[10] French officials also opted to abstain on the vote concerning the Irish resolution of 1960, which was not in the end adopted on the grounds that it was not a disarmament measure.[11,12] Interestingly, even the US objected to the Irish draft of 1959 on the basis that it contained commitments that could not be verified that would last for an indefinite duration, and because

> nuclear powers cannot expect other nations indefinitely to deny to themselves such weapons as they may believe are required for their defence if they, the nuclear powers, refuse to accept the responsibility for halting their own build-up of nuclear weapons and refuse to begin the process of their destruction.[13]

Irish officials, in defending the resolution's lack of disarmament provisions, explained that the

> resolution took account of the difficulties of the nuclear powers – the fact that their defence now depended upon nuclear weapons, that there was no certain method of inspection and control, and that a secretly retained stockpile of nuclear weapons would give an unscrupulous state the power to dominate the world.[14]

India, while objecting to the principle of nuclear retention, would eventually vote for the resolution on the basis that, "it was the least that we could obtain".[15] The resolution was ultimately adopted by the UNGA with 68 votes in favour, no votes against, and a number of important countries, including the US and France, abstaining.[16]

In 1961 Ireland again put forward a resolution on non-proliferation. This time the resolution included provisions for inspection and control. The resolution also held states that possessed nuclear weapons responsible for securing an international agreement. It also called upon states not possessing nuclear weapons not to acquire them. This time, in the context of growing concern about proliferation – particularly in the context of the souring of the Soviet-China relationship – the resolution was adopted unanimously and had the support of both the Soviet Union and the US. Both Moscow and Washington also issued declarations on non-dissemination in 1961.[17] Importantly for the negotiations that followed, these declarations differed in that the American version was based upon the premise that states possessing nuclear weapons would not relinquish 'control' over such weapons to states not owning them, whereas the Soviet draft was based upon 'possession'. This subtle distinction related to the US plans for a multilateral nuclear force (MNF) in the context of NATO, which is explored further in the following.[18]

In April 1963, the US sent to the USSR a "draft non-transfer declaration" in which the nuclear powers would have

> solemnly declared that they will not transfer any nuclear weapons directly, or indirectly through a military alliance, into the national control of individual states not now possessing such weapons, and that they will not assist such states in the manufacture of such weapons.[19]

This draft would also see non-nuclear signatories agree not to manufacture or acquire nuclear weapons. The US also communicated to the Soviet Union that a non-proliferation agreement would not preclude the pursuit of an MNF.[20] These steps were taken in the context of the break in China-Russia relations, which is explored further in the following. Moscow evidently came to regret the nuclear assistance that it had provided to China and to appreciate the need to forego providing nuclear assistance.

The effect of the Chinese nuclear test

The Chinese nuclear test in 1964 focused minds on the problem of proliferation. China's nuclear programme had benefited from Soviet assistance from 1954, which provided scientists and equipment provided in the late 1950s and Stalin actively considering the transfer of a model nuclear weapon in 1960 before the relationship soured around 1961.[21] The US and USSR were negotiating the Partial Test Ban Treaty (PTBT) at this point, which prompted the Soviet leadership to write to China to inform them that they were postponing nuclear cooperation.[22] The reasons attributed for the souring include Russia's perceived view that China did not reciprocate in strategic exchanges as well as difficult relations between Mao and the Soviet Premier.[23]

By 1961, sufficient concern had emerged about China's nuclear aspirations for possible preventative action to be discussed between the US and the Soviet Union, but Moscow expressed the view that the programme was already too far along for acquisition to be prevented.[24] Indeed, China's response to the USSR's decision to limit cooperation was to commit to the goal of breaking the nuclear monopoly of China's adversaries within ten years.[25] This goal proved obtainable despite the setback of losing Soviet patronage largely because of the depth of previous assistance provided by Moscow.[26]

At the time of China's test, the Johnson administration lacked a coherent non-proliferation policy. IAEA safeguards were extended to power reactors in 1964, but the WSG states had not agreed to go beyond a case-by-case approach regarding safeguards on bilateral assistance, with the French government, in particular, holding the line for a national based approach. The policies of Atoms for Peace were still in force and the Johnson administration was grappling with a plan for nuclear weapons sharing in an effort to promote European unity against the Soviet threat and discourage European state proliferation through the multilateral nuclear force (MNF) – also abbreviated

MLF – concept, which conventional wisdom in the US believed was compatible with or unrelated to the nuclear spread problem.[27,28] On 20 April 1964, National Security Action Memo (NSAM) 294 stated that the policy of the US was to

> oppose the development of nuclear forces by additional states, other than those whose forces would be assigned as part of a NATO nuclear force, targeted in accordance with NATO plans and, except where supreme national interests were at stake, used only for the defense purposes of the Alliance.[29]

Following the Chinese test, and in an effort to head off onward proliferation, President Johnson offered security guarantees to any state threatened by nuclear China, stating that, "the nations that do not seek nuclear weapons can be sure that, if they need our strong support against some threat of nuclear blackmail, then they will have it".[30] However, not all nations were prepared to leave their security in US hands, with the traditionally non-aligned India, in particular, expressing reservations.[31]

While US officials were still wedded to the principles of the Atoms for Peace initiative, it was recognised that action must be taken to address the proliferation challenge. It was in this context that President Johnson launched the Gilpatric Committee in late 1964, which was tasked to "examine the problem in its broadest ramifications" – a relatively free mandate to explore issues around non-proliferation.[32]

The committee concluded that, "preventing the further spread of nuclear weapons [was] clearly in the national interest despite the difficult decisions [that would] be required".[33] As a result, the committee recommended that the US should take three types of action: "negotiation of formal multilateral agreements; the application of influence on individual nations considering nuclear weapons acquisition, by ourselves and in conjunction with others; and example [sic] by our own policies and actions".[34] Regarding peaceful uses, the committee concluded that fissile material would become more widely available for industrial uses but that the US should "in all cases insist on adequate safeguards for all peaceful programs" and that PNE "should [not] be allowed to jeopardise a comprehensive test ban treaty".[35] The committee thus expressly supported working with the Soviet Union to prevent proliferation because it "probably shares with us a strong interest in preventing the further spread of nuclear weapons".[36] This was in recognition that "the dangers of proliferation affect all countries, creating a widespread common interest in early and effective steps to halt the nuclear spread".[37]

These policy conclusions and proposed courses of action were radical for the 1960s. As the previous chapter noted, the US had not, until this point, expressly set out a non-proliferation strategy and in the earlier part of the decade, the US was actively considering nuclear sharing to aid fighting the Cold War. Nuclear proliferation was not considered abhorrent or even necessarily undesirable. Indeed, the committee's report addresses this point head-on, arguing that,

> although one might be tempted to accept Indian or Japanese nuclear weapons to counterbalance those of China, we do not believe that the spread of nuclear weapons would or could be stopped there. An Indian or Japanese decision to build nuclear weapons would probably produce a chain reaction of similar decisions by other countries, such as Pakistan, Israel, and the United Arab Republic (UAR).[38]

The committee's conclusions were thus based on an assessment that, "the world is fast approaching a point of no return in the prospects of controlling the spread of nuclear weapons" and that, "the spread of nuclear weapons poses an increasingly grave threat to the security of the United States", with the potential for "additional nuclear powers – perhaps some in this hemisphere – individually possessing the capability to destroy millions of American lives".[39]

As radical and forward looking as the Gilpatric committee was, the report failed almost entirely to address the issue of peaceful uses of nuclear energy and non-proliferation trade controls. The limited inclusion of supply-side measures in the report did not mean that the committee did not consider the matters at length, however, and further study was undertaken. Much of the second meeting of the committee focused on the issue of export controls of technology to France – a fact that would set the scene for a follow-up study on the subject. In the wake of the report and in the context of the French nuclear weapons programme, the US conducted a review of its export policy which took as its starting point the belief that US denial of technology could not prevent weapons acquisition but likewise should not support it. As such, the policy direction that resulted from the review was to seek to prevent exports that would assist a weapons programme while not encumbering legitimate trade or commerce so as not to undermine existing bilateral relations). NASM 294 also addressed the issue of technological support "barring the appearance of assistance to the French weapons program" (but with the tacit assumption that such measures could not prevent the programme).[40]

The Gilpatric Committee's findings did not result in an immediate change to US policy or an end to the implementation of the Atoms for Peace concept. As Brands has argued, for example, not all of the committee's recommendations were accepted. In particular, the implications of the committee's findings for the MLF – that it should be traded off in pursuit of a non-proliferation treaty – proved divisive within the administration.[41] Nonetheless, by the end of 1965, Johnson had authorised exploratory discussions with the Soviet Union on the nuclear spread problem and would ultimately forego MLF in pursuit of an NPT. The US and its allies lifted the Coordinating Committee for Multilateral Export Controls (COCOM) restrictions on the supply of nuclear technology to Soviet Bloc countries in 1965.[42] This was a sign of confidence in the IAEA Safeguards system and contributed to the development of a pragmatic working relationship with the Soviet Union.[43] At the very least, the Gilpatric Committee provided the headroom within the US policymaking community to take such action.

It can be argued that the Gilpatric committee's findings mark the beginning of an emergence of a non-proliferation norm. Indeed, it was also felt by the administration that a disarmament speech delivered by Robert Kennedy on 23 June 1965 was probably informed by unauthorised access to the Gilpatric Report, thus suggesting that the committee had an impact on the domestic political narrative in the US.[44] Committee recommendations that were acted upon included talking with the Soviet Union on the 'nuclear spread problem' and prioritising non-proliferation over the formation of the MLF. It is notable that the committee's work did not benefit from insight into Soviet thinking and it could only assume that Moscow might be open to a non-proliferation agreement after the Chinese test and the deterioration of the Sino-Soviet relationship. In retrospect, greater communication between the US and the USSR might have highlighted common interests in non-proliferation earlier in the process. By mid-1964, the conceptual challenges with the Atoms for Peace initiative were thus becoming apparent and efforts would soon be made to address them.

Negotiating the NPT

The General Assembly again picked up the issue following the Chinese nuclear test in its 1965 session. The Chinese test had focused minds on the problem of the spread of nuclear weapons resulting in a more determined atmosphere for non-proliferation measures within the General Assembly. During 1965, the General Assembly adopted Resolution 2028 (XX) setting out the principles of a non-proliferation treaty from the perspective of non-aligned states.[45] This resolution recognised that, "the danger now exists that an increase in the number of States possessing nuclear weapons may occur" and called for "an international agreement under which nuclear states do not relinquish control of nuclear weapons nor transmit information for their manufacture", and under which non-nuclear states undertake "not to manufacture or otherwise acquire control of such weapons".[46]

Specifically, Resolution 2028 (XX) stated:

- the treaty should be void of any loop-holes which might permit nuclear or non-nuclear powers to proliferate directly or indirectly, nuclear weapons in any form;
- the treaty should embody an acceptable balance of mutual responsibilities and obligations of the nuclear and non-nuclear powers;
- the treaty should be a step towards the achievement of general and complete disarmament, and more particularly, nuclear disarmament;

- there should be acceptable and workable provisions to ensure the effectiveness of the treaty; and
- nothing in the treaty should adversely affect the right of any group of States to conclude regional treaties in order to ensure the total absence of nuclear weapons in their territories.

The UAR would build upon these principles in an important statement to the Eighteen Nation Disarmament Commission as a third view (in addition to the views of the two Superpowers) about the objective of the NPT.[47] This statement set out a plan that involved identifying the objectives of a non-proliferation treaty, including consideration from the outset of the question of

> whether there is at this stage real readiness and a sincere desire to put the names of our respective Governments on a formal treaty which binds us all, nuclear and non-nuclear powers [and] whether the political atmosphere is auspicious enough for the conclusion of an international instrument of such a magnitude.

The UAR believed it should also be viewed as a permanent international obligation free from so-called "escape clauses". Finally, it should be viewed as "a step towards reaching agreement on the prohibition of the use of, and destruction of, all nuclear weapons".[48]

MLF and the NPT

An important parallel discussion concerned the proposals for a MLF. The US had begun consideration of a MLF in the Eisenhower administration. The basic concept was to give US allies a role in the employment of US nuclear weapons. The objectives were multiple. The policy would provide reassurance to European allies that the US would intervene if the Soviet Union was to attack.[49] The policy was thus central to the NATO structure and to the perceived ability of the US to fight the Cold War. At the same time, the policy was intended to reduce the likelihood that more European states, and in particular Western Germany, would pursue an independent nuclear weapons capability. The policy would become central to the discussions between the Soviet Union and the US on the merits, and indeed the overall purpose, of a non-proliferation treaty.

From the US perspective, the purpose of a non-proliferation treaty would be to prevent more states from acquiring an independent nuclear capability. From the Soviet perspective, the purpose of a non-proliferation treaty would be to agree that nuclear weapons states would not share nuclear weapons with allies. These were two separate concepts for non-proliferation, and the perceived elements required of a treaty for each concept also differed. For the US objectives to be met, a treaty would have to include measures to ensure compliance among third countries – that is, safeguards. The US Joint Chiefs of Staff (JCS) advocated pushing for the inclusion of safeguards only if it did not prevent the treaty itself from moving forward. This perhaps indicated that the JCS subscribed more to the Soviet objectives for the treaty.[50] For the Soviet objectives to be met, the treaty would have to include language to commit nuclear weapons states not to share nuclear weapons with allies, or, as Soviet Officials put it, measures to prevent "physical access" to nuclear weapons produced in other states.[51] Indeed, the Soviet Union did not support the draft Irish resolution in 1959 because it did not prohibit states from having nuclear weapons owned by other states on their territories – an argument intended to oppose NATO nuclear sharing plans.[52] These divergent views were based on self-interest: the US wanted to ensure the Soviet Union did not pass nuclear weapons technology on to other states such as China, whereas the Soviet Union wanted to ensure that the US did not give West Germany access to nuclear weapons. The scope of a potential compromise solution was thus clear – and indeed was foreseen by the Gilpatric Committee – but would require the US to give up on the MLF and require the Soviet Union to agree to include safeguards.

Negotiations between the US and the Soviet Union began in earnest in 1965, with MLF and safeguards issues proving to be some of the key points of contention. The MLF concept was envisioned as a way to satisfy a political desire in NATO states to have some direct influence over the employment of nuclear weapons and in the early 1970s, the MLF concept was seen as a central mechanism through which to ensure a united alliance. However, somewhat helpfully from the perspective of negotiating a non-proliferation treaty, the MLF concept ran into roadblocks in the 1960s in parallel to the negotiations with the Soviets on the NPT with the result that the US would eventually be willing to abandon the MLF concept and conclude the NPT with Russia.

Writing in 1965, General Andre Beaufre, who had been the French representative to the NATO Standing Committee Group, former Chief of Staff at NATO's SHAPE, and director of the Institut Français D'analyse Stratégique commented:[53]

> For the Americans, the leading partners in the alliance and controllers of 98 per cent of its nuclear capability, the desire in Europe to share in decisions relating to the planning and use of nuclear weapons has posed a specific problem: they have recognised that desire as politically and psychologically legitimate but, at the technical level, they have been unwilling to accept any solution to the problem other than the retention of nuclear control in the hands of the President of the United States.

Beaufre went on to set out how the position of the US, while consistent with American law, was at odds with other NATO allies. He argued that France sought influence on all of NATO's nuclear policymaking rather than just influence over systems under joint key and that West Germany too wanted direct involvement in nuclear decision making given that it would be on German territory that war would most likely take place.[54] The practical effect of this was for the US to reconsider the MLF concept and, ultimately, be willing to abandon the proposal. In reality, it appears the Johnson administration was not particularly committed to the MLF concept. For example, one administration official noted in a letter to the President that, it was "not clear how much support for the MLF there actually was … [it was being] pushed by junior officials in the State Department".[55] As an alternative, the focus of the US came to rest on a 'two key system' instead of MLF.[56] This would see the deployment of some US nuclear weapons under joint control with European allies. But the US would deny allies either access to the nuclear weapons know-how or the ability to use these weapons without the consent of the US President. These systems thus provided a means to more closely align allies with the US.

The US carefully handled the process of informing states that it would not go ahead with MLF. It was particularly concerned about the reaction in West Germany, which it feared might pursue its own nuclear weapons programme. Henry Kissinger was dispatched to West Germany by President Johnson to evaluate the response of senior officials and provide reassurance concerning sharing arrangements under NATO.[57] With the MLF issue effectively resolved, the safeguards issue easily followed and steps could be taken to socialise the draft treaty with other states. Thus, by the time that the UNGA took up the non-spread issue in 1966, MLF was becoming less of a barrier to an agreement between the US and the Soviet Union. Several rounds of drafts would be needed before language acceptable to the US and the Soviet Union could be achieved. The differences between the drafts primarily involved the language on nuclear sharing and whether non-nuclear weapons states could have access to the nuclear weapons of others. One notable proposal of the Soviet Union, which was rejected by the US on the grounds that it could prevent cooperation with countries such as West Germany on nuclear power topics, involved the following language:[58]

> Parties to the Treaty possessing nuclear weapons undertake not to provide assistance—directly or indirectly, through third States or groups of States—to States not at present possessing nuclear weapons in the manufacture, in preparations for the manufacture or in the testing of such weapons and not to transmit to them any kind of manufacturing, research or other information or documentation which can be employed for purposes of the manufacture or use of nuclear weapons.

Non-nuclear weapons states and the 'three pillars'

In parallel to discussions between the Soviet Union and the US, other states sought to influence the direction of the non-spread discussions. The initial focus of these discussions was around the UNGA session in 1965. UNGA resolution 2028 (XX) was adopted during this session, after which the focus of the discussions switched to the ENDC. The US and the USSR were the convening powers of the ENDC, which had been established by the UNGA in 1961. During the course of the negotiations of the draft treaty at the ENDC, both countries had tabled drafts, reflecting the different concepts for an NPT. In August 1967, the US and the USSR submitted identical drafts to the ENDC for consideration, although the draft only had a placeholder for safeguards due to concerns from European states, which are explored in the following. Up to this point, the focus of negotiations had been on finding a compromise between the two main parties on the issues of nuclear sharing and safeguards. The submission of the draft text to the ENDC thus provided an opportunity for a cross-section of states – including non-nuclear weapons states – to comment on the draft before the text was put to the UNGA.

It should be noted that despite the enthusiasm of states such as Ireland, the creation of the NPT was not a priority for many states. As Lt General L.M. Burns, the Canadian representative to the ENDC noted.[59]

> But the governments of some Member States had determined that they would not engage themselves not to "proliferate" nuclear weapons. Other governments were of two minds about adhering, and most of the less developed nations which neither had nuclear weapons nor any hope of producing them were indifferent. All this added up to a profound lack of enthusiasm for the measure and created resistance to including language in the resolution, which would have seemed to bind those voting for it to accept the Treaty.

A number of specific amendments were suggested by the other ENDC delegates and were incorporated into an updated draft submitted to the ENDC by the sponsoring powers. Further comments from the ENDC were incorporated into the draft submitted to the General Assembly.[60] The majority of these suggestions were intended to bring 'balance' to the treaty between the nuclear weapons states and the non-nuclear weapons states.

One important amendment made at the request of the Mexican delegation (with the endorsement of Sweden, the UAE, and Ethiopia) was to move language on the "inalienable right" – with associated language for peaceful uses of atomic energy – from the non-binding preamble to the operative paragraphs of the treaty.[61] The US – and also apparently the USSR – was open to such suggestions to secure the support of the members of the ENDC for the treaty when it was submitted to the General Assembly.[62] A US official writing to inform the Secretary of State of this change noted: "We have for some time envisioned that we would at some point have to make such changes to give the treaty more balance between the nuclear and non-nuclear states … These changes represent a fallback for which we have been preparing. The reaction of the Soviet delegation at Geneva has been sympathetic to this approach and we believe several useful amendments can be worked out".[63] It was as a result of this that the following Mexican language was included in the operative paragraphs of the treaty:[64]

> An expression of the right of parties to develop research, production and use of nuclear energy for peaceful purposes without discrimination and encouragement of the fullest possible exchanges of scientific and technical information for peaceful uses of nuclear energy
>
> An undertaking by parties to cooperate to ensure that potential benefits from any peaceful application of nuclear explosions will be made available through appropriate international procedures to non-nuclear-weapon-parties on a non-discriminatory basis
>
> A statement that nothing affects the right of any group of states to conclude regional treaties in order to assure total absence of nuclear weapons in their respective territories
>
> An undertaking by parties to pursue negotiations to arrive at further agreements regarding cessation of the nuclear arms race as well as agreement on general and complete disarmament under strict and effective international control.

As a result of the Mexican proposal, language was also accepted into the draft concerning nuclear disarmament. Specifically, the language requires states to negotiate in good faith towards general and complete disarmament. This made the treaty consistent with most of the main provisions of 2028 (XX).

For the US – and by extension the Soviet Union – there are signs that the changes introduced by the ENDC were seen as superficial and non-substantive. For example, in the NSC memorandum to President Nixon recommending that he sign the NPT, the article-by-article review of the treaty described the disarmament article as "hortatory", and article IV concerning peaceful uses as potentially causing future problems as states might claim the US had "an obligation to exchange information on subjects of U-235 isotope separation" but that the US would not have to honour these.[65] The treaty was subsequently adopted by the General Assembly, indicating the concessions were sufficient to satisfy all parties.

Despite the apparently relaxed approach that the US took with regards to the language on peaceful uses and disarmament, both articles would later prove to be challenging from a non-proliferation perspective. On peaceful uses, it was recognised in the US memo, for example, that a state could claim that it had the right to enrich uranium or separate plutonium – that is, that the inalienable right extended not only to the uses of atomic energy but also to the prerequisite steps in the use of atomic energy – even though this was not supported by the US.[66] During the negotiation of the NPT, certain states, including West Germany, set out their expectation that the treaty would not prohibit the acquisition of enrichment or reprocessing.[67] This argument was later used by a number of states – including most recently Iran – to defend the right to enrich and to challenge the legitimacy of international nuclear trade controls. A lack of progress on the "hortatory" disarmament article would also frustrate later efforts to complement the safeguards measures that were included in the NPT.

These limitations of the NPT must be clearly understood in the context of its adoption. As conceptualised by the US and the Soviet Union, the NPT was primarily conceived as an agreement between the nuclear weapons states not to transfer nuclear weapons capabilities to other states. The treaty also evolved to restrict the ability of other states to acquire nuclear weapons. However, from the perspective of the US and the USSR, this was a secondary benefit to the concessions from the other Superpower not to transfer nuclear weapons to third states.

In this context, it is valid to ask why states agreed to the NPT text at all given that, from one perspective, it bound states not to transfer nuclear weapons to others, to negotiate toward disarmament, and to enable full exploitation of the nuclear fuel cycle; whereas from another perspective it did only the first of these. Evidently, the ambiguity of the NPT's provisions was important in achieving the compromise as in the example of West Germany mentioned earlier. However, there was also a clear risk of such ambiguity in that the treaty could end up assuring no one and thus undermine the non-proliferation concept. Nonetheless, there were factors working in the treaty's favour. These included the widely held view that something had to be done to arrest proliferation, particularly in the context of China's test and broader public anxiety about nuclear weapons and nuclear testing. Second, the treaty had provisions for verification and enforcement that could potentially stop states from cheating. Finally, because the NPT did not detail the verification provisions that would ultimately be used to enforce the treaty, states could agree to the text of the NPT while reserving their decision on whether to sign it until these actual provisions were negotiated. Overall, therefore, the NPT was an important development in the non-proliferation sphere but still marked only the beginning of a broader process of establishing an effective non-proliferation regime.

Controls and the NPT

> The treaty should be void of any loop holes which might permit nuclear or non-nuclear powers to proliferate, directly or indirectly, nuclear weapons in any form.[68]

The absence of an international control mechanism for atomic energy, as had been envisioned in the 1940s, has been considered a serious loophole in the NPT.[69] In its absence, the NPT has had to rely on three sets of measures to ensure non-proliferation. The first is the non-proliferation commitment of state parties. The second involved the safeguards to be enacted on non- nuclear weapons state's nuclear fuel cycles. The third is the controls to be enacted on transferred nuclear technologies (i.e., international trade controls).

The non-proliferation commitments of states were set out in Articles I and II, which imposed an obligation on the nuclear weapons states not to transfer or otherwise assist non-nuclear weapons states to seek or receive assistance to obtain nuclear weapons. Increasing signatures would have the effect of expanding the coverage of the commitment. The second set of controls built into the NPT were safeguards. The principles guiding safeguards adoption were set out in the ENDC. The main principle was:

> For all non-nuclear-weapon parties, there should be safeguards of such a nature that all parties can have confidence in their effectiveness. Therefore, safeguards established by an agreement negotiated and concluded with the IAEA in accordance with the Statute of the IAEA and the Agency's safeguards system must enable the IAEA to carry out its responsibilities of providing assurances that no diversion is taking place.[70]

Three weeks after the NPT entered into force in 1970, the IAEA established a safeguards committee to devise a system of safeguards to implement the NPT. Ultimately, the NPT would build upon the safeguards framework created by the Atoms for Peace initiative but substantially expand the responsibility of the IAEA, which had hitherto safeguarded only a relatively small number of reactors.[71] The European States, and in particular France, were reluctant to agree to overly intrusive measures because it was felt this would jeopardise the Euratom negotiations with the IAEA concerning safeguards.[72]

David Fischer notes that:

> The Euratom delegations succeeded in sustaining the principle, implicit in the NPT, that safeguards should be applied only to nuclear material (and not, as provided in INFCIRC 66, also to plant and equipment) and in limiting the access of inspectors, during routine inspections, to previously agreed 'strategic points'. In simple language, this meant that IAEA inspectors would normally – i.e. during routine inspections – verify only nuclear material at locations that had been declared by the State and would do so by access that would be limited to pre-defined strategic points in the plant concerned – but the strategic points would be so defined as [all] points necessary for the Agency to accomplish its task of applying safeguards to all nuclear material in the State.[73]

The motivation of the collective Euratom membership was complex. Darryl Howlett notes Euratom had established its own safeguards system and begun nuclear cooperation between Euratom members before IAEA safeguards had matured.[74] As such, the Euratom states were reluctant to give up on what they considered to be an effective safeguards system for their own needs.[75] Howlett further notes that the Euratom states were able to muster a number of arguments in support of this position, including the fact that Euratom safeguards were better suited to a mixed block involving NWS and NNWS and that Euratom safeguards were more effective than either IAEA or US bilateral safeguards. The converse view, as noted by Howlett, was that the Euratom system was one of self-inspection that could not provide confidence to states such as the USSR that states like West Germany were not pursuing nuclear weapons.[76] In negotiations between Euratom and the IAEA, a compromise solution was reached in which the IAEA would conduct 'spot checks' to confirm the effectiveness of Euratom safeguards. However, this compromise did not change the fact that the Euratom states had limited the effectiveness of NPT safeguards to strengthen their own position.

This led to practical considerations that would limit the scope of IAEA safeguards: unless the responsibilities of the IAEA were well-defined, the Agency would simply not have the resources to implement the NPT's requirements. For this reason, the IAEA safeguards system was designed only to ensure the non-diversion of nuclear materials. This involved establishing points at which material balance could be monitored to detect the diversion of nuclear material in a timely fashion.[77] This was not within the scope of the safeguards system to detect undeclared activities, although an allowance was included for 'special inspections' should information on such activities come to light.[78]

While the NPT safeguards system leveraged the safeguards infrastructure created at the IAEA through the Atoms for Peace initiative, there are important differences between the two: under Atoms for Peace, states could maintain parallel safeguarded and unsafeguarded facilities; but non-nuclear weapons state parties to the NPT were required to place all nuclear facilities under safeguards.

Interestingly, during negotiations over the NPT, the UAR proposed an amendment in recognition that, "it was not enough for the governments and the official organs engaged in nuclear activities to respect the provisions of the treaty in all good faith" as "certain companies, firms or other bodies which are independent of the state" could also become involved in proliferation. The US and the Soviet Union worked to limit the number of amendments to the draft text and rejected this amendment partly because they felt it was covered in articles I and II and partly because, in the US at least, commercial involvement in nuclear energy was strictly controlled.[79] In the decades that followed and as later chapters highlight, the challenge of non-state actors involved in nuclear trade would indeed become a problem, particularly as a result of the globalisation of the international manufacturing base.

International nuclear trade controls

The third set of controls implicitly included in the NPT were export controls. Article III.2 required safeguards on "equipment or material especially designed or prepared for the processing, use or production of special fissionable material".

> III.2. Each State Party to the Treaty undertakes not to provide: (a) source or special fissionable material, or (b) equipment or material especially designed or prepared for the processing, use or production of special fissionable material, to any non-nuclear-weapon State for peaceful purposes, unless the source or special fissionable material shall be subject to the safeguards required by this Article.

This had the effect of, legally at least, ending the potential option for states inside the NPT to maintain parallel safeguarded and non-safeguarded programmes while also receiving technology from international suppliers that were also party to the NPT. It did not, of course, apply to states such as India and Pakistan that remained outside of the NPT. By 1974, the NPT had around 80 parties, thus highlighting that many non-NPT states could still pursue nuclear weapons by acquiring capability with only limited safeguards.

Importantly, the NPT itself did not contain a definition of the term "especially designed for" as contained in Article III.2 of the NPT. This level of detail would have been difficult to negotiate due to its technical nature and, from an American and Soviet perspective, would have been unnecessary for their primary purpose of having assurances that states would not seek nor supply nuclear assistance. Nonetheless, for states to implement the treaty, it would be necessary to adopt national legislation in order to ensure that the actions of commercial entities did not lead to a state becoming non-compliant. To this end, a committee of NPT signatories came together to define these technologies on a "trigger list" – a list of technologies the export of which would trigger a requirement for safeguards. This committee, named after its first chairman, Claude Zangger, created a list of 10 technologies, the export of which would be prohibited in the absence of safeguards.[80] The Zangger committee list was not exhaustive and has been described as a "lowest common denominator" approach, with part of the rationale for limiting the list being a desire not to provide a "blueprint for making a bomb".[81,82] The list initially included the following technologies when specifically designed for a nuclear end use: reactor pressure vessels, reactor control rods, isotope separation plants, primary coolant pumps, reactor fuel charging and discharge machines, zirconium tubes, irradiated fuel element choppers, main dissolving tanks, irradiated fuel storage and transportation containers. The Zangger list was drawn up to support the implementation of the NPT, but this approach did not include France, which remained outside the treaty, and it did not restrict exports provided they were subject to safeguards, which was a problem for enrichment and reprocessing.[83]

The three sets of controls were designed to collectively restrain the ability of NPT state parties to develop nuclear weapons. However, this limited scope meant that the NPT did not meet the principle set out in General Resolution 2028 (XX) of being 'loophole'-free. Indeed, there were substantial loopholes that would later be exploited by some states. The primary reason for this was the interest of the European States in limiting IAEA safeguards in order to minimise the safeguards to be applied in Europe under Euratom.

Non-signatories

The NPT was only binding only on countries that signed and ratified it and there was perhaps little expectation that the treaty would become universal. Notable early objectors to the treaty included France, which objected to the NPT for a number of reasons, including opposing US pressure, the way the treaty was negotiated between the US and USSR (without consulting France), and a desire not to be constrained in relation either to nuclear supply or the maintenance of its nuclear weapons infrastructure. Additionally, in the words of Harald Muller,

> French opposition to the NPT thus was not only a serious defence of the French deterrent against a suspected United States diplomatic encirclement tactic, it also permitted Paris the delight of denouncing and sabotaging a beloved object of United States diplomacy, and, therefore, to take a much-desired small revenge for what had been perceived as a series of United States insults against La Grande Nation.[84]

Less than a quarter of all states had signed the NPT at the time it came into force in 1970, leaving more than 100 states outside the treaty's limitations. The nature of the NPT meant it was in the interests of signatories to encourage non-signatories to adhere to the treaty's requirements and ultimately to sign up to the treaty itself. There was concern that countries such as West Germany would refuse to sign the NPT in the face of what could be considered an increased security threat, particularly following the soviet invasion of Czechoslovakia in 1968.[85] The US and UK thus undertook a coordinated diplomatic effort to increase adherence.[86] Numerous studies were also undertaken in countries such as the US of those states thought capable of pursuing nuclear weapons. The result was a prioritised effort to encourage a handful of key states to adopt the treaty. These states included West Germany, Japan, India, and Pakistan, all of which were identified as states that had the capability and possible interest to pursue nuclear weapons.[87]

The US invested substantial diplomatic effort to broaden participation in the NPT. Beyond alleviating diplomatic pressure, however, there were few specific incentives for states to adhere to the NPT. Potential suppliers of nuclear technologies maintained a common front as established through the WSG, but this only required that exports be subject to safeguards on a case-by-case basis, not that recipient state accept 'full scope' safeguards on their entire nuclear infrastructures. States outside of the NPT could thus continue to benefit from international nuclear assistance while maintaining parallel indigenous nuclear facilities or even a weapons programme.

India and the NPT

The fact that the initial take-up of the NPT was slow raises important questions in the context of this book, including why uptake was slow and what the perceived costs and benefits of NPT membership were at the time. In considering these questions, it is useful to examine India's decision making within the NPT, given that India opted against signing. It used arguments about encroachments on the use of civil nuclear power, rather than an interest in acquiring nuclear weapons to justify staying outside the NPT, despite being suspected of its options open to acquire nuclear weapons if a decision was made to do so.[88]

In an effort to prevent India from testing a nuclear device, one particular strategy pursued by the US was to encourage India to be at the forefront of efforts to draft the NPT and to get the treaty adopted. In fact, US Ambassador Bowles believed that if the US helped India lead the effort to conclude the NPT while simultaneously helping build India's scientific prestige, there was a good chance India would remain non-nuclear.[89] In 1965, therefore, the US considered assisting India with plutonium recycling, thorium recycling, the development of Torbay as a regional centre for study and training, and providing rocketry.[90] Evidently, if such cooperation went ahead, it would have benefited any Indian strategic weapons programme in the longer term, but it had been hoped that this problem would be alleviated by India's participation in the NPT. However, any reliance on the US would have undermined India's non-aligned status, which was central to the country's political identity at the time. India thus rejected such offers despite, or perhaps because, the NPT did not address India's security concerns *vis-à-vis* China which was a key strategic rival and which had tested its first nuclear device in 1964.

The US intelligence and diplomatic community closely followed India's public and non-public consideration of a possible test from 1972 to 1974.[91] Officials from the US, UK, and Canada met to consider what action to take to prevent a PNE and to consider how to respond should such a test be undertaken. Kissinger initiated a National Security Study under Memorandum 156 (NSSM156) of 5 July 1972.[92] The study considered a wide variety of actions, including terminating all cooperation and exports in the nuclear field, suspending all nuclear cooperation and exports of nuclear equipment, seeking renewed and strengthened assurances that US-supplied plutonium for Tarapur would not be used in any nuclear explosive device, and suspending all active contracts except for the Tarapur fuel supply. The US also considered the implications for the future provision of non-nuclear assistance, for cooperation with India's space and missile programmes, and for technology transfer to India.[93] These potential actions were communicated to Delhi but were clearly were insufficient to prevent the PNE.

The response of the western nuclear suppliers to the PNE was primarily to limit future cooperation on nuclear technology and the provision of aid to India and other states not a party to the NPT.[94,95,96] Tarapur meant that a clean break would be problematic. For this reason, the US considered linking the provision of fuel for[97] to a commitment from India to conduct no further tests.[98] In 1974, Secretary of State Henry Kissinger supported the provision of a heavy water production facility from Germany to India, which was not listed on the Zangger committee trigger list. The Soviet Union also shipped 200 tonnes of heavy water to India in 1975. Joseph Nye Jr., President Carter's special representative on non-proliferation, expressly linked India's decision not to conduct further tests with the decision of the US not to take a punitive approach by withholding cooperation.[99] Nonetheless, US assistance would ultimately be cut off as a result of the Nuclear Non-proliferation Act (NNPA) adopted by Congress in 1978.[100] The NNPA, which is examined later in the book, was adopted by Congress in the wake of India's nuclear test and in the context of growing concerns about nuclear proliferation to other countries, including Pakistan. Despite these measures, India was able to secure some fuel for the reactor from overseas sources until the early 1990s when, as discussed later, the NSG would eventually agree on full-scope safeguards as a condition of supply.

The NNPA of 1978 had effects beyond India. It raised questions in all countries that were, or could, receive assistance from the US over the certainty and reliability of the US as a fuel supplier. There was a concern that if states began to doubt fuel assurances, then they would be more likely to embark on domestic fuel production, potentially including enrichment and reprocessing. It was for this reason that Gerald Smith, who was by this point President Carter's Special Representative on non-proliferation matters, stated that he was "determined not to be associated with [the] legislation" even though he was bound to uphold it.[101] Smith came to believe that the US subsequently became viewed as an "unreliable and unpredictable" supplier.[102] This problem was compounded in the early 1980s when the US moved to a commercial imperative; ahead of which recipient countries over-ordered enriched uranium so as to secure a national surplus and hedge against future supply uncertainty. This exacerbated the problem, however, that the US could not keep up with the orders.[103]

Collective action and the NPT: understanding its limitations

The NPT was a major milestone in the evolution of nuclear non-proliferation trade controls and it is generally seen as the 'cornerstone' of the non-proliferation regime. Nonetheless, the treaty and its implementation through IAEA safeguards were far from 'loophole-free' because its coverage was not universal, and its measures were somewhat constrained. Before examining the effect of the limitations in the NPT and the efforts taken to overcome these in the 1970s and 1980s, it is useful to recap why the NPT was limited in effect by briefly examining it through the lens of the CAP framework.

The NPT originated primarily because of two activities: the bilateral US/Soviet non-spread agreement reached following China's nuclear test and the Irish resolutions, which involved dozens of states in decisions. Agreement between the US and USSR was relatively easy once the issue of nuclear proliferation was separated from other strategic issues such as the MLF. However, achieving ENDC support for the text was complicated by the fact that some of the ENDC states had vested interests, such as acquiring nuclear weapons. This problem was compounded further in relation to NPT safeguards, with States like India and the Euratom states exercising their influence to water down controls.

In order to balance out the distribution of benefits contained in the NPT and thus make it acceptable to the developing world, the US and the USSR agreed to the inclusion of language on peaceful uses and disarmament in the operative paragraphs. While there were clear signs that this language was deliberately left vague to prevent binding commitments, the language effectively locked in the principles of Atoms for Peace for the life of the NPT.

Face-to-face discussions were key in overcoming the distrust between the USSR and the US and in negotiating the NPT as well as IAEA safeguards. Such discussions confirmed the assumption of the Gilpatric committee that non-proliferation was a common interest of the US and Soviet Union.

Overall, then, the prospect of perceived benefits and vested interests were the primary factors the NPT emerged not being loophole-free when it was agreed in 1968.

Beyond the NPT: evolution of the non-proliferation regime after the Indian PNE

In the immediate aftermath of Smiling Buddha, the US initiated a fundamental review of its nuclear non-proliferation policy. As Chapter 3 highlighted, the Indian test had used technology supplied under the US-initiated Atoms for Peace initiative – notably a reactor supplied by Canada and heavy water supplied under licence from the US. Indeed, at least some of this technology had been supplied in the knowledge that India was keeping its options open to acquire nuclear weapons and that India intended to indigenously duplicate some of the facilities with the effect that these would not be subject to IAEA safeguards. While the NPT had helped to differentiate countries that had an interest in nuclear weapons from countries that probably did not, the Indian PNE made it apparent that something major needed to be done to control nuclear transfers to countries that remained outside of the NPT.

A review was initiated by President Ford under National Security Study Memorandum 202 dated 23 May 1974. To inform this, a parallel study was undertaken by the State Department under Secretary of State Kissinger. The studies identified a range of policy options that could contribute to the goal of non-proliferation. This included "intensified national policy", such as reaffirming high-level support for the NPT (including prompt US ratification), "aggressive" implementation of policies "intended to increase universality of IAEA safeguards applications by securing multilateral guidelines on nuclear export controls", and consultation with Canada and other nuclear suppliers on the subject of cooperation with India with a view to securing assurances regarding the non-use of nuclear exports for peaceful nuclear explosions.[104] Studies would also be undertaken on US policy towards PNEs, security assurances, and sanctions. State Department planners went further, expressly calling this a non-proliferation strategy, the purpose of which was to: "1, strengthen political, legal and security-related inhibitions against proliferation, and 2, deny nations the full range of material, equipment, services, and technology needed to produce nuclear explosives".[105]

Kissinger's suppliers group

As a direct outcome of the State Department's strategising over the problem of proliferation, the US decided to pursue meetings with those countries capable of supplying nuclear technology with the objective of achieving a common front on conditions of supply. Despite the emphatic nature of the US non-proliferation initiatives, there were evident limitations to the extent to which Washington was willing to utilise political capital to bring about collective action against proliferation, at least in the absence of willing allies and partners. For example, as the following quote from Kissinger highlights, there were limitations to how far the US could go in pursuit of non-proliferation goals.

> New conditions of nuclear supply, however desirable, should not be imposed by the US unilaterally but rather pursued and adopted multilaterally. I must stress that a unilateral approach will damage us politically, with our allies and partners, and will lead the US to lose both commercially and in non-proliferation terms, as other less committed nations preempt the nuclear market. It should be recognised that if the suppliers, many of whom are also our allies, do not wish to follow a US initiative voluntarily, then we will either have to coerce them or jeopardise our non-proliferation policy. Clearly, we should not select a strategy which could so easily trap us in such a dilemma. At the same time, we should continue to make best diplomatic efforts to make non-proliferation gains, as I believe we have in our proposed nuclear agreements with Egypt and Israel and in our current negotiations with Iran.[106,107]

In this context, the purpose envisioned for the suppliers meeting was principally to coordinate between states in relation to exports to non-NPT states. The following points were included in the *note verbale* sent by the US inviting countries to participate in the meeting, although a caveat was included to indicate this was only an indicative list.[108]

1 Nuclear cooperation would be undertaken with non-nuclear weapons states only under agreements as to peaceful uses, which would explicitly exclude use in any nuclear explosive device.

2 Nuclear supply would be undertaken only when covered by IAEA safeguards, with appropriate provisions for duration and coverage of produced nuclear material.
3 Supply of weapons-grade material, or of uranium enrichment or chemical reprocessing equipment or technology, to non-nuclear-weapon states should be subject to special restraint. Such special restraint might include supply only for multinational enterprises or only to those non-nuclear weapons states which have accepted IAEA safeguards on their entire nuclear fuel cycle.
4 Nuclear supply would include appropriate requirements for the physical protection of materials and facilities against theft, seizure, or sabotage.
5 Stringent conditions might be developed on the supply of sensitive nuclear material, equipment or technology to countries or regions where such exports would contribute to particular risks of conflict or instability.

In considering the countries to invite to the discussion, the State Department did not simply draw upon the list of "western suppliers" that had been meeting since the late 1950s but instead conducted an analysis based upon the ability of states to supply nuclear technology. The US wanted to keep the suppliers group small in order to maximise the likelihood of success and the initiative remaining secret.[109] The two factors combined to result in an initial list of 7 invitees: the UK, the US, the USSR, France, the FRG, Canada, and Japan. The group would expand to 15 in 1976 after the Carter administration took office and after an initial agreement among the participating states on an expanded membership and control list. The additional states were Belgium, Czechoslovakia, the German Democratic Republic, Italy, the Netherlands, and Sweden. Switzerland had been invited to join at the June meeting but opted to defer joining until it had ratified the NPT.[110]

The participation status of four particular states is worthy of note. First, the US invited the Soviet Union to participate. This is perhaps not surprising given that the US and the Soviet Union had found common ground on non-proliferation during the NPT negotiations. Second, a great deal of significance was placed on French participation. France did not sign the NPT as a matter of principle and the conventional observation was that France could provide assistance to states outside of safeguards. France had agreed to behave as though it was a party to the NPT, with the French delegate to the UNGA in 1968 stating that: "France, for its part, which will not sign the non-proliferation treaty, will behave in the future in this field exactly as the States adhering to the Treaty".[111] France's decision not to sign was viewed primarily as an example of de Gaullean foreign policy characterised by a desire to assert independence from the US.[112]

At this time, France was engaged in supplying nuclear states which were outside of the NPT, including the transfer of a reprocessing plant to Pakistan. France agreed to participate in the NSG meetings but with the caveat from the outset that it would continue its policy of considering exports on a case-by-case basis. Given that this was the position that France took at the WSG meeting in 1959, the French agreement to participate and its reserved position should not have been particularly surprising.

The third country of note was China which was not invited to participate in the suppliers' group meetings. The US assessed that China was not at the time capable of nuclear exports. One US official noted:

> No approach to the PRC is included. While the PRC has criticized the NPT as a US-Soviet condominium, it is not a manufacturer of commercial nuclear equipment and has not been an exporter of nuclear materials. While it might choose to export some nuclear materials in the future, an approach at this time to head off the possibility would not seem productive. In any event, notwithstanding its negative stance on the NPT, the PRC would appear to have no reason to contribute to the further spread of nuclear explosives.[113]

A British Foreign Office Minister also noted in official correspondence in November 1977:

> The People's Republic of China is aware of the Group's existence but has never given any indication of interest in joining. We have not seen any indication that they intend to export nuclear equipment or technology. The Chinese have consistently said that they do not object if others acquire nuclear weapons but that they will not be the ones to help them do so.[114]

This decision may have been significant as China would soon enter into nuclear cooperation with Pakistan, including on nuclear weapons issues. (Given Nixon's trip to China in 1972, which lead to the 'opening of China' and the new phase of US-China relations that followed, Beijing could potentially have been receptive to an invitation to participate at that time). However, there are no indications that this option was explored at the time.[115]

A final country of note is India. Kissinger did reach out to India in 1974 to propose discussions on nuclear exports and the latter did agree to pursue a policy of restraint concerning nuclear exports. India did not respond to Kissinger's overtures for a dialogue on the matter before the NSG discussions concluded in 1976.[116]

Over the course of the supplier discussions, a key point of contention related to the nature of safeguards to be applied to exports. The UK proposed that full-scope safeguards be made a condition of supply, and its position was supported by Canada and others. Full Scope Safeguards would prevent cooperation with states such as India, which were keeping their nuclear options open and would have the effect of imposing the same rules in transfer to NPT states and NPT states alike. France did not agree to this position. At the NSG meeting, the French representative's position was summarised as follows by the UK FCO:

> The problem for France was a political one. She could not make accession to the NPT a condition for cooperation with other countries. This would be a form of pressure. It was a matter of sovereignty. France could not exert pressure on others to accede to the NPT when she had not done so herself.[117]

Canada was among the countries that took the firmest position on the issue – a viewpoint doubtless driven by lessons learned from having supplied India a reactor with inadequate safeguards.

An important area where an agreement was not reached in the NSG discussions in the 1970s related to the creation of a working party to consider the implementation of the guidelines, including the possibility of making them legally binding. The possibility of such a working party was discussed at the April 1977 meeting of the NSG. However, an agreement was not reached because of a concern that its creation would provide an excuse for states not to reach a conclusion on several pending issues, including Canadian proposals to amend the trigger list and the question of full-scope safeguards.[118] This idea would be overtaken by the International Nuclear Fuel Cycle Evaluation Programme (INFCE), as discussed in the following. Another policy where there was a lack of consensus related to enrichment and reprocessing. The participants could only agree to encourage rather than make mandatory the development of multinational regional facilities (as opposed to national facilities).[119] The reason for this was France's commercial and strategic interest in exporting reprocessing capabilities to Pakistan, which is examined in the following. There were also limitations in the control list agreed upon by the NSG participants. The NSG states agreed not to supply more than the apparently arbitrary amount of 500 kg of zirconium without the application of safeguards. For example, India "almost immediately arranged to acquire 495 kilograms of zirconium tubing from Germany, despite Canadian pressure on Germany to prevent the transfer".[120] But Germany could not do so given that the amount was below the agreed threshold. Such transfers acted to undermine confidence in the controls that were in place.

The participating states did take some action to align their policies to those discussed at the meeting. Under much US pressure, the US obtained a copy of a letter from French Foreign Minister Guiringaud to the Council for French Nuclear Policy that outlined French thinking on export control issues in October 1976.[121] This proposal would set out "four imperatives" of any French policy in this field: to maintain French export capacity; to appear acceptable to the third world; to avoid endangering French natural uranium supply; and to "include maximum restraints on the dissemination of sensitive technologies and materials as well as legal provisions aimed at discouraging the development of military potential".[122] French officials said that they participated in the NSG discussions in the 1970s in order to "harmonise rules concerning non-proliferation with a view to avoiding distortion between the supplier countries".[123] Despite this apparent progress, France continued to resist pressure to agree to full-scope safeguards as a condition of supply and by September 1977 made the case that to accept such a provision before the conclusion of INFCE would be to prejudice the initiative before it began.[124] France was thus continuing the policy it had pursued since the 1950s of being willing to talk but ultimately acting to keep its options open even though France would at this time quietly agree to cancel the transfer of a reprocessing capability to Pakistan as examined in the Pakistan episode which follows.

The meetings of the NSG thus had some effect in coordinating the policies of nuclear suppliers. However, the vested interests of some states prevented more comprehensive measures from being adopted. In particular, France's interest in exporting reprocessing capabilities, as well as its desire not to be seen to bow to US pressure, limited the scope of the agreement, which played into broader French foreign policy at the time *vis-à-vis* relations with the US and the country's rationale for remaining outside of the NPT.[125] France was thus driven primarily by geostrategic imperatives reasons and national pride rather than commercial factors, given that it subsequently cancelled the reprocessing export to Pakistan.

Varying approaches of the Ford, Carter, and Reagan administrations

Non-proliferation and domestic politics during the Ford administration

In parallel to the supplier's meetings in London, non-proliferation and trade controls became an increasingly important issue in US domestic politics during the 1970s. This would result in different administrations taking different approaches to non-proliferation and would affect the continuation of the meetings of the NSG. As such, it is useful to briefly examine the different approaches of the Ford, Carter, and Reagan administrations. The politicising of non-proliferation in the US started with the 1976 Presidential election. During a presidential debate between then-Governor Carter and President Ford, the former stated:

> I also know that as far as the human beings on this Earth are concerned, that the non-proliferation of atomic weapons is number one. Only in the last few days, with the election approaching, has Mr. Ford taken any interest in a non-proliferation movement.[126]

Carter was a former naval nuclear engineer and could talk with authority on nuclear issues. When he launched his bid for the presidency, the Ford team felt a need to respond head-on to the criticism from Carter and launched another study chaired by Robert Fri. The study was rushed and delivered its findings within six weeks because of the forthcoming election. The rush may have undermined the study's robustness and made it more susceptible to the influence of special interest groups and lobbyists. For example, early drafts of the study came out strongly in favour of a substantial investment in US reprocessing capabilities, leading the State Department to comment, "Which I understand was the product of ERDA advocates and ACDA critics of reprocessing and which was inadequately reviewed by Fri (with no input solicited from the Department) before being circulated to agencies".[127] The option to reprocess was left in the final report, but a decision on the matter deferred for further study. Ultimately it would not matter. Ford lost the election and, upon taking office, President Carter pursued a policy of limiting reprocessing, something he ultimately prioritised over realising maximum value from the NSG process. The domestic political environment in the US, therefore, had a direct impact on the supplier discussions, with a 1976 meeting partially paralysed while the Fri study was undertaken.[128].

The Ford administration's initial policies on non-proliferation were a continuation of the Nixon administration. Nixon was sceptical about non-proliferation measures but did ultimately agree to sign the NPT on behalf of the US.[129] Kissinger, who served in both the Nixon and Ford administrations, was sceptical of non-proliferation primarily because he believed the US could not stop states from pursuing nuclear weapons if the state's security situation was perceived to require them. This belief was possibly based on an insufficient understanding of the difficulties associated with acquiring nuclear weapons. As late as March 1974, Kissinger is said to have asked aids, "what exactly is a reprocessing plant?".[130] William Burr has documented Kissinger's evolving view of non-proliferation following the Indian test, which saw him support the adoption of a US non-proliferation strategy, including the establishment of a suppliers group.[131] The Indian test, therefore, spurred both the development of a non-proliferation norm and a belief that something could be done to frustrate the acquisition of nuclear weapons. This willingness to take action was moderated by a view that the US should go only as far as others were willing to go, for example, in preventing sensitive technology transfers. For the same reason, Kissinger was reluctant to use US leverage to have states sign the NPT.[132]

It is notable that the Ford administration, and Kissinger in particular, sought to establish what appeared to be a new forum for discussion among suppliers rather than building on the WSG. However, by reinventing the forum, the US was able to include countries such as the Soviet Union, which had not participated in the WSG meetings but with whom Washington had cooperated in concluding the NPT.

By the end of the Ford administration in January 1977, the NSG had been meeting for approximately two years and had agreed to an expanded list of controlled items over which safeguards would be applied as a condition of transfer. The NSG had not at this time agreed on numerous other issues, including the question of whether full-scope safeguards would be required as a condition of supply, whether the group should be expanded to include 'customers' (perhaps as part of a two-tier structure) or whether the group should include controls on so-called grey areas – technologies later to be known as 'dual-use goods'. The NSG's expanded trigger list had also not been published. Overall, therefore, it must be concluded that while Kissinger's suppliers group laid a promising foundation for international cooperation on nuclear trade controls, its contribution at this point was limited. Nonetheless, a forum had been established and progress made in terms of agreeing on a more complete control list.

Carter administration's non-proliferation policy

President Carter took office in January 1977 after a campaign in which non-proliferation, and reprocessing in particular, were important issues. Given this prominence, the new administration had to be seen to act on reprocessing. In practice, this involved resetting US domestic policy on reprocessing, seeking to dissuade France from exporting reprocessing capability to Pakistan, and taking other initiatives to discourage the pursuit of reprocessing more generally. This approach was to have implications for the future functioning of the NSG.

During the 1976 presidential election campaign, Carter argued that the Ford administration's policy was weak, particularly on reprocessing.[133] As such, Carter clearly believed, therefore, that he came to office with a mandate and a desire to strengthen US non-proliferation policy.[134]

The Carter administration quickly set about to strengthen the non-proliferation policy, including through completion of the work of the NSG. However, the primary focus of the administration's efforts was to curtail the so-called plutonium economy, something largely pursued outside of the NSG.[135] The diplomatic mechanisms for this were bilateral, particularly with France, unilateral and eventually multilateral, through the creation of the INFCE.[136] Unilateral action centred on plans to cancel the development of US facilitates related to the so-called plutonium economy, which included a demonstration breeder reactor and reprocessing capabilities. Carter also opted to restrain cooperation and exports to countries not implementing full-scope safeguards – a requirement later written into US law through the NNPA, which also strengthened other aspects of non-proliferation issues, including increased funding and support to the IAEA.[137] Carter also stated that he would increase US enrichment capacity to provide reassurance that the US could meet uranium supply commitments.[138]

The Carter administration's policy led to uncertainty in capitals around the world about the reliability and predictability of the US as a supplier of nuclear technology and assistance, prompting Gerard Smith to resign from his role as Ambassador-at-Large because he "was between the White House, the State Department and Congress".[139] As the so-called market-based approach to non-proliferation was reliant on surety of supply, there was a clear concern that states might pursue their own enrichment, reprocessing and conversion capabilities.[140,141]

The risk was particularly acute for states outside the NPT, such as India and Pakistan, which anyway had reasons to pursue indigenous fuel cycle facilities. INFCE was a mechanism intended to build international support for the Carter administration view of the so-called plutonium economy, but its results were disappointing, in part because it was recognised there could be no 'technical fixes' to the proliferation problem even if fuel cycle choices can influence the proliferation risk.[142] The dissatisfaction of customer states in the US policy led Gerard Smith to begin a discussion with other countries on creating an international plutonium store. Smith was concerned about the effect of US policy and the NNPA on the view of the US as a reliable supplier, which led to his raising the plutonium bank option. However, he was judged to have exceeded his mandate and thus recalled and rebuked. He would later write about his concerns over the Carter administration's non-proliferation policy.[143] A final aspect of Carter's policy concerned the Soviet invasion of Afghanistan in 1979. Prevailing literature suggests that Carter relaxed his position *vis-à-vis* Pakistan's nuclear programme to secure the support of Pakistan as an ally.[144] The Reagan administration would later follow suit.

With regards to the NSG, the suppliers had already agreed on an expanded control list and expanded the size of the group before Carter took office. However, the group had not yet published its guidelines and several issues, as set out, remained outstanding. The Carter administration participated in some further meetings of the suppliers group and steered the group's work towards completion. At the meetings in 1977, the group's members agreed to publish the control list through the IAEA. The rationale for publishing the transfer guidelines, as noted by the UK chair, was as follows:

> By demonstrating their willingness to come out more into the open, Supplier Governments should now be in a stronger position to justify the role of the Suppliers Group as part of the wider international strategy of non-proliferation. This is all the more important as the focus of non-proliferation discussions begins to turn toward INFCE, at whose opening conference in Washington next month the Suppliers Governments may be outnumbered by developing countries and other non-suppliers.[145]

This move to conclude the group's work suggested that it had failed to reach consensus on several issues, including that of full-scope safeguards as a condition of supply, group expansion and the issue of dual-use technologies. In short, the group made little progress during the Carter period in comparison with the Ford administration. The primary reason for this was a sense that further progress in the NSG could not be made absent French willingness to agree to the adoption of full-scope safeguards as a condition of supply.

Further meetings of the group could potentially have overcome these issues. The question of why further meetings were not held is complex. Tadeusz Strulak, who served as the chairman of the NSG in 1992, has noted that:

> In my opinion, the major cause of the group's inactivity was the unwillingness of some NSG suppliers to move beyond the conditions for nuclear exports established in 1977. The motive behind this unwillingness was commercial interest.[146]

Joseph Nye, who was Carter's special representative for non-proliferation issues, attributes the decision to a US desire not to press the French too hard after France decided not to export the reprocessing plant to Pakistan. The US felt that trying to secure further concessions through the NSG would push France too far. According to Nye, the US used INFCE – a Carter-era international forum intended to explore the utility of reprocessing to civil nuclear fuel cycles – to 'put the issue into the long grass'.[147] It is certainly the case that administration officials placed the INFCE programme ahead of the suppliers group in terms of the administration's policy. The primary reason appears to relate to the central purpose of INCFE in relation to US domestic politics: the pursuit of INFCE helped to deliver upon President Carter's election rhetoric to curb the use of reprocessing. US officials also stated that no further supplier group meetings would be held until INFCE had concluded and the 1980 NPT Revcon had taken place. If this was the primary driver, however, the conclusion reached by INFCE highlights flaws in the administration's policy as the findings of the study were seen as a blow to Carter's position against plutonium recycling. Indeed, Ambassador Gerard Smith, representative of the President on non-proliferation and disarmament, found himself in a difficult position after INFCE concluded. He was quietly, and with the blessing of President Carter, exploring whether states would be willing to enter into further non-proliferation commitments if US surety of supply was strengthened by, for example, creating an international bank of separated plutonium that states could draw upon – a policy that would have been in stark contrast to the election commitment to prevent the practice.[148] Another possibility is that the supplier meetings were put on hold because of the adverse reaction of recipient states to the concept. This would have had the advantage of allowing the supplier states to engage recipient states in a dialogue about their fuel cycle choices. Whatever the principal driver was for suspending the suppliers meetings, the decision had a clear and significant impact on international efforts to control proliferation.

Reagan's non-proliferation policy

Before examining the effects of international efforts to advance nuclear trade controls during the 1970s and 1980s through an examination of the Pakistan case, it is useful to briefly introduce Reagan's non-proliferation policy. During the 1980 presidential campaign, Reagan famously said that 'non-proliferation was none of our business'.[149] After winning the election, his transition team also put forward a non-proliferation policy which was rather weak in nature.[150] That said, on taking office, Reagan's staff worked to devise a new non-proliferation policy which sought to further both non-proliferation and broader US geostrategic interests. This policy was enunciated in NSDD39 of 4 June 1982.[151] The starting point was the view that the US needed to restore its position as a reliable nuclear supplier, which had been damaged in the previous years. The administration's concern was that uncertainty of US supply might drive other countries to pursue indigenous enrichment and reprocessing capabilities. The US thus expanded its enrichment capacity and became prepared to support reprocessing overseas on a case-by-case basis. This allowed the administration the political space to support reprocessing for Japan, although the reprocessing itself would be done in Europe on Japan's behalf. The administration also entered into security and economic cooperation with Pakistan based on its assurance that it would not exceed 5% enrichment of uranium. This was used to justify the waiver under US law for the provision of aid to Pakistan in 1984 and beyond.[152] Nonetheless, as the examination of Pakistan's nuclear programme illustrates, the Reagan administration's policy would be shaped largely by other events, including the need to sustain a strategic relationship with Pakistan following the Soviet invasion of Afghanistan and countering Iran in the context of the Iran-Iraq war.[153] Washington's approach to these two issues was to have a direct and negative impact on international efforts to block Pakistan and, as Chapter 5 examines, Iraq nuclear programme.

International nuclear trade controls and Pakistan's nuclear weapons programme

The evolution of Pakistan's nuclear weapons programme in the 1970s and 1980 provides an important reference point to help illustrate the nature and shortcomings of international nuclear trade controls as these evolved in the 1970s. Pakistan had benefited from Atoms for Peace in the late 1950s and 1960s, but it largely lacked a nuclear fuel cycle capability. From the 1970s, however, Pakistan invested time and resources to achieve a nuclear weapons capability, a process directly influenced by India's PNE in 1974. Pakistan furthered its programme by acquiring goods and material from the international marketplace. Both countries also benefited, to some extent, by the US turning a blind eye to Pakistan's nuclear activities for competing geostrategic reasons.[154]

Pakistan's nuclear programme pre-1974

There is no evidence to suggest that Pakistan was seeking to pursue nuclear weapons in the 1950s, but it is likely that its pursuit of nuclear technology was to some extent driven by keeping the option open to do so at a later date. The Pakistan Atomic Energy Commission (PAEC) was created in 1956.[155] And in 1959, Pakistan signed a nuclear cooperation agreement with the US.[156] This agreement enabled Pakistan to acquire an HEU-fuelled pool-type research reactor – which, as discussed in the following, was not well suited to plutonium production – from the US with the associated safeguards agreement entering into force on 5 March 1962.[157] It is notable that even at this point, Pakistani officials appeared to want to keep the option open to acquire nuclear weapons, with the chairman of the PAEC pushing for the supply of a type of reactor that was suited to plutonium production, the CP-5. Pakistan could not afford this reactor and the US was reluctant to supply it apparently because of the associated proliferation risks.[158] Pakistan was also interested in obtaining a pressurised heavy water reactor of the CANDU-type from Canada, which could have been used for weapons production, but again the price tag proved too great.[159]

It was not until 1965 that Pakistan's first reactor, the US-supplied PARR 1 – a 5MW research reactor fuelled with 20% enriched uranium – went critical.[160] The design of the reactor meant it was not suitable for plutonium production and so Pakistan's nuclear infrastructure in the mid-1960s remained a long way from being capable of supporting a nuclear weapons effort. However, in the wake of the Chinese nuclear test in 1964, Pakistani officials doubtless took stock of whether India was progressing toward a point at which it could follow suit.[161] It is in this context that Bhutto's famous quote of 1965 – when relations between India and Pakistan were extremely poor – is significant: "If India builds the bomb, Pakistan will eat grass or leaves, even go hungry, but we will get one of our own. We have no alternative … atom bomb for atom bomb".[162] There are also claims that Pakistan began to pursue Chinese support for its weapons efforts as early as 1965 in the immediate aftermath of the first Chinese test, but there are no grounds to believe China provided such support before 1977, as discussed in the following.[163]

This apparent dual interest in procuring nuclear facilities for civil purposes while also developing the option to acquire nuclear weapons appears to have manifested itself in Pakistan's other negotiations with nuclear suppliers from the mid-1960s. When Pakistan negotiated for the supply of the Karachi Nuclear Power Plant (KANUPP), a CANDU-type reactor, in 1965, Pakistani officials pushed Canada to supply the reactor without IAEA safeguards on the basis of equality with the terms granted to India for its CANDU reactor, a decade earlier.[164] However, Canada refused to give way on the safeguards requirement unless Pakistan paid for the reactor in full, as India had done.[165] The Canadian logic appears to have been that it was happy to supply a reactor with potential for use in weapons production but did not want to be left with ownership of a reactor that was producing weapons-grade material in a foreign country.[166]

Ultimately, Pakistan did accept safeguards after Sultan Mohammad Khan, then Pakistani Ambassador to Canada expressed support for the deal on the grounds that, "the power plant was for civil use and practically free [of cost]".[167] However, the same official evidently felt that accepting safeguards did not constrain Pakistan's options and went on to say that,

> Should a situation develop where we could not allow inspections, then we would have to face the problem of finding a non-Canadian source of fuel, and it would be up to our nuclear scientists to develop ways and means to keep the nuclear plant operational.[168]

This statement clearly highlights the limitations of inspections as a non-proliferation mechanism at the time. The reactor was completed in 1971 with the safeguards agreement entering into force on 17 October 1969.[169]

Pakistani fuel cycle choices after 1974

The 1970s brought a new landscape for Pakistan. Protests in Eastern Pakistan resulted in a revolt and then Indian intervention, resulting in a loss of nearly half of the country. As Feroz Khan noted,

> A Pakistani military crackdown on March 25, 1971, would prove to be the proverbial last straw. The strike on Bengali dissidents morphed into a civil war, and refugees poured into India. For the second time in a quarter-century, the subcontinent was about to witness a bloody partition.[170]

Some argue these events prompted Pakistan's leadership to take the decision to pursue nuclear weapons. Feroz Khan, for example, argues that, "Ultimately, Pakistan's humiliation [at the Indian intervention to end the Pakistani civil war] would lay the foundation for a shift in the once-peaceful nature of the nuclear programme".[171] President Bhutto began to actively lay the foundations for a weapons programme at a conference of Pakistan nuclear scientists in January 1972, the same conference at which Munir Ahmed Khan was appointed to head the PAEC.[172] These interests intensified when India conducted its PNE in 1974, with the Defence Committee of the Pakistani Cabinet purportedly giving the go-ahead to develop nuclear weapons.[173]

Following the Indian test, it appears that Pakistan's leadership decided that the country should become a fully latent nuclear weapons state by acquiring a complete nuclear fuel cycle before its ability to do so became too constrained by the increasing coverage of international trade controls.[174] This was an ambitious objective given that Pakistan's nuclear infrastructure was very limited in 1974, despite having had access to technology under the Atoms for Peace initiative. Pakistan had three reactors, all of which were subject to safeguards and only two of which were potentially suitable for plutonium production, as set out in the following. To use either reactor for plutonium production, Pakistan would have had to withdraw it from safeguards, secure a source of natural uranium and develop a capability to manufacture fuel.

Pakistan also had the option of developing an indigenous plutonium route through the construction of an indigenous plutonium production reactor, although this could not be accomplished in the short term. Pakistan had the option of pursuing the enrichment route. This would involve developing an enrichment technology, such as the gas centrifuge, and constructing uranium conversion facilities. An indigenous centrifuge effort which began in the 1960s had made no real progress by the mid-1970s.[175]

Munir Ahmad Khan is thought to have decided to pursue both the uranium and the plutonium route when he took office in 1972. However, given Pakistan's lack of indigenous capacity, this required the import of complete facilities from the international marketplace at a time when potential suppliers were beginning to toughen controls in the wake of the India test. Pakistan's efforts to access advanced enrichment, plutonium production, and weaponisation capacity after 1974 are explored in the following in order to shed important light on the limitations and failings of international controls as they stood in the 1970s and 1980s.

Uranium

Uranium deposits had been identified in Pakistan in the 1950s, but these were not exploited until 1978, when mining, milling, and fuel fabrication began to ramp up.[176] The total amount of uranium mined is thought to have been less than 500 tons over the period 1978–1999 when extraction at Pakistan's primary site ended. Pakistan, therefore, had only very limited stocks of uranium in the late 1970s and early 1980s. As discussed in the following, this likely explains, at least in part, Pakistan's decision not to withdraw the KANUPP from safeguards. By leaving the reactor within safeguards, Pakistan could acquire safeguarded uranium from the international marketplace leaving the indigenous uranium, which was not subject to safeguards, to be used in its enrichment programme, and then in Pakistan's plutonium production reactor. Indeed, despite Western Supplier Group controls, Pakistan was also successful in procuring uranium from other countries in the 1970s for use in KANUPP. This included acquiring safeguarded uranium from South Africa via the Federal Republic of Germany (FRG) and from Niger.[177] Pakistan is also thought to have obtained quantities of unsafeguarded uranium and Uranium Hexafluoride (UF6) – the form of uranium needed for use in centrifuge enrichment – in the 1970s. This included procuring 30 kg of UF6 illicitly via its embassy in Paris in 1978.[178] When combined with indigenous sources, this would likely have been enough for Pakistan's immediate weapons-related requirements via the enrichment route.

Plutonium

Pakistan had three reactors in 1974: the US-supplied PARR-1 reactor, an indigenously constructed reactor based on Chinese technology known as PARR-2, and the Canadian-supplied KANUPP reactor. PARR-1 was a 10MW pool-type research reactor fuelled with 20% enriched fuel that Pakistan procured in the 1960s under the Atoms for Peace initiative from the US. To enable the sale, Pakistan concluded a trilateral safeguards agreement with the IAEA and the US government in 1962.[179,180] The reactor's modest power rating and design made it impractical for the production of significant quantities of plutonium. PARR-2 was a 30 kW miniature neutron source supplied by China that went critical in 1974.[181] It is fuelled with 1 kg of HEU and, because of its size, could not be used for plutonium production.[182] KANUPP was a large (100 MWe) heavy water reactor supplied by Canada in the late 1960s and early 1970s.[183] Construction began in 1966 and finished in 1971 when the reactor went critical.[184] The reactor was a commercial power generating reactor, meaning that during standard operation, it would produce reactor-grade plutonium rather than weapons-grade plutonium. The reactor was capable of producing significant quantities of plutonium with some estimates up to 200 kg of reactor-grade plutonium per year, or enough for several nuclear weapons.[185] A pressure tube reactor like KANUPP could be operated in a manner that would result in the production of weapons-grade plutonium, but this would require it to be powered down frequently, which would be detectable by satellites via thermal signature and would compromise the reactor's electricity-generating capability.

The reactor was supplied under IAEA safeguards which prevented Pakistan from using the facility for weapons production so long as Pakistan did not break its agreement with Canada and the IAEA by withdrawing the reactor from safeguards. The safeguards on all of Pakistan's nuclear facilities were based upon INFCIRC66 (updated to INFCIRC 66 Rev 2). This required that the facility and any foreign-supplied fuel be subject to safeguards for the purpose of ensuring they were not used for the purpose of developing nuclear explosive devices. As discussed earlier, it is likely that Pakistan also calculated that the removal of KANUPP from safeguards would be counterproductive as it would require a significant proportion of Pakistan's indigenous uranium to fuel the reactor, reducing the amount of uranium available for use in the other parts of the fuel cycle. Despite these safeguards, Pakistan could have opted to irradiate indigenously-produced fuel in the reactor and reprocess this to extract plutonium for weapons purposes without violating its safeguards agreement, as India had.[186] Pakistan did, however, agree to put domestically-manufactured fuel for KANUPP under safeguards. Again, this likely was driven by a desire to assure uranium suppliers that fuel supplied to KANUPP would not be diverted.[187]

Feroz Khan concluded from interviews with those involved in Pakistan's programme that there was never a plan to divert fuel from KANUPP because of the 'unwarranted controversy' this would generate.[188] CIA officials noted in one memo to the director of the CIA in 1982 that, "the sticking point is 'unsafeguarded reprocessing'. He [Zia, the president of Pakistan] would characterize the beginning of reprocessing as being authorised under IAEA rules, but this would quickly turn into an international brouhaha".[189]

To continue using the reactor after Canada decided to stop providing supplies in the mid-1970s following the Indian PNE, Pakistan pursued alternative sources of uranium fuel and heavy water. Pakistan had sought to procure around 8 tons of heavy water from West German firm NUKEM in 1973. The procurement was channelled through Pakland Corporation, an arm of PAEC, in order to disguise its true end use.[190,191] Later, there was also an alleged transfer of fissile material from NUKEM to Pakistan, although as noted in the following, there are reasons to believe this alleged transfer did not take place.[192]

As discussed earlier, Pakistan procured uranium under safeguards from South Africa and Niger. With regards to fuel manufacture and heavy water, it appears Pakistan had three main options: to produce the fuel and heavy water indigenously, to procure the materiel openly or covertly from an NSG member state, or to procure it from a country outside of the NSG.

When Pakistan purchased the reactor from Canada in the 1960s, the sale included the provision of both fuel and heavy water. Pakistan had ordered a fuel fabrication plant for KANUPP in 1973, but Canada stopped the shipment at the last minute in line with its NSG commitments.[193] The decision by Canada to cut supplies to Pakistan in the mid-1970s left Pakistan with no immediate alternatives and resulted in the reactor being under-utilised for part of the decade.[194]

Pakistan instead pursued the development of an indigenous fuel fabrication capability which was achieved through foreign procurements and possibly with foreign assistance. The procured materials for this effort included two shipments of 400 kg of zirconium procured via its embassy in Norway in 1978–1979, which was below the 500 kg control threshold set by the Zangger committee's lists.[195] The Norwegian government, therefore, approved the export licences and the British government conceded that no rules had been broken as 400 kg was below the control threshold at the time.[196] Pakistan was also able to acquire in the early 1980s, "18 metric tonnes of zircaloy tubing, plate, and rods for the manufacture of fuel assemblies, plus an electron beam and laser welding apparatus, vacuum ovens and sintering ovens for processing nuclear fuel materials", from the German company Neue Technologien GmbH without the required licences having been sought from the German authorities.[197]

US-led efforts to restrict the supply of zirconium did begin to have success, however. In 1979, the Norwegian government eventually blocked the export of zirconium to Pakistan, as did the West German government the following year.[198] But by the mid-1980s, PAEC documents purportedly began to indicate that Pakistan had located domestic reserves of zirconium, possibly negating the need to import.[199] When combined with procurement of an arc-remelting furnace, electron beam welder, and a pellet pressing facility from Germany in

1986, Pakistan likely had everything required to manufacture zirconium and fuel indigenously.[200]

French reprocessing plant

Perhaps no aspect of Pakistan's nuclear programme received greater attention in the 1970s than the proposed procurement of a reprocessing facility from France. Munir Ahmad Khan approached France over the supply of a reprocessing plant in 1972. An agreement was reached in 1976 over the supply of a reprocessing plant with a capacity of 100 tons, around the same time as a safeguards agreement for the facility was concluded with the IAEA.[201]

The full rationale behind this effort to procure a reprocessing plant from France is not yet fully understood. It would have been completed years before Pakistan had reactor fuel that could be reprocessed, and its capacity greatly exceeded what would be required for Pakistan's reactor needs, at least in the medium term. It is in this context that the following comments from President Bhutto's information minister appear significant:

> Bhutto himself was of the view that the work at Kahuta laboratories (the enrichment effort) should be kept concealed from the world by focusing attention on the purchase of the reprocessing plant.[202]

The lack of a coherent rationale associated with Pakistan's pursuit of the reprocessing facility concerned the US in particular, with the proposed transfer in direct conflict with the US non-proliferation strategy of the time. While the facility was to be put under safeguards, the US was concerned about the potential use of the facility in the production of weapons should Pakistan withdraw from the safeguards, and also about the possibility that Pakistan could create an unsafeguarded indigenous copy.

The French government's policy on the reactor sale changed during the period from 1972 to 1978 in direct response to discussions in the NSG and under bilateral US pressure. Before opting to cancel the contract, France had attempted to introduce a requirement that the supplied plant would be capable only of separating mixed fissile materials, which would not be suitable for use in weapons.[203]

The US only had a limited ability to influence French decision making on the reprocessing plant transfer because France remained outside of the NPT and the belief in Paris that proliferation concerns over its nuclear sales were addressed by the inclusion of safeguards. The UK and US were also concerned that pressuring Pakistan could potentially result in Pakistan's withdrawal from the Central Treaty Organisation (CENTO), a Cold War era alliance involving Iran, Iraq, Pakistan, Turkey, and the UK.[204,205]

Under increasing US diplomatic pressure, the French eventually agreed to cancel the sale. Even after taking the decision to cancel, France was reluctant to renege on the contract in order to avoid a legal liability and the reputational damage that would result. This was despite the fact that the US had apparently offered to underwrite any losses.[206] Ultimately, France announced the cancellation of the contract after President Bhutto was toppled from power by a coup in 1977.

While the decision by France not to honour the contract for the reprocessing plant did not prevent Pakistan from developing a reprocessing capability, it did delay the effort substantially. In parallel to seeking the facility from France, Pakistan had already acquired a gram-quantity plutonium separation facility developed with British assistance earlier in the 1970s and had been pursuing a smaller-scale effort called "New Labs" with Belgian assistance.[207] At the Pakistan Institute of Nuclear Science and Technology (PINSTECH), Pakistan had a small underground facility for solvent extraction in the basement. By 1983, Pakistan was also nearing completion of the "New Labs" reprocessing facility, which was also located on the PINSTECH site.[208] The facility had benefited from European design assistance as well as "specialised handing equipment such as manipulators and a waste handling system" from various suppliers.[209] Pakistan pursued both indigenous efforts to scale up the reprocessing capabilities at the PINSTECH facility.[210] It was also thought to have taken steps to complete the French reprocessing facility as Pakistan did receive many of the facility drawings, but these efforts proved to be unsuccessful because the facility was never completed.[211]

Chinese assistance to Pakistan's weapons programme

Another important aspect of Pakistan's nuclear programme in the 1970s was the assistance provided by China. China accepted something of a unique position in the 1970s as it was perhaps the only potential nuclear supplier not engaged in the NPT or the NSG. China was not thought by the US to be involved in foreign nuclear transfers as late as the 1970s, which was one of the reasons it was not invited to join the NSG process.[212]

Chinese assistance was certainly important to Pakistan's pursuit of nuclear weapons in the late 1970s and early 1980s, although any study of the contribution that China made must be heavily caveated because there continues to be a lack of transparency about the nature and scope of this cooperation. The US believed that China signed a scientific and technical cooperation protocol with Pakistan on the 29 January 1977, with Chinese technicians arriving at KANUPP soon after.[213] China, for its part, has denied assisting Pakistan with its weapons programme.[214] It nonetheless also widely accepted that at some point between 1977 and 1983, China provided Pakistan with a nuclear weapons design – a design that was subsequently sold on by the A.Q. Khan network.[215]

It is unclear exactly what drove China to cooperate with Pakistan and to provide a weapons design. Some have speculated that China needed Pakistan as an ally, with China relying on Pakistan's support to claim its seat on the UN Security Council, for example.[216] China might also have been leveraging

Pakistan as an ally against India. Others have speculated that China wanted access to the URENCO centrifuge technology that Khan had taken to Pakistan from Europe, and which is examined further in the following.[217] Pakistan could also have given China access to the partially-constructed French reprocessing plant.

The technical value of the Chinese cooperation remains unclear. While China does appear to have given Pakistan a weapons design, Beijing had no experience of heavy water reactors or of the URENCO enrichment technology that Pakistan used. Additionally, it was not until the 1990s that Pakistan's plutonium production reactors became operational. China's cooperation with Pakistan was ultimately curtailed in the 1990s. It appears that the primary driver for China to engage in non-proliferation was its desire to engage the US in nuclear cooperation, but it is also possible that the US could have embarrassed China by confronting Chinese officials over the weapons design.[218] Pakistan's cooperation with China would ultimately be curtailed in the 1980s.

By the 1990s, China began to prioritise the fulfilment of its own nuclear energy needs, resulting in a desire to receive technology and facilities from international suppliers. China, therefore, set about negotiating a nuclear cooperation agreement with the US. Conditions for the conclusion of an agreement with China were laid down by President Reagan under National Security Decision Directive 76 and included: a Chinese commitment to adhere to international norms in its nuclear export practices; conclusion of an agreement for cooperation with China which includes the provisions required by US law as well as procedures for assuring that US exports are used only for peaceful purposes; and convincing assurances that China will not assist any country to develop or acquire any nuclear explosive device.[219] Importantly, the US conditioned completion of this nuclear cooperation agreement on China, ending nuclear weapons cooperation with Pakistan. This resulted in the Chinese Premier making the following statement on non-proliferation at a Whitehouse State Dinner for the Chinese Premier in 1984 and which was subsequently published through the Xinhua news agency:

> China has always opposed the arms race, particularly the nuclear arms race, and stands for the complete prohibition and thorough destruction of nuclear weapons. We have long declared that China will never be the first to use nuclear weapons. We are critical of the discriminatory treaty on the non-proliferation of nuclear weapons. But we do not advocate or encourage nuclear proliferation. We do not engage in nuclear proliferation ourselves nor do we help other countries develop nuclear weapons. We actively support all proposals that are truly helpful to realizing nuclear disarmament, terminating the nuclear arms race and eliminating the threat of nuclear war.[220,221]

This statement allowed for the conclusion of the nuclear cooperation agreement. In the years that followed, China has gradually aligned itself to the international trade controls of the export control regimes in the decades which followed, including the NSG. In this case, it thus appears that Reagan's market-based approach to non-proliferation yielded positive results.

A.Q. Khan and the Uranium route

Pakistan began the pursuit of enrichment technology in 1967 using designs obtained from Italy and expertise gained by Pakistani scientists working overseas, although these efforts saw few results.[222] In 1974, after India's nuclear explosion, Abdul Qadeer Khan (A.Q. Khan), a Pakistani scientist working for a contractor at the URENCO enrichment plant in the Netherlands, offered to assist Pakistan's leadership in taking forward the centrifuge programme. This offer was accepted and the enrichment effort was renewed.[223]

Khan had been working with URENCO contractor FDO in the early 1970s in a role that involved engineering and translation work.[224] This role gave Khan some access to URENCO's Almelo site. This was against the security policy of the URENCO partners, which permitted foreigners access to nothing higher than "confidential" information.[225] In fact, the Dutch government had protected information on the centrifuge technology a decade before at the request of the US government, which was specifically concerned about the risk that a foreign worker could gain access to the designs.[226]

Following his offer, Khan met with President Bhutto and it was agreed to set up 'Project 706' based on the technological know-how that Khan had provided.[227] Khan himself briefly returned to Europe, but upon visiting to check progress in 1975, was asked by the President to take over the programme after Khan reported that it had made little progress.[228] On 31 July 1976, Khan was put in charge of the project under the auspices of the Engineering Research Laboratories, reporting directly to the President.[229]

Khan brought to Pakistan a list of URENCO suppliers and possibly designs for the G1, G2, and G4 centrifuges.[230] He also led the creation of a complex network to acquire goods for the programme.[231] While Khan's theft of centrifuge designs was illegal under Dutch law, it should be noted that there were no restrictions on the movement of people at this time in relation to proliferation concerns. Under the Atoms for Peace initiative, the overseas study of nuclear technology issues was actually encouraged. Khan was not the only Pakistani engineer or scientist that had been residing overseas before returning to Pakistan and supporting the country's enrichment effort. Others included Dr. Farooq Hashmi, who trained in metallurgy at Southampton University and became deputy director of the Engineering Research Laboratories, and Dr. Alam, a British-educated computer programmer and mathematician.[232]

Pakistan's renewed centrifuge programme initially focused on the so-called P1 centrifuge with a short aluminium rotor and the P2 with a longer aluminium rotor with maraging steel bellows. Later work would move over to the P3 and P4 centrifuge in the mid-1980s, which used several maraging steel segments joined together.[233] However, Pakistan's industrial capacity was not sufficient to manufacture the thousands of parts and components needed to construct cascades of centrifuges. The technical barriers were such that, without external assistance and technology, the programme would be unable to progress. Indeed, Khan's approach to indigenising enrichment largely involved procuring components from overseas. Khan himself has observed:

> It was not possible for us to make each and every piece of equipment or components within the country. Attempts to do so would have killed the project in the initial stages. We devised a strategy by which we would go all out to buy everything that we needed in the open market to lay the foundation of a good infrastructure and would then switch over to indigenous production as and when we had to.[234]

Khan, who had an extensive knowledge of European industry, set about acquiring goods from European companies. In many cases, Khan had long-term relationships with potential suppliers:

> My long stay in Europe and intimate knowledge of the various countries and their manufacturing firms was an asset. Within three years, we had put up prototypes of centrifuges and were going at full speed to build the facilities at Kahuta ... I took full advantage of the willingness of western companies to do business and decided to make purchases from the open market.[235]

Dr. Shafiq, the son of the Army officer who oversaw the construction of the Kahuta site and a close business associate of the Khan family, has reflected:

> Everything came from the UK, Germany and France and was openly transacted. The companies would tell their governments, "These silly buggers in Pakistan want to spend billions" and their governments would say "If these silly buggers have got the cash, then let them have it". We would say vacuum pumps; we need them for oil and gas, etc. It was all going to Kahuta.[236]

A particularly important procurement attempt for the enrichment programme was for inverters, which were not subject to export control, from the UK firm Emerson in 1977.[237] The Pakistani government placed an order for 100 inverters with the firm Emerson Electric Ltd of Swindon, with at least one of the orders placed through the Pakistan embassy in Berlin.[238,239] A repeat order of 100 inverters was submitted in 1978. The company brought this order to the attention of British authorities.

Based on the revelations that uncontrolled UK goods were being sought by Pakistan for use in a weapons programme, a debate began amongst UK government officials about how to respond. The debate focused on the so-called 'dual-use' dilemma. Many of the points made would be echoed by officials in other countries struggling with the same problem. These included: a belief that the UK should not act alone in controlling such goods to Pakistan; a recognition that UK exports should not be used to support another country's nuclear weapons programme; a recognition of the challenge associated with controlling dual-use items; a realisation that existing laws did not allow for the controlling of dual-use goods; and a recognition that controls on dual-use goods could have an impact upon legitimate markets commerce.[240] In response to these challenges, the UK approach was summed up by one British official as follows:

> [We] understand that some essential items covered in general terms by the Export of Goods Control Order cannot be individually defined for purposes of export control; control procedures may thus be ineffective in such cases. This is worrying – notably, at present, in the context of Pakistan. Officials should be ready to respond quickly and flexibly to seek the cooperation of manufacturers and shippers in denying Pakistan such items. I am reassured to learn that there are informal interdepartmental arrangements to deal with this problem on a case-by-case basis and that they have proved effective; there is a need for them to continue. I believe these arrangements also cover occasional informal approaches to manufacturers and shippers to seek their cooperation in denying the Pakistanis specific non-controlled centrifuge-related items and materials which might have an important bearing on the Pakistani programme. The extension of the Export of Goods Control Order, as proposed, should substantially reduce the occasion for these particular approaches.[241]

There were different views on the question of controlling dual-use items within the UK. For example, David Owen, Foreign Secretary, noted:

> My reservations about the effectiveness in this case of using export controls as a means of preventing proliferation and my misgivings about the probable effect of this course on non-nuclear trade are as strong as when we discussed this matter on 21 September [1979]. However, in the light of the meeting which officials held with Emersons and the subsequent official discussions I recognise that the only practicable way of preventing this export seem to be to impose export controls on inverters and therefore acquiesce in the conclusions set out in Para 11 of Gen 74 (78) 9. In acquiescing, I assume that export licences will be withheld in any future cases only if the inverters in question could be used, and are likely to be used, with gas centrifuges.[242]

Ultimately, in late 1978 UK officials agreed that nuclear-capable inverters should be controlled for export to Pakistan.[243] In fact, an examination of records from several government departments shows a general consensus that dual-use goods should not be exported to Pakistan's nuclear programme, although the Department of Trade was hesitant about controlling goods unless other states also did the same.[244] Importantly, however, the UK opted not to approach members of the NSG regarding controls on inverters, but instead, to approach on a bilateral basis those countries that it considered could be alternative suppliers for the inverters and which would view the request to control the items with sympathy.[245] The list included the US, Switzerland, Japan, the Netherlands, France, Australia, Canada, Austria, Sweden, and Italy.[246]

The key reason given in UK internal correspondence for this bilateral approach rather than raising the issue relates to the need for, "caution in making any approach to the Russians which would create the temptation to exploit the situation for political reasons despite their generally tough position on non-proliferation questions".[247] In effect, therefore, the UK was concerned that sharing intelligence with the Soviet Union would be used against the UK's broader interests in the context of the Cold War.

Still, despite the mechanism used, Pakistan was not able to procure the inverters from mainstream manufacturers and it turned instead to other manufacturing states, including Turkey. Pakistan would also procure inverter parts from Canada, although one shipment of these parts was seized by Canadian customs.[248]

The UK also set about considering what other "grey areas" – or dual-use items – should be subject to control. While reluctant to control any such items, the Department of Trade did concede that some controls were necessary, but resisted controls on goods such as maraging steel – a key chokepoint material in centrifuge production, because of the legitimate market for this material.[249]

Had the NSG continued meeting, the suppliers involved could potentially have taken collective action to respond to Pakistani proliferation. However, once the Carter administration received French assurances that it would cancel the transfer of the reprocessing capability to Pakistan, the US opted to suspend NSG meetings until at least after INCFE had concluded. Ultimately, therefore, the decision to suspend meetings was a missed opportunity in the context of strengthening international efforts to prevent proliferation. In the absence of a coordinated international response to Pakistan's procurement of dual-use technologies, progress on the adoption of controls on dual-use technologies was slow, thus allowing Pakistan to engage in extensive illicit procurement. Pakistan's procurement modus operandi was based on several elements, including targeting countries with poor national enforcement of export controls. It also included the use of covert procurement practices, such as the use of embassies to circumvent controls.

Pakistan and controls on enrichment

By the time British officials had uncovered Pakistan's enrichment effort in 1978, as a result of procurement attempts for British-made inverters, Pakistan had already acquired most of what would be needed to enrich uranium.[250] However, the hesitation about discussing Pakistan with NSG countries in

1978 meant that there was no immediate multilateral coordination of controls, with the result that the NSG was not leveraged as a useful forum for controlling enrichment technology to Pakistan. Indeed, the first successful separation of uranium isotopes took place sometime between 4 April and 4 June 1978.[251] Pakistan did suffer setbacks after this point, however, including the loss of thousands of centrifuges because of an earthquake. But in 1984, Khan claimed that Pakistan had mastered enrichment even though other Pakistani officials claimed not to be enriching beyond 5%.[252,253]

By the early 1980s, concern about Pakistan's enrichment program did prompt efforts to control enrichment technology, but it would prove to the Zangger Committee rather than the NSG that was used as the main forum for this. In this context, it is useful to briefly examine why this was the case.

Britain opted to limit the adoption of dual-use controls, in the first instance, to inverters, and the UK and US were still corresponding to coordinate their own controls as late as March 1980, with the US exerting pressure upon the UK to introduce controls on 'specialised aluminium' and maraging steel.[254] The reason for the delay seems to have related to bureaucratic resistance to the idea of controlling dual-use technologies and technical challenges in defining control language. While this delay in coordinating would benefit Pakistan, which was able to continue procuring goods for its nuclear programme, there was some success. US intelligence enabled France to prevent a shipment of 9,000 of 10,000 bellows from French firm Calorstatto to Pakistan in 1979.[255] By 1979, France had also moved to control the export of inverters to Pakistan in line with the diplomatic request from the UK.[256] However, there was no move at this time to control dual-use technologies more broadly.

In March 1981, US senator Alan Cranston said on the floor of the Senate that his sources in the executive branch had told him that Pakistan and India were preparing for nuclear tests, which could take place as soon as later that year.[257] This announcement understandably caused some consternation and it was in this context that the US called at short notice for an informal meeting of the NSG in June 1981 on the side-lines of the IAEA board of governors meeting in Vienna.[258,259] At this meeting, which only lasted for 45 minutes, it was agreed that there was a need to coordinate controls. The UK had anyway been talking to the Netherlands and Germany – its partners on the URENCO project – about what could usefully be added to export control lists and therefore took the initiative.

The UK convened a meeting of 'western countries' to consider controls on enrichment technology in June and September 1981.[260] After contact with the Soviet Union, the UK then tabled a proposal to the Zangger Committee in September 1981.[261]

It appears that it was for reasons of engaging Switzerland in the process that the UK would put its proposal on export control of centrifuge technology to the Zangger Committee on the 16th of September. It is interesting to note that the Soviet Union welcomed the proposal, but it said it regretted the fact that it was put to the Zangger Committee rather than the NSG. In justifying its position, the UK made the following points at the meeting.[262]

- The Zangger committee could be more effective because its membership was wider.
- Moreover, it draws its authority from formal commitments entered into by signatories of the NPT.
- It was consequently less open to criticism by the G77 as a discriminatory organisation of the nuclear haves and have-nots.

However, privately, the UK also told the Soviet Union that "Switzerland is one of the most reluctant countries to introduce controls, but is much more likely to be helpful in the Zangger Committee, where Swiss national and personal prestige are involved, than in an NSG format".[263] The decision to use the Zangger Committee rather than the NSG thus appears to have been driven as much by personality as it was anything else. It seems that the UK was thus performing a form of 'forum shopping' in jumping between forums based upon its sense on in which it would most likely find success. One important footnote to this point is that France, while not a member of the Zangger Committee, had made it known that it would abide by anything the Zangger Committee decided. Thus, French participation was not contingent on the type of forum as it had been in the 1970s.[264]

Use of the Zangger Committee as the basis of the centrifuge controls provided a broad base for the measures but was constrained by the fact that the mandate of the Zangger Committee was to interpret Article III.2 of the NPT. As such, the basis of expanded controls would be items described as 'especially designed and prepared for a nuclear end use. Ahead of the September meeting, the US prepared a legal memorandum in which it was argued that this phrase, and in particular the use of the word 'especially' provided some leeway in controlling items not uniquely designed and prepared for a nuclear end use.

The 1980s thus saw advancement in centrifuge controls, specifically in response to Pakistan's nuclear activity. However, this was undertaken largely through the Zangger Committee rather than the NSG. While the UK put forward its reasons for choosing Zangger over the NSG, perhaps the overall impression that results from examining this period is that states were somewhat agnostic about the forums used for agreeing on nuclear export controls. In 1981 alone, there was an informal meeting of the NSG, a meeting of 'western suppliers' (which was not described as being a continuation of the western suppliers group meetings of the 1950s and 1960), and meetings of the Zangger Committee in which controls on some dual-use items were pursued.

The role of Switzerland was important in this period. Claude Zangger admitted at the informal NSG meeting in 1981 that Swiss companies were involved in supplying enrichment-related equipment to Pakistan.[265] This continued in the years that followed and in 1987, the Swiss government raided a firm that was manufacturing desublimers for UF6 that were apparently designed to hold highly enriched uranium and destined for Pakistan, thus undermining Pakistan's claims of peaceful intent.[266] Interestingly, the Swiss firm was subcontracted by Leybold and is not thought to have known that the goods were destined for Pakistan.[267]

The gradually expanding national controls did prevent some of Pakistan's procurements. Even by 1980, the coverage of laws was beginning to improve, much to Khan's frustration. "They are even stopping nails and screws", he wrote to Aziz, a Pakistani based in Canada who would later be arrested for involvement in the transfer of zirconium to Pakistan.[268] Nonetheless, despite the discovery of the Pakistani programme and the national moves to increase controls, Pakistan managed to continue procuring materials for its fuel cycle after 1980, with procurement for Pakistan's plutonium and weaponisation activities being particularly important.

In 1987, the Reagan administration secured an undertaking from Pakistan's leadership that covert procurement from the US would stop. This was necessary partly because of the Solarz amendment to the Foreign Assistance Act, which would require the US administration to cut off aid to Pakistan if it was found to have acquired goods from the US for use in a nuclear weapons programme.[269] One case of note came to light in the US with the arrest of Arshed Pervez in the US in July 1987. The Pervez case involved a Canadian-Pakistani national who attempted to bribe a US customs official in order to facilitate the export of maraging steel and beryllium to Pakistan for use in its enrichment programme.[270] American officials raised the case with Pakistani officials who were apologetic for the embarrassment the case had caused in the US, with Zia claiming to have given an order for procurement in the US to end.[271] The case might thus have been an early sign that Khan's organisation would act outside the control of Pakistan's political leadership. A US official recounted that, "after the initial discussion with the Pakistanis, we noted a shift in emphasis from procurement of weapons components themselves to procurement of machinery necessary for their procurement".[272] This thus highlights that Pakistan was sensitive to the consequences of its procurement activity but that it was determined to move forward with the programme regardless.

Evaluating the failures of international nuclear trade controls: insights from Pakistan

How was it that despite the negotiation of the NPT and creation of the NSG, Pakistan was able to develop a full nuclear fuel cycle and a robust and multifaceted nuclear weapons programme within ten years from taking a firm political decision to acquire nuclear weapons in 1974. While the knowledge that Khan brought back from URENCO's enrichment programme was evidently important, Pakistan still had to import most of the materials and components required to consult the centrifuge cascades required to produce highly enriched uranium for weapons.

Re-examining the Pakistan case has highlighted a number of limitations that existed in international nuclear trade controls in the 1970s and 1980s. One important contributing factor during this period were the variations in American leadership and priorities on nuclear trade controls across the Ford, Carter, and Reagan administrations. Variation in approaches had a direct impact on the subsequent evolution of the non-proliferation regime.

First, the differing approaches of the Ford, Carter, and Reagan administrations were inconsistent on the nuclear trade control issue. Across the three administration's the US had gone from a position of supporting to opposing and then back to supporting reprocessing. This damaged the reputation of the US as a reliable commercial nuclear supplier. After the NSG published its guidelines, the Carter Administration decided against holding further meetings of the suppliers until after INFCE concluded. While US leadership had focused attention on non-proliferation issues following the Chinese test and helped to develop a non-proliferation norm, the subsequent sporadic leadership limited efforts to resolve underlying structural issues with the non-proliferation regime. The nuclear programme of states including Pakistan and Iraq advanced as a result.

Second, despite the differing approaches of the US Presidents, both the Carter and Reagan administrations were consistent in putting US geopolitical interests *vis-à-vis* the Cold War ahead of US non-proliferation interests. The US consistently certified Pakistan as not pursuing nuclear weapons, for example.

Third, there were limitations to the trade control regime in this period. For example, dual-use items were not included on either the Zangger or the NSG lists. In fact, Dr. Claud Zangger expressly noted: "We found that what was being imported was not on the list. It was on the periphery. There was no legal basis for us to deny a licence to export".[273] Given that the UK had begun to discuss the issue of 'grey areas' during the NSG meetings in the 1970s, it is clear the decision to cease meetings of the NSG in 1977 undermined the possibility that collective action would be taken to coordinate controls on dual-use technology.

The overall conclusion from this examination of Pakistan's nuclear weapons programme is that international trade controls, as they constituted in the 1970s and 1980s, were not capable of preventing proliferation regardless of whether or not the state in question was a party to the NPT. Efforts to strengthen controls did accelerate throughout the 1970s, particularly after the Indian PNE and the detection of Pakistan's clandestine efforts, but the pace of adoption and the coverage of controls were not sufficient to prevent Pakistan from becoming a latent nuclear weapons state by 1983.[274] As argued, this was a direct consequence of the decision to suspend meetings of the NSG. Moreover, compelling national security imperatives interfered with non-proliferation efforts in the Pakistan case as a consequence of US efforts to counter the Soviet Union's action in Afghanistan. In the end, the international trade control arrangements put in place over the course of the 1970s were not capable of overcoming competing interests and limitations.

Pakistan was able to acquire the parts and materials for its nuclear weapons programme through hundreds of procurements from overseas. In many cases, the governments in supplier countries had knowledge of Pakistan's efforts and initiatives. For example, the US sent over 100 specific demarches to the West German government about exports to Pakistan.[275] Indeed, the sheer number of cases involving German companies raises the question of whether the German State was complicit, although there is no evidence of systematic collusion by the German authorities in the supply of goods to Pakistan's nuclear programme. However, German law, like those of most countries, did not prohibit most of the procurement discussed in this chapter, at least in the 1970s and early 1980s. It also appears that Pakistan actively targeted Germany because of its weak laws on trade control its advanced industrial base. Part of the challenge was that some governments, including Germany, focused overtly on materials. Indeed, one German official reportedly said in relation to controls: "We're interested in the [nuclear] material, not the facilities".[276]

If the NSG had continued the meeting, it is possible that a coordinated response to such illicit procurement practices could have resulted in a more effective international effort to counter the advancement of Pakistan's weapons programme. While bilateral diplomacy and demarches did succeed in preventing some exports, they were largely ineffective in inducing states to prevent shipments to Pakistan. The primary reason for this – as the resistance of UK officials to control materials such as maraging steel demonstrates – was that supplier states were reluctant to stop shipments to Pakistan unless they were confident that other states would also prevent them. The concern for these – as evidenced in the UK – was that national businesses could be disadvantaged *vis-à-vis* international competitors that may not have been subject to the same controls.

Findings and conclusion

The purpose of this chapter was to examine how non-proliferation controls evolved in the 1964–1980 period. This period was an important and formative one for international nuclear trade controls. The period included numerous important developments, including the conclusion of the NPT and the formation of the NSG. It also included important proliferation episodes, including perhaps most notably in relation to Pakistan. In the context of the overall research question of this book, it is argued that controls evolved in a sub-optimal way in this period in at least two regards. First, the NPT text was not 'loophole-free' even though this was one of the objectives set for the treaty. Second, the NSG did not agree on full-scope safeguards as a condition of supply or controls on dual-use items.

This final section of this chapter presents findings from examining these developments through the lens of the CAP framework. The framework's propositions are examined in turn in the following. The chapter then draws broader conclusions about the sub-optimal development of controls in the period.

Findings

The CAP framework includes propositions related to core and structural factors, imperatives and technological factors. Findings from examining these factors in this period are presented in turn.

It is apparent that both structural and core factors were significant in determining why the regimes evolved in this way but so too were domestic politics – particularly in the US. This concluding section of this chapter will briefly highlight insights gleaned through the research framework and will draw broader findings from efforts to agree on controls in the post-war period.

Structural factors

- Number of actors: grew dramatically during this period. This was partly a result of Atoms for Peace, which increased the number of states with vested interests in nuclear issues. However, once the US and Soviet Union agreed on a 'non-proliferation' that suited both sides, the proliferation as a policy problem itself transformed from a bilateral question to one that required cooperation among many states. The approach taken was to negotiate a text for a treaty first on a bilateral basis, then on a multilateral basis and finally on a global basis with minimum concessions offered at each stage of expansion. This was an effective strategy to develop a treaty, although the approach did frustrate leaders in key nuclear states that were not consulted, including France. The treaty was a compromise, but it provided a solid foundation on which to build. However, a similar strategy employed to the development of safeguards was less effective. In both cases, the involvement of states with substantial vested interests – India in the case of the NPT and the European States in the context of safeguards – served to substantially undermine the completeness of these measures.
- The homogeneity of states, or lack thereof, was a barrier to achieving a loop–hole free NPT despite there being widespread support for this objective. Key issues included the non-alignment of certain states, including India and, to some extent, France. The broader geopolitical outlook of these states made them resistant to adherence and implementing broad non-proliferation commitments. India, in particular, felt it represented non-aligned and developing countries and exploited this status to push for less stringent trade controls to facilitate increased transfers. The attitudes of such state drove the need for secrecy within the NSG process and contributed to a suspension of NSG meetings after 1977.

- The distribution of benefits appears to have been a factor in influencing both the NPT discussions and the non-proliferation landscape in the 1970s. The concession to include the inalienable right language – and indeed clauses on disarmament – in the NPT provided some reassurance that states would not lose out as a result of signing the treaty. However, the absence of a requirement for full-scope safeguards as a condition of supply meant that states outside the treaty could achieve many of the benefits of state parties while also keeping open their nuclear weapons options. As the NSG did not agree to full-scope safeguards as a condition of supply, the benefits associated with NPT adherence were not clear: states could benefit from nuclear trade whether or not they signed up to the NPT. On the positive side, the Chinese and later Indian tests demonstrated that non-proliferation was a benefit worth pursuing. Evidently, states such as France had most to lose economically as a result of NSG controls, which drove the French reluctance to cancel reprocessing plant exports.
- The ability to hold face-to-face communications was essential to moving non-proliferation controls forward in the period, but the lack of opportunities was counterproductive. In-person discussions between US and Soviet experts highlighted the common interest of both states in non-proliferation. This eventually paved the way for the US and the USSR to cooperate on non-proliferation issues. The ability to hold face-to-face discussions within the NSG process, and later as part of INFCE, facilitated a common understanding of issues. However, the inability to hold formal NSG meetings after 1976 significantly hindered efforts to coordinate controls which, for example, had a direct knock-on effect on the progress of Pakistan's nuclear weapons programmes.
- Information on past actions: the rumours circulating about unsafeguarded transfers risked undermining international control in this period. However, these rumours combined with concern following the Chinese and Indian tests also drove the adoption of controls. Further meetings of the NSG might well have increased cooperation, particularly in the context of countering proliferation, including, for example, Pakistan's enrichment programme. A key challenge this introduced was that no multilateral process existed after 1977 through which states could assure one-another that trade controls were being implemented. This affected both the willingness for states to expand controls as well as individual licensing decisions. On the positive side, the existence of international safeguards – particularly INFCIRC 154 safeguards – adopted for NPT states increased the confidence of states that others were not seeking nuclear weapons and thus provided some confidence that NNWS states did not want to pursue nuclear weapons. However, such measures were not sufficient to stop Israel, which destroyed Iraq's Osiraq reactor in 1980 because of concerns that it could be used to produce plutonium for nuclear weapons.

- How actors are linked: the bipolar character of the Cold War clearly was helpful in the creation of the NPT. Once the Superpowers agreed on a definition of non-proliferation that was in their mutual interest, many aligned states quickly fell into line. However, this same advantage made non-aligned and independently minded states – including France – anxious and hesitant about the concept, which worked to the detriment of non-proliferation efforts.

Core factors

- Norms: The lack of an agreed understanding of the concept of non-proliferation meant that a norm did not exist prior to the mid-1960s. For the USSR, non-proliferation was about preventing nuclear sharing. For the US, it was about preventing state-sponsored nuclear weapons cooperation. With the Chinese nuclear test, understanding of the issue solidified and the common benefit of preventing further nuclear proliferation became apparent. However, the focus of this emerging norm, and the definition of non-proliferation, concerned the non-diversion of fissile material only. US efforts to broaden the definition to include enrichment and reprocessing were ultimately unsuccessful. Norms, therefore, were of limited relevance in the period.
- Relational: It is notable that relations between key states seem to have been an important secondary factor in influencing the evolution of international nuclear trade controls in this period. The Superpowers – despite a lack of trust – ultimately realised the sense of cooperation on achieving the common interest of a non-spread treaty, for example. This was facilitated by face-to-face discussions between experts at key points, as well as some information on how other states might act based upon past actions.
- Imperatives: The imperatives of non-proliferation, disarmament and peaceful uses continued to play an important role in shaping nuclear policies in this period. These became embedded into the NPT and thus shaped the future nuclear policy landscape. It is notable that, despite this, the US appears to have believed that the NPT did not impose a binding obligation concerning nuclear disarmament. The US evidently also believed that the NPT did not require the US to transfer enrichment and reprocessing capability to other states. The US launched INFCE to examine how to balance these imperatives through technical approaches, but the key finding of INFCE was that there are no technical fixes to the duality of nuclear technology and nuclear fuel cycles.

Technology issues

The emergence of gas centrifuge enrichment technology was a key factor in this period. The lack of controls on dual-use materials and items with applications in gas centrifuge enrichment allowed states such as Pakistan to acquire enrichment capability with little international meddling. The focus of the US on reducing interest in reprocessing in the latter part of the 1970s worked to the detriment of advancing controls on enrichment. The reasons for this related primarily to US domestic politics, specifically the domestic political narrative that had gained momentum during the Carter vs Ford presidential election campaign against reprocessing because it proved a nuclear proliferation risk. From this examination of the evolution of controls in the 1960s, it appears that structural and technological factors were the most important to the evolution of controls.

Overall, structural factors were relevant in the period but in a different way from the Atoms for Peace era when geostrategic rivalries impeded the evolution of controls. In this period, common ground was found between the Superpowers on the issue of 'non-spread' before and after the Chinese nuclear test in 1964. China's pursuit of nuclear weapons after the Sino-Soviet split highlighted to countries like the USSR, the US, Canada, France, and the UK, the risks associated with ostensibly civil nuclear cooperation and the undesirability of an expanded number of nuclear-armed states. Once this common ground was established, the two Superpowers came to share an interest in pursuing policies to counter nuclear spread. As the chapter highlighted, one difficult issue related to the MLF concept and nuclear sharing within NATO. However, after the MLF declined in prominence, it became possible to define proliferation in a way that was compatible with both states' interests. Despite the common ground between the Superpowers, competition between them continued and this had an impact on international nuclear trade controls. In particular, the US placed strategic competition with Moscow in the context of the Soviet invasion of Afghanistan ahead of non-proliferation *vis-à-vis* Pakistan.

Broader conclusions

The period from 1964 did see a substantial evolution in international nuclear trade controls. This included the drafting of the NPT and the creation of the NSG – all measures intended to control aspects of trade and cooperation that had been facilitated through the Atoms for Peace initiative. Despite the advancement in controls and the cooperation that developed between the US and the Soviet Union as well as other states, a variety of factors combined to prevent these controls from preventing nuclear proliferation in some important contexts.

The most important measure adopted during the period was the NPT, which evolved to become the cornerstone of the non-proliferation regime. The NPT's origins lay with mounting nuclear concerns in the 1950s, which resulted in Ireland putting forward a General Assembly resolution in 1959. The Chinese nuclear test in 1964 focused minds in the US and USSR *vis-à-vis* nuclear spread and negotiations for an NPT followed. These negotiations would ultimately progress towards a conclusion after the US agreed to give up on MLF and when the USSR agreed to make concessions on safeguards. To conclude the NPT, certain concessions were made to non-nuclear weapons states, including in relation to peaceful uses and disarmament. Importantly, while there was an aspiration for the NPT to be 'loophole-free', there was no prospect of the NPT including measures related to 'international control' without progress on disarmament. The safeguards system that was concluded instead can be considered a pragmatic but imperfect solution: while it applied to all declared nuclear facilities of a state, the IAEA's mandate was largely limited to ensuring the 'correctness' of a state's declaration.

Another issue with the NPT approach was that it only applied to states that opted to sign up to it. While the proliferation risks associated with as Pakistan were relatively well understood, there continued to be substantial gaps in and limitations with the non-proliferation regime and trade controls which meant, for example, that Pakistan could continue to fuel its programme by acquiring goods from the international marketplace. With the Pakistan case, in particular, it appears the priority the US placed on preventing the reprocessing plant transfer came at the detriment of efforts to counter its enrichment programme. In this context, it is possible that further meetings of the NSG in the 1970s would have allowed the regime to be more responsive to the actions of proliferators. The main reason this did not happen was twofold. The first was related to domestic politics in the US, which resulted in efforts to discourage reprocessing being prioritised over further meetings of the NSG. The second was a concern about sharing intelligence about Pakistan with the Soviet Union in the context of the Cold War.

Overall, therefore, while there was progress in the development of international nuclear trade controls in the period, certain factors acted to restrain the effectiveness of the controls that were adopted. At one level, it was the lack of disarmament that meant that the system was not based on 'international control'. At another level, it was more practical issues that prevented the full use being made of the available controls. There was agreement that the NPT should be free from loopholes, for example, but such loopholes were not prevented in the subsequent safeguards agreement. These structural problems were compounded by the variation in the policies of the Nixon, Ford, Carter, and Reagan administration concerning non-proliferation. The variation in policy saw the US become viewed as an 'unreliable supplier' of nuclear assistance and resulted in a discontinuance of the meetings of the NSG. Partly as a result of the lack of continuity on US policy, the underlying structural problems with the non-proliferation regime were not addressed.

As a result, while the underpinning architecture of the non-proliferation regime was formed in the 1960s and the 1970s, this architecture would not be sufficient to comprehensively address the problem of proliferation. Many of the gaps in the non-proliferation regime from the 1970s would eventually be addressed in the 1990s and 2000s but not before revelations about Iraq and customers of the A.Q. Khan proliferation network, which are explored in Chapter 5.

Ultimately, therefore, the 1970s and 1980s saw an alignment of structural factors that allowed the Superpowers to cooperate on non-proliferation matters on a global basis while also limiting the action that could be taken in response to specific county proliferation concerns. The moves to introduce non-proliferation measures also introduced new structural issues, including an increase in the number of states involved and thus additional and competing geostrategic and commercial interests.

While key technology holders were generally willing to forgo helping others obtain nuclear weapons, they were less willing to accept controls on their own programmes. US leadership gradually overcame some vested interests to secure non-proliferation agreements. However, US policy was inconsistent between administrations and opportunities to use forums such as the NSG to build trust among states were lost. As a result, much of the momentum of the 1970s was lost by the end of the decade. US leadership on non-proliferation in the 1970s must ultimately be viewed as a failure.

Notes

1 Lewis, J.W. and Litai, W., *China builds the bomb. Stanford University Press, 1988*

2 For example, Gerard Smith, who would later be US ambassador-at-large for non-proliferation, notes that:

> By the beginning of 1950, the Cold War between the United States and the Soviet Union was reaching a new level of intensity. Within months, it escalated further with the outbreak of the Korean War. The atmosphere in Washington was tense. Since 1945 and the failure of the Baruch plan (the U.S. proposal for international control of atomic energy), two key events in the nuclear arena had contributed to the general deterioration in relations between the former wartime allies. Most portentous for U.S. security, Moscow had demonstrated its own nuclear capability, exploding an atomic device in August 1949. Then the U.S. program itself was compromised. It was learned in February 1950 that British scientist Klaus Fuchs, who worked on both fission and fusion designs at the Los Alamos weapons laboratory, had been a spy for the Soviets.
>
> (Ibid., Smith, 'Disarming Diplomat', p. 2)

3 The Bravo incident refers to a nuclear explosion which resulted in substantial fallout. The fallout irradiated the crew of a Japanese fishing vessel. Jacobs, R., "The Bravo Test and the death and life of the global ecosystem in the early Anthropocene", *The Asia Pacific Journal*, vol. 13, issue 29, no. 1, 20 July 2015.

4 Ibid., Smith, *Disarming diplomat,* p. 7.

5 Ibid., Smith, *Disarming diplomat*, p. 26.

6 Ibid., Smith, *Disarming diplomat,* p. 61/62.

7 Ireland's role can be attributed to the neutral activism of Foreign Minister, Frank Aiken. "Frank Aiken and Irish activism at the United Nations, 1957–61", *The International History Review*, vol. 6, no. 2, May 1984, pp. 210–231. www.jstor.org/stable/40105371.

8 Ibid., Shaker, *The nuclear non-proliferation treaty*, p. 29.
9 Ibid.
10 Ibid., Shaker, *The nuclear non-proliferation treaty*, p. 31.
11 Ibid., Shaker, p. 39.
12 It should be noted that France was at this point pursuing its own nuclear weapons program, with its first nuclear test taking place on 13 February 1960.
13 Ibid., Shaker, p. 45.
14 Ibid., Shaker, p. 43.
15 Ibid., Shaker, p. 46.
16 Ibid.
17 Ibid., Shaker, *The nuclear non-proliferation treaty*, p. 50.
18 Ibid.
19 "Briefing for the Gilpatric Committee on Nuclear non-proliferation", 1 December 1964. GWDNSA.
20 Ibid., Shaker.
21 Zhihua, S., and Yafeng, X., 'Between aid and restriction: Changing Soviet policies toward China's nuclear weapons program: 1954–1960', Wilson Centre.
22 Ibid., Lewis, J.W. and Litai, W., 'China builds the bomb', p. 64.
23 For example, China is said to have refused permission for a USSR radio system for submarine communication to be deployed on Chinese territory in 1958. Ibid.
24 Ibid.
25 Ibid.
26 For a fuller overview of USSR/Chinese cooperation, see Lewis, J., and Litai, X., *China Builds the Bomb.*
27 The MLF concept was devised after Sputnik and involved joint operation of nuclear weapon delivery platforms with European allies. Initially, the plan called the joint operation of a submarine-based deterrent, but this was changed to a surface ship platform solution. A central perceived benefit of the plan was that it could be leveraged to encourage the Federal Republic of Germany to forego nuclear weapons. "Committee on nuclear proliferation minutes of discussion: second meeting" 13–14 December 1964, Roswell Gilpatric Papers, President's Taskforce on non-proliferation, correspondence October 1965–March 1967, JFKPL (2120).
28 The view that MLF was unrelated to the nuclear spread problem was expressed by Secretary Rusk as expressed during a White House meeting on non-proliferation in July 1965 after the Gilpatric report had been delivered. It was also the view of Gerard Smith as expressed in his memoir. The counterargument noted by Brands in his own exploration of the relevant archives was that the Soviet Union would not agree to collective action to limit the spread of nuclear weapons unless the problem of West Germany was addressed. During the negotiations over a text of the NPT, MLF would prove to be a key issue for the Soviets. Meeting minutes entitled "non-proliferation", 9 July 1965, Nuclear Non-proliferation, Unpublished files, (box 7), GWNSA.
29 NSAM294, 20 April 1964, Roswell Gilpatric Personal Papers: President's Task Force on Nuclear Proliferation – correspondence April–September 1965 JFKPL (2123).
30 Memorandum for members of the committee on non-proliferation, 30 December 1964, Subject: committee meeting – 7–8 January 1965, Roswell Gilpatric Personal Papers Box 010-010, JFKPL.

31 "Memorandum for Mr Gilpatric from Henry S. Rowen (Deputy Assistant Secretary): Comments on possible Antiproliferation actions", 7 January 1965, Roswell Gilpatric Personal Papers Box 010-010, JFKPL (2325).
32 "National Security Action Memorandum No 320", 25 November 1964. Located in Roswell Gilpatric Personal Papers: President's Task Force on Nuclear Proliferation correspondence April–September 1965 (2190), JFKPL.
33 Gilpatric Committee report.
34 Ibid.
35 Ibid.
36 Ibid.
37 Ibid.
38 Ibid., Gilpatric Committee report.
39 Gilpatric Committee report ("A report to the President by the committee on nuclear proliferation", 21 January 1965).
40 "US Nuclear Export Controls: Policy and Procedures. Nuclear non-proliferation" Gilpatric Report – 1306. p. 536. Committee on nuclear proliferation – minutes of discussions – second meeting – 1–4 December 1964. Roswell Gilpatric Personal Papers: President's Task Force on Nuclear Proliferation – correspondence April–September 1965 JFKPL (2117).
41 Meeting minutes entitled "non-proliferation", 9 July 1965, Nuclear Non-proliferation, Unpublished files, (box 7), GWDNSA.
42 COCOM was a US-led initiative to coordinate export controls from allied nations against the Soviet Bloc. On the history of COCOM, see Hunt, C., "Multilateral cooperation in export controls – the role of COCOM", *University of Toledo Law Review,* 14, 1982–1983.
43 AB 48/1061, BNA.
44 "Senator Robert Kennedy's Statement on nuclear proliferation", 22 June 1965. GWDNSA.
45 Ibid., Shaker, *The nuclear non-proliferation treaty*, vol. 1, p. 22.
46 Ownership of the treaty concept would later prove to be an important issue, with the US making an effort to encourage India to take ownership of the concept to help to encourage that country's commitment to the treaty.
47 The UAR was a short-lived union between Egypt and Syria in the period 1958–1961.
48 Ibid., Shaker, *The nuclear non-proliferation treaty*, vol. 1, p. 70.
49 The need for such reassurance to the European Allies of the United States was a continuing theme of US diplomacy in the period. The US spent considerable time working to assure Germany and even France that the US would intervene in a conflict.
50 "ACDA Position Paper on Non-proliferation (U)", 15 January 1966. GWDNSA.
51 Letter from W. Rostow to the President of the United States, Saturday, 8 April 1967. GWDNSA.
52 Ibid., Shaker, *The nuclear non-proliferation treaty*, vol. 1, p. 39.
53 Beaufre, A., 'The Sharing of Nuclear Responsibilities: A Problem in Need of Solution', *International Affairs*, Royal Institute of International Affairs 1944, vol. 41, no. 3, 1965, pp. 411–419. doi: 10.2307/2609803.
54 Ibid.
55 "Letter from Chet Helifield to the President of the United States", 3 October 1964. GWDSNA. (66).

56 "Adrian Fisher's Proposed Non-proliferation Treaty Language – Information Memorandum", 30 August 1966. GWDNSA. (217).
57 Summary of Conversation in Germany – 24–30 January 1966. GWDSNA. (1326).
58 Burns, E.L.M. 'The Nonproliferation Treaty: Its Negotiation and Prospects', *International Organization,* 23, no. 4, 1969, pp. 788–807. www.jstor.org/stable/2705898.
59 Ibid.
60 For an overview of the Negotiating history of the NPT, see Shaker, *The nuclear non-proliferation treaty*, vol. 1.
61 "Status Report on NPT Negotiations – Information Memorandum", William C. Foster, 10/11/1969. RG59, Office of European Affairs, box (2414). USNARA.
62 Ibid.
63 Ibid.
64 "Memorandum for the Secretary of State: Status Report on the NPT Negotiations – information memorandum", William C. Foster, 11/10/69. Folder "Memos". USNARA.
65 "Provisions of the NPT and Associated Problems", 28 January 1969. NSC Meeting Non-proliferation Treaty 1/29/69, National Security Council ("H") files, Meeting Files (1969–1974), National Security Council Meetings, Nixon Presidential Materials, Box H-019. RNPL.
66 Ibid.
67 Ibid., Shaker, *The nuclear non-proliferation treaty*, vol. 1, p. 337.
68 "Principle (a)" of General Assembly Resolution 2028 (XX). UN General Assembly, New York, 1959.
69 Ibid., Shaker, *The nuclear non-proliferation treaty*, vol. 1, p. 76.
70 Ibid., p. 202.
71 Ibid., p. 227.
72 Community Discussions of NPT Verification Arrangements, 9 May 1969, Euratom – IAEA Safeguards (NPT), General Records of the Department of State. USNARA.
73 Fischer, D., History of the International Atomic Energy Agency the first forty years, International Atomic Energy Agency. p. 256.
74 Howlett, D., *EURATOM and nuclear safeguards*, Macmillan. 1990. doi: 10.1007/978-1-349-10382-9.
75 Ibid.
76 Ibid.
77 Ibid., p. 252.
78 Ibid., p. 253.
79 Ibid., p. 283.
80 Note: While the Zangger committee was the first effort to defined article III (2) of the non-proliferation treaty, Zangger-like groups of states had since the 1950s coordinated policy's with regards to nuclear exports. See for example, FCO96/991 (non-proliferation grey areas) "Zangger committee: Items for the trigger list". BNA.
81 FCO 66/751 (United States Proposal for Common Nuclear Export Policies): FCO telegram from Ottawa to Canberra, 13 February 1975, BNA.
82 FCO 66/949.168 Nuclear Power Matters in Pakistan: Pakistan Nuclear Weapons Development, BNA.

83 "Analytical Staff Meeting on Non-proliferation Strategy", Memo from Winston Lord to the Secretary, 31 July 1974, The Winston Lord Files, RG59, USNARA.
84 Muller, H., 'Falling into line? France and the NPT', Programme for promoting nuclear non-proliferation, Occasional Paper No 6, Centre for International Policy Studies, Department of Politics, University of Southampton May 1990.
85 See for example, Günter Bischof, Stefan Karner, and Peter Ruggenthaler, The Prague Spring and the Warsaw Pact Invasion of Czechoslovakia in 1968 annex 9: Secretary of Defense staff meeting, 26 August 1968, p. 474. 2010.
86 Ibid., "recommended EUR Position for Secretary's Meeting – Briefing Memorandum".
87 Notably, despite being able to join the treaty as a nuclear weapons state because it had conducted a nuclear weapons test before the arbitrary date given in the NPT of 1 January 1967, France also opted not to join the treaty, although France did agree to behave as though it had done so. Ibid., Shaker, *The nuclear non-proliferation treaty*, vol. II. p. 340.
88 "Study requested by NSSM 13", 1 March 1969, NSSM 13, Box H-134, NSC H-files, RNPL.
89 "Recent nuclear developments in India", 18 January 1965, GWDNSA.
90 Telegram 04656 Rusk to New Delhi, Karachi, London, 12 January 1965. GWDSNA. (J5)
91 For a chronology of US understanding of the Indian test, see: 'The Nixon Administration and the Indian Nuclear Program, 1972–1974', GWDSNA.
92 NSM156, 5 July 1972.
93 National Security Study Memorandum 156: Indian Nuclear Development (Revised and Updated), 30 May 1974, Folder NSSM-156 [2 of 2], Box H-192, National Security Council Institution ("H") files, RRNL.
94 Letter from Alastair Gillespie to the Honourable A.J. MacEachen, 9 March 1976, Uranium export controls & nuclear safeguards – general – 1975–1976, File 260-14. LAC (8109).
95 Statement Discourse, Secretary of State for External Affairs, 22 December 1976, Uranium export controls & nuclear safeguards – general – 1975–1976, File 260-14. LAC (8062).
96 "Nuclear Export Policy Toward India", Alfred and Samuel to Kissenger, 26 December 1974, the Winston Lord Files, Department of State, USNARA.
97 Ibid.
98 "Longer Term U.S. Enriched Uranium Supply Policy". The Winston Lord Files. Box 344. RG59, Department of State. USNARA.
99 Nye, J.S., 'Nonproliferation: A Long-Term Strategy', *Foreign Affairs*, April 1978. www.foreignaffairs.com/articles/29147/joseph-s-nye/nonproliferation-a-long-term-strategy. www.jstor.org/stable/20039921.
100 "No Fuel for Tarapur", *The Washington Post*, 22 September 1980.
101 Ibid., Smith, 'Disarming Diplomat', p. 193.
102 Ibid., p. 201.
103 "Longer Term U.S. Enriched Uranium Supply Policy". The Winston Lord Files. RG59 Box 344, USNARA.
104 "National Security Study Memorandum (NSSM) 202 on Nuclear Proliferation", 23 May 1974, History and Public Policy Program Digital Archive, Nixon Presidential Library, National Security Council Institutional Files, Study

Memorandums (1969–1974), Box H-205. Obtained by Fundação Getúlio Vargas. Available online at: http://digitalarchive.wilsoncenter.org/document/115172.

105 "Analytical Staff Meeting on Non-proliferation Strategy", Memo from Winston Lord to the Secretary, 31 July 1974, The Winston Lord Files, RG59, USNARA.

106 "Nuclear Policy Review and Non-Proliferation Initiatives", Memo from Henry A. Kissinger to the President, 6 September 1976, the Winston Lord Files, RG59, USNARA.

107 Note: The reference to Egypt and Israel in Kissinger's quote relates to a plan of the Ford administration to sell nuclear reactors to both countries in exchange for them undertaking non-proliferation commitments. Both countries submitted requests to the US for support in constructing power reactors. US officials advised that

> A positive decision would afford an appropriate opportunity for the US to reaffirm its desire to guard against the further spread of nuclear weapons, while continuing to support peaceful applications of nuclear power through the imposition of meaningful bilateral controls and international safeguards – which were not operative on the Canadian-supplied CIRUS research reactor that we believe provided the plutonium for India's test. We would expect that Egypt and Israel would, at this juncture, be especially interested in assuring each other, the world community, and the US of their intention to use nuclear power peacefully by accepting credible controls.

And

> "IAEA safeguards should deter diversion of material to a weapons program but this system has certain shortcomings, particular when applied to the cases in question, and we believe could be substantially strengthened by the inclusion of certain special conditions in our bilateral agreements with both countries … Nevertheless, the condition of IAEA safeguards and special bilateral conditions would offer substantially more effective legal, political and technical impediments to the clandestine diversion of material or the open abrogation of any commitments than would be provided by likely controls imposed by non-US suppliers to the middle east.
>
> "Nuclear Energy Cooperation with Egypt and Israel", Winston Lord Files. RG59, Box 344, USNARA.

108 "Nuclear Safeguards for Indians", Memo from Winston Lord to the Secretary, 9 November 1974, The Winston Lord Files, Department of State, USNARA.

109 The initially secret WSG meetings had become public knowledge, causing a degree of consternation for states such as South Africa.

110 FCO66/844: Nuclear Suppliers: 3–4 June 1976, BNA.

111 As read in Shaker, *The nuclear non-proliferation treaty,* vol. II, p. 796.

112 By the 1990s, however, this position was less relevant and began to be counterproductive to French interests, particularly with regards to new disarmament initiatives in the Middle East launched in 1991, which led France to sign. "France will sign 1968 nuclear pact", *New York Times*, 4 June 1991.

113 "Analytical Staff Meeting on Non-proliferation Strategy", Memo from Winston Lord to the Secretary, 31 July 1974, The Winston Lord Files, RG59, Department of State. USNARA.

114 Letter from John Tomlinson MP to Nigel Foreman Esq MP. 30 November 1976. FCO 66/911, "Nuclear Suppliers Group Policy". BSA.
115 See for example, Burr, W., 'Nixon's Trip to China', GWDSNA, 11 December 2003. Available online at: https://nsarchive2.gwu.edu/NSAEBB/NSAEBB106/ (Accessed 4 February 2018).
116 Ibid., Perkovich, *India's nuclear bomb*, pp. 185–198.
117 'UK Record of Seventh Nuclear Suppliers Meeting at Riverwalk House' on 28–29 April 1977, FCO 66/913 "Nuclear Suppliers Group Policy" BSA.
118 Ibid.
119 "Nuclear suppliers conference", memorandum from Helmut Sonnenfeldt to the secretary, 31 October 1975. TTB/PNE/NPT. Country and Subject Files, 1973–1976. RG0059, Department of State. Container 11. USNARA.
120 "Memorandum to Cabinet – nuclear cooperation with India", 12 February 1975, Sale of nuclear reactor – India, Minister Energy Mines & Resources Canada, 252-2-1, LCA.
121 "Probable result of French Nuclear Policy Review: memorandum from Winston Lord to Deputy Secretary", 9 October 1976, RG59 Box 344. USNARA.
122 Ibid.
123 Letter from to J.A. Thomson Esq "Nuclear Suppliers Cooperation: the French attitude", 7 July 1975. FCO 66 /754, BSA.
124 "Ottawa TELNO 552: Nuclear Suppliers Meeting", 14 September 1977. FCO 66/914, Nuclear Suppliers Group: Policy. BSA.
125 See for example, Muller, H. "Falling into line? France and the NPT", Programme for promoting nuclear non-proliferation, Occasional Paper No 6, Centre for International Policy Studies, Department of Politics, University of Southampton May 1990.
126 Transcript: "Debate with President Gerard Ford (Foreign and Defense Issues) (October 6 1976) Jimmy Carter".
127 "Next steps in White House Nuclear Policy Review", memorandum from Winston Lord to the Deputy Secretary. 18/08/1976. RG59 Box 344, Policy planning council, policy planning staff, director's files (Winston Lord), General Records of the Department of State. USNARA.
128 Some have argued that this whole period was a 'lost period' in relation to non-proliferation. See for example, Cameron J., and Rabinowitz, Or., 'Eight lost years? Nixon, Ford, Kissinger and the non-proliferation regime, 1969–1977', *Journal of Strategic Studies*, 05 January 2016. pp. 839–866. doi: https://doi.org/10.1080/01402390.2015.1101682.
129 Brown, W.L., 'Presidential leadership and U.S. nonproliferation policy' *Presidential Studies Quarterly*, vol. 24, no. 3, 1994, pp. 563–575. doi: www.jstor.org/stable/27551284.
130 Burr, W., 'A scheme of control: The United States and the origins of the Nuclear Suppliers Group, 1974–1976', *The International History Review*, 20 January 2014, pp. 252–276. doi: https://doi.org/10.1080/07075332.2013.864690.
131 Ibid., Brown, W.L., 'Presidential leadership and U.S. nonproliferation policy'. www.jstor.org/stable/27551284.
132 Ibid., Burr, 'A scheme of control'.
133 Tiseo, A., 'The Carter Administration and its non-proliferation Policies: the road to INFCE', Humana Mente, *Journal of Philosophical Studies*, 16, 2011, pp. 60–64.

134 Ibid.
135 Cross, F.B., and Smith, C.V., 'The Reagan administration's non-proliferation policy', *Catholic University Law Review*, vol. 33, no. 3, Spring, 1984.
136 Smith, G., and Rathjens, G.W., 'Reassessing nuclear non-proliferation policy', *Foreign Affairs*, 1 March 1981.
137 Ibid., Tiseo.
138 Cross, F.B., and Smith, C.V., 'The Reagan administration's non-proliferation policy', Catholic *University Law Review*, vol. 33, no. 3 Spring, 1984.
139 Ibid., Smith, *Disarming Diplomat*, p. 201.
140 Ibid., Burr 'A scheme of control'.
141 Ibid., Brown 'Presidential Leadership'.
142 Smith, G., and Rathjens, G.W., 'Reassessing nuclear non-proliferation policy', *Foreign Affairs*, Spring 1981.
143 Ibid.
144 Ibid., Brown 'Presidential Leadership'.
145 "Nuclear Suppliers Meeting On 20/21 September", FCO 66/914, Nuclear Suppliers Group: Policy. BSA.
146 Strulak, T., 'The Nuclear Suppliers Group', *The Nonproliferation Review*, Fall 1993.
147 Interview with Joseph Nye Jr., 1 April 2015.
148 NLC-43-13-16-1-2 "Memorandum of Conversation", 10 July 1980 Paris, JCPL.
149 Ronald Reagan said this during the campaign before aids called an impromptu press conference to clarify the candidate's views. See: "Nonproliferation debate: Carter hit hard, but did Reagan miss opportunity?" *The Christian Science Monitor*, 30 October 1980.
150 Recommendation for the Reagan administration: Non-proliferation policy. Non-proliferation Coordinating Committee. Boggs, Danny J; Files – OA 11475, 11476 (Box 47). RRPL.
151 NSDD 39: US Policy on Foreign Reprocessing and Use of Plutonium Subject to US Control. 4 June 1982.
152 Soffer to Ating Secretary, 'Pakistan Certification Requirement in Section 620 (e) of the Foreign Assistance Act', 18 October 1985, Box 91880, Tahir-Kheli, Shirin Files, RRPL.
153 NSDD 144: US Policy towards the Iran–Iraq War. 26 November 1983.
154 While it could be argued that other states also turned a blind eye to Pakistan's programmes, the continued issuing of presidential waivers to allow the continuation of aid to the Mudahadin to aid their fight against the Soviets in Afghanistan assign particular responsibility to the United States.
155 'Pakistan's Nuclear Weapons Program: Personnel and Organizations', Directorate of Intelligence, November 1985, as found in GWDSNA.
156 FCO 096/952, 'Pakistan Cooperation, Agreement of cooperation between the government of the United States of America and the Government of Pakistan', 5 March 1959, FCO Files, BSA.
157 PARR-1 was supplied under a trilateral safeguards agreement between the US, Pakistan and the IAEA. This agreement applied only to the reactor supplied by the US. In 1965, the IAEA concluded the model bilateral safeguards agreement for non-NPT states which was published as INFCIRC 66, which Pakistan subsequently agreed with the Agency. INFCIRC 66 provides for the safeguarding

of reactors supplied by international partners. INFCIRC 66 was updated after the NPT came into force but without changing its underpinning characteristics. NFCIRC/66/Rev.1, IAEA, 12/09/1967.

158 Ibid., Rehmanm, *Long road to Chagai*, Ebook Location 586.

159 Ibid.

160 Koch, A., and Topping, J., 'Pakistan's Nuclear Weapons Program: A Status Report', *The Non-proliferation Review*, Spring/Summer 1997. https://doi.org/10.1080/10736709708436685.

161 The Chinese test was not likely to be perceived as a direct threat to Pakistan as China and Pakistan shared significant common interests. However, Pakistan doubtless feared that India would follow China's lead.

162 As read in Levy, A., and Scott-Clark, C., *Deception: Pakistan, the United States, and the secret trade in nuclear weapons*, Walker & Company, New York, 2007, p. 18.

163 Ibid., See Levy A., and Scott-Clark, C., *Deception*, p. 60.

164 Ibid., Rehmanm, *Long road to Chagai*, Location 622.

165 Ibid., Khan, F.H., *Eating grass*, p. 54.

166 It is possible that Canada's negotiators were obfuscating their desire for Pakistan to accept stricter safeguards knowing that Pakistan could not afford the higher price offered for an unsafeguarded reactor.

167 As read in ibid., Khan, F.H., *Eating grass*, p. 55.

168 Ibid.

169 INFCIRC 135, IAEA, 13 November 1969.

170 Ibid., Khan, F.H., *Eating grass*, p. 70.

171 Ibid.

172 Chaudhri, M.A., 'Pakistan's Nuclear History: Separating myth from reality', *Defence Journal*, May 2006, vol. 9, no. 10.

173 Rehmanm, *Long road to Chagai*, Ebook location 967.

174 Summarising a JIC report on the Pakistani nuclear program, R. Alston, for example, comments, "Pakistan appears to have accelerated her programme of overseas purchases to lessen the risk of facing delays as a result of any embargo that may be imposed by key foreign supplier countries". FCO96/949.101, R. Alston, Joint Nuclear Unit, "Pakistan: Nuclear Weapons Development", 1 March 1979, FCO Files, BSA.

175 Chaudhri, M.A., 'Pakistan's nuclear history: Separating myth from reality', *Defence Journal*, May 2006, vol. 9, no. 10 and Khan, F., *Eating Grass*, p. 82.

176 Mian, Z., Nayyar, H., and Rajaraman, R., 'Exploring Uranium Resource Constraints on Fissile Material Production in Pakistan', *Science and Global Security*, no. 17, 2009, pp. 77–108. https://doi.org/10.1080/08929880902975834.

177 "Nuclear Safeguards – Pakistan, South Africa, China", Memo from Cyrus Vance to the Assistant to the President for National Security Affairs, Department of State, 14 July 1977.

178 Hibbs, M., 'US repeatedly warned Germany on Nuclear Exports to Pakistan', *Nuclear Fuel*, 6 March 1989.

179 Chaudhri, M.A., 'Pakistan's Nuclear History: Separating myth from reality', *Defence Journal*, May 2006, vol. 9, no. 10.

180 For details of PARR-1, see IAEA's Research Reactors Database.

181 For details of PARR-2, see IAEA Research Reactor Database.

182 Koch, A., and Topping, J., 'Pakistan's Nuclear Weapons Program: A Status Report', The *Non-proliferation Review*, Spring/Summer 1997. https://doi.org/10.1080/10736709708436685.
183 See KANUPP (Karachi Nuclear Power Plant), IAEA Power Reactor Information System.
184 Ibid.
185 Ibid., Khan, F.H., *Eating grass*, p. 194.
186 Department of State internal paper: "The Pakistani Nuclear Program", 23 June 1983, GWDNSA.
187 Ibid., Khan, F.H., *Eating grass*, p. 194.
188 Ibid.
189 Memo from Hans Heymann, Jr to the Director of Central Intelligence, DC6 December 1982.
190 Hibbs, M., 'U.S. Repeatedly Warned Germany on Nuclear Exports to Pakistan', *Nuclear fuel*, 29 May 1989.
191 This may have been the procurement of 990 kg of heavy water facilitated by Butt, which was slightly below the 1000 kg threshold that would trigger a safeguards requirement. Ibid., Rehmanm, *Long road to Chagai*, Ebook location 1393.
192 Interview with Mark Hibbs, 24 February 2018.
193 Khan, M.A., "How Pakistan Made Nuclear Fuel", The Nation, 7 February 1998, as read in ibid., Khan, F.H., *Eating grass*, p. 105.
194 Mian, Z., 'Some issues associated with Pakistan's Karachi Nuclear Power Plant (KANUPP)', Sustainable Development Policy Institute (SDPI), Working Paper Series # 51 2000.
195 FCO96/1105.134 'Pakistan Nuclear', Letter from M.T. Jones to R J Alston, Joint Nuclear Dept, 16 April 1980.
196 Ibid.
197 'Five charged in Germany export case', *Nuclear Fuel*, vol. 15, no. 3, 5 February 1990, p. 9.
198 'Report on Diplomatic Actions Taken Concerning Foreign, Nuclear-related Supplies to Pakistan', Memorandum from Richard L. Williamson (Arms Control and Disarmament Agency) to Chairman, Joint Atomic Energy Intelligence Committee's Working Group on Nuclear Non-proliferation, 14 August 1981.
199 Hibbs, M., "Official confirms Pakistan will develop indigenous fuel cycle for its reactors", *Nuclear Fuel*, 30 June 1999.
200 Hibbs, M., 'Prosecutors link tritium plant to Pakistan weapons program', *Nuclear Fuel*, 1 May 1989.
201 Ibid., Malik, *Dr A.Q. Khan and the Islamic Atomic Bomb*, p. 185.
202 Niazi, M.K., 'Aur Line Kat Gayee', Chapter 9: Unknown factors about the reprocessing plant, Pakistan, 1987, as read in Adrian Levy and Catherine Scott-Clark, *Deception: Pakistan, the United States, and the secret trade in nuclear weapons*, Walker & Company, New York, 2007, p. 46.
203 Ibid., Rehmanm, *Long road to Chagai*, Ebook location 770.
204 Letter from P.J. Weston to R.J. Alston Esq, Joint Nuclear Unit, 'Pakistan Nuclear Developments', 22 December 1978.
205 In 1978, Zia had told American officials that he was "doubtful that the organisation could play a useful role", so it is unclear how effective use of CENTO as a bargaining chip in negotiations could have been. American Embassy, Islamabad

to Secretary of State, "Ambassador's talks with Gen Zia", cable ref 050740Z, 05 September 1978.

206 See for example, Department of State Cable 235372 "Congressional Consultations on Pakistan", September 1978.

207 Ibid., Rehmanm, *Long road to Chagai*, Ebook location 789.

208 Department of State internal paper: 'The Pakistani Nuclear Program', 23 June 1983, GWDSNA.

209 Ibid.

210 Ibid.

211 Ibid.

212 Cyrus Vance to The Assistant to the President for National Security Affairs, "Nuclear Safeguards – Pakistan, South Africa, China, 14 July 1977, Winston Lord Files, USNARA.

213 "A review of the evidence of Chinese involvement in Pakistan's nuclear weapons programme", Central Intelligence Agency, Office of Political Analysis, 7 December 1979.

214 Memo from Deputy Director for National Foreign Assessment to Chistine Dodson, Staff Secretary, National Security Council, "A review of the evidence of Chinese involvement in Pakistan's Nuclear Weapons Program", 7 December 1979.

215 General Walter Vernon of the US National Security Office is reported to have confronted President Zia with a copy of the design during a visit to Islamabad in 1985. Ibid., Rehmanm, *Long road to Chagai,* Ebook location 112.

216 Ibid., See Levy A., and Scott-Clark, C., *Deception*, p. 61.

217 Chaudhri, M.A., 'Pakistan's Nuclear History: Separating myth from reality', *Defence Journal*, May 2006, vol. 9, no. 10.

218 See for example, 'Talking points for Secretary Baldridge: Nuclear Cooperation Agreement Negotiations', 1 November 1984.

219 Memorandum from Assistant Secretary of State for East Asian and Pacific Affairs Paul Wolfowitz to Deputy Secretary of State Kenneth Dam, "The Secretary's Meeting with Premier Zhao - Nuclear Cooperation", 10 January 1984, with attachments, Secret Source: State Department FOIA release. Digital National Security Archives.

220 US Embassy China cable 00644 to State Department, "Premier Zhao's Statement on Non-Proliferation Published in Beijing", 12 January 1984, Confidential Source: State Department FOIA Release.

221 Cryptically, a US cable reporting this statement has a handwritten note added to it stating: "this is not precisely what he said" without providing further details.

222 Chaudhri, M.A., 'Pakistan's Nuclear History: Separating myth from reality', *Defence Journal*, May 2006, vol. 9, no. 10 and ibid., Khan, F.H., *Eating grass*, p. 82.

223 Ibid., Khan, F.H., *Eating grass*, p. 82.

224 Levy A., and Scott-Clark, C., *Deception*, p. 26.

225 FCO 96/1077, 'The Khan Affair', Report of the Inter-ministerial working part responsible for investigation "the Khan Affair", October 1979, FCO Files, BSA.

226 "Visit of United States Gas Centrifuge Team to Germany", Position Paper, July 1960, US Atomic Energy Commission.

227 Ibid., Malik, *Dr A Q Khan and the Islamic Bomb*, p. 61.

228 Ibid., p. 62.

229 Ibid., p. 63.

230 Levy A., and Scott-Clark, C., *Deception,* p. 3.

231 According to David Albright, the P1 centrifuge is a near-direct copy of the German G1 centrifuge, the P2 is a near replica of the G2 centrifuge, and the P3 is a near replica of the G4 centrifuge. Ibid., Albright, 'Peddling Peril'.
232 Ibid., Levy A., and Scott-Clark, C., *Deception*, p. 35.
233 "Pakistan developed more powerful centrifuges", *Nuclear Fuel*, 29 January 2007.
234 A.Q. Khan, as quoted in, *Dr A.Q. Khan and the Islamic Atomic Bomb*, Hurmat Publication (PVT) Ltd, 1992, p. 77.
235 Ibid., pp. 74–75.
236 As read in Adrian Levy and Catherine Scott-Clark, *Deception*, p. 45.
237 FCO 37/2114, "Pakistan Inverters", Letter From R.J. Alston, Joint Nuclear Unit, to Mr Moberly, 12 December 1978, BSA.
238 Moberly, R.J. Alston, Joint Nuclear Unit, 'Pakistan Inverters', 12 December 1978, FCO Files, BSA.
239 FCO 96/1077, 'The Khan Affair', Report of the Inter-ministerial working part responsible for investigation "the Khan Affair", October 1979, FCO Files, BSA.
240 Letter from Douglas Hurd MP, Minister of State FCO to Cecil Parkinson MP, "Control of Nuclear Exports", 14 August 1979. FCO 96/949 'Nuclear Power Matters in Pakistan', BSA.
241 Ibid.
242 'Inverters for Pakistan', Letter from Secretary of State, 10 October 1978, FCO37/2114 part G (The nuclear policy of Pakistan), BSA.
243 Moberly, R.J. Alston, Joint Nuclear Unit, "Pakistan Inverters", 12 December 1978, FCO Files, BSA.
244 Letter from Cecil Parkinson to Mr Douglas Hurd CBE MP 'Control of Nuclear Exports'. 28 August 1979. FCO 96/949 'Nuclear Power Matters in Pakistan', BSA.
245 Ibid.
246 Cable: 'Inverters for Pakistan', October 1978 FCO37/2113 'The nuclear policy of Pakistan'. BSA.
247 Ibid.
248 Weissman, S., and Krosney, H., *The Islamic bomb*, Times Books, 1981, p. 216.
249 Letter from Cecil Parkinson, Department of Trae to Douglas Hurd, Minister of State, Foreign and Commonwealth Office, 28 August 1979. FCO 96/959: Nuclear Power Matters in Pakistan, BSA.
250 Kemp argues that inverters were not specific enough to allow the enrichment use to be concluded. Instead, he argues that it was procurement of a soft magnetic alloy that resulted in the US concluding that Pakistan was pursuing uranium enrichment. See Kemp, R.S., "The nonproliferation Emperor has no clothes: The gas centrifuge, supply-side controls, and the future of nuclear proliferation". *International Security*, vol. 38, no. 4, Spring, 2014, pp. 39–78.
251 Henny Khan (AQ Khan's wife) said in an interview that Khan had told her of their success on the 4 April (As read in Deception: Pakistan, the United States, and the secret trade in nuclear weapons, p. 51), but Zahid Malik in his book, "A.Q. Khan and the Islamic bomb" says it was 4th June.
252 "Scientist Affirms Pakistan Capable of Uranium Enrichment, Weapons Production", Nawa-I-Waqt, 10 February 1984, translated in JPRS-TND, 5 March 1984, p. 32 and as read in Spector, S., *Nuclear ambitions*, Westview Press, 1990.
253 Ibid., Khan, F.H., *Eating grass*, p. 157.
254 FCO 96/1105, Note from M.A. Pakenham to R J Alston covering US "Note Verbal on UK Nuclear Export Controls", 18 March 1980, FCO Files, BSA.

255 "Report on Diplomatic Actions Taken Concerning Foreign, Nuclear-related Supplies to Pakistan", Memorandum from Richard L. Williamson (Arms Control and Disarmament Agency) to Chairman, Joint Atomic Energy Intelligence Committee's Working Group on Nuclear Non-proliferation, 14 August 1981.
256 Ibid.
257 "Cranston Says India and Pakistan Are Preparing For Nuclear Testing", New York Times, 28 April 1981. Available online at: www.nytimes.com/1981/04/28/world/cranston-says-india-and-pakistan-are-preparing-for-nuclear-testing.html (Accessed 31 January 2019).
258 FCO 151/47, p. 95.
259 FCO 96/1331.
260 Halsey, M.D.K., "Aide Memoire, Centrifuge Export Controls", 2 July 1982.
261 Ibid.
262 FCO 151/47, BNA.
263 Ibid.
264 FCO 151/47 BNA p. 148.
265 Ibid.
266 Hibbs, M., 'Components for Pakistan were intended for high-enriched U', *Nuclear Fuel*, 18 May 1987.
267 Ibid.
268 Letter from A.Q. Khan to Aziz, As Read in Levy A., and Scott-Clark, C., *Deception*, p. 66.
269 'The Solarz Amendment', Pakistan, Nuclear Pervez Case (box 91880), Tahir-Kheli, Shirin R: files. RRPL.
270 For details of the case, see Burr, W, 'Pakistan's Illegal Nuclear Procurement Exposed in 1987', GWDNSA.
271 Telegram from US Embassy Islamabad to State Department 'The Pervez Case – Talk with the Foreign Secretary', 22 July 1987. Pakis, Nuclear Pervez Case (box 91880), Tahir-Kheli, Shirin R: files. RRPL.
272 Department of State internal paper: 'The Pakistani Nuclear Program', 23 June 1983, GWDSNA.
273 Dr. Zangger, as quoted in Weissman, S., and Krosney, H., *The Islamic bomb*, Times Books, 1981, p. 191.
274 Department of State internal paper: 'The Pakistani Nuclear Program', 23 June 1983, GWDNSA.
275 'U.S. repeatedly warned Germany on Nuclear Exports to Pakistan', 6 March 1989, *Nuclear Fuel*, NUF, vol. 14, no. 5, pp. 12, English, Copyright 1989 McGraw-Hill, Inc.
276 'West German non-proliferation policy could complicate Pakistan reactor sale', 5 March 1990, *Nuclear Fuel*, NUF, vol. 15, no. 5, p. 7, English, Copyright 1990 McGraw-Hill, Inc.

Bibliography

"A review of the evidence of Chinese involvement in Pakistan's nuclear weapons programme", Central Intelligence Agency, Office of Political Analysis, 7 December 1979.

AB 48/1061, BNA.

"ACDA Position Paper on Non-proliferation (U)", 15 January 1966. GWDNSA.

Albright, D. *Peddling peril: How the secret nuclear trade arms America's enemies*, Free Press, 2012.

American Embassy, Islamabad to Secretary of State, "Ambassador's talks with Gen Zia", cable ref 050740Z, 05 September 1978.

"Analytical Staff Meeting on Non-proliferation Strategy", Memo from Winston Lord to the Secretary, 31 July 1974, The Winston Lord Files, RG59, USNARA.

"Briefing for the Gilpatric Committee on Nuclear non-proliferation", 1 December 1964. GWDNSA.

"Adrian Fisher's Proposed Non-proliferation Treaty Language – Information Memorandum", 30 August 1966. GWDNSA. (217).

Beaufre, A. The sharing of nuclear responsibilities: A problem in need of solution. *International Affairs*, Royal Institute of International Affairs 1944, vol. 41, no. 3 1965, pp. 411–419. doi: 10.2307/2609803.

Brown, W.L. Presidential leadership and U.S. nonproliferation policy. *Presidential Studies Quarterly*, vol. 24, no. 3, 1994, pp. 563–575. www.jstor.org/stable/27551284.

Burns, E.L.M. The nonproliferation treaty: Its negotiation and prospects. *International Organization,* vol. 23, no. 4, 1969, pp. 788–807. www.jstor.org/stable/2705898.

Burr, W. A scheme of control: The United States and the origins of the nuclear suppliers group, 1974–1976, *The International History Review*, vol. 36, no. 2, 20 January 2014, pp. 252–276, doi: https://doi.org/10.1080/07075332.2013.864690.

Burr, W. 'Nixon's Trip to China', GWDSNA, 11 December 2003. Available online at: https://nsarchive2.gwu.edu/NSAEBB/NSAEBB106/ (Accessed 4 February 2018).

Burr, W. 'Pakistan's Illegal Nuclear Procurement Exposed in 1987', GWDNSA.

Cable: 'Inverters for Pakistan', October 1978 FCO37/2113 'The nuclear policy of Pakistan'. BSA.

Cameron, J., & Rabinowitz, O. Eight lost years? Nixon, Ford, Kissinger and the non-proliferation regime, 1969–1977. *Journal of Strategic Studies*, vol. 40, no. 6, 05 January 2016, pp. 839–866. doi: https://doi.org/10.1080/01402390.2015.1101682.

Chaudhri, M.A. Pakistan's nuclear history: Separating myth from reality. *Defence Journal*, vol. 9, no. 10, May 2006.

"Committee on nuclear proliferation minutes of discussion: Second meeting" 13–14 December 1964, Roswell Gilpatric Papers, President's Taskforce on non-proliferation, correspondence October 1965–March 1967, JFKPL (2120).

Community Discussions of NPT Verification Arrangements, 9 May 1969, Euratom – IAEA Safeguards (NPT), General Records of the Department of State. USNARA.

"Cranston Says India and Pakistan Are Preparing For Nuclear Testing", New York Times, 28 April 1981. Available online at: www.nytimes.com/1981/04/28/world/cranston-says-india-and-pakistan-are-preparing-for-nuclear-testing.html (Accessed 31 January 2019).

Cross, F.B., & Smith, C.V. The Reagan administration's non-proliferation policy. *Catholic University Law Review*, vol. 33, no. 3, Spring 1984.

Cyrus Vance to The Assistant to the President for National Security Affairs, "Nuclear Safeguards – Pakistan, South Africa, China, 14 July 1977", Winston Lord Files, USNARA.

"Debate with President Gerard Ford (Foreign and Defense Issues) (6 October 1976) Jimmy Carter".

Department of State Cable 235372 "Congressional Consultations on Pakistan", September 1978.

Department of State internal paper: 'The Pakistani Nuclear Program', 23 June 1983, GWDSNA.

Dr A.Q. Khan and the Islamic Atomic Bomb, Hurmat Publication (PVT) Ltd, 1992.

FCO 37/2114, "Pakistan Inverters", Letter From R.J. Alston, Joint Nuclear Unit, to Mr. Moberly, 12 December 1978, BSA.

FCO 66/751 (United States Proposal for Common Nuclear Export Policies): FCO telegram from Ottawa to Canberra, 13 February 1975, BNA.

FCO66/844: Nuclear Suppliers: 3–4 June 1976, BNA.

FCO 66/949.168 Nuclear Power Matters in Pakistan: Pakistan Nuclear Weapons Development, BNA.

FCO 096/952, 'Pakistan Cooperation, Agreement of cooperation between the government of the United States of America and the Government of Pakistan', 5 March 1959, FCO Files, BSA.

FCO96/991 (non-proliferation grey areas) "Zangger committee: Items for the trigger list". BNA.

FCO96/1105.134 'Pakistan Nuclear', Letter from M.T. Jones to R.J. Alston, Joint Nuclear Dept., 16 April 1980.

FCO 96/1105, Note from M.A. Pakenham to R.J. Alston covering US "Note Verbal on UK Nuclear Export Controls", 18 March 1980, FCO Files, BSA.

FCO 96/1077, 'The Khan Affair', Report of the Inter-ministerial working part responsible for investigation "the Khan Affair", October 1979, FCO Files, BSA.

Fischer, D., History of the International Atomic Energy Agency the first forty years, International Atomic Energy Agency.

Five charged in Germany export case. *Nuclear Fuel*, vol. 15, no. 3, p. 9, 5 February 1990.

"France will sign 1968 nuclear pact", *New York Times*, 4 June 1991.

Frank Aiken and Irish activism at the United Nations, 1957–61. *The International History Review*, vol. 6, no. 2, May 1984, pp. 210–231. www.jstor.org/stable/40105371.

Gilpatric Committee report "A report to the President by the committee on nuclear proliferation", 21 January 1965.

Günter, B., Stefan, K., & Peter R. The Prague Spring and the Warsaw Pact Invasion of Czechoslovakia in 1968 annex 9: Secretary of Defense staff meeting, 26 August 1968, p. 474. 2010.

Halsey, M.D.K. "Aide Memoire, Centrifuge Export Controls", 2 July 1982.

Hibbs, M. Components for Pakistan were intended for high-enriched U. *Nuclear Fuel*, 18 May 1987.

Hibbs, M. Official confirms Pakistan will develop indigenous fuel cycle for its reactors. *Nuclear Fuel*, 30 June 1999.

Hibbs, M. Prosecutors link tritium plant to Pakistan weapons program. *Nuclear Fuel*, 1 May 1989.

Hibbs, M. US repeatedly warned Germany on nuclear exports to Pakistan. *Nuclear Fuel*, 6 March 1989.

Howlett, D. *EURATOM and nuclear safeguards*, Macmillan. 1990. doi: 10.1007/978-1-349-10382-9.

Hunt, C. Multilateral Cooperation in Export Controls – the role of COCOM, *University of Toledo Law Review* 14, 1982–1983.

INFCIRC 135, IAEA, 13 November 1969.

'Inverters for Pakistan', Letter from Secretary of State, 10 October 1978, FCO37/2114 part G (The nuclear policy of Pakistan), BSA.

Jacobs, R. The bravo test and the death and life of the global ecosystem in the early anthropocene. *Asia Pacific Journal*, vol. 13, no. 29.1, 20 July 2015, pp. 1–17.

Kemp, R.S. The nonproliferation emperor has no clothes: The gas centrifuge, supply-side controls, and the future of nuclear proliferation. *International Security*, vol. 38, no. 4, Spring 2014, pp. 39–78.

Khan, F. *Eating grass: The making of the Pakistani bomb*. Stanford Security Studies, 7 November 2012.

Koch, A., & Topping, J. Pakistan's nuclear weapons program: A status report. *The Non-Proliferation Review*, Spring/Summer, 1997. doi: https://doi.org/10.1080/10736709708436685.

Letter from Alastair Gillespie to the Honourable A.J. MacEachen, 9 March 1976, Uranium export controls & nuclear safeguards – general – 1975–1976, File 260-14. LAC (8109).

Letter from John Tomlinson MP to Nigel Foreman Esq. MP. 30 November 1976. FCO 66/911, "Nuclear Suppliers Group Policy". BSA.

Letter to J.A. Thomson Esq. "Nuclear Suppliers Cooperation: the French attitude", 7 July 1975. FCO 66 /754, BSA.

Letter from Cecil Parkinson to Mr. Douglas Hurd CBE MP 'Control of Nuclear Exports'. 28 August 1979. FCO 96/949 'Nuclear Power Matters in Pakistan', BSA.

Letter from Cecil Parkinson, Department of Trae to Douglas Hurd, Minister of State, Foreign and Commonwealth Office, 28 August 1979. FCO 96/959: Nuclear Power Matters in Pakistan, BSA.

"Letter from Chet Helifield to the President of the United States", 3 October 1964. GWDSNA. (66).

Letter from Douglas Hurd MP, Minister of State FCO to Cecil Parkinson MP, "Control of Nuclear Exports", 14 August 1979. FCO 96/949 'Nuclear Power Matters in Pakistan', BSA.

Letter from P.J. Weston to R.J. Alston Esq, Joint Nuclear Unit, 'Pakistan Nuclear Developments', 22 December 1978.

Levy, A., & Scott-Clark, C. *Deception: Pakistan, the United States, and the secret trade in nuclear weapons*, Walker & Company, 2007.

Lewis, J., & Litai, X. *China builds the bomb*, Stanford University Press, 1988 Paper 380, The International Institute for Strategic Studies, 2006.

"Longer Term U.S. Enriched Uranium Supply Policy". The Winston Lord Files. Box 344. RG59, Department of State. USNARA.

Malik. *Dr. A.Q. Khan and the Islamic Atomic Bomb*, p. 185.

Meeting minutes entitled "non-proliferation", 9 July 1965, Nuclear Non-proliferation, Unpublished files, (box 7), GWNSA.

Memo from Deputy Director for National Foreign Assessment to Chistine Dodson, Staff Secretary, National Security Council, "A review of the evidence of Chinese involvement in Pakistan's Nuclear Weapons Program", 7 December 1979.

Memo from Hans, H. Jr., to the Director of Central Intelligence, "DC6" December 1982.

Memorandum from Assistant Secretary of State for East Asian and Pacific Affairs Paul Wolfowitz to Deputy Secretary of State Kenneth Dam, "The Secretary's Meeting with Premier Zhao – Nuclear Cooperation", 10 January 1984, with attachments, Secret Source: State Department FOIA release. Digital National Security Archives.

Memorandum for Members of the committee on non-proliferation, 30 December 1964, Subject: committee meeting – 7–8 January 1965, Roswell Gilpatric Personal Papers Box 010-010, JFKPL.

"Memorandum for Mr Gilpatric from Henry S. Rowen (Deputy Assistant Secretary): Comments on possible Antiproliferation actions", 7 January 1965, Roswell Gilpatric Personal Papers Box 010-010, JFKPL (2325).

"Memorandum for the Secretary of State: Status Report on the NPT Negotiations – information memorandum", William C. Foster, 11/10/69. Folder "Memos". USNARA.

"Memorandum to Cabinet – nuclear cooperation with India", 12 February 1975, Sale of nuclear reactor – India, Minister Energy Mines & Resources Canada, 252-2-1, LCA.

Mian, Z. 'Some issues associated with Pakistan's Karachi Nuclear Power Plant (KANUPP)', Sustainable Development Policy Institute (SDPI), Working Paper Series # 51 2000.

Mian, Z., Nayyar, H., & Rajaraman, R. Exploring Uranium resource constraints on fissile material production in Pakistan. *Science and Global Security*, vol. 17, no. 2–3, 2009, pp. 77–108. doi: https://doi.org/10.1080/08929880902975834.

Moberly, to Alston, R.J. Joint Nuclear Unit, "Pakistan Inverters", 12 December 1978, FCO Files, BSA.

Muller, H. 'Falling into line? France and the NPT', Programme for promoting nuclear non-proliferation, Occasional Paper No. 6, Centre for International Policy Studies, Department of Politics, University of Southampton. May 1990.

"National Security Action Memorandum No 320", 25 November 1964. Located in Roswell Gilpatric Personal Papers: President's Task Force on Nuclear Proliferation – correspondence April–September 1965 (2190), JFKPL.

National Security Study Memorandum 156: Indian Nuclear Development (Revised and Updated), 30 May 1974, Folder NSSM-156 [2 of 2], Box H-192, National Security Council Institution ("H") files, RRNL.

"Next steps in White House Nuclear Policy Review", memorandum from Winston Lord to the Deputy Secretary. 18/08/1976. RG59 Box 344, Policy planning council, policy planning staff, director's files (Winston Lord), General Records of the Department of State. USNARA.

NLC-43-13-16-1-2 "Memorandum of Conversation", 10 July 1980 Paris, JCPL.

"No Fuel for Tarapur", *The Washington Post*, 22 September 1980.

NSAM294, 20 April 1964, Roswell Gilpatric Personal Papers: President's Task Force on Nuclear Proliferation – correspondence April–September 1965 JFKPL (2123).

NSDD 39: US Policy on Foreign Reprocessing and Use of Plutonium Subject to US Control. 4 June 1982.

NSDD 144: US Policy towards the Iran-Iraq War. 26 November 1983.

NSM156, 5 July 1972.

"National Security Study Memorandum (NSSM) 202 on Nuclear Proliferation", 23 May 1974, History and Public Policy Program Digital Archive, Nixon Presidential Library, National Security Council Institutional Files, Study Memorandums (1969–1974), Box H-205. Obtained by Fundação Getúlio Vargas. doi: http://digitalarchive.wilsoncenter.org/document/115172.

Nonproliferation debate: Carter hit hard, but did Reagan miss opportunity? *The Christian Science Monitor*, 30 October 1980.

"Nuclear Energy Cooperation with Egypt and Israel", Winston Lord Files. RG59, Box 344, USNARA.

"Nuclear Export Policy Toward India", Alfred and Samuel to Kissinger, 26 December 1974, the Winston Lord Files, Department of State, USNARA.

"Nuclear Policy Review and Non-Proliferation Initiatives", Memo from Henry A. Kissinger to the President, 6 September 1976, the Winston Lord Files, RG59, USNARA.
"Nuclear Safeguards – Pakistan, South Africa, China", Memo from Cyrus Vance to the Assistant to the President for National Security Affairs, Department of State, 14 July 1977.
"Nuclear Safeguards for Indians", Memo from Winston Lord to the Secretary, 9 November 1974, The Winston Lord Files, Department of State, USNARA.
"Nuclear suppliers conference", memorandum from Helmut Sonnenfeldt to the secretary, 31 October 1975. TTB/PNE/NPT. Country and Subject Files, 1973–1976. RG0059, Department of State. Container 11. USNARA.
"Nuclear Suppliers Meeting on 20/21 September", FCO 66/914, Nuclear Suppliers Group: Policy. BSA.
Nye, J.S. Nonproliferation: A long-term strategy. *Foreign Affairs*, April 1978 www.foreignaffairs.com/articles/29147/joseph-s-nye/nonproliferation-a-long-term-strategy. www.jstor.org/stable/20039921.
Perkovich, G. *India's nuclear bomb: The impact on global proliferation*, University of California Press, February 2002.
"Ottawa TELNO 552: Nuclear Suppliers Meeting, 14 September 1977". FCO 66/914, Nuclear Suppliers Group: Policy. BSA.
"Pakistan: Nuclear Weapons Development", 1 March 1979, FCO Files, BSA.
'Pakistan's Nuclear Weapons Program: Personnel and Organizations', Directorate of Intelligence, November 1985, as found in GWDSNA.
Pakistan developed more powerful centrifuges. *Nuclear Fuel*, 29 January 2007.
"Principle (a)" of General Assembly Resolution 2028 (XX). UN General Assembly, New York, 1959.
"Probable result of French Nuclear Policy Review: memorandum from Winston Lord to Deputy Secretary", 9 October 1976, RG59 Box 344. USNARA.
"Recent nuclear developments in India", 18 January 1965, GWDNSA.
Recommendation for the Reagan administration: Non-proliferation policy. Non-proliferation Coordinating Committee. Boggs, Danny J; Files – OA 11475, 11476 (Box 47). RRPL.
Rehman, S.U. *Long road to Chagai*, Ebook Location 586.
'Report on Diplomatic Actions Taken Concerning Foreign, Nuclear-related Supplies to Pakistan', Memorandum from Richard L. Williamson (Arms Control and Disarmament Agency) to Chairman, Joint Atomic Energy Intelligence Committee's Working Group on Nuclear Non-proliferation, 14 August 1981.
Roswell Gilpatric Personal Papers: President's Task Force on Nuclear Proliferation – correspondence April–September 1965 JFKPL (2117).
Shaker, M.I. *The nuclear non-proliferation treaty: Origin and implementation – 1959–1979*. Volumes 1–3. Oceana Publications Inc., 1980.
"Senator Robert Kennedy's Statement on nuclear proliferation", 22 June 1965. GWDNSA.
Smith, G. *Disarming diplomat: The memoirs of ambassador Gerard C. Smith, arms control negotiator*, Madison Books, 1996.
Smith, G., & Rathjens, G.W. Reassessing nuclear non-proliferation policy. *Foreign Affairs*, 1 March 1981.
Soffer to Ating Secretary, 'Pakistan Certification Requirement in Section 620 (e) of the Foreign Assistance Act', 18 October 1985, Box 91880, Tahir-Kheli, Shirin Files, RRPL.

Spector, S. *Nuclear ambitions*. Westview Press, 1990.
Statement Discourse, Secretary of State for External Affairs, 22 December 1976, Uranium export controls & nuclear safeguards – general – 1975–1976, File 260-14. LAC (8062).
"Status Report on NPT Negotiations – Information Memorandum", William C. Foster, 10/11/1969. RG59, Office of European Affairs, box (2414). USNARA.
Strulak, T. The nuclear suppliers group. *The Non-Proliferation Review*, Fall, 1993.
"Study requested by NSSM 13", 1 March 1969, NSSM 13, Box H-134, NSC H-files, RNPL.
Summary of Conversation in Germany – 24–30 January 1966. GWDSNA. (1326).
'Talking points for Secretary Baldridge: Nuclear Cooperation Agreement Negotiations', 1 November 1984.
Telegram 04656 Rusk to New Delhi, Karachi, London, 12 January 1965. GWDSNA. (J5).
Telegram from US Embassy Islamabad to State Department 'The Pervez Case – Talk with the Foreign Secretary', 22 July 1987. Pakis, Nuclear Pervez Case (box 91880), Tahir-Kheli, Shirin R: files. RRPL.
Tiseo, A. The Carter administration and its non-proliferation policies: The road to INFCE. Humana mente. *Journal of Philosophical Studies*, 16, 2011, pp. 60–64.
'The Nixon Administration and the Indian Nuclear Program, 1972–1974', GWDSNA.
"The Pakistani Nuclear Program", 23 June 1983, GWDNSA.
'The Solarz Amendment', Pakis, Nuclear Pervez Case (box 91880), Tahir-Kheli, Shirin R: files. RRPL.
'UK Record of Seventh Nuclear Suppliers Meeting at Riverwalk House' on 28–29 April 1977, FCO 66/913 "Nuclear Suppliers Group Policy". BSA.
US Embassy China cable 00644 to State Department, "Premier Zhao's Statement on Non-Proliferation Published in Beijing", 12 January 1984, Confidential Source: State Department FOIA Release.
U.S. repeatedly warned Germany on nuclear exports to Pakistan. 6 March 1989, *Nuclear Fuel*, NUF, vol. 14, no. 5, pp. 12, English, Copyright 1989 McGraw-Hill, Inc.
"Visit of United States Gas Centrifuge Team to Germany", Position Paper, July 1960, US Atomic Energy Commission.
Weissman, S., & Krosney, H. *The Islamic bomb*, Times Books, 1981.
West German non-proliferation policy could complicate Pakistan reactor sale. 5 March 1990, *Nuclear Fuel*, NUF, Vol. 15, No. 5 p. 7, English, Copyright 1990 McGraw-Hill, Inc.
Zhihua, S., & Yafeng, X. *Between aid and restriction: Changing Soviet policies toward China's nuclear weapons program: 1954–1960*. Wilson Centre, 2012.

5 International nuclear trade controls after the Cold War

The end of the Cold War and the disintegration of the USSR had a significant impact on many aspects of international security, including the role of international nuclear trade controls. Following the Gulf War of 1990–1991, the shock of the discovery of Iraq's expansive nuclear programme by international inspectors produced significant impetus to improve controls but this effort was restrained by these underpinning structural factors. Despite President Bush's hopes for a new world order, the main argument of this chapter is that the end of the Cold War did not bring to a conclusion the non-proliferation collective action problem, which had less to do with a lack of consensus between the Superpowers than it had to do with hold over structural factors.

This chapter examines developments in the immediate post-Cold War context during the period from approximately 1990 to 2000. During this period, the UN Security Council responded to Iraq's invasion of Kuwait which paved the way for the US to address one of the legacies of the Cold War – Iraq's possession of Weapons of Mass Destruction (WMD). It was during this period that revelations about failed trade controls *vis-à-vis* Iraq in the 1980s came to light. This pushed the American policymaking community to place priority on improving international trade controls, which resulted in the reinvigoration of the Nuclear Suppliers Group (NSG) and adoption of the IAEA Additional Protocol.

The main argument of the chapter is that while non-proliferation controls in this period were considerably tightened as a result of the Iraqi revelations, the opportunity for expanded controls that was realised related more to *ad hoc* and voluntary measures than universal treaties. It is shown that there are a number of practical and political reasons for this, including the priority assigned to securing the future of the Nuclear Non-Proliferation Treaty (NPT), which was given higher priority than that given for enacting new universal measures in this period. As will be shown through the examination of the AQ Khan network in Chapter 6, the *ad hoc* approach taken in this period was suboptimal as proliferation networks were able to leverage countries outside of the control regime to facilitate their proliferation-related activities.

DOI: 10.4324/9781003194262-5

The chapter proceeds by examining the Iraq episode because it was a fundamental driver of the new emphasis placed on nuclear trade controls in the post-Cold War period. It then considers the shock Iraq caused to governments working toward preventing proliferation and then examines the nature of the international policy response.

Non-proliferation and the end of the Cold War

Iraq had been quietly pursuing nuclear weapons for more than a decade when the case came to a head in late 1990 and early 1991 shortly after the end of the Cold War and the collapse of the Soviet Union. While concern about Iraq's intentions persisted beyond this period, it is the nuclear programme up to 1991 that is of interest to this chapter as it was revelations about Iraq in 1990 and 1991 that provided the 'shock' to the non-proliferation system that resulted in significant reform. While it is primarily Iraq's programme from Israel's destruction of the Osiraq reactor in 1981 onwards that is of greatest relevance to this chapter, it is useful to provide further context by briefly examining Iraq's nuclear programme before 1981. This pre-1981 examination highlights that Iraq pursued nuclear weapons as an NPT Non-Nuclear Weapons State party.

There remains debate about when exactly Iraq became interested in acquiring nuclear weapons. The lack of clarity is explained in part because Iraq underwent numerous changes of government in the second half of the 20th century. The monarch, King Faisal II, was overthrown in a military coup led by Abd-al-Karim Qasim and Abdul Salam Arif in 1958.

General Afir[1] then ousted Qasim in a coup in 1963.[2] A Bathist coup saw Ahmad Hasan al-Bakr become leader in 1968.[3] And Saddam Hussein succeeded Al-Bakr in 1979.[4] Braut-Hegghammer identifies the period 1973–1981 as the period in which Iraq's intentions were most ambiguous, while noting that one individual closely associated with the programme dated the aspiration to the early 1970s.[5,6] Nonetheless, any interest in nuclear weapons at this point would have been provisional as Iraq only had the IRT2000 reactor (later upgraded to 5000MW in 1978), which was not usable for plutonium production and which was subject to IAEA safeguards.[7] Whether Iraq had decided to pursue nuclear weapons or simply wished to achieve the capability to acquire them should a decision be taken to do so, Iraq pursued the plutonium route in the 1970s. This involved seeking to import reactors and reprocessing capabilities from outside the country. Iraq also sought uranium in raw and fabricated forms.

From the early 1970s, Iraq sought to procure a mid-sized research reactor from an international supplier. Iraq agreed a deal with France in 1976 during the period in which the NSG was meeting. Iraq had sought a heavy water reactor, but France opted instead to offer a pool-type research reactor, which was viewed as being less suited to plutonium production.[8] France believed this version to be proliferation-resistant for a variety of reasons. First, Iraq would have in its possession at any one time only around one weapon's-load of enriched uranium suitable for weapons use, and plutonium production would require dozens of cycles of fuel rod insertion and removal to extract this. Second, the reactor was to be subject to IAEA safeguards that should have detected the diversion of the fuel rods in good time for preventive action to be taken. Third, Iraq had signed a full-scope (comprehensive) safeguards agreement with the IAEA, meaning that all the country's declared nuclear facilities had to be subject to IAEA inspection.[9] Proliferation concerns were thus influencing French thinking on reactor sales in the mid-1970s.

Iraq had also sought to procure large quantities of uranium in the 1970s. This included 1,767 kg of uranium dioxide (UO_2) enriched to 2.6% from Italy in 1982, 4,006 kg of natural uranium from Italy in 1979 in the form of UO_2 powder and 508 kg of UO_2 as pressed pellets for use in its Experimental Research Laboratory for Fuel Fabrication (ERLFF)[10]; and also in 1979, 6,005 kg of depleted uranium as UO_2 powder. This procurement of depleted uranium fuel pins carried with it a significant proliferation risk as they would be particularly suited for use in plutonium production. The depleted uranium was to be supplied in the form of fuel pins which could be used in the Osiraq reactor.[11,12] Iraq also imported several hundred thousand tonnes of yellow cake from Niger, Brazil and Portugal, all countries outside of the NSG at the time, and thus not party to its informal rules in the period 1979–1982.[13]

While the majority of the uranium Iraq procured was subject to safeguards, the depleted uranium clandestinely formed into fuel pins was exempt from safeguards because of the reluctance of producer states to control this material as examined in previous chapters. Iraq may have intended to irradiate this material in the Osiraq reactor and then separate the plutonium from the irradiated fuel that would likely have been detected as a result of Iraq's safeguards.

Concern about Iraqi uranium imports outside of safeguards was compounded by Iraq's pursuit of a reprocessing capability. In the period 1976–1978, Iraq purchased hot cells and other equipment valued at several million dollars. Italy stated that its "London group" obligations had been met in relation to this transfer because Iraq had a full-scope safeguards agreement with the IAEA.[14] Matthew Fuhrmann argues that Italy's assistance to Iraq was motivated by its economic and oil interests.[15]

Given that many of Iraq's procurements were either covered by safeguards or acquired legitimately without safeguards, a key question that arises from Iraqi procurements in the 1970s is whether the IAEA safeguards measures in place were sufficient to ensure that Iraq could not acquire nuclear weapons. As a country that had brought into force the NPT, Iraq had concluded a full-scope safeguards agreement with the IAEA based upon INFCIRC 153.[16] In internal correspondence, British officials described the safeguards requirements as follows in 1981:

> In broad terms Iraq is required to place under IAEA safeguards all nuclear materials in every nuclear activity that it conducts. In the case of nuclear

> material of a composition and purity not suitable for fuel fabrication without further processing (e.g. yellow cake), Iraq is required to inform the IAEA about all imports and exports. All other nuclear material (natural and enriched uranium, plutonium) are subject to the full range of IAEA safeguards. All production of such material and every movement of such material (except very small quantities) must be recorded and reported to the IAEA). Well before such material is introduced into a new facility the IAEA must be given the information about the design of the facility that it needs to carry out effective safeguards.[17]

However, as Feldman has highlighted, there were numerous limitations and exceptions to the safeguards, which were, in effect, intended primarily to detect the diversion of declared material rather than to identify undeclared activities.[18] These limitations and exceptions included the lack of safeguards on imported yellow cake and lack of continuous monitoring of the Osiraq reactor, which could have allowed for the insertion of uranium "targets" for production of materials relevant to weapons production. Iraq also had the right to withdraw material from safeguards for a temporary purpose so that it could, for example, conduct experiments. Although the reactor was subject to IAEA safeguards, Israel would go on to claim that the facility could be used for the production of plutonium without the knowledge of the IAEA. Specific technical claims were made to support this supposition, but the Agency provided a rebuttal to its member states that was described as "fairly convincing" by British officials.[19]

While there may have been a number of reasons that Israel decided to strike the Osiraq reactor in 1981, the attack must be viewed as an expression of Israel's lack of confidence in the NPT and its associated system of IAEA-administered safeguards. This lack of confidence may have resulted from one of two concerns: either that safeguards were viewed as an ineffective instrument to detect and deter diversion and misuse, or that Iraq could withdraw from the NPT at a later date. Of course, no enforcement had been built into the NPT and the UN Security Council had not been active on the non-proliferation issue up to this point. Israel thus expressed the view that safeguards could not prevent the Osiraq reactor from being used to irradiate natural or depleted uranium. While Iraq may not have been able to use the Osiraq reactor for the production of material for nuclear weapons without withdrawing from the NPT, it may well have had aspirations to do so at some later date. That said, a US Defence Intelligence Agency (DIA) assessment of 1983 found "no identifiable nuclear weapons program in Iraq", although the DIA believed Iraq would "probably pursue nuclear weapons".[20,21] While this would be a violation of Iraq's NPT commitments, Iraq could and later would have developed parallel facilities that the safeguards architecture would be poorly suited to detecting. Ultimately, therefore, the Israeli strike may have set back Iraq's nuclear efforts. However, in the absence of a more robust safeguards regime, the strike would not prevent Iraq from pursuing nuclear weapons through clandestine means.

Iraq's programme post-Osiraq

From 1979 onwards, Iraq was increasingly viewed as a pariah state by Western governments, with Saddam Hussein's seizure of power leading to growing concerns about the country's future direction. The Tehran Embassy siege and hostage crises, combined with increased concerns about state-sponsored terrorism, resulted in President Carter declaring both Iran and Iraq to be state sponsors of terrorism pursuant to US law.[22] On 22 September 1980, Iraq launched an attack against Iran, sparking a war that would last eight years and bring the country to near financial ruin. During this time, WMD became a central pillar of Iraq's military action and of projected capabilities with Iraq using chemical weapons against both the Kurds and Iran during the 1980s.[23]

These factors, together with the destruction of Osiraq, meant that Iraq would have to re-evaluate its nuclear fuel cycle if its programme was to move forward. The most fundamental question was whether to continue pursuit of nuclear technology, and if so, whether to do it within our out-with the NPT. Not to do so would be viewed as a victory for Israel whereas simply replacing the reactors could result in Israel's continued use of force. Moreover, diplomatic favour was with Iraq following the Israeli strike and withdrawal from the NPT could give credence to the Israeli decision to conduct the strike.[24] In the end, Saddam opted for a middle ground: keeping Iraq in the NPT while quietly pursuing nuclear weapons through covert means. This gave Saddam considerable manoeuvring room. Saddam pressed France to supply another reactor while also calling for outside assistance from Arab states to acquire nuclear weapons.[25]

In search for a solution

Nuclear suppliers were reluctant to provide reactors to Iraq, particularly without substantial modification, to reduce proliferation risks. Saddam was able to utilise this reluctance to score diplomatic points with states in the non-aligned movement by highlighting that Iraq had a right to such technology under the NPT.[26] For example, from 1984, Iraq worked to develop and construct an indigenous 40MW heavy water moderated and cooled reactor. This project was pursued after it became apparent that France would not rebuild Osiraq.[27] However, the reactor design was never taken beyond theoretical studies, likely a result of Iraq's lack of indigenous know-how and technical capacity. While Iraq reprocessed the fuel of the IRT5000 reactor during the period 1988–1990 – which had been supplied by the Soviet Union in 1963 – in breach of its safeguards agreement with the IAEA as part of its nuclear weapons R&D plan, the reactor route proved impossible to pursue without international assistance.[28]

Despite Iraq's lack of progress in this field, it did make progress in developing an indigenous enrichment capability, pursuing diffusion, centrifuge, and, most successfully, electromagnetic isotope separation (EMIS) techniques.

Iraq's diffusion effort began in 1982 and, by 1985, Iraq saw some early progress, with Mahdi Obeidi, an Iraqi scientist, successfully creating a candidate material for the diffusion barrier made from aluminium oxide.[29,30] Iraq found, however, that acquisition of "compressors and diffusers of such varying specifications [as would be required in a] production-scale diffusion plant would be impossible for Iraq" simply because of the size of the undertaking and facilities that this would involve.[31] Iraqi officials also noted that, "even if [Iraq] could purchase and manufacture the massive amount of equipment needed, it would be nearly impossible to keep such a large-scale project secret from the eyes of the international community".[32] Diffusion was thus not pursued beyond laboratory-scale research and experimentation.[33]

Iraq commenced its gas centrifuge programme in 1987 with the aim of achieving a production rate of 10 kg of Highly Enriched Uranium (HEU) per year.[34] Lacking time and capability to start from scratch, Iraqi engineers searched the world for centrifuge designs. This included visiting US libraries in pursuit of unclassified but sensitive designs for the Zippe-type centrifuge. Documents related to these designs were eventually acquired but Iraq was unable to fully recreate the design because of a lack of access to relevant components and a lack of expertise.[35] Initially, Iraqi engineers were unable to produce most centrifuge components, in large part because of a lack of a capable industrial base. Iraq focused on developing subcritical single-cylinder designs rather than more complex supercritical designs that would comprise multiple cylinders "simply because there were more design details available for that machine".[36] In pursuit of further detailed designs and related expertise, Iraqi officials next approached European companies associated with centrifuge production. Major companies including MAN New Technology, a German firm which manufactured centrifuges for Urenco, were unwilling to provide the required access without official clearances – presumably having been alerted to the dangers by Khan's efforts – but ex-employees were accessible for hire as consultants.[37] Iraq also bought out Western firms to assist its nuclear program. One such firm, H&H, sent several such individuals to Iraq, some of whom purportedly arrived in Iraq with centrifuge designs in a briefcase and detailed knowledge of centrifuge production in exchange for around US$1m.[38,39,40] With the support of such individuals, Iraq learned to overcome rotor dynamics and bearing design issues, which are among the hardest engineering challenges associated with uranium enrichment.[41] Iraq became capable of manufacturing stationary components but had to seek to import rotary components from overseas. Iraq also sought production equipment, such as Computer Numerically Control machine tools.[42] Iraq needed to obtain grade 350 maraging steel for its centrifuge programme and approached European suppliers with a cover story related to making artillery tubes. In one case, 'Malik' – a middleman who evidently had suspicious about Iraq's true intentions for the material – facilitated the delivery of 100 tonnes of maraging steel from an unnamed British source for around US$7m.[43] Iraq also received flow-forming machines from H&H for flow forming of maraging steel rotors.[44]

Subsequent to the coalition's ejection of Iraqi forces from Kuwait in 1991 and the UN inspections that followed, it was revealed that H&H had supplied nine flow-forming machines to Iraq.[45] Three had been exported with licences from the German government for non-nuclear uses in Iraq.[46] Sometime before 1988, Iraq accepted an offer for the supply of carbon fibre rotors from Karl-Heinz Schaap, a former employee of MAN Technologien GmbH.[47] Schaab ran his own consulting company, Rosch GmbH, and was later convicted in absentia for providing designs to Iraq, but only received a suspended sentence.[48] Schaab is also thought to have sold to Iraq other centrifuge designs, including for the advanced TC-11 centrifuge.[49]

Through the provision of this technology, and many other procurements, by the end of 1989, Iraq had managed to develop a series of sub-critical centrifuge designs based on carbon fibre rotors. The procured components included 50 rotor centrifuges manufactured by German firm Rosch.[50] Iraqi officials also sought desublimers from German firm Interatom GmbH, which had also supplied URENCO.[51] Iraq bought quantities of samarium-cobalt – a specialist material used to produce centrifuge magnets – from the UK in 1990.[52] Inwako GmbH, Bonn, supplied Iraq about 125 AlNiCo ring magnets for top bearings.[53] Another firm, Technology Development Group Ltd based in London, also provided ring magnets to Iraq.[54] German firm Inwako was also thought to have supplied AlNiCo magnets for top bearing assemblies. Another German firm was thought to have supplied 240,000 dual-use ferritic magnets for manufacturing motor stators in centrifuges.[55]

Iraq built a workshop which was said to be capable of manufacturing up to 200 centrifuges per year, although by the time of its discovery, the facility was not producing centrifuges at scale.[56] A total of 22 Iraqi technicians also trained with Siemens in Germany to master the production of aluminium pipework for use in centrifuge cascades.[57] Iraq obtained an annealing furnace from Leybold.[58] Leybold also provided an electron beam furnace between 1979 and 1982.[59] VAT – the Swedish valve manufacturer that would become an infamous element of the AQ Khan network – may also have sold valves to Iraq.[60] Iraq bought a British-made mass spectrometer, from the firm, VG Elemental, which was a dual-use off-the-shelf item.[61] The item required a licence for export to Iraq, but none was sought.

By the time of the 1990–1991 Gulf War, Iraq's centrifuge programme remained in the development phase. Obeidi, the head of the programme, claimed, in a book written after the 2003 invasion, that Iraq succeeded in enriching a small amount of uranium in a single centrifuge in 1989.[62] Indeed, Iraq lacked the materials needed to construct even a small cascade, meaning that a crash programme to acquire nuclear weapons could not have relied on this route.

A final aspect of Iraq's interest in centrifuges was its contact with AQ Khan whose proliferation supply network is explored in Chapter 6. Iraqi documents suggest that Khan offered to sell Iraq centrifuge technologies in 1990 after the country's invasion of Kuwait.[63] The reason the deal did not go ahead is not entirely clear, but international scrutiny and concerns about the possibility of Khan's approach being a sting operation appeared to contribute to this outcome. Moreover, as mentioned above, Iraqi officials claim they had a functional centrifuge design and it was parts they needed at that time. Had Khan been in a position to provide functional centrifuges in a short period, it might have been possible for Iraq to acquire nuclear weapons before the Gulf War. The Khan network was not selling either completed nuclear weapons or even functioning centrifuge cascade. Instead, the Khan network was selling parts which could be manufactured before assembly into centrifuges and cascades. Even with Khan's designs, it would have taken Iraq a considerable time to manufacture centrifuges. The Khan network thus did not offer Iraq a quick route to the bomb.

A route to success? The calutron programme

From 1982, Iraq increasingly concentrated its enrichment efforts on EMIS.[64] The first phase concentrated on research and development using "R40" magnet separation chambers (half production scale). The second phase beginning in 1983 was devoted to development of R50 and R100 pre-production scale units as well as 1:5 scale model units. From 1985, one R50 and three R100 units were put into operation, with none of these units achieving more than 20% of design capacity. Design work for phase 3 was finalised in 1987, which would see the use of 70 R120 separators for 20% enrichment and 20R60 separators for production of HEU (93%), giving an HEU yield of 15 kg per year (around enough for one bomb). Installation and commissioning of the R120 separators at Al Tarmiya commenced in 1990, with eight being installed and under limited operation by the time of the 1990–1991 Gulf War.[65] Much of the EMIS equipment was buried at the Tuwaitha Fire Station to avoid detection and allow Iraq to re-establish its programme when circumstances allow before being uncovered by the inspectors.[66]

There are signs that much of the equipment that Iraq needed for the calutrons came from the international marketplace. The US believed that equipment procured as power supplies for induction welding equipment was used to power the calutrons.[67] The calutrons were not subject to export control and none of the archive materials examined in the course of this research suggested that controls existed on such technology. This suggested control on such technology were not discussed in the main export control and non-proliferation forums even though this was, in effect, a second world war technology.

Iraq's easy circumvention of controls

The fact that Iraq's programme advanced to the extent it did in secret while also procuring goods from the international marketplace raises important questions about the effectiveness of controls in this period. Iraq lacked the indigenous capability to produce most of the materials and equipment required for its programmes. As a result, Iraq needed to import much of this from international suppliers. Unlike Iraq's earlier procurement of nuclear reactors, reprocessing capabilities and uranium, many of Iraq's procurements after the destruction of Osiraq were not covered on the control lists of the NSG, which only covered a list of items 'specifically designed' for nuclear use at the time it stopped meeting in 1977. This was despite the fact that several countries had introduced controls on dual-use technologies in the late 1970s and over the course of the 1980s in response to Pakistan's attempts to acquire dual-use technologies for its enrichment programme, although the coverage of these was extremely limited, often only applying to Pakistan. Moreover, only a handful of countries had, as Chapter 4 highlighted, adopted the measures which meant Iraq could feasibly work around such controls.

The decision by Iraq to pursue a clandestine nuclear programme drove the need to establish elaborate procurement pathways through which to acquire goods. The goal was not necessarily to hide the entire effort, but instead to provide sufficient obfuscation to allow the majority of the transactions to succeed. To enable this, Iraq established a complicated network of entities and a number of procurement routes through which to acquire goods. This included dispersing the nuclear programme amongst Iraq's legitimate activities, including using its petrochemical programme as a cover.[68]

Iraq also utilised diplomatic missions for its illicit procurement actions, with one official claiming that more than US$10bn passed through a special bank account held by a diplomat of the Iraqi embassy in Germany, which resulted in "every major German company [being] at his beck and call, along with his network of black marketers, smugglers, and front companies".[69] The Iraqi ambassador to the UN complained "you guys in Baghdad seem to regard it as your personal purchasing and shipping headquarters".[70] Iraq also made extensive use of front companies to procure goods from innocent (or ignorant) suppliers or to evade intelligence agencies.[71] In some cases, the supplier companies appear to have known the true end-use of procured technologies.[72] Additionally, in some cases, as exemplified by H&H, Iraq appears to have bought out failing Western companies.[73] This allowed Iraqi officials to influence the decisions made by the company, including on whether to fulfil questionable orders.

The techniques utilised by Iraq bore similarities to those used by Khan's network to acquire technology for the Pakistani programme. As in the Pakistan case, there are signs that Western intelligence agencies were aware of the scale of Iraq's activities and network.[74] Indeed, many procurements were blocked, particularly towards the end of the period. For example, Iraq ordered, via Rosch, materials and equipment – including a filament winding machine – required to produce carbon fibre centrifuge rotors, although the shipment was blocked in 1990 by the adoption of sanctions. These goods in 1991 made it to Jordan via Singapore but did not make it to Iraq.[75] In 2000–2001, staff from this carbon fibre project would later contribute to Iraq's efforts to use carbon fibre in missile applications.[76] A shipment of centrifuge end-cap forgings, which appears to have been destined for Iraq's nuclear programme, was confiscated by customs at Frankfurt airport. Three Swiss firms – Schmiedemeccanica, Biasca and Schaeublin SA, Bevilard – were also put on trial for exporting end-caps to Iraq.[77] The trial, however, collapsed due to errors by the prosecutor.[78] US authorities seized 27 cases of valves from CVC Products Inc which were suitable for use in centrifuge enrichment.[79]

Given that many of Iraq's procurements involved German suppliers, questions arose of whether Germany's export controls were effective, and if not, why not? Mark Hibbs attributed the limitations of Germany's export controls in this period to a complex interplay of factors, including a powerful German industrial lobby which sought, with some success, to minimise the intrusiveness of controls; a legalistic approach to export which saw government and companies deem many questionable transfers legal; and a small number of unscrupulous businessmen who were willing to exploit the loopholes, and in some cases even break the law, for profit and related incentives.[80] Hibbs also noted that the embarrassment resulting from such cases, and from related foreign demarches, lead to the German foreign minister, with the blessing of the Chancellor, taking over responsibility for aspects of Germany's non-proliferation policy. This included a decision in the late 1980s by Germany to adopt a unilateral requirement for full-scope safeguards as a condition of supply for nuclear materials and equipment.[81] It can thus be concluded that the embarrassing cases of the 1980s led to the establishment of a non-proliferation norm in Germany's trade controls. This norm, in turn, overcame some of the inertia that had restricted implementation of effective controls even before the public revelations about Iraq's programme that would reinforce this approach among other suppliers.[82]

More broadly, within the Western community, there does appear to have been a trend toward turning a blind eye to Iraq's activities. That Western intelligence agencies had knowledge and were prepared to act to stop goods from reaching Iraq raises questions about why more shipments were not stopped. There appears to be no single answer to this question. A former intelligence official from the UK who described the two parallel networks maintained by Iraq stated, for example, that Iraq simply was not a priority for his agency in the late 1980s, when efforts were focused on the rapidly changing situation in the Soviet Union.[83] In many countries, the laws did not allow for the stopping of uncontrolled items (i.e., countries had no 'catch-all control'), and controls had not been extended to dual-use goods at this time. For commercial actors, the potential profit involved with supplying Iraq seems to have been a common driver. In some cases, including the UK arms to Iraq scandal, it is known that governments turned a blind eye to Iraqi procurement under pressure from firms with a minister in one case implicitly approving a company's plan to ship goods to Turkey in the knowledge they would end up in Iraq.[84]

In practice, Western policy had to carefully balance a number of issues. The US, for example, was concerned about the possibility of either Iraq or

Iran moving closer to the Soviet Union. The US also wished to see an end to rule of the Islamic Republic in Iran. Moreover, the US wanted to ensure the availability of Iranian and Gulf oil.[85] The net effect of these competing foreign policy interests was that the US was formally neutral on the Iran–Iraq war.[86] Despite this, the US did quietly provide some support to Iraq at key junctures and failed to take determined action against Iraq's use of chemical weapons.[87] The US was thus, in effect, willing to turn something of a blind eye to the activities of both countries in pursuit of its largest foreign policy goals.

The Iraq 'shock'

By the time of the 1990–1991 Gulf War, Iraq had made progress in its indigenous nuclear programme particularly through the EMIS route. However, this programme had not allowed Iraq to produce nuclear weapons and would soon be overtaken by events. Nonetheless, the public outing of the programme would provide major impetus to collective action *vis-a-vis* strengthening international controls.

After eight years of conflict, the Iraq–Iran war ended in August 1988 with a ceasefire enshrined in UNSCR 598.[88] The situation on the ground had been a near stalemate although Iran showed signs of making advances. The resources of both countries were dwindling. Primarily, as a result of the economic situation in Iraq, which had become desperate because of the war, Iraq invaded Kuwait on 2 August 1990 using long-standing territorial disputes in its narrative to justify the action. The Security Council promptly responded with the adoption of UNSCR 660, which demanded that Iraq withdraw military forces immediately. Four days later, sanctions were imposed under UNSCR 661 on 6 August, establishing a near total trade boycott on Iraq.[89] Iraq did not comply with these UN resolutions.[90,91] The end result was Operation Desert Storm which was launched on 17 January 1991 under the authority of UNSCR 678.[92] The US-lead UN coalition forces ejected Iraqi forces from Kuwait but did not proceed deep into Iraq to threaten the Saddam regime itself.

Desert Storm resulted in a much fuller discovery of the scale of Iraq's clandestine nuclear programme. The discovery led to the development of both Iraq-centric measures to reform international nuclear trade controls.

Iraq-centric measures

While the measures adopted by the UNSC *vis-a-vis* Iraq were largely beyond nuclear trade controls, it is useful to briefly examine the main provisions as the experience of adopting such measures would influence subsequent actions by the Security Council, including UNSCR 1540. UNSCR 687 of 8 April 1991 tasked the IAEA and established a new United Nations Special Commission (UNSCOM) with inspecting and supervising the destruction of Iraq's WMD capabilities. The resolution also placed restrictions on Iraq's ability to export oil and to import "dual-use" items.[93] The Security Council required Iraq to submit a full final and complete declaration of its WMD and missile programmes in order to aid inspectors in verifying their dismantlement, but from Iraq's first declaration on 18 April 1991, the country provided incomplete information. The Security Council continued to push Iraq to provide a full declaration, adopting resolution 707 in August 1991 for this purpose, a demand that Iraq continued to avoid. In late 1993, it appeared that Iraq was ready to respond fully to the UN's requirements after the Vice President sent a letter to the Security Council in which it was proposed that Iraq would cooperate more fully in exchange for a partial lifting of the oil embargo.[94,95] The adoption of UNSCR 986 did not mark the beginning of full transparency from Iraq, however. In the years that followed, the defection of Hussein Kamel al-Majid on 7 August 1995 lead to a string of further revelations about undisclosed activities.[96] Kamel was Saddam's son-in-law and had responsibilities for the country's WMD programmes. Further revelations also came to light from Jordan regarding Iraqi attempts to acquire missile guidance equipment, and from UNSCOM itself which found that Iraq had attempted to smuggle SCUD assemblies from Yemen.[97] While outside the scope of this book, it is notable that Iraq continued to obfuscate with inspectors until the 2003 invasion of the country. Despite the later allegations, there are no signs that the country resumed its nuclear weapons programme. It did, however, undertake prohibited missile activity.[98]

Reforming international nuclear trade controls post-Iraq

The discovery of the role played by Western companies in supplying Iraq's nuclear programme, together with the ongoing nature of the crisis, ensured that international attention to enhancing trade controls was sustained for several years. This attention was influenced further by the end of the Cold War and the rise in prominence of proliferation as a Western security concern. Moreover, as a NNWS party to the NPT, Iraq's nuclear programme stood out as a stark violation of the treaty and so robust action was needed in order to restore its credibility. These factors combined to drive substantial international efforts to tackle the challenge of enforcing effective controls on the spread of sensitive items. The primary initiatives here involved the increased involvement of the UNSC in non-proliferation matters, the resumption of NSG meetings and the reform of NSG guidelines to include dual-use items, and the creation of the IAEA's model Additional Protocol.

Nuclear Suppliers Group

The NSG became the focus of a concerted effort to improve international trade controls following the discovery of Iraq's programme. The first true meeting of the NSG since 1970s took place in 1991 in a much-changed international environment. During the NSG's meetings in 1992, 27 countries attended.[99] This included the original 15 members from the 1970s and an additional 12 countries that had informed the IAEA of their intent to adhere to the NSG guidelines.[100]

A key focus of the 1991–1992 meetings was the dual-use issue.[101] This occurred against the backdrop of large-scale illicit procurements by Iraq and Pakistan, and the removal of certain nuclear-related items from the COCOM list, which had disbanded in 1994 as a result of the end of the Cold War.[102] At its 1991 meeting, the NSG created a working group to draw up multilateral arrangements to control nuclear-related dual-use exports which met four times over a nine-month period to January 1992.[103] Consensus was reached by February 1992 ahead of the regime's 1992 plenary, which was the first meeting at which a public statement was issued.[104] The working group designed a separate but complementary NSG regime for dual-use items. Such was the proposed separateness of the dual-use regime from the NSG, that questions were raised about whether the same point of contact could act for both regimes, and whether the same membership rules would apply for both. By 1992, these questions resolved themselves through a *de facto* harmonisation of the two regimes under the auspices of the NSG.[105]

Records of the 1992 meetings, in particular, highlight the challenges associated with reaching agreement on dual-use items. While there was a recognised imperative to control dual-use items, there were also specific commercial and national interests that challenged the adoption of such controls. The UK Ministry of Defence, for example, was concerned that NSG members might apply the guidelines to transfers to nuclear weapons states as well as non-NPT states. This could have made it more difficult to procure items for the UK's nuclear weapons programme.[106] The UK, like other countries, was content with the outcome, however, and felt that it would not have been possible to go further than had been agreed. There are, nonetheless, signs that specific countries sought to protect domestic industries. For example, a UK official noted:

> Consensus was ultimately reached on a list of 65 dual-use items to which the regime will apply, and a number of potential additions to the existing INFCIRC 254. Computers is not amongst these. Agreement on machine tools, carbon fibre and nickel powder was only reached after discussions in the plenary. The outcome on machine tools is the best that could be achieved given the clear split of opinion but there is agreement to an early review of the parameters. The proposals to delete nickel powder were surprising and one we accepted with reservations. The outcome on these two items enabled consensus to be achieved on the inclusion of carbon fibre.[107]

The public statement of the meeting noted: "following a year of intensive negotiations, the participants adopted a comprehensive arrangement to control the export of these [dual-use] items. The arrangement, which consists of a set of guidelines and a list of some 65 items to be controlled, will be incorporated into the Nuclear Suppliers guidelines".[108]

At the meeting, participating states also agreed a common policy of "requiring the application of full-scope IAEA safeguards to all current and future nuclear activities as a necessary condition for all significant, new nuclear exports to non-nuclear weapon states" (i.e., full-scope safeguards as a condition of supply).[109] This decision must be examined in the context of the 1990s. Following the discovery of Iraq's nuclear weapons programme, a political consensus emerged around strengthening implementation of controls. For example, France joined the NPT as a NWS in 1991. France's decision came in the context of the discovery of Iraq's programme and a desire to launch new non-proliferation and disarmament initiatives, including initiatives focused on the Middle East. The holdover from the foreign policy of de Gaulle on the NPT made less sense in the post-Cold War era and could have been counterproductive for France as it would have undermined French credibility on disarmament issues in the eyes of other countries.[110]

Additionally, several important countries, including the US (through the Nuclear Non-Proliferation Act of 1978) and Germany, had anyway adopted a unilateral requirement for full-scope safeguards as a condition of supply as noted above. With France an NPT signatory, all NSG members were now parties to the NPT. It thus became easier for the NSG states to set a requirement of full-scope safeguards as a condition of supply without affecting trade with members of the group. As a result, British officials noted after the 1992 NSG meeting that:

> Although the majority of NSG members had already announced some form of full-scope safeguards, the terms varied and the implementation has been patchy. This agreement [for full scope safeguards as condition of supply] establishes a valuable common, and reasonably high, standard for future supply. Perhaps more importantly it marks a common public commitment [redacted], although with a concession to cover supplies to other [Commonwealth of Independent States] countries until they establish safeguards. [111,112]

This policy was later endorsed by the 1995 NPT review and extension conference.[113] At the NSG meeting in April 1992, several other important developments were agreed immediately. For example, Japan became the point of contact for administering controls on dual-use items.[114]

Strengthening safeguards

The Iraq episode also caused states and the IAEA secretariat to review safeguards, including as relevant to international nuclear trade controls. The Iraq case provided some diplomatic space for this. For example, at the 1990

NPT Review Conference, the committee reviewing Article III of the NPT made a number of recommendations. These included:[115]

- that the NPT parties consider further improvements in measures to prevent the diversion of nuclear technology and services;
- that states engaged in consultations to ensure appropriate coordination of their controls on the export of items, such as tritium, not identified in AIII.2 but still relevant to nuclear weapons proliferation and therefore the NPT as a whole; and
- that nuclear supplier states, as a necessary condition for the transfer of relevant nuclear suppliers to non-nuclear weapons states, the acceptance of safeguards on all of their current and future nuclear activities.

Following the Iraq revelations, the IAEA commenced a far-reaching effort to strengthen the system of IAEA safeguards in 1993 through a process known as 'programme 93+2'. Lessons learned from Iraq included:[116]

- the NPT, with associated INFCIRC 154 safeguards, was not enough to ensure Iraq's nuclear programme was peaceful in nature. There was a clear example of the 'loophole' in the NPT discussed in Chapter 4. Iraq had unsafeguarded nuclear activities in buildings directly next to safeguarded facilities to which the IAEA had no knowledge or right of access;
- as a result of this, exports to Iraq could have been used for safeguarded or unsafeguarded activities. At the time, the IAEA only tracked the transfer of fissile material;
- Iraq had assembled its uranium enrichment programme primarily through the acquisition of dual-use goods which were not subject to control; and
- the IAEA had no knowledge of dual-use goods exports to Iraq and no mandate to monitor trade or open source information.

The outcomes identified through this process focused on measures designed to improve the IAEA's ability to detect undeclared nuclear materials and activities in states with Comprehensive Safeguards Agreements (CSAs). Certain measures could be implemented under the IAEA's existing authority under CSA (e.g., the use of environmental sampling and satellite imagery). However, new powers were also identified that could not be enacted under CSAs. This included "access to other buildings on the site of a facility, and additional declarations from the State regarding nuclear-related research and development".[117] Importantly for this book, it also included a trade component. States with an AP provide trade data to the IAEA. The IAEA Broad of Governors approved a model "Additional Protocol" in 1997.[118,119]

The model AP includes provisions on broader information and broader access including:[120,121]

- information to the state's nuclear fuel cycle research and development activity;
- information on all parts of the state's nuclear fuel cycle from uranium mines to nuclear waste;
- information on the manufacturing and exporting of sensitive nuclear-related equipment and material;
- access to any building on a nuclear site at short notice;
- access to any state-declared location related to the nuclear fuel cycle; and
- access to any other locations for the collection of environmental samples.

Acceptance of such measures could have allowed the IAEA to reach its 'broader conclusion' (BC) that all nuclear activity in the country was peaceful in nature. One potential benefit of the BC was that suppliers could have more confidence that a state was not seeking nuclear weapons. There are signs that this benefit was seen in practice. Despite this, the fact that the Additional Protocol was not mandatory limited the trade benefit of concluding such a measure with the IAEA.[122]

It is notable that with the exception of the requirement for full-scope safeguards as a condition of supply, the initiatives to strengthen the non-proliferation regime were undertaken or enacted only by a limited number of countries: there was no broader consensus in the international community that existing or new non-proliferation measures should be universalised. While it might be expected, it is still notable that the changes to the controls were adopted by members of the NSG and not through an additional NPT, for example. It is also notable that the Additional Protocol was not a mandatory measure. Had international consensus around the need for a stronger non-proliferation regime existed, this might not have been the case. The NSG did not, and has still not, adopted the Additional Protocol as a condition of supply because of the views of Brazil and Argentina, which continue to resist this measure without progress being made on disarmament.[123] This raises the question of why there was not broader consensus for the adoption of stronger non-proliferation measures following the discovery of Iraq's programme, particularly given the relatively united front of the major powers. There appears to be no single answer to this question. However, there are a number of factors that point toward an answer. Hibbs noted, for example, that one important factor was the 1995 NPT Review Conference (Revcon) at which states were focused not on expanding controls but on achieving the extension of the NPT, which originally had a 25-year life.[124] Hibbs also noted other factors of relevance, including a concern about the IAEA's ability to rapidly expand its activity given its actions in Iraq and South Africa and its frozen safeguards budget.[125]

Findings and conclusions

The purpose of this chapter was to examine the evolution of non-proliferation controls from approximately 1990 to 2000. This was an important period for the evolution of non-proliferation controls. The discovery of the scale of Iraq's clandestine nuclear programme in 1991 was a substantial shock that provided major impetus to the improvement of international nuclear trade controls. While numerous measures were adopted that were intended to fill specific gaps in the non-proliferation trade control regime, an overall argument of this book is that the measures adopted in this period were sub-optimal as they were largely based on a voluntary rather than a universal basis. As Chapter 6 will examine, this approach specifically left open pathways for proliferation networks – such as the AQ Khan network – to spread proliferation-sensitive technologies to numerous countries. In this context, the purpose of this final section of this chapter is to briefly highlight insights gleaned through the research framework into the question of why controls evolved in a sub-optimal, *ad hoc* way in this period.

Findings

The Collective Action Problem (CAP) framework includes propositions related to core and structural factors, imperatives, and technological factors. Findings from examining these factors in this period are presented in turn.

Structural factors

- The number and types of actors involved: There are few signs that the increase in the number of states participating in the NSG made achieving consensus more difficult. For example, the increased number of states involved did not constrain NSG plenary decision-making in the 1991–1992 period.
- Heterogeneity of participations: The end of the Cold War increased homogeneity to a substantial degree in the 1990s by removing East–West tensions. The unipolarity that followed did not allow the US a free hand in dictating non-proliferation measures, however. In particular, non-aligned states resisted the US unipolarity, including with regard to non-proliferation measures such as the Additional Protocol.
- Whether benefits were fully shared: There was a dichotomy in benefits – or at least the perceived benefits – following the Cold War. For the US and European states, the benefit being sought was the objective of non-proliferation. For non-aligned states, however, the principal benefit being sought was disarmament. These priorities were increasingly incompatible.

At the same time, NPT states pressed to protect the benefit associated with NPT membership – that is, the right to engage in civil nuclear cooperation with other states. It was for this reason that the NSG's decision to require full-scope safeguards as a condition of supply was acceptable to the non-aligned states, who might otherwise have been expected to object to a policy of technology denial. Iraq had also used Israel's destruction of Osiraq to reinforce the point that non-nuclear weapons under the NPT had full rights to use atomic energy for peaceful purposes. Finally, the fact that the Additional Protocol was not mandatory limited its utility both from a trade and trade control perspective.

- Face-to-face communications: Such communications had an important and helpful effect in relation to international nuclear trade controls. Forums such as the NSG allowed for steady progress on implementation of non-proliferation controls. High-level face-to-face discussions in the NSG plenary, for example, overcame national reluctance to control some dual-use items such as machine tools even where there was reluctance on behalf of some officials to control such items.
- Information on past actions: Political embarrassment that had resulted from inadequate controls at the national level. This was a key driver in the improvements to non-proliferation controls that took place in the 1990s. Embarrassment at past actions also drove some states, including Germany, to take unilateral action to improve national controls. Finally, recognition of the importance of learning from past actions also drove the regularisation of meetings of the NSG.
- How actors are linked: Linkages in the international community were directly tied to the evolution and limitation of non-proliferation controls in this period. The closer alignment of the US, Russia, and the European states at the end of the Cold War allowed for progress on controls. At the same time, the non-alignment of certain countries was a barrier to broader (or even global) cooperation.

Core factors

- Normative: The discovery of Iraq's programme and the international furore which resulted was key to reinforcing the non-proliferation norm. By this point, the non-proliferation norm had become well established particularly among the main nuclear exporters' states. This was aided by the public disclosure of problematic transfers in countries such as Germany in the 1980s and 1990s and, ultimately, by the Iraq shock.
- Trust: While the renewed meetings of the NSG helped build trust among states in the 1990s, the question of trust appears to have been a secondary factor compared to the structural factors discussed above. States were willing to adopt controls on dual-use goods. If there was mistrust that states would implement commitments, US leadership in the NSG and the

non-proliferation imperative was sufficient to overcome these in the context of the Iraq shock.

- Technological change: There are few signs that technological advancement had a significant impact on the evolution of controls in this period. Indeed, the main proliferation pathways of Iraq related to older rather than newer technologies. It is unclear why EMIS was not controlled by export controls as the technology was not mentioned in relevant regime meetings. It is possible that officials simply did not understand the proliferation potential of the approach. Additionally, there was no concept of 'catchall controls' in this era, which could allow non-controlled items to be stopped if destined for use in nuclear weapons.[126]

Imperatives

In this period, all three imperatives, non-proliferation, disarmament, and peaceful uses, continued to be present. It appears that structural factors rather than core factors principally affected the balance between these imperatives over this period. The imperative of civil uses of nuclear energy required the NSG to balance non-proliferation and commercial interests particularly when controls were extended to dual-use items. This resulted in some items being left off the control lists.

- Non-proliferation: This imperative overtook other imperatives to some extent after Iraq allowing controls to be extended to dual-use items and full-scope safeguards to be required as a condition of supply. However, this imperative was not sufficient to overcome other imperatives to mandate conclusion of additional protocols for states developing civil nuclear programmes.
- Disarmament: This imperative took a back seat in this period but was still important. A lack of progress on disarmament and concern about the future of the NPT constrained NSG action on topics such as requiring the additional protocol as a condition of supply.

Overall, therefore, while the end of the Cold War and the Iraq shock led to improvements in aspects of nuclear trade control governance, the underlying structural limitations of the regime from atoms for peace continued to persist. Concentrated international action following a substantial shock was insufficient to overcome the non-proliferation trade control collective action problem, meaning that these structural factors persisted into the new millennium. As Chapter 6 illustrates, other proliferators would take advantage of the known limitations to the regime and trade controls.

Broader conclusions

The discovery of the scale of Iraq's clandestine nuclear programme in 1991 was a substantial shock that provided major impetus to the improvement of international nuclear trade controls. The improvements were substantial, with a new regime within the NSG being created to control dual-use items and additional measures adopted through the IAEA. Despite the progress that was made, the geographical adoption of controls was limited as the decision to require full-scope safeguards and to control dual-use goods in the context of the NSG meant that such controls only applied to those countries that were NSG participants. This gap in coverage would later be exploited by the AQ Khan network and is explored in Chapter 6. The 1990s drew to a close with known limitations to the international nuclear trade control regime persisting.

Notes

1 Iraq profile – timeline, BBC, 21 May 2018.
2 Ibid.
3 Ibid.
4 Ibid.
5 Ibid.
6 Braut-Hegghammer, M., 'Revisiting Osirak: Preventive Attacks and Nuclear Proliferation Risks', *International Security*, vol. 36, no. 1, Summer 2011, pp. 101–132. www.jstor.org/stable/41289690.
7 IAEA Iraq decommissioning project, "IRT5000 reactor".
8 For a discussion of the proliferation potential of the Osiraq reactor, see Vandenbroucke, L., The Israeli Strike Against OSIRAQ: the dynamics of fear and proliferation in the Middle East., Air University Review, September–October 1984.
9 See INFCIRC172, 22 February 1973; available online at www.iaea.org/Publications/Documents/Infcircs/Others/infcirc172.pdf.
10 S/1997/771, p. 25 annex 1 – The acquisition of weapons-usable nuclear material.
11 Evron, Y., *Israel's Nuclear Dilemma*, Cornell University Press: 1994. Ithaca, NY, as read in http://nuclearweaponarchive.org/Iraq/IraqRefs.html#Evron94.
12 Barnaby, F., *How Nuclear Weapons Spread*, Routledge, ISBN 0-415-076749, as read in http://nuclearweaponarchive.org/Iraq/IraqRefs.html#Evron94.
13 S/1997/779 Annex 1 – The acquisition of weapons-usable nuclear material.
14 FCO 96/1122.73 'Iraq's nuclear programme', Letter to RG Alston, Joint Nuclear Unit (FCO), from British Embassy, Rome. BNA.
15 Fuhrmann, M., Atomic Assistance: How 'Atoms for Peace' Programs Caused Nuclear Instability. Cornell University Press. www.jstor.org/stable/10.7591/j.cttn34vg.
16 INFCIRC 153 "The Structure and content of agreements between the Agency and States required in connection with the Treaty of the Non-proliferation of Nuclear Weapons", July 1972.
17 FCO 8/4179 – Iraq Nuclear Energy Part C: R.I.T. Cromartie to D K Haskell Esq, Nuclear Energy Dept: Safeguards and the Iraqi Nuclear Centre (31 December 1981), BNA.
18 Feldman, S., 'The Bombing of Osiraq-Revisited', *International Security*, vol. 7, no. 2, August 1982, pp. 114–142. doi: https://doi.org/10.2307/2538435.
19 FCO 8/4179 – Iraq nuclear energy Part C: R.I.T. Cromartie to D K Haskell Esq, Nuclear Energy Dept: Safeguards and the Iraqi Nuclear Centre (31 December 1981), BSA.

20 As read in 'The Iraq nuclear programme: Progress despite setbacks', Directorate of Intelligence, June 1983, available online in redacted from via GWDNSA: www.2.gwu.edu/~nsarchiv/NSAEBB/NSAEBB82/iraq19.pdf.
21 "Shaking Hands with Saddam Hussein: The U.S. Tilts towards Iraq, 1980–1984", National Security Achieve Electronic Briefing Book No. 82, GWDNSA, February 2009.
22 "State sponsor of terrorism" is a feature of numerous US laws, including the Export Control Act, (1940) Foreign Assistance Act, and Arms Export Control Act (1976), with Iraq first being designated in 1978. See US Federal Register via the National Achieves, available online at www.archives.gov/federal-register/ (accessed 14 June 2021).
23 See UNSCR 612 adopted 9 May 1998 following Secretary-General's report into the use of chemical weapons in the Iran–Iraq war.
24 The UN Security Council condemned Israel's actions in Security Council Resolution 487 and General Assembly Resolution 36/27.
25 As read in "The Iraq nuclear programme: Progress despite setbacks", Directorate of Intelligence, June 1983, available online in redacted from via GWDNSA: www.2.gwu.edu/~nsarchiv/NSAEBB/NSAEBB82/iraq19.pdf.
26 See for example, Muller, H., "Falling into line? France and the NPT", Programme for promoting nuclear non-proliferation, Occasional Paper No 6, Centre for International Policy Studies, Department of Politics, University of Southampton May 1990.
27 S/1997/779: The indigenous reactor – project 182, p. 53.
28 S/1997/779: The production and separation of plutonium, p. 53.
29 S/1997/779: Development of indigenous uranium enrichment capabilities – gaseous diffusion uranium enrichment, p. 35.
30 Other countries relied upon nickel powder for this barrier, but Iraq had no ability to manufacture the prerequisite nickel powder. Obeidi, M., *Bomb In My Garden*, p. 53.
31 Ibid.
32 Ibid.
33 S/1997/779: Development of indigenous uranium enrichment capabilities – gaseous diffusion uranium enrichment, p. 35.
34 Ibid., p. 38.
35 Source used in this section: Obeidi, M., *Bomb In My Garden*, p. 67.
36 S/1997/779, p. 9 para 24.
37 Ibid., Obeidi, M., *Bomb In My Garden*, p. 88.
38 S/1997/779:Development of indigenous uranium enrichment capabilities – gas centrifuge uranium enrichment, p. 39.
39 Source used in this section: Obeidi, M., *Bomb In My Garden*, p. 69.
40 Hibbs, M., 'Iraqi Centrifuges Incomplete On Eve of Serial Production', *Nucleonics Week*, vol. 33, no. 4, 23 January 1992.
41 S/1997/779:Development of indigenous uranium enrichment capabilities – gas centrifuge uranium enrichment, p. 38.
42 Ibid., p. 40.
43 Source used in this section: Obeidi, M., *Bomb In My Garden*, chapter 3.
44 S/1997/779: Development of indigenous uranium enrichment capabilities – gas centrifuge uranium enrichment, p. 41.

45 Comprehensive report of the special advisor to the DCI on Iraq's WMD, CIA, 30 September 2004, vol. 2.
46 Hibbs, M., 'Report Says Centrifuge Know-How May Have Been Transferred to Iraq', *Nuclear Fuel*, vol. 15, no. 22, 29 October 1990.
47 Hibbs, M., 'German Expert Wanted by Authorities for Giving Iraq Carbon Centrifuge Rotors', *Nuclear Fuel*, vol. 17, no. 23, 9 November 1992.
48 Hibbs, M., 'Ex-MAN Gas Centrifuge Expert Said Higher-Ups Helped Iraq'. *Nuclear Fuel*, vol. 23, no. 6, 23 March 1998.
49 Ibid.
50 S/1997/779: Development of indigenous uranium enrichment capabilities – gas centrifuge uranium enrichment, p. 40.
51 Hibbs, M., 'Iraq Sought UF6 Know-How in 1989', *Nuclear Fuel*, vol. 15, no. 26, 24 December 1990.
52 Hibbs, M., 'Iraqi Centrifuges Incomplete on Eve of Serial Production', *Nucleonics Week*, vol. 33, no. 4, 23 January 1992.
53 Ibid.
54 Hibbs, M., 'No Centrifuge Plant in Iraq, But Investigators Seek Know-How Source', *Nucleonics Week*, vol. 31, no. 42, 18 October 1990.
55 Hibbs, M., 'Iraqi Centrifuges Incomplete on Eve of Serial Production', *Nucleonics Week*, vol. 33, no. 4, 23 January 1992.
56 Hibbs, M., 'Iraqi-Made Centrifuge Rotors Didn't Work, Inspectors Told', *Nuclear Fuel*, vol. 16, no. 17, 19 August 1981.
57 Ibid., 1996.
58 Hibbs, M., 'Agencies Trace Some Iraqi URENCO Know-How to Pakistan Re-Export', *Nuclear Fuel*, vol. 32, no. 48, 28 November 1991.
59 Ibid., no. 48, 28 November 1991.
60 Hibbs, M., 'Second Iraqi Defector Led IAEA to Document Trove', *Nuclear Fuel*, vol. 32, no. 40, 3 October 1991.
61 Hibbs, M., 'Spectrometer Sought by Iran Is Dual-Use Off-The-Shelf Item', *Nuclear Fuel*, vol. 22, no. 18, 8 September 1997.
62 Obeidi, M., The Bomb in My Garden.
63 See Albright, D., and Corey, H., 'Documents Indicate A.Q. Khan Offered Nuclear Weapons Designs to Iraq in 1990: Did He Approach Other Countries?', February 2004, ISIS.
64 Albright, D., 'Iraq's Programs to Make Highly Enriched Uranium and Plutonium for Nuclear Weapons Prior to the Gulf War', 1997 updated in October 2001.
65 S/1997/779: Development of indigenous uranium enrichment capabilities – electromagnetic isotope separation, p. 35.
66 S/1997/779, p. 5.
67 Hibbs, M., 'U.S. Believes Iraq Has Built Magnetic Isotope Enrichment Plant', *Nucleonics Week*, vol. 32, no. 25, 20 June 1991.
68 The overarching name for Iraq's clandestine nuclear weapons related effort was Petrochemical Project3 (PC3). PC3 included at least a dozen "projects". "Projects Managed by the Iraqi Nuclear Weapons Program Known as PC-3", Federation of American Scientists Central Intelligence Agency Gulflink Collection, August 1991, www.fas.org.
69 Hamza, K., *Saddam's Bombmaker: The Terrifying Inside Story of the Iraqi Nuclear and Biological Weapons Agenda*, Scribner, 2000, p. 202.

70 Ibid.

71 For example, one official noted,

> At Atomic Energy we'd perfected that art of acquiring sensitive foreign technology by routing purchase orders through universities or ministries such as oil, industry, agriculture, and even health. I should have suspected that an even more secretive agency might use us for the same purpose. But to tell the truth, it didn't occur to me at the time. We were too busy scheming to use everybody else.
>
> Ibid., Hamza, *Saddam's Bombmaker*, p. 150

72 For example, Hamza noted,

> By early afternoon, Hamid reported that the Germans were eager to make the foundry sale [for purifying uranium] but that our cover story was a bust. In fact, he said, the Germans had burst out laughing when they heard the story about tungsten.
>
> (Hamza, K., 'Saddam's Bombmaker: The Terrifying Inside Story of the Iraqi Nuclear and Biological Weapons Agenda', Scribner, 2000, p. 209

73 Interview with former UK government official, 1 October 2014.

74 For example, one former official interviewed by the author stated that one Western intelligence agency had two organograms for Iraq's procurement networks: one covering the active network and one for the backup network. The same official also mentioned a list of Western firms that it was known had been acquired by Iraqi entities to support its nuclear program.

75 S/1997/779:Development of indigenous uranium enrichment capabilities – gas centrifuge uranium enrichment, p. 42.

76 Comprehensive report of the special advisor to the DCI on Iraq's WMD, CIA, 30 September 2004, vol. 2.

77 Hibbs, M., 'Trail of Iraqi Nuclear Commerce Leads To Two Swiss Companies', *Nucleonics Week*, vol. 31 no. 34, 23 August 1990.

78 Hibbs, M., "Swiss Drop Cases Against Firms Aiding Iraqi Centrifuge Effort', *Nucleonics Week*, Vol 13, No 17, 23 April 1992.

79 Hibbs, M., 'Customs Officials Say Iraq Is Shopping For Centrifuge U Enrichment Hardware', *Nuclear Fuel*, vol. 15, no. 17, 20 August 1990.

80 Interview with Mark Hibbs, 23 February 2018.

81 Ibid.

82 Hibbs noted the importance of a Bundestag investigation into German exports in achieving reform. Ironically, Hibbs noted that this investigation started almost accidently with an alleged transfer of fissile material from NUKAM to Pakistan, which, he believes, after talking to all the key persons involved, did not in fact take place. Interview with Mark Hibbs, 23 February 2018.

83 Interview with former UK government official, 1 October 2014.

84 Ibid.

85 See for example, Fortier and Teicher to McFarlane, *Memorandum: U.S Policy Toward Iran*, 11 June 1985.

86 Shaking Hands with Saddam Hussein: The U.S. Tilts toward Iraq, 1980–1984 National Security Archive Electronic Briefing Book No. 82 George Washington Digital National Security Archive.

87 Ibid.

88 UNSCR 598, United Nations Security Council, New York, 20 July 1987.

89 The resolution includes the following operational paragraph:

> Decides that all States shall not make available to the Government of Iraq or to any commercial, industrial or public utility undertaking in Iraq or Kuwait, any funds or any other financial or economic resources and shall prevent their nationals and any persons within their territories from removing from their territories or otherwise making available to that Government or to any such undertaking any such funds or resources and from remitting any other funds to persons or bodies within Iraq or Kuwait, except payments exclusively for strictly medical or humanitarian purposes and, in humanitarian circumstances, foodstuffs ...
>
> (Extract from UNSCR661)

90 The adoption of sanctions was a first for the international community and put to test the vision of collective security set out by Woodrow Wilson some 80 years before. Because the adoption of international sanctions was unprecedented, it is apparent that Saddam could not have predicted the effect that the sanctions would have on Iraq. Indeed, Iraq had been subject to restrictions since the country's designation as a state sponsor of terrorism in 1979, and during the Iran–Iraq war, restrictions had also been imposed. Saddam's experience of sanctions during the preceding decade would have influenced his expectations about the level of impact that the UN sanctions would have on Iraq.

91 While the need for military force to expel Iraqi forces from Kuwait highlights clearly that the adoption of UN resolutions (including on sanctions) alone were not enough to pursued Saddam to withdraw his forces, it is not clear that there was a collective expectation amongst policymakers that sanctions would cause this to happen; for example, US Secretary of State Baker stated: "no one can tell you that the sanctions alone will ever be able to impose a high enough cost on Saddam Hussein to get him to withdraw". As read in Hurst, S., The United States and Iraq Since 1979, Hegemony, Oil and War, Edinburgh University Press Ltd, 2009, pp. 75–77; doi: 10.3366/edinburgh/9780748627677.001.0001.

92 United Nations Security Council Resolution 678.

93 UNSCR 687, United Nations Security Council, New York, 8 April 1991.

94 Comprehensive report of the special advisor to the DCI on Iraq's WMD, CIA, 30 September 2004, vol. 1.

95 This was the foundation of what would become known as the oil for food programme, which was adopted by the Security Council through resolution 986 on 14 April 1995.

96 Ibid., 2004, p. 48.

97 Cordesman, A., *Iraq and the War of Sanctions: Convention Threats and Weapon of Mass Destruction*, p. 216.

98 In one significant case, acting on an intelligence tip, UN inspectors intercepted a shipment of 240 Russian-made gyroscopes and recovered hundreds of additional components from the Tigris River. Investigations revealed that the shipments were part of a massive procurement of advanced ballistic missile technologies from the programmes of the former Soviet Union which was commissioned by Iraqi officials. Orlov, V., and Potter, W., 'The Mystery of the Sunken Gyros', *The Bulletin of the Atomic Scientists*, vol. 54, no. 6, November/December 1998. Iraq

also attempted to purchase chemicals for use in propellants, including expressing interest in AZ-11 liquid propellant to be procured through Ukraine. Iraq, because of the embargo, could not acquire these chemicals openly. Comprehensive report of the special advisor to the DCI on Iraq's WMD, CIA, 30 September 2004: vol. 1, Regime Finance and Procurement – chapter 3.

99 The countries were as follows: Australia, Austria, Belgium, Bulgaria, Canada, Czech and Slovak, Denmark, Finland, France, Germany, Greece, Hungary, Ireland, Italy, Japan, Luxembourg, Netherlands, Norway, Poland, Portugal, Romania, Russia, Spain, Sweden, Switzerland, United Kingdom, and the United States of America. Press statement of nuclear suppliers meeting: meeting of states adhering to the nuclear suppliers guidelines, 3 April 1992.

100 US Department of State, "Briefing on Nuclear Suppliers Group", 9 June 1993, Honolulu, Hawaii. GWDSNA.

101 This section draws largely on files released to the author under the UK's Freedom of Information Act. NPN83/10, "Nuclear Suppliers Group (NSG) Dual-use exports, Part A and B. UK Foreign and Commonwealth Office".

102 Ibid.

103 Ibid.

104 Ibid.

105 Ibid.

106 Ibid.

107 Nunn to Smith, 21 January 1992, 'NSG working group on a multi-lateral regime for nuclear sensitive dual use goods: final meeting in Interlaken', 13–17 January 1992. NPN83/10, 'Nuclear Suppliers Group (NSG) Dual-use exports, Part A and B'. UK Foreign and Commonwealth Office.

108 "Press statement of nuclear suppliers meeting: meeting of states adhering to the nuclear suppliers guidelines", 3 April 1992.

109 Ibid.

110 "France will sign 1968 nuclear pact", *New York Times*, 4 June 1991.

111 Donnelly to Coluden, "Meeting of the Nuclear Suppliers' Group (NSG): Warsaw 31 March – 3 April", 6 April 1992. NPN83/10, "Nuclear Suppliers Group (NSG) Dual-use exports, Part A and B". UK Foreign and Commonwealth Office. BNA.

112 The redacted section likely relates to Russia. Questions arose in the NSG about whether to treaty the Former Soviet Union states with nuclear weapons as nuclear weapons states for the purpose of controls or whether to treat them as non-nuclear weapons states. It was decided to treat them as non-nuclear weapons states but with a temporary exception, particularly for safety-related items, until safeguards were in place. Ibid.

113 INFCIRC539/Rev 6: Communication received from the permanent mission of Argentina to the International Atomic Energy Agency on Behalf of the Participant governments of the Nuclear Suppliers Group, 22 January 2015.

114 "Press statement of nuclear suppliers meeting: meeting of states adhering to the nuclear suppliers guidelines", 3 April 1992.

115 As read in INFCIRC 539 rev 6.

116 See for example, Jennekens, J., Parsick R., and von Baeckmann, A., 'Strengthening the international safeguards system: An overview of proposals to further improve the effectiveness and efficiency of the IAEA's safeguards system', IAEA Bulletin, vol. 34, no. 1, pp. 6–10, 1992.

"Strengthening the effectiveness and improving the efficiency of the safeguards system: a report by the Director General", GC(39)/17, 22 August 1995.

Blix, H., "Verification of nuclear non-proliferation: Securing the future", *IAEA Bulletin*, vol. 34-1, March 1992. Available online at: www.iaea.org/sites/default/files/publications/magazines/bulletin/bull34-1/34103580205.pdf (Accessed 31 December 2017). Harrer, G., "Verifying nuclear dismantlement in Iraq", *Trust & Verify*, VERTIC. April–June 2014, Number 145.

117 "Additional Protocol", Website of the IAEA.

118 Ibid.

119 Technically, there is one model additional protocol which is used as the basis of negotiations with individual states over the country-specific additional protocol.

120 This language is based upon the language used by the IAEA to explain the Additional Protocol to states. See "Additional Protocol – Ensuring that all Nuclear Material Remains in Peaceful Activities", IAEA.

121 INFCIRC 540, Model Protocol Additional. To the Agreement Between State (S) and the International Atomic Energy Agency for the Application of Safeguards. Available online at: www.iaea.org/sites/default/files/infcirc540.pdf (Accessed 27 November 2020).

122 The author, who was responsible for assessing the proliferation risk of all nuclear and dual-use transfers from the UK, recalls that implementation of an AP and the existence of a Broader Conclusion were relevant factors used in estimating the risk of nuclear-related transfers of export licence applications.

123 See for example, Kassenova, T., "Brazil, Argentina, and the Politics of Global Nonproliferation and Nuclear Safeguards", http://carnegieendowment.org/2016/11/29/brazil-argentina-and-politics-of-global-nonproliferation-and-nuclear-safeguards-pub-66286.

124 Interview with Mark Hibbs, 23 February 2018.

125 Ibid.

126 Such catchall controls were introduced in the NSG in 2004.

Bibliography

"Additional Protocol – Ensuring that all Nuclear Material Remains in Peaceful Activities", *IAEA*. Available online at: www.iaea.org/sites/default/files/sg-ap.pdf (accessed 14 June 2021).

Albright, D. 'Iraq's Programs to Make Highly Enriched Uranium and Plutonium for Nuclear Weapons Prior to the Gulf War', 1997, updated in October 2001.

Albright, D., & Corey, H. 'Documents Indicate A.Q. Khan Offered Nuclear Weapons Designs to Iraq in 1990: Did He Approach Other Countries?', February 2004, ISIS.Barnaby, F. How Nuclear Weapons Spread. Routledge, ISBN 0-415-076749 as read in http://nuclearweaponarchive.org/Iraq/IraqRefs.html#Evron94.

Blix, H. "Verification of Nuclear Non-Proliferation: Securing the Future", *IAEA Bulletin*, vol. 34-1, March 1992. Available online at: www.iaea.org/sites/default/files/publications/magazines/bulletin/bull34-1/34103580205.pdf (Accessed 31 December 2017).

Braut-Hegghammer, M. Revisiting Osiraq: Preventive attacks and nuclear proliferation risks, *International Security*, vol. 36, no. 1, Summer, 2011, pp. 101–132. www.jstor.org/stable/41289690.

Comprehensive report of the special advisor to the DCI on Iraq's WMD, CIA, 30 September 2004, Volume 1.
Comprehensive report of the special advisor to the DCI on Iraq's WMD, CIA, 30 September 2004, Volume 2.
Cordesman, A. *Iraq and the war of sanctions: Convention threats and weapon of mass destruction*. Praeger, 1999.
Donnelly to Coluden. "Meeting of the Nuclear Suppliers Group (NSG): Warsaw 31 March–3 April", 6 April 1992. NPN83/10, Nuclear Suppliers Group (NSG) Dual-use exports, Part A and B. UK Foreign and Commonwealth Office. BNA.
Evron, Y. *Israel's nuclear dilemma*, Cornell University Press, 1994. Ithaca, NY. As read in http://nuclearweaponarchive.org/Iraq/IraqRefs.html#Evron94.
FCO 8/4179 – Iraq Nuclear Energy Part C: R.I.T. Cromartie to D K Haskell Esq, Nuclear Energy Dept: Safeguards and the Iraqi Nuclear Centre (31 December 1981), BNA.
FCO 96/1122.73 'Iraq's nuclear programme', Letter to RG Alston, Joint Nuclear Unit (FCO), from British Embassy, Rome. BNA.
Feldman, S. The bombing of Osiraq-revisited, *International Security*, vol. 7, no 2, August 1982, pp. 114–142. doi: https://doi.org/10.2307/2538435.
"France will sign 1968 nuclear pact", *New York Times*, 4 June 1991.
Fuhrmann, M. *Atomic assistance: How 'atoms for peace' programs caused nuclear instability*, Cornell University Press. www.jstor.org/stable/10.7591/j.cttn34vg.
Harrer, G. "Verifying Nuclear Dismantlement in Iraq", Trust & Verify, VERTIC. April–June 2014, Number 145.
Hamza, K. *Saddam's bombmaker: The terrifying inside story of the Iraqi nuclear and biological weapons agenda, Scribner*, 2000. p. 202.
Hibbs, M. Iraqi-made centrifuge rotors didn't work, inspectors Told, *Nuclear Fuel*, vol. 16, no. 17, 19 August 1981.
Hibbs, M. Customs officials say Iraq is shopping for centrifuge U enrichment hardware, *Nuclear Fuel*, vol. 15, no. 17, 20 August 1990.
Hibbs, M. Trail of Iraqi nuclear commerce leads to two Swiss companies, *Nucleonics Week*, vol. 31, no. 34, 23 August 1990.
Hibbs, M. Report says centrifuge know-how may have been transferred to Iraq, *Nuclear Fuel*, vol. 15, no. 22, 29 October 1990.
Hibbs, M. No centrifuge plant in Iraq, but investigators seek know-how source, *Nucleonics Week*, vol. 31, no. 42, 18 October 1990.
Hibbs, M. Iraq sought UF6 know-how in 1989, *Nuclear Fuel*, vol. 15, no. 26, 24 December 1990.
Hibbs, M. U.S. believes Iraq has built magnetic isotope enrichment plant, *Nucleonics Week*, vol. 32, no. 25, 20 June 1991.
Hibbs, M. Second Iraqi defector led IAEA to document trove, *Nuclear Fuel*, vol. 32, no. 40, 3 October 1991.
Hibbs, M. Agencies trace some Iraqi URENCO know-how to Pakistan re-export, *Nuclear Fuel*, vol. 32, no. 48, 28 November 1991.
Hibbs, M. Iraqi centrifuges incomplete on eve of serial production, *Nucleonics Week*, vol. 33, no. 4, 23 January 1992.
Hibbs, M. Swiss drop cases against firms aiding Iraqi centrifuge effort, *Nucleonics Week*, vol. 13, no. 17, 23 April 1992.
Hibbs, M. German expert wanted by authorities for giving Iraq carbon centrifuge rotors, *Nuclear Fuel*, vol. 17, no. 23, 9 November 1992.

Hibbs, M. Spectrometer sought by Iran is dual-use off-the-shelf item, *Nuclear Fuel*, vol. 22, no. 18, 8 September 1997.

Hibbs, M. Ex-MAN gas centrifuge expert said higher-ups helped Iraq. *Nuclear Fuel*, vol. 23, no. 6, 23 March 1998.

IAEA Iraq decommissioning project, "IRT5000 reactor". Available online at: www.ns.iaea.org/projects/iraq/.

INFCIRC 153. The structure and content of agreements between the Agency and States required in connection with the Treaty of the Non-proliferation of Nuclear Weapons, July 1972.

INFCIRC539/Rev 6: Communication received from the permanent mission of Argentina to the International Atomic Energy Agency on Behalf of the Participant governments of the Nuclear Suppliers Group, 22 January 2015.

INFCIRC 540, Model Protocol Additional. To the Agreement Between State (S) and the International Atomic Energy Agency for the Application of Safeguards. Available online at: www.iaea.org/sites/default/files/infcirc540.pdf (Accessed 27 November 2020).

INFCIRC172, 22 February 1973. Available online at: www.iaea.org/Publications/Documents/Infcircs/Others/infcirc172.pdf.

Iraq profile – timeline, *BBC*, 21 May 2018.

Jennekens, J., Parsick R., & von Baeckmann, A. Strengthening the international safeguards system: An overview of proposals to further improve the effectiveness and efficiency of the IAEA's safeguards system, *IAEA Bulletin*, vol. 34, no. 1, pp. 6–10, 1992.

Kassenova, T. "Brazil, Argentina, and the Politics of Global Nonproliferation and Nuclear Safeguards". Available online at: http://carnegieendowment.org/2016/11/29/brazil-argentina-and-politics-of-global-nonproliferation-and-nuclear-safeguards-pub-66286.

Muller, H. Falling into line? France and the NPT, Programme for promoting nuclear non-proliferation, Occasional Paper No 6, Centre for International Policy Studies, Department of Politics, University of Southampton, May 1990.

NPN83/10, "Nuclear Suppliers Group (NSG) Dual-use exports, Part A and B. UK Foreign and Commonwealth Office.

Nunn to Smith, 21 January 1992, NSG working group on a multi-lateral regime for nuclear sensitive dual use goods: Final meeting in Interlaken, 13–17 January 1992.

Obeidi, M. *The bomb in my garden: The secrets of Saddam's nuclear mastermind*, John Wiley & Sons, Inc, 2004.

Orlov, V., & Potter, W. The mystery of the sunken gyros, *The Bulletin of the Atomic Scientists*, vol. 54, no. 6, November/December 1998, pp. 34–39.

"Press statement of nuclear suppliers meeting: meeting of states adhering to the nuclear suppliers guidelines", 3 April 1992.

S/1997/771: Annex 1 – The acquisition of weapons-usable nuclear material, p. 25.

"Shaking Hands with Saddam Hussein: The U.S. Tilts towards Iraq, 1980–1984", National Security Achieve Electronic Briefing Book No. 82, GWDNSA, February 2009.

"State sponsor of terrorism" is a feature of numerous US laws, including the Export Control Act (1940), Foreign Assistance Act, and Arms Export Control Act (1976), with Iraq first being designated in 1978. See US Federal Register via the National Achieves. Available online at: www.archives.gov/federal-register/ (accessed 14 June 2014).

"Strengthening the effectiveness and improving the efficiency of the safeguards system: A report by the Director General", GC(39)/17, 22 August 1995.
'The Iraq nuclear programme: Progress despite setbacks', Directorate of Intelligence, June 1983; available online in redacted from via GWDNSA: Available online at: www.2.gwu.edu/~nsarchiv/NSAEBB/NSAEBB82/iraq19.pdf.
UNSCR 598, United Nations Security Council, New York, 20 July 1987.
UNSCR 687, United Nations Security Council, New York, 8 April 1991.
US Department of State, "Briefing on Nuclear Suppliers Group", 9 June 1993, Honolulu, Hawaii. GWDSNA.
Vandenbroucke, L. The Israeli strike against OSIRAQ: The dynamics of fear and proliferation in the Middle East. Air University Review, September–October 1984.

6 Universalising non-proliferation trade controls

International nuclear trade controls and the broader non-proliferation regime were considerably strengthened in the decade after the Cold War. However, underlying structural flaws remained and both the coverage and scope of trade controls varied across states as they had not been universalised. The result was that controls proved to be incapable of preventing further proliferation episodes, notably involving Iran, Libya, and North Korea, much of which was facilitated by the AQ Khan proliferation network. The limitations became apparent just prior to the 9/11 terrorist attacks in the US, which subsequently led to increased fears about the acquisition and use of weapons of mass destruction by terrorists and not just state actors.

In this context, the US again sought to exert leadership to strengthen international nuclear trade controls. As in the 1970s, US efforts focused on leveraging support from small numbers of states, including nuclear suppliers and the members of the UN Security Council to have a broader effect. It is demonstrated that despite efforts to universalise international nuclear trade controls in this period through the adoption of measures such as UNSCR 1540, the suboptimal evolution of controls continued because many states did not take action to implement measures. The reasons for this vary between states but include pursuit of other priorities such as economic development over trade control, and ideological positions which promoted the imperative of disarmament over the imperative of non-proliferation.

The purpose of this chapter is to examine this interplay of factors in the context of the research framework. The adoption of binding Chapter VII resolutions in relation to non-proliferation allowed the permanent members of the Security Council – which largely shared the non-proliferation goal – to adopt measures that would be binding on all states, thus potentially helping to overcome the non-proliferation collective action problem. At the same time, however, the veto power of the individual P5 states afforded them control over the non-proliferation actions pursued by the UN, as well as a bargaining chip that could be used to pursue narrower self-interest.

The chapter begins by examining the AQ Khan proliferation network and its role in facilitating the clandestine nuclear programmes of Iran, Libya, and the Democratic People's Republic of Korea (DPRK).[1]

DOI: 10.4324/9781003194262-6

It then examines the steps taken in response to the discovery and public outing of the programme, including the adoption of 1540, the Proliferation Security Initiative (PSI), and other relevant measures. This includes an examination of how 1540 affected the actions of two particular states – Malaysia and Indonesia – in implementing non-proliferation trade controls for the first time. Finally, the chapter examines the Nuclear Suppliers Group (NSG) exemption granted to India in 2008 in order to provide insight into how broader factors affected non-proliferation trade controls after the adoption of UNSCR 1540.

AQ Khan's proliferation network

The limitations of international nuclear trade controls in the 1990s are well illustrated through an examination of the AQ Khan network. From around 1983, Khan, whose role in Pakistan's nuclear programme was examined in Chapter 4, refocused his attention away from supporting Pakistan's enrichment programme towards selling associated technology and components to other countries. Over the course of more than 15 years, at least four countries gained access from the network to centrifuge designs – and in some cases, parts, materials, complete centrifuges, and even weapons designs. Those countries include, in order, China, Iran, Libya, and North Korea, although other countries were also offered the technology, including Iraq, as noted earlier.

To illustrate the impact of the Khan network, the Iranian, Libyan, and North Korean episodes are examined in some depth following a brief overview of the network's structure. The whole episode thus highlights the limitations of the nuclear trade controls as these existed at the beginning of the 21st century. Libya was, however, the first substantial sale for the Khan network, and while there is some question about the complicity (or at least awareness) of the Pakistani State in the previous sales, it is perhaps the Libya episode that came closest to being a straightforward commercial transaction. The Pakistani government and related political parties claimed that it was not aware of Khan's actions which may suggest monetary reward rather than geopolitical interest as a motivation for Khan.[2] However, his role in leading one of the key Pakistani nuclear facilities, together with his use of Pakistani diplomatic and military assets in the sales and the earlier claims from the 1970s of a secret agreement between Pakistan and Libya related to nuclear weapons procurement, challenges the credibility of claims by the Pakistani government that Khan acted without authority. This uncertainty is compounded by the fact that the Pakistani government refused to allow the IAEA, or other international authorities, access to Khan following his house arrest in 2004.[3] It should also be noted that Pakistan, as a non-NPT state, would not have violated any international commitment by transferring nuclear weapons know-how to other states.

The network

The AQ Khan proliferation network is perhaps best described as a one-stop shop for a nuclear weapons programme.[4] On a commercial basis, it offered designs, components, and know-how to states in relation to everything from uranium enrichment and conversation to weaponisation. The network was international in scope and complex in nature. There remains ambiguity about aspects of the network, such as whether Khan himself directed all of its operations and where the network of complicit actors ended and legitimate suppliers began. The network evolved over time in terms of purpose, which was originally to supply Pakistan's programmes, as well its membership and location. The network has been extensively documented elsewhere, although the full scope of the network and its activities will likely never be fully known.[5] Speaking in 2004, the Director General of the IAEA Mohamed ElBaradei noted:

> It's mind-boggling. All I know is there's at least more than 30 companies in 30 countries all over the globe involved in this fantastic, sophisticated illicit trafficking network with Mr A.Q. Khan acting as C.E.O.[6]

Despite a substantial body of work that has been produced after the fact to understand the network, there are signs that intelligence agencies largely missed the network's activity until the early 2000s. For example, the Congressional Research Service noted in 2005, "Despite the existence of intelligence information and rumors in the open literature concerning significant Pakistani contacts with radical states known to be seeking nuclear weapons, Congress has received little information on this issue in unclassified reports from intelligence agencies".[7]

From what is known about the network, its main elements were as follows.

- A number of individuals associated with the network were based in South Africa, where some of the goods were also manufactured. The individuals based in South Africa included Gerhard Wisser, Daniel Geiger of Krislch Engineering, and Johan A.M Meyer of Roxound Engineering Works who had previously produced goods for South Africa's enrichment programme.[8]
- Henk Slebos was a Dutch businessman who procured goods from across Europe to fulfil orders from Khan's network.[9]
- Peter Griffin was originally based in the UK before moving to Dubai.[10]
- There were at least two companies in Turkey associated with the network: EKA Electronik owned by Selim Alguadis, and ETI Electronic.[11]
- The network's original hub was in the UAE, specifically Dubai, before it was moved to Malaysia. There were a number of associated organisations based in the UAE, including Bin Belailah Enterprises owned by S

Mohammed Farooq, the SMB Group owned by Tahir, Desert Electrical Equipment owned by the Tinners, and Gulf Technical Industry owned by Peter Griffin. Tahir brokered a substantial agreement with Malaysian-based SCOMI Precision Engineering Ltd for the manufacture and supply of components.[12]

- The Tinners owned a number of companies in Switzerland and facilitated access for the network to other Switzerland-based companies before members of the Tinner family moved to the UAE to run aspects of the network. Companies owned by the Tinners in Switzerland included Phitech AG, Cemog AG, and Tracoscchieiz AZ.[13]
- While not part of the network as such, Gerhard Wisser, a representative of Leybold Heraeus in South Africa, was complicit with the network and falsified documents submitted to Leybold Heraeus in an attempt to secure an order.

From the above description, it can be seen that the network operated in countries with export control laws and mature intelligence capabilities, including the UK and Germany, as well as countries without them such as Malaysia and the UAE. This leads to questions about how the network was able to function and why it was not detected before its transfers to Libya? For example, the CRS noted in 2005 that, "The IAEA reported in February 2004 that Libya began receiving centrifuge components from A.Q. Khan in 1997. Yet, the Section 721 reports did not contain any text about a Libyan nuclear program until 2000".[14] There seems to be no single answer to these questions. Many of the cases examined were not subject to national export controls. Even when export control violations did take place, it was often difficult for enforcement authorities to take action or bring cases against the individuals concerned. Overall, however, the success of the Khan network, as examined through the customers' programmes in the following, highlights the continued inadequacy of nuclear trade controls as they existed in the 1990s.

Iran

There remains some ambiguity about when Khan sold to Iran some of the items it received via the network. However, the centrifuge designs Iran obtained would be central to the country's nuclear programme in the years ahead. It is thus helpful to examine Khan's assistance in the context of Iran's broader nuclear effort. It should be noted that the country had little infrastructure suited to a nuclear weapons programme prior to Khan's intervention.

Iran had pursued an indigenous enrichment programme in the mid-1980s, with its first procurements efforts dated from around 1984–1985.[15] Around 1986–1987, a deal was brokered between the Khan network and Iranian officials. The deal involved the exchange of between US$5–10m for designs for the P1 centrifuge that Khan had taken from URENCO in the 1970s and a few disassembled centrifuges and an assortment of parts.[16] Unlike Libya, Iran decided to manufacture the centrifuges indigenously rather than procuring centrifuge cascades from the Khan network. This meant that Iran was not dependent on Khan for ongoing support but also required Iran to devise an alternative plan to acquire the needed parts, material, and equipment. As early as 1985, Iran had begun to acquire key component manufacturing capabilities, such as flow-forming equipment.[17] Using illicit procurement practices, Iran was able to acquire components, parts, and materials from the international marketplace in the years that followed. In 1988, for example, Iran ordered 50 vacuum pumps from Leybold, an order that received a German export licence.[18] Iran also bought 120 valves intended for use in uranium enrichment from Leybold around this time.

At some point between 1994 and 1996, Iran is thought to have received a complete set of design drawings from Khan for the P2 centrifuge[19], apparently as compensation for the poor quality of P1 parts previously supplied.[20] Iran lacked the capability to manufacture maraging steel required for the production of the P2 centrifuge so instead contracted with a private company in Iran which experimented, in 1999 or 2000, with the production of a short subcritical centrifuge made from carbon fibre. Iran failed to declare the P2 work to the IAEA in 2003 at the time when Iran had declared other aspects of its programme and promised full transparency.

The Khan network was not Iran's only source of outside assistance. In the mid-1990s, Russia went ahead with the contract to finish the Bushehr Light Water Reactor. This reactor, which is unsuited to, and therefore, unlikely to be used for, plutonium production had been started by German companies which subsequently pulled out.[21] China relented to US pressure not to sell Iran a turnkey project to establish a uranium conversion capability (see the following). Because Bushehr is a power reactor, and not suited to weapons production, the supply of fuel for the reactor was exempted from UN sanctions on Iran at the insistence of Moscow, which wanted to proceed with the sale while also supporting the adoption of UN sanctions.[22] Russia had also entered into a contract to supply fuel for the reactor for many years and to return spent fuel to Russia for disposal. Iran would nonetheless cite the need to fuel its reactors as part of its justification for pursuing uranium enrichment.[23]

The data sold by the AQ Khan network thus provided Iran with the means for pursuing its nuclear programme despite the fact that international suppliers had opted to limit sales with this country. It also gave Iran the means to pursue an undeclared programme away from IAEA oversight.

Libya

Like Iran, Libya would ultimately turn to the Khan network for nuclear assistance. Libya had an interest in nuclear weapons in the 1970s and 1980s.[24] During this period, Libya acquired a small research reactor from the Soviet Union, but this was not suitable for the production of plutonium for use in nuclear weapons. It was reported in this period that Libya had provided finance to Pakistan for development of the Pakistani nuclear weapons programme with the apparent understanding that Pakistan would make nuclear weapons available to Libya if requested.[25] If such an agreement did exist, it appears that when Muhammad Zia-ul-Haq took office in 1978, he opted not to follow through on it as there is no evidence of such a transfer or arrangement.

The Khan network's sales to Libya

Khan had apparently offered to sell enrichment capabilities to Libya in 1984 but Gaddafi opted not to take up the offer at the time.[26] Instead, like Iraq, Libya also hired a former employee of the European firm, Man New Technologies (a URENCO subcontractor), to develop a centrifuge enrichment capability for Libya. This individual is said to have left Libya in 1992 without having produced a working system.[27] Khan then renewed the offer around 1989.[28] An agreement was reached by 1991 for the supply of the P1 centrifuges, although these transfers had not taken place by the time that UN sanctions were imposed on Libya as a result of the Lockerbie bombing in 1993.[29] Some of the equipment that Khan's network had been collecting for Libya is thought to have been sent to Iran instead to provide bridge funding for Khan's network.[30] By the latter half of the 1990s, Libya was ready to reinvigorate its effort, with officials apparently agreeing to procure some 5,000 centrifuges, expandable to 10,000 machines at a later date, as well as associated equipment and material.[31]

To fulfil this sale, Khan is thought to have divided the work between members of his network by holding a meeting attended by the Sweden-based Tinners taking on responsibility for centrifuge components; South Africa-based Gotthad Lerch taking on responsibility for producing feed and withdrawal systems; and Tahir who was based in the UAE and Malaysia. Lerch would subcontract work to Wisser and Geiges in South Africa and the network would also engage Turkey-based Selim Alguadis to produce frequency changers. Turkish national Gunes Cire and his son also produced centrifuge motors. Peter Griffin, and his son Paul, who owned Gulf Technical Industries (GTI) in Dubai, was in charge of assembling a centrifuge production workshop ordered by Libya. Tahir states that all of these individuals were aware that the plant was destined for Libya.[32]

The network used companies and addresses in Dubai when procuring items from elsewhere, and members of the network-maintained companies and facilities there. This included SMB Computers owned by Tahir and Desert Electrical Equipment owned by the Tinners.[33] In 2001, Tahir would also establish a relationship with the Malaysian-based Scomi Group for the manufacture of centrifuge components, after which Malaysia would become an increasing focus for the network's activities.[34] Specialist metals were procured through the Singapore-based Bikar Metal Asia Pte Ltd, which in turn sought the goods from specialist manufacturers and suppliers.[35] The Tinners also subcontracted numerous Switzerland-based companies to manufacture centrifuge items. The Netherlands-based Henk Slebos also procured items for the network over a number of years, including specialist MKS pressure transducers.[36] It was the combination of complicit Western businessmen with entities based in jurisdictions that did not have effective export controls that enabled the network to evade international nuclear trade controls.

Western intelligence agencies had been tracking aspects of the network for a number of years. In 2003, some centrifuges and parts had begun to arrive in Libya. However, a major shipment was to be dispatched to Libya in October 2003. This shipment, on the BBC China, was intercepted by the Germans and Italians based on US intelligence and diverted to port where hundreds of centrifuge parts were unloaded in an Italian port.[37] Libya was still some years away from operating the cascades, never mind producing enriched uranium, when the shipment was intercepted. The UK and US were able to utilise the seizure of this equipment as part of their efforts to persuade Gadhafi to abandon pursuit of WMD programmes.

North Korea

Less is known about Khan's transfers to North Korea than to Iran and Libya. Indeed, little is presently known about many aspects of North Korea's nuclear programme, including from where it procured key components.[38] Based on existing accounts, it appears that Khan's relationship with North Korea took shape in the 1990s. Khan is believed to have been involved in the transfer of No Dong missiles from the DPRK to Pakistan.[39] This relationship is believed to have evolved to one involving nuclear supply by the late 1990s or the year 2000, when Khan's network is thought to have transferred "two dozen P1 and P2 centrifuges and measuring equipment" to the DPRK.[40]

Responding to the Khan network

There are several issues highlighted by the role of the Khan network that are directly relevant to understanding the continued limitations of controls during this period.

First, Iran, Libya, and North Korea were all NNWS parties to the NPT but had opted not to conclude an Additional Protocol with the IAEA. Such an agreement would have made it more likely that the Agency would have detected their respective clandestine activities. However, for all three countries, the chosen path to nuclear weapons did not leave the country reliant on authorised imports from other states so the lack of overt assistance can be considered inconsequential.

Second, the Khan network succeeded in procuring and producing much of what was required for Libya's programme, which was the only known programme to buy a complete capability. This was accomplished using a number of actions to evade controls including the use of front companies in states such as the UAE and Malaysia, which at this point had to date not enacted export control measures and were outside of the NSG. These companies utilised a range of techniques to evade controls when buying items manufactured in states that did have controls.

Third, the Khan network demonstrated that more countries were capable of supplying nuclear-related items than had previously been the case. The ability of countries such as the UAE and Malaysia to act as nuclear suppliers was a new development even if these countries were principally being used to form parts from materials produced elsewhere rather than manufacture the underlying materials. This highlighted the need to extend nuclear trade controls to all states rather than just to states known to manufacture nuclear goods.

There are no signs that any states were overly complicit in selling technology to the network with the knowledge that it was destined to Libya, although the Malaysian companies had close ties to the country's leadership.[41] Intelligence agencies followed some of the network's activities. But, overall, it must be concluded that international nuclear trade controls were poorly suited to the task of stopping the type of activity that Libya and the Khan network had undertaken primarily because the control regime in place was too narrowly implemented.

A wide variety of lessons were learned from the Khan network although it took some time for many of these to emerge given the complex and secret nature of the network. In a seminal speech at the National Defence University in 2004, President George W. Bush announced that the US would pursue the following seven initiatives in order to prevent future state and non-state proliferation:[42]

- the work of the Proliferation Security Initiative be expanded to address more than shipments and transfers;
- all nations to strengthen the laws and international controls that govern proliferation;
- expand our efforts to keep weapons from the Cold War and other dangerous materials out of the wrong hands;
- the world's leading nuclear exporters should ensure that states have reliable access at reasonable cost to fuel for civilian reactors, so long as those states renounce enrichment and reprocessing;
- only states that have signed the Additional Protocol be allowed to import equipment for their civilian nuclear programmes;
- the creation of a special committee of the IAEA Board which will focus intensively on safeguards and verification; and
- countries under investigation for violating nuclear non-proliferation obligations are currently allowed to serve on the IAEA Board of Governors.

The agenda President Bush put forward was ambitious and held the potential to have profound implications for the future of non-proliferation trade controls. Perhaps the most significant initiative that subsequently came to fruition was the adoption of a UNSCR 1540. It is notable, however, that a number of elements of the President's speech did not come to pass. For example, there was no immediate consensus on the issue of enrichment and reprocessing or on the issue of requiring the Additional Protocol as a condition of supply. These issues were discussed within the NSG. However, it took more than a decade for the NSG to reach consensus on the issue of enrichment and reprocessing.[43] The primary reason for this was that countries such as Brazil and Argentina, which were members of the NSG but not parties to an Additional Protocol, were not willing to accept additional constraints on their own nuclear programmes. The reasons for this are not yet fully understood and are somewhat complex. Kassenova, for example, notes that while it is often the lack of progress on disarmament that is presented as the principal reason South American countries do not support enhanced non-proliferation controls, "at closer examination, lack of progress on the disarmament front does not appear to serve as the primary concern for either Brazil or Argentina. Instead both countries appear to be more concerned that developing countries' access to nuclear technology might become hostage to the non-proliferation goals of developed countries".[44]

UNSCR 1540 as foundation for international nuclear trade controls

The P5 had gained experience of working through the UN Security Council as a result of the Iraq episode in the 1990s. It was in this context that US and British officials began to explore whether the Security Council could in some way be used to tackle the problem of proliferation involving non-state actors, as had been so clearly illustrated by the Khan network.[45] The advantage of a Security Council resolution was that it could incorporate measures under Chapter VII of the UN Charter (threats to international peace and security) which would be binding on all states.[46] A Security Council resolution could, therefore, provide the mandatory international legal basis for those states that were willing to enact export control and related measures.

The G8 had recently adopted the 'Kananaskis Principles', which contained many of the elements that would later be included in UNSCR1540.[47] These principles were used as the starting point for a draft resolution.[48] Resolution 1540 would require states to implement a variety of measures in order to prevent non-state actor involvement in proliferation. These measures include the creation and maintenance of a system of export controls, broader controls, and physical security measures around WMD and related materials. China, however, was not a participant in the G8 and was confronted with the principles for the first time in the form of a draft Security Council resolution. It is thus understandable that China was hesitant about the implications of what became 1540. Indeed, Chinese official statements on the PSI had stated that: " ... the international community including China remains concerned about the possibility that the interdiction activities taken by PSI participants might go beyond the international law".[49] China had earlier opted not to adhere to the PSI. As to the reason for this, Onderco and Hooft noted that:

> China is most explicitly concerned about the transparency and consequences of interdiction procedures at the heart of the PSI, which could impede the passage of Chinese ships in the territorial waters of PSI-endorsing states. [119] But the PSI is considered a broader impingement on Chinese sovereignty and great power status. The 2003 Chinese white paper on non-proliferation maintained that 'either the improvement of the existing regime or the establishment of a new regime should be based on the universal participation of all countries and on their decisions made through a democratic process'.[50]

It was in this context that China insisted in changes to the 1540 draft. Specifically, the draft removed reference to interdiction and the use of intelligence in order to address China's concern. China's concerns could have prevented its adoption, and so the US agreed to remove these elements in order to secure Beijing's support for of the resolution.[51]

While the post 9/11 climate made most states amenable to the idea of taking actions that could prevent the use of WMD, the Security Council has rarely – if ever – adopted resolutions of this type requiring states to enact domestic legislation other than sanctions resolutions. Perhaps understandably then the reaction of states outside of the Security Council to the resolution was mixed. The specific scope of 1540 was somewhat helpful with this: the resolution technically targets 'non-state actor' involvement in proliferation, where a non-state actor is defined as an "individual or entity, not acting under the lawful authority of any State in conducting activities which come within the scope of this resolution".[52] This scope was important for two main reasons. First, narrowing the scope of targets to non-state actors helped to diffuse concerns that the resolution could infringe on the sovereignty of states as all states would likely support the assertion that non-state actors should not be able to acquire and use WMD. Second, in the preceding years, it had increasingly been individuals and companies not connected with the state that had facilitated proliferation. Targeting the resolution in this way thus brought such actors directly into the scope of the non-proliferation regime and nuclear trade controls.

To pre-empt negative views of the resolution from damaging its implementation, an open debate was scheduled by the Security Council at which more than a quarter of the UN's membership spoke.[53] The views expressed by the representatives were diverse: while there was general support for the resolution's objectives, reservations about the resolution were also expressed including on the grounds that it did not include disarmament provisions and, importantly, that it was a Security Council initiative rather than a General Assembly measure.[54] India, for example, stated:

> Our recognition of the time imperative in seeking resource through the Security Council does not, however, obscure our more basic concerns over the increasing tendency of the Council in recent years to assume new and wider powers of legislation on behalf of the international community, with its resolutions binding on all states. In the present instance, the Council seeks to both define the non-proliferation regime and monitor its implementation. But who will monitor the monitors? We are concerned that the exercise of legislative functions by the Council, combined with recourse to Chapter VII mandates, could disrupt the balance of power between the General Assembly and the Security Council, as enshrined in the Charter.[55]

India's position must be understood against the backstop of the country's traditional non-aligned status and its longer term desire for a seat on the Security Council. It could be expected that India would have reservations about any UNSC action that it viewed as infringing on its sovereignty while not having a seat of its own. This did not prevent enactment of the resolution, but the negative connotations associated with the method through which the resolution was adopted could have undermined the willingness of states to enact its measures. More than a decade on, it seems this concern has abated or not come to pass with more and more countries citing 1540 as the reason for their adoption of controls.[56]

When the resolution was adopted, there was no expectation that substantial resources would be available to support its implementation – at least through the UN system.[57] Cupitt noted that 1540 had overcome this, to some extent, by deciding not to use the 1540 committee to 'hound' states into compliance.[58] Indeed, he noted that "virtually every state had expressed, formally or otherwise, often in multiple settings, this commitment to implement the resolution".[59] In practice, such resources have been made available in the years since 1540 was adopted on either a bilateral or multilateral basis or through a related UN trust fund, and coordinated by the UN Secretariat, notably through the Global Partnership, and the 1540 Group of Experts.[60] Perhaps, as a result of this sustained investment in capacity building, the institutionalisation of 1540 through regional forums such as ASEAN and the European Union, and the work of the 1540 Committee, and associated group of experts, the resolution appears to have been increasingly accepted as an important and enduring tool of international security.[61] As a result of 1540, then it can be argued that substantial global progress was made in implementing non-proliferation trade controls.[62]

Requirements and implementation

While the primary purpose of 1540 relates to non-state actors, its measures are nonetheless relevant to national efforts to preventing the proliferation of nuclear weapons by states. In part, this is because many states have become reliant on goods and technologies procured through non-state actors to take forward their nuclear programmes. Additionally, however, the practical implementation of 1540 involves the creation and enforcement of a requirement not to export nuclear-related items without authorisation – a requirement that exists whether the end-use is for a non-state actor or for a government. Because of this, it can be argued that 1540 constitutes a universally binding supplement to the main non-proliferation regime.

It is notable that acceptance of 1540 appears to be broad when measured by the reporting to the 1540 Committee. Indeed, as of 1 January 2017, 172 of 193 UN member states had reported to the UN on implementation as required by the resolution.[63] This contrasts with measures such as the IAEA's Additional Protocol which is currently implemented by around 129 states with notable absentees, including Argentina, Brazil, and (formally at least) Iran.[64]

Nevertheless, national implementation of resolution 1540 varies considerably as highlighted in the 2016 comprehensive review its implementation conducted by the 1540 Committee.[65] Many states have not taken action to implement aspects of the resolution's requirements, such as enacting export controls on dual-use items. Implementation is particularly weak in Africa, South America, and parts of Asia where WMD concerns are not among the foremost issues facing the state.[66] The resolution itself does allow for variation in implementation between states, with implementation of specific provisions usually required to be "effective and appropriate" – that is, good enough in the national context. As many states do not hold WMD or manufacture "related materials" (a term which can be taken to mean dual-use goods), it could be argued that for most states, it is enough to have in place reactive measures to stop shipments of WMD-related items through the countries' territory. This said, the discussion on what 'appropriate and effective' means in practice is only now beginning well over a decade after the resolution was first adopted.[67] It is informative to briefly examine the cases of Malaysia and Indonesia to appreciate the different types of responses to 1540 and to understand why some states have responded and others have not.

New export control implementers: the case of Malaysia

A particularly important and illustrative country that introduced export controls after the adoption of 1540 is Malaysia. Malaysia was one of the countries exploited by the AQ Khan proliferation network and subsequently adopted the Strategic Trade Management Act in 2010. In the context of the research question and conceptual framework, it is valuable to examine the factors that lead Malaysia to adopt controls.

In February 2004, Royal Malaysian Police issued a 12-page report on its investigations into the Khan network of companies and individuals involved in the procurement and manufacture of the items intercepted on the BBC China *en route* to Libya. Malaysia was central to the network with Malaysian company SCOMI Precision engineering (SCOPE) manufacturing many of the most sensitive items from equipment and material procured from the international marketplace. SCOPE is notable not least because the company was owned by the son of the then Malaysia Prime Minister, Abdullah Ahmad Badawi.[68] At the time, Malaysia had no export control measures and the actions of the network in exporting the goods from Malaysia to Libya were not illegal. The Police Report therefore concluded:

> From the explanation above, it is clear that SCOPE has not violated any law under the NPT, Additional Protocol and also the Malaysian law under the AEL (Act 304).[69]

Under pressure from the US, Malaysia began to draft an export control act as early as 2005. However, Mohamed Shahabar Abdul Kareem, Malaysia's first strategic trade controller, recounts that this early draft floated around different Malaysian government departments without a clear champion to drive it toward adoption.[70] This changed in 2010 after the Malaysian Prime Minister was invited to President Barack Obama's inaugural Nuclear Security Summit. The Summit process was notable because it was held at head of government level and the idea of 'gift baskets' emerged where it was hoped each attending government would bring something substantial to the table. The Malaysian government decided to deliver upon the export control act as a part of its gift basket, thus facilitating the rapid adoption of the law in Malaysia.[71] Shahabar notes that there were other drivers for adoption. He cites specifically Malaysia's obligations under UNSCR1540, its economic interests – which he believes were furthered through the adoption of export controls – and the 'external push' provided in particular by the US.[72]

The act was unique to Malaysia but based loosely upon the Singapore Strategic Goods (Control) Act of 2002, which had been adopted prior to the enactment of 1540, but which was subsequently revised to reflect 1540's requirements.[73] The Malaysian act controls "the export, transshipment, transit and brokering of strategic items, including arms and related material, and other activities that will or may facilitate the design, development and production of weapons of mass destruction and their delivery systems and to provide for other matters connected therewith, consistent with Malaysia's national security and international obligations".[74] Unusually, Malaysia opted to include the death penalty as one of the punishments that could be imposed for violating the act.[75] This likely reflects the level of national embarrassment that resulted from the SCOMI case. Malaysia set up a dedicated team in its Ministry of Trade and Industry under a Strategic Trade Controller to enforce the law.

Malaysia is exactly the type of country that the US and the UK drafters of 1540 sought to influence. However, as Malaysia's first strategic trade controller noted, it was not the adoption of 1540 that cleared the logjams preventing adoption of the law, but the external push provided by the Obama administration that succeeded in securing Prime Ministerial support. Malaysia also saw economic advantages to enacting export controls, although this appears to have been a secondary consideration.[76]

The case of Indonesia

In contrast to Malaysia, neighbouring Indonesia has taken little action to implement the requirements of 1540. Indonesian officials are known to be sceptical about the need to enact trade controls because the country is not a substantial producer of dual-use goods.[77] Andy Rachmianto, Director for International Security and Disarmament in Indonesia's Foreign Affairs Ministry, summarised Indonesia's position as follows:

> As a developing country, Indonesia is focusing on economic and trade development. Therefore, export and import of goods, including strategic ones, are important. Despite Indonesia not being a member of any of the export control regimes, it is aware of the potential risks caused by the possible misuse of dual-use technologies and materials, in particular for proliferation. Therefore, Indonesia has adopted an array of laws and regulations that govern its export and import control system. Furthermore, Indonesia considers that existing nonproliferation instruments, particularly the Nuclear Nonproliferation Treaty (NPT), the Chemical Weapons Convention (CWC), and the Biological and Toxic Weapons Convention (BTWC), are critical elements to counter the proliferation of Weapons of Mass Destruction (WMD).[78]

It should be noted that despite this sentiment, Indonesia has adopted a range of laws that can contribute to the implementation of the requirements of 1540 but does not implement export controls on dual-use goods as required by the resolution.[79]

Rachmianto proceeded to note two main concerns about the nature of export controls. First, that export controls could hamper Indonesia's import and export of dual-use goods and technology; and second, that the regimes were formulated in a selective, non-inclusive, and limited manner outside the existing UN framework.[80]

In the case of Indonesia, at least, it is clear that while 1540 has helped to frame the context in which the country considers strategic trade controls, it has been insufficient on its own, to motivate the country to take action to meet the resolution's requirements.

UN Security Council sanctions

A final aspect of the universalisation of non-proliferation trade controls began in the mid-2000s, when the UN Security Council adopted resolutions under Article VII of the UN Charter that contained universally binding sanctions provisions over the actions of the DPRK and Iran until 2015 with the adoption of the Joint Comprehensive Plan of Action. In addition to ordering the countries to halt aspects of their nuclear programmes, the resolutions also imposed a number of trade-related restricts.[81] These included prohibitions on the import and export of various nuclear-related, missile-related, and dual-use items to and from each country. Additional measures involved 'designations' and asset freezes on certain individuals and entities involved in the countries' strategic programmes.[82]

Beyond these restrictive measures, the UN resolutions included a number of measures related to monitoring compliance with the resolutions. In the case of both countries, this included:

1 a requirement for states to report suspected violations of the UNSC;
2 the creation of a 'sanctions committee' as a subsidiary body of the Security Council and a related panel of independent experts; and
3 a requirement for all states to report how they were implementing the resolution's requirements.

While there was clearly a political aspect to the invocation of UN sanctions, Jonathan Brewer – who was the British member of the UN's Iran sanctions panel of experts between 2010 and 2015 – noted that the purpose of sanctions was to "ensure [implementation of] relevant controls to a common standard" in a way that had not been achieved through export controls alone.[83] There are signs that the resolutions have generally been implemented by states.[84] Licensing authorities are not known to have authorised the export of prohibited goods to either the DPRK or Iran in violation of the resolution's requirements. Despite this, however, there have been a number of limitations around the implementation of the resolutions including.

1 In both cases, it is unclear how many states actually implemented the resolution's requirements and to what extent. Many states did not submit implementation reports to the committee as required by the resolutions.[85] Moreover, a subjective review of the content of the matrix reports published by the 1540 committee on each country suggests that the quality of the reports varied considerably.[86] Nonetheless, in the case of Iran, at least, Brewer noted that most key states did implement the measures.[87]
2 Both the DPRK and Iran engaged in widespread efforts to evade the sanctions, including most notably through the use of illicit procurement practices as was widely documented in relevant Panel of Expert reports. Some states, including the UK, the US, and France, undertook proactive measures to counter Iranian illicit trade. This included an expansive 'demarche' campaign acting upon a substantial body of classified intelligence information about Iranian illicit procurement.
3 There are reasons to believe that numerous known cases of illicit procurement were not reported to the UN despite the requirement for such cases to be reported. The reasons for this are unclear but likely relate to a

number of factors including technical ambiguity, ongoing national level prosecutions, and a political desire in some states not to report such diplomatically sensitive issues to the UN Security Council.[88]

The UN resolutions on Iran and the DPRK raised the question of whether many of these specific measures could be built into the non-proliferation regime more generally, or whether they were only relevant in a country-specific sense. For example, certain elements of these points could be implemented by states on a voluntary basis and perhaps coordinated through the NSG. However, it appears that there is at present little appetite for broader application of enhanced control measures to other countries.[89] Key here are the fractious politics associated with the NPT review process and with IAEA safeguards.[90] The origins of these politics are largely beyond the scope of this book but it is useful to examine them briefly.

The NPT was extended indefinitely in 1995 on its 25th anniversary. The extension was predicated on a number of factors including progress on disarmament and progress on creating a WMD-free zone in the Middle East. Approaching the 25th anniversary of the indefinite extension, many State Parties feel that insufficient progress has been realised in the intervening years. This has resulted in several failures to reach consensus documents at the five yearly review conferences. Most recently, the frustrations resulting from the lack of progress on disarmament contributed to the adoption of the Treaty on the Prohibitions of nuclear weapons.[91] Another manifestation of the frustration relate to the role of the mandate of the IAEA. The IAEA's Board of Governors and its member states are hesitant about increasing the Agency's safeguards mandate. The practical effect of this has been that the IAEA's Secretariat maintains distance from trade control issues. Additionally, IAEA member states have viewed proposals to optimise safeguards, including the so-called "State Level Concept" with suspicion.[92] Hibbs also argues that forums such as the NSG are becoming increasingly political in part as a result of the politics outlined earlier but perhaps more so given the NSG waiver for India and the membership applications to India and Pakistan. The political body of the NSG has been fixated on these issues in recent years potentially to the detriment of other issues. As a result of these factors, it is unclear whether the gradual progress that has been made on non-proliferation trade controls will be sustained.

It should also be noted that the Security Council was generally not united with regard to the Iran portfolio during the sanctions period. While all permanent members of the Security Council voted for, or at least did not against, the sanctions resolutions that have been adopted and the measures that have been adopted can be descried as 'lowest common denominator' in that they had to be acceptable to all permanent members of the Security Council.[93] Not satisfied with such 'lowest common denominator' measures taken by the Security Council, several countries led by the US took additional measures intended to supplement UN sanctions. For example, the US and EU also both adopted additional lists of designated entities and additional lists of technologies, the export of which is prohibited to Iran.[94]

During the sanctions period, Iran effectively rejected the authority of the Security Council to limit its nuclear programme by continuing activities that were problematic such as enrichment and the procurement of certain dual-use items. Iran also highlighted that its activities have been within the letter, if not the spirit, of the country's international commitments including with regard to the NPT.[95] Iran highlights that as an NNWS signatory to the NPT with an inalienable right to civil nuclear energy, it has the right to a civil nuclear programme.[96] Iran, therefore, did not cease procuring items for its nuclear programme after the revelations in 2003 and despite the UN sanctions. As mentioned, it was in this context that Iran used a variety of illicit procurement techniques, where Iran imported hundreds of shipments for its nuclear programme during this period.[97]

From this examination, it is apparent that while UN sanctions have complemented international nuclear trade controls, the use of such measures is a highly political act. Given that the overall nuclear landscape was difficult and politicised in this period, the contribution of such measures has been limited in scope. As a result, it appears unlikely that such measures, while valuable in specific cases, will have broader application to the problem of nuclear proliferation in the future.

The US–India nuclear deal and its significance for nuclear trade controls

On face value, the adoption of 1540 in 2004 and the subsequent UNSCRs on Iran and DPRK gives the impression that the UNSC had taken control of the non-proliferation issues. However, the UNSC is a body that relies on consensus among its permanent members each of which has its own interests that worked against non-proliferation efforts. A final indicative episode concerning the universalisation of non-proliferation relates to the US–India nuclear deal.

The India case (and indeed the Pakistan case) highlights that states continue to take national decisions related to nuclear trade controls based upon their perception of self-interest. Numerous states evidently supported the NSG exemption for India based upon a combination of the economic value of trade that could result or the importance of India (or indeed, the US) as a strategic partner. China's decisions to engage in questionable nuclear cooperation with Pakistan and to support Pakistan's entry into the NSG are also clearly in the country's own strategic interests. By supporting Pakistan, China strengthened its relationship with Pakistan while, at the same time, the US strengthened its relations with India.

As already mentioned, India and Pakistan had been cut off from the international nuclear market by the NSG's decision to require full-scope safeguards as a condition of supply in the early 1990s. They also conducted nuclear tests in 1998, which resulted in further isolation and sanctions. Following the 9/

11 attacks, US security priorities shifted towards counterterrorism efforts, paving the way for the NATO-led invasion of Afghanistan and the coalition's invasion of Iraq and the toppling of Saddam's regime. The US also intensified its non-proliferation efforts through more proactive measures.[98] It was at this time the Bush administration began to recognise the geostrategic importance of India. However, the non-proliferation issue was a key point of contention between the US and India and it became clear that broader accommodation to be reached between the two States, an arrangement would need to be reached on non-proliferation matters.

It was in this context that the idea for a bilateral US–India agreement arose. The US believed that by reaching an agreement with India, it could secure a geo-strategically important ally while also boosting its nuclear export market. The Bush administration also put forward the argument that any assistance would be subject to safeguards and therefore could not contribute to India's nuclear weapons programme. India, on the other hand, would gain technology for its civil nuclear sector, which had lagged behind Indian aspirations because of India's inability to acquire uranium.

The US negotiators had to ensure that cooperation could be presented as being civil in nature if it was to receive the support of Congress and other governments. The US and India thus negotiated a separation of India's civil and military nuclear programmes as well as a range of other non-proliferation commitments.[99]

The negotiations were complicated by the nature of the Indian nuclear fuel cycle, which had evolved quite differently in nature to that of any other country. Because India needed its limited and finite sources of indigenous uranium for its weapons programme, India had for many decades sought to utilise its plentiful supplies of thorium for use in its nuclear fuel cycle through a complex three-phase fuel cycle in which the thorium would be turned into uranium 233 in reactors. India would resist placing this part of its fuel cycle under IAEA safeguards. Resolution of these issues would require negotiation between India and the IAEA.[100]

The staging for the agreement was necessarily complex. As a provision of the US Atomic Energy Act, the US had to negotiate a nuclear cooperation agreement – a 123 agreement – with India in addition to the US–India agreement, and India had to have in place an agreement and additional protocol with the IAEA before the 123 agreement could enter into force. As a result, the US–India agreement took a number of years to conclude and some of the discussions progressed multilaterally rather than just bilaterally between the US and India. The sequence was as follows.[101]

- 2005: President Bush and Prime Minister Singh announce intention to enter a bilateral nuclear agreement.
- 2006: Hyde act passage in the US which allowed for the conclusion of a nuclear cooperation agreement between the US and India without India signing the NPT.

- 2007: The US and India release text of 123 agreement.
- 2008: NSG exemption for India agreed.
- 2008: US–India agreement reached.

India was evidently keen to conclude an agreement with the US but held a strong line in the negotiations with the US and IAEA. India resisted declaring this novel fuel cycle as 'civil' under the separation plan and thus making it subject to IAEA safeguards.[102] India also resisted other non-proliferation measures, such as ratifying the Comprehensive Test Ban Treaty. The US obtained certain commitments from India, including a voluntary moratorium on testing, but ultimately reached agreement with India with these points not being fully addressed.

The NSG waiver

For the US to resume cooperation with India on nuclear issues, an exemption to the full-scope safeguards requirement reached among the members of the NSG in 1992 would be required. It was recognised that this would be politically and diplomatically challenging not least because the NPT had itself been indefinitely renewed in 1995 after the NSG adopted the requirement. The 1995 NPT review conference expressly welcomed the NSG's actions in adopting a full-scope safeguards requirement as it limited the benefits of nuclear commerce to NPT partners even though the conference was critical of the NSG, in particular for its lack of transparency.[103]

It is notable that despite this international consensus on maintaining a requirement for full-scope safeguards, Russia opted to export fuel valued at $700m to the Tarapur reactors in India through an exemption that existed for nuclear safety. The NSG guidelines allowed for export "in exceptional cases when they are deemed essential for the safe operation of existing facilities".[104] The use of the safety clause by Russia was likely one of the factors that led the US to reconsider its position regarding India.

The US mobilised its diplomatic and political leverage to secure international support for the exemption despite widespread opposition. Despite the backing of the US and other key states such as the UK, there was substantial opposition to the exemption, particularly from the traditionally anti-nuclear states of Ireland, Austria, and New Zealand.[105] China also opposed the waiver but ultimately relented after a phone call from President Bush to President Hu Jintao.[106]

The US pushed for an exemption for India while opposing similar treatment of other non-NPT states (meaning Israel and Pakistan). The rationale for opposing Pakistan likely relates to that country's questionable proliferation record, and the actions of the AQ Khan network in particular. However, the case of Israel is perhaps a more interesting one for examination, given Israel's close relationship with the US. Hibbs attributes the decision of the US to pursue an exemption for India rather than a broader approach for non-NPT states to the diplomatic and political uproar that would likely result from Arab states if an exemption was granted to Israel.[107] The NSG ultimately agreed to the waiver in August 2008.

Despite this, Pakistan has benefited from some civil nuclear commerce. In recent years, China has proceeded with transferring a number of nuclear reactors to Pakistan despite the NSG requirement for full-scope safeguards.[108] China has claimed that this is permissible under a so-called grandfathering provision. The provision relates to when China joined the NSG in 2002. China stated at the time that it considered any existing contracts to be exempt from the requirement for full-scope safeguards. By using this provision to cover the construction of new facilities, China is evidently pushing the bounds of what is reasonably permissible. However, given that the US–India deal was designed in part to balance China, there is a clear strategic driver for China to continue cooperation with Pakistan in responding to the emerging US–India alliance to help in balancing the emerging US–India alliance.

Implications of the India deal the future of international trade controls

As the non-proliferation regime nears universal coverage, questions have arisen about how to manage relations with the small number of countries remaining outside of the regime, with questions about India and Pakistan being most active.[109] Such states naturally want to engage in nuclear cooperation with the international marketplace to benefit their own programmes. Such cooperation can also be in the economic and technical cooperation interests of exporting states. However, such cooperation runs counter to the universalisation of non-proliferation controls which would otherwise see such programmes cut off until the state joins the NPT. In examining the Indian waiver, it is apparent the US put its strategic and commercial interests ahead of its broader non-proliferation interests. In doing so, the US did secure certain non-proliferation commitments from India, including a test moratorium and a commitment to implement export controls. Whether these benefits outweigh the potential costs to the non-proliferation regime is not possible to assess objectively. However, given that the US–India deal has resulted in Indian moves to implement export controls, it has at least helped in moving such measures toward universalisation.

Conclusions: universalising non-proliferation trade controls

The purpose of this chapter was to examine efforts to universalise non-proliferation controls following the discovery of the AQ Khan network as well as the nuclear programmes of Iran and Libya. The discovery of these programs highlighted the limitations of the non-proliferation regime and trade controls as these existed in 2003 and spurred systemic efforts to address the limitations of controls. However, the chapter demonstrates that the sub-optimal evolution of controls continued primarily as implementation of controls at the national level proved insufficient. In this context, this concluding section of the chapter will briefly highlight insights gleaned through the research framework and will draw broader findings from efforts to agree controls in the post-war period.

Findings

The loose research framework includes propositions related to core and structural factors, imperatives, and technological factors. Findings from examining these factors in this period are presented in turn.

Structural factors

- Number of actors involved: This period saw a rapid increase in new potential nuclear supplier states as the case of the Khan network demonstrated. This expansion did make implementation of controls more difficult as these states had no legal basis or capacity to implement controls. The adoption of externally binding measures such as 1540 helped to address this, including by reinforcing a non-proliferation norm, but, ultimately, it was political pressure from the US that led states such as Malaysia to adopt controls rather than the existence of 1540 itself. This expansion of states also meant that states with ideologically different outlooks were involved in the non-proliferation regime for the first time with Indonesia being an example of this.
- Heterogeneity of participants: The homogeneity of states decreased with the growing involvement of non-aligned states and the global south in non-proliferation measures. This meant that the interests and perceived benefits being sought by different parties evolved significantly and became more complex as more states became involved. Even the adoption of binding measures such as 1540 was not enough to overcome the reluctance of some states, including Indonesia, to adopt controls.
- Whether benefits are subtractive or fully shared: More actors recognised the benefits of international nuclear trade controls following the discovery of Iraq's programmes and following the AQ Khan network revelations. This made it easier to achieve consensus around controls and helped to justify external regulation in the form of UNSCRs. However, as noted, this did not result in all states adopting controls and some states, such as Indonesia, were still reluctant to accept controls. Moreover, nuclear suppliers, including the US, were still willing to trade off non-proliferation interests in favour of geopolitical and commercial interests as in the case of the NSG waiver to India.
- The ability for face-to-face communications to take place: It is difficult to evaluate the importance of face-to-face communications as forums such as the NSG do not appear to have played a decisive role in this period. Bilateral face-to-face meetings were essential for the US in getting

China to support the adoption of UNSCR1540 and it was important that all states had the opportunity to express their views on the resolution through an open debate. However, face-to-face communications were at the same time much more common in this period than they had been during the Cold War so it is less clear how important any specific face-to-face meeting was in achieving strengthened international nuclear trade controls.

- Information about past actions and trust among suppliers: These factors do not appear to have been important in this period as the key mechanism of proliferation involved non-state actors and new supplier states with whom no information on past actions was available. Nonetheless, lessons were clearly learned from previous periods in relation to, for example, the need to control dual-use items and the need to deposit information with the IAEA. Indeed, it seems likely that the moves to universalise controls could have been undertaken without the difficult experiences of the previous periods.
- How actors are linked: The NPT became the central linking mechanism in this period as its coverage expanded. This raised tensions with countries outside of the NPT and eventually led to efforts to engage countries such as India into the non-proliferation regime, all be it for other reasons including geopolitical and commercial interests.

Core factors

- The existence of a non-proliferation norm: A non-proliferation norm did exist in this period, which stopped overt state-authorised transfers for the purpose of proliferation. This norm did not, initially at least, apply to non-state actors (i.e., companies and individuals), which was one of the gaps 1540 sought to fill. Moreover, problematically, as the US–India deal and the Chinese arrangement with Pakistan demonstrated, key nuclear states were willing to trade off this norm against other geostrategic interests.
- Technological change including proliferation 'shocks': Nuclear technology did not evolve *per se* in this period, but factors related to globalisation and the expansion of the manufacturing base, with the introduction of new suppliers like Malaysia and the UAE, did change the status quo. The focus of controls was on evolving to meet these challenges but this was complicated, as noted earlier, by the increased number of states potentially involved.

Imperatives

- Uses of atomic energy imperative: Demand for nuclear power for both peaceful and military purposes continued in this period. The number of countries pursuing civil nuclear power production expanded particularly as a consequence of the so-called 'nuclear renaissance', but this was not a central aspect of the evolution of non-proliferation controls in this period.[110] NPT states believed in their inalienable right to the full nuclear fuel cycle with certain states choosing to exercise this right, such as Iran. International nuclear trade controls were accepted but only in as much as they did not interfere with these rights.

- Non-proliferation imperative: The discovery of the AQ Khan network and 1540 solidified the non-proliferation imperative. However, as examination of the India episode highlights, key states continued to place other interests above non-proliferation interests even in this period.
- Disarmament imperative: The lack of progress on disarmament continued to affect the willingness of states to accept additional non-proliferation commitments, including most notably the Additional Protocol. As the AP includes trade provisions, this had the effect of limiting the utility of international nuclear trade controls. One important reason that this became a prominent issue was that states such as Indonesia prioritised disarmament and to some extent peaceful uses more than non-proliferation. In this context, the lack of progress on disarmament is the key barrier to the universalisation of non-proliferation controls.

From this summary of the factors that informed nuclear trade controls in this period, it is apparent that 1540 did help solidify an international trade control norm on a global basis. This allowed for a relatively unified response to the proliferation challenges posed by countries such as Iran and the DPRK. However, away from these high-level principles, practical issues frequently overrode state's commitments to non-proliferation. These practical issues included the real challenges associated with enforcing effective export controls at the national level. Another set of practical issues are related to the question of how to deal with countries such as India, which possess nuclear weapons and are not likely to join the NPT as non-nuclear weapons states. In the case of the latter, in particular, the tendency of many states was to put bilateral and geostrategic and commercial interests ahead of higher-level non-proliferation principles, such as in relation to the US–India deal and subsequent NSG exemption. Ultimately, therefore, it appears the limitations of international trade controls from the Atoms for Peace era continued through this period despite concerted efforts to universalise non-proliferation controls.

Notes

1 Khan's is also known to have sold enrichment technology to North Korea. However, less information is currently available in the public domain about this case.

2 'Nuclear proliferation: PPP denies AQ Khan's allegations', *Pakistan Tribute*, 16 September 2016.

3 'Disgraced atomic scientist disowns confession', *The Guardian*, 30 May 2008.

4 While it is somewhat difficult to attribute this phrase to any one individual, an early use of this phrase was by Mark Fitzpatrick in 2007. See Congressional Hearing Serial No. 110–97, 27 June 2007: *A.Q. Khan's Nuclear Wal-mart: Out of business or under new management?* Statement of Mr Mark Fitzpatrick, Senior Fellow for Non-proliferation, International Institute for Strategic.

5 Perhaps, the most comprehensive account of the Khan network and its activities was produced by Albright, 'Peddling Peril'. Albright notes that there are numerous unknowns associated with his account, exacerbated by the fact that the Pakistan government has denied the IAEA and other authorities access to A.Q. Khan. The description of the network is based on Albright's account. Albright's account drew on a broad variety of primary source information, including some sources reviewed in the drafting of this book, including a Malaysian police report into the Khan network.

6 Interview of Mohamed ElBaradei on BBC Hardtalk, 30 September 2003.

7 For example, a number of Congressional Research Service reports have examined the network and its implications and a number of books have been published examining the network's scope, including David Albright's Peddling Peril, "Pakistan's Nuclear Proliferation Activities and the Recommendations of the 9/11 Commission: U.S. Policy Constraints and Options", *CRS Report for Congress*, Updated 24 May 2005.

8 Albright, *Peddling Peril*, pp. 110–114.

9 Ibid.

10 Ibid.

11 Ibid.

12 Ibid.

13 Ibid.

14 "Pakistan's Nuclear Proliferation Activities and the Recommendations of the 9/11 Commission: U.S. Policy Constraints and Options", *CRS Report for Congress*, Updated 24 May 2005, p. 21.

15 Albright, D., *Peddling Peril*, p. 72.

16 Ibid., p. 78.

17 Ibid., p. 73.

18 Ibid., p. 81.

19 GOV/2004/11: Implementation of the NPT Safeguards agreement in the Islamic Republic of Iran, The International Atomic Energy Agency, 13 March 2004 (para 44).

20 GOV/2007/58: Implementation of the NPT Safeguards agreement in the Islamic Republic of Iran, The International Atomic Energy Agency, 15 November 2007 (para 19).

21 As a light water power reactor, the Busher reactor is not suited to production of plutonium suited for use in nuclear weapons. The reactor is subject to IAEA safeguards and Iran and Russia agreed that the spent fuel would be returned to Russia after its use in the reactor. See "BUSHEHR NUCLEAR POWER PLANT (BNPP)", NTI website.

22 See for example, "Russia may get OK to build reactor for Iran: Country would be exempt from U.N. sanctions imposed by Tehran", NBC News, 17 October 2006.

23 See for example, "Iran Says It Needs More 20%-Enriched Fuel", *Arms Control Association*, 3 May 2011.

24 For an overview of the Libya case, see Bowen, W. *Libya and Nuclear Proliferation: stepping back from the brink*, Adelphi Paper 380, The International

Institute for Strategic Studies, 2006. On Iran and North Korea, see Shen D., Can Sanctions Stop Proliferation?, *The Washington Quarterly*, vol. 31, no. 3, pp. 89–100, doi: 10.1162/wash.2008.31.3.89. On Iraq, see Lopez, G., and Cortright, D., 'Containing Iraq: Sanctions Worked', *Foreign Affairs*, vol. 83, no. 4, July–August, 2004, pp. 90–103.

25 Panorama, Project 706: The Islamic Bomb. Broadcast 6th of June 1980.
26 Albright, D., *Peddling Peril*, p. 116.
27 Ibid.
28 Ibid.
29 Ibid., p. 117.
30 Ibid., p. 117.
31 Ibid., p. 116.
32 Ibid.
33 Ibid.
34 Ibid.
35 Ibid.
36 Ibid.
37 "Cooperation in the Libya WMD Disarmament Case", *Studies in Intelligence*, vol. 61, no. 4 (Extracts, December 2017), Tobey, W.; ibid.
38 There have been a handful of documented transfers of nuclear-related items to DPRK. See for example, Albright, D., '*Peddling Peril: How the secret nuclear trade arms America's enemies*', Free Press, 2012 (pp. 154–168).
39 Ibid., Albright, *Peddling Peril*, p. 160.
40 Ibid.
41 The Malaysian company, SCOMI, was operated by the son of the Malaysian Prime Minister. "Malaysia PM's son in nuclear link", BBC, 5 February 2004.
42 "President Announces New Measures to Counter the Threat of WMD: Remarks by the President on Weapons of Mass Destruction Proliferation", Office of the Press Secretary, 11 February 2004. https://georgewbush-whitehouse.archives.gov/news/releases/2004/02/20040211-4.html.
43 Viski, A., "The Revised Nuclear Suppliers Group Guidelines: A European Perspective", EU Non-proliferation Consortium, Non-proliferation Papers, No 15, May 2012.
44 See for example, Kassenova, T., "Brazil, Argentina, and the Politics of Global Nonproliferation and Nuclear Safeguards", 29 November 2016.
45 This account is based primarily upon a recent original history of the origins of resolution 1540 drafted by William Toby in a volume co-edited by the author of this book. Interviews were also conducted with Toby to inform this section. Toby, W., 'A History of United Nations Security Council Resolution 1540', in *Preventing the Proliferation of WMDs: Measuring the Success of UN Security Council Resolution 1540*, Palgrave Pivot Series. doi: 10.1007/978-3-319-72203-0.
46 Charter of the United Nations, UN.
47 The Global Partnership program gradually refocused its efforts away from dealing with from dealing with the legacy of the Soviet Union's WMD programmes towards countering such emergent threats following the September 9/11 attacks in 2001. The Global Partnership was a somewhat effective forum for this as it involved most of the governments with the greatest capacity for WMD non-proliferation. See for example, Heyes, A., Bowen, W., and Chalmers, H., *The Global Partnership against WMD: Success and shortcomings of G8 Threat Reduction since 9/11*, RUSI Whitehall Paper 68.

48 Cupitt, R.T., 'Capstone and Mortar: Notes on the creation of UNSCR1540', *1540 Compass*.
49 The Proliferation Security Initiative, Ministry of Foreign Affairs, People's Republic of China.
50 Onderco, M., and Hooft., Why is the Proliferation Security Initiative a Problematic Solution?, *The Chinese Journal of International Politics*, vol. 9, no. 1, 1 March 2016, pp. 81–108, doi: https://doi.org/10.1093/cjip/pov013.
51 Toby, W., 'A History of United Nations Security Council Resolution 1540', in Salisbury, D., Stewart, I., and Viski., A. *Preventing the proliferation of WMDs: Measuring the success of UN Security Council Resolution 1540*, Palgrave. doi: 10.1007/978-3-319-72203-0.
52 UNSCR1540, UN Security Council, New York. 28 April 2004.
53 UN Security Council, Minutes of the 4950th meeting, Thursday, 22 April 2004, 9:50 a.m. New York.
54 Ibid.
55 See UNSC, '4950th meeting, Thursday 22 April 2004. Doc S/PV. 4950. As read in Corell, H., "The Mandate of the United Nations Security Council in a Changing World", *International law and changing perceptions of security*. Brill Books. doi: https://doi.org/10.1163/9789004274587
56 The author has observed this on numerous countries when undertaking capacity building on export controls on behalf of the EU.
57 Interview with Will Tobey.
58 It is unclear how and when the 1540 committee took a decision not to 'hound' states into compliance. Indeed, it is possible that this modality of working was a not a result of an active decision but instead an emergent way of working.
59 Interview with Rick Cupitt 22 February 2018. Salisbury, D., Stewart, I., and Viski., A. *Preventing the proliferation of WMDs: Measuring the success of UN Security Council Resolution 1540*, Palgrave. 2018. doi: 10.1007/978-3-319-72203-0.
60 UNODA website, 'The Role of the UN Office for Disarmament Affairs (UNODA) in support of the Committee established pursuant to Security Council Resolution 1540 (2004)'.
61 For example, at a civil society event on resolution 1540 co-hosted by the author in New Delhi, India, in February 2014, the view was expressed that the resolution was "here to stay".
62 Measuring the effectiveness of UNSCR 1540 is challenging. Nonetheless, the 2016 report of the Comprehensive Review of the resolution's implementation notes: While, overall, progress has been made with implementation of resolution 1540 (2004), there remains more to be done to accomplish the objective of full implementation of the resolution, which is a long-term task that requires continuous efforts at the national, regional, and international levels. See S/2016/1038, Report of the Security Council established pursuant to resolution 1540 (2004).
63 Frequently Asked Questions on Resolution 1540 (2004).
64 Information courtesy of the IAEA. "Additional Protocol".
65 See S/2016/1038, Report of the Security Council established pursuant to resolution 1540 (2004).
66 Salisbury, D., Stewart, I., and Viski., A. *Preventing the proliferation of WMDs: Measuring the success of UN Security Council Resolution 1540*, Palgrave. doi: 10.1007/978-3-319-72203-0.

67 See for example, Dill, C., and Stewart, I., 'Defining Effective Strategic Trade Controls at the National Level'. *Strategic Trade Review*, no. 01, Autumn, 2015. Report "Identification of effective implementation practices by examining UNSCR1540 (2004) after a decade of its existence", Institute for Defence Studies and Analyses, Institute for Strategic Studies, King's College London in collaboration with the United Nations Office for Disarmament Affairs. 25–26 February 2014.
68 "Malaysian Opposition Accuses Prime Minister of Nepotism", *LA Times*, 24 February 2004.
69 "Press Release by Inspector General of Police in Relation to Investigation on the Alleged Production of Components for Libya's Uranium Enrichment Programme", February 2004.
70 Kareem, M.S.A., 'Implementation and Enforcement of Strategic Trade Controls in Malaysia', *Strategic Trade Review*, vol. 2, no. 2, Spring, 2016.
71 Ibid.
72 Ibid.
73 Strategic Goods (Control) Act, 2002.
74 Ibid., Kareem, M.S.A.
75 Ibid.
76 Ibid.
77 Rachmianto, A., 'Indonesia's Approach to Strategic Trade Controls: The Perspective of a Developing and Archipelagic Country'. *Strategic Trade Review*, vol. 2, no. 2, Spring, 2016.
78 Ibid.
79 See for example, '1540 Committee Matrix of Indonesia', United Nations, New York.
80 Ibid.
81 See for example, UNSCR 1929, UN Security Council, New York, 2010 (Iran) and UNSCR 1718, UN Security Council, New York, 2006 (North Korea).
82 The restrictions were laid down in UNSCR 1737, UNSCR 1747, UNSCR 1803, and UNSCR1929.
83 Interview with Jonathan Brewer, 20 February 2018.
84 Ibid.
85 For example, the UNSC Committee established pursuant to UNSCR1718 reports:

> As of 16 February 2018, 2 Member States have submitted reports on the implementation of resolution 2397 (2017), 53 Member States have submitted reports on the implementation of resolution 2375 (2017), 56 Member States have submitted reports on the implementation of resolution 2371 (2017), 97 Member States have submitted reports on the implementation of resolution 2321 (2016), and 106 Member States on the implementation of resolution 2270 (2016).
>
> (See www.un.org/sc/suborg/en/sanctions/1718/implementation-reports)

86 For example, the Algeria report includes numerous question marks intended to indicate that it was not possible to establish whether or not the country had taken action on specific measures. Algeria 1540 Matrix Report.
87 Interview with Jonathan Brewer, 20 February 2018.

88 For example, the illicit procurement and export of MKS pressure transducers from MKS Shanghai Limited to Iran was not reported to the UN Panel of Experts. See "Chinese Citizen's Involvement in the Supply of MKS Pressure Transducers to Iran: Preventing a Reoccurrence", 30 April 2014. Available online at: http://isis-online.org/uploads/isis-reports/documents/MKS_China_30Apr2014-final.pdf.

89 Laura Rockwood noted that the IAEA and Iran might, in due course, find that certain specific measures might be implemented more generally for efficiency reasons but believed the landscape was not right for broader adoption of such controls. Interview with Laura Rockwood, 24 February 2018.

90 See for example, Hibbs, M., 'The Unspectacular Future of the IAEA Additional Protocol'. Available online at: http://carnegieendowment.org/2012/04/26/unspectacular-future-of-iaea-additional-protocol-pub-47964.

91 Potter, W., "Disarmament Diplomacy and the Nuclear Ban Treaty", *Survival*, vol. 59, no. 4, pp. 75–108, doi: 10.1080/00396338.2017.1349786.

92 For example, Laura Rockwood has noted, 'Rather than being received as intended – as a blueprint for the next logical step in the evolution of safeguards – the paper and, more specifically, the concept it described triggered a decidedly vitriolic response'. Rockwood, L., 'The IAEA's State Level Concept and the Law of Unintended Consequences'. Available online at: www.armscontrol.org/act/2014_09/Features/The-IAEAs-State-Level-Concept-and-the-Law-of-Unintended-Consequences.

93 See for example, McMahon, R., "Iran, the United Nations, and Sanctions". Available online at: www.cfr.org/backgrounder/iran-united-nations-and-sanctions, 4 April 2006.

94 See Council Regulation (EU) No 961/2010 of 25 October 2010.

95 The question of whether Iran violated the NPT is a complex one that has been much debated. For media coverage of the issue, see "NPT 101: Is Iran violating the nuclear treaty?". Available online at: www.csmonitor.com/World/Middle-East/2010/0504/NPT-101-Is-Iran-violating-the-nuclear-treaty, 4 May 2010. For research on the topic, see "Iran's Nuclear Program: Tehran's Compliance with International Obligations", *Congressional Research Service*. 19 September 2017.

96 "Iran Says It Has 'Inalienable Right' to Enrich Uranium", Bloomberg, 29 June 2012.

97 See for example, Stewart, I., and Gillard, N., 'Iran's illicit procurement: Past, present and future', 24 July 2015.

98 See for example, James A. Russel and James J. Wirtz, *Globalization and WMD proliferation: Terrorism, Transnational networks and international security*. Routledge Global Security Studies, 2008.

99 The need for India to separate its civil and military nuclear programmes was recognised in the 2005 Joint Statement by George W Bush and Manmohan Singh. "Joint Statement by President George W. Bush and Prime Minister Manmohan Singh", White House Press Release, Office of the Press Secretary, Washington, DC, 18 July 2005.

100 See for example, "CRS Report for Congress: India's Nuclear Separation Plan: Issues and Views", Updated 22 December 2016.

101 This timeline is based on the timeline produced by the Times of India. Chronology of the Indo-US nuclear deal, *Times of India*, 9 October 2008.

102 INFCIRC731, 2008.

103 Hibbs, M., 'The future of the Nuclear Suppliers Group', Carnegie Endowment for International Peace, 2011.

104 As read in Hibbs M, "The Future of the Nuclear Suppliers Group", Carnegie Endowment for International Peace, 2011.
105 As read in 'Nuclear Supplier Group gives India unique "waiver", but only after row between Delhi and Beijing'.
106 Ibid.
107 Hibbs M, "The Future of the Nuclear Suppliers Group", Carnegie Endowment for International Peace", 2011.
108 See for example, Hibbs, M., "China, Pakistan, and the Nuclear Suppliers Group", Carnegie Endowment for International Peace, June 2010.
109 At present, there are five such countries: India, Pakistan, Israel, South Korea, and South Sudan.
110 The extent to which there is a nuclear renaissance is unclear particularly in the post-Fukushima context. However, there are signs that Asian countries, in particular, are increasingly relying on nuclear power as a part of an energy balance. Hibbs, M., 'The Nuclear Renaissance?' Carnegie Endowment for International Peace, 30 November 2016.

Bibliography

Albright, D. *Peddling Peril: How the secret nuclear trade arms America's enemies*. Free Press, 2012.

Bowen, W. *Libya and nuclear proliferation: Stepping back from the brink*, Adelphi Paper 380. The International Institute for Strategic Studies, 2006.

"BUSHEHR NUCLEAR POWER PLANT (BNPP)", NTI website.

Chinese Citizen's Involvement in the Supply of MKS Pressure Transducers to Iran: Preventing a Reoccurrence, 30 April 2014. Available online at: http://isis-online.org/uploads/isis-reports/documents/MKS_China_30Apr2014-final.pdf.

Chronology of the Indo-US nuclear deal, *Times of India*, 9 Oct 2008.

Cooperation in the Libya WMD disarmament case, *Studies in Intelligence*, vol. 61, no. 4, pp. 31–42, 2017.

Corell, H. "The Mandate of the United Nations Security Council in a changing world", In *International law and changing perceptions of security*. Brill Books. doi: https://doi.org/10.1163/9789004274587."CRS Report for Congress: India's Nuclear Separation Plan: Issues and Views", Updated 22 December 2016.

Cupitt, R.T. 'Capstone and Mortar: Notes on the creation of UNSCR1540', 1540 Compass.

Dill, C., & Stewart, I. Defining effective strategic trade controls at the national level. *Strategic Trade Review*, vol. 1, no. 1, pp. 4–17, Autumn, 2015.

GOV/2004/11: Implementation of the NPT Safeguards agreement in the Islamic Republic of Iran. The International Atomic Energy Agency, 13 March 2004.

GOV/2007/58: Implementation of the NPT Safeguards agreement in the Islamic Republic of Iran. The International Atomic Energy Agency, 15 November 2007.

Hibbs, M. "China, Pakistan, and the Nuclear Suppliers Group", Carnegie Endowment for International Peace, June 2010.

Hibbs, M. 'The future of the Nuclear Suppliers Group', Carnegie Endowment for International Peace, 2011.

Hibbs, M. 'The Nuclear Renaissance?', Carnegie Endowment for International Peace, 30 November 2016.

Hibbs, M. 'The Unspectacular Future of the IAEA Additional Protocol', 2012. Available online at: http://carnegieendowment.org/2012/04/26/unspectacular-future-of-iaea-additional-protocol-pub-47964.
Heyes, A., Bowen, W., & Chalmers, H. The Global Partnership against WMD: Success and shortcomings of G8 Threat Reduction since 9/11, RUSI Whitehall Paper 68.
"Iran Says It Needs More 20%-Enriched Fuel", Arms Control Association, 3 May 2011.
"Iran Says It Has 'Inalienable Right' to Enrich Uranium", Bloomberg, 29 June 2012.
"Iran's Nuclear Program: Tehran's Compliance with International Obligations", Congressional Research Service. 19 September 2017.
"Joint Statement by President George W. Bush and Prime Minister Manmohan Singh", White House Press Release, Office of the Press Secretary, Washington, DC, 18 July 2005.
Kareem, M.S.A. Implementation and enforcement of strategic trade controls in Malaysia', *Strategic Trade Review*, vol. 2, no. 2, Spring, 2016, pp. 104–117.
Kassenova, T. "Brazil, Argentina, and the Politics of Global Nonproliferation and Nuclear Safeguards", 29 November 2016. Available online at: https://carnegieendowment.org/2016/11/29/brazil-argentina-and-politics-of-global-nonproliferation-and-nuclear-safeguards-pub-66286 (Accessed 14 June 2021).
Lopez, G., & Cortright, D. Containing Iraq: Sanctions worked, *Foreign Affairs*, vol. 83, no. 4, July–August, 2004.
"Malaysia PM's son in nuclear link", *BBC*, 5 February 2004.
"Malaysian Opposition Accuses Prime Minister of Nepotism", *LA Times*, 24 February 2004.
McMahon, R. "Iran, the United Nations, and Sanctions", 4 April 2006. Available online at: www.cfr.org/backgrounder/iran-united-nations-and-sanctions.
"NPT 101: Is Iran violating the nuclear treaty?", 4 May 2010. Available online at: www.csmonitor.com/World/Middle-East/2010/0504/NPT-101-Is-Iran-violating-the-nuclear-treaty.
Onderco, M., & Hooft P. Why is the proliferation security initiative a problematic solution?, *The Chinese Journal of International Politics*, vol. 9, no. 1, 1 March 2016, pp. 81–108. doi: https://doi.org/10.1093/cjip/pov013.
"Pakistan's Nuclear Proliferation Activities and the Recommendations of the 9/11 Commission: U.S. Policy Constraints and Options", CRS report for Congress, Updated 24 May 2005, p. 21.
Panorama, Project 706: The Islamic Bomb. Broadcast 6 June 1980.
Potter, W. Disarmament diplomacy and the nuclear ban treaty, *Survival*, vol. 59, no. 4, pp. 75–108. doi: 10.1080/00396338.2017.1349786.
"President Announces New Measures to Counter the Threat of WMD: Remarks by the President on Weapons of Mass Destruction Proliferation", Office of the Press Secretary, 11 February 2004. Available online at: https://georgewbush-whitehouse.archives.gov/news/releases/2004/02/20040211-4.html.
"Press Release by Inspector General of Police in Relation to Investigation on the Alleged Production of Components for Libya's Uranium Enrichment Programme", February 2004.
Rachmianto, A. Indonesia's approach to strategic trade controls: The perspective of a developing and archipelagic country. *Strategic Trade Review*, vol. 2, no. 2, pp. 130–139, Spring, 2016.

"Russia may get OK to build reactor for Iran: Country would be exempt from U.N. sanctions imposed by Tehran", *NBC News*, 17 October 2006.

S/2016/1038, Report of the Security Council established pursuant to resolution 1540 (2004).

Salisbury, D., Stewart, I., & Viski, A. Preventing the Proliferation of WMDs: Measuring the Success of UN Security Council Resolution 1540, Palgrave. doi: 10.1007/978-3-319-72203-0.

Shen, D. Can sanctions stop proliferation?, *The Washington Quarterly*, vol. 31, no. 3, pp. 89–100, Summer, 2008.

Stewart, I., & Gillard, N. 'Iran's illicit procurement: Past, present and future', 24 July 2015. doi: 10.1162/wash.2008.31.3.89.

The Proliferation Security Initiative, Ministry of Foreign Affairs, People's Republic of China.

Toby, W. 'A History of United Nations Security Council Resolution 1540'. In *Preventing the Proliferation of WMDs: Measuring the Success of UN Security Council Resolution 1540*, Palgrave Pivot Series. doi: 10.1007/978-3-319-72203-0.

UN Security Council, Minutes of the 4950th meeting, Thursday, 22 April 2004, 9:50 a.m. New York.

UNODA website, 'The Role of the UN Office for Disarmament Affairs (UNODA) in support of the Committee established pursuant to Security Council Resolution 1540 (2004)'.

UNSCR1540, UN Security Council, New York, 28 April 2004.

UNSCR 1718, UN Security Council, New York, 2006.

UNSCR 1929, UN Security Council, New York, 2010.

Viski, A. "The Revised Nuclear Suppliers Group Guidelines: A European Perspective", EU Non-proliferation Consortium, Non-proliferation Papers, No 15, May 2012.

7 Conclusions

This book has sought to identify and understand the factors that have influenced the evolution of international nuclear trade controls over time. In particular, it sought to address the question: *why have nuclear non-proliferation trade controls evolved in a sub-optimal fashion since the dawn of the nuclear age?* This suboptimal evolution, as the previous chapters have demonstrated, is both relative and absolute; in each period of study, decisions were taken that resulted in a sub-optimal system of control while, simultaneously, implementation of conceived systems of control that were considered to be more complete and effective proved out of reach for the entire period of study.

In explaining this, a central argument of this book is that there has been a non-proliferation collective action problem and that this affected the evolution of controls. Given this, relevant factors from collective action literature were used as propositions in a loose framework which was used to examine a number of important episodes. Episode selection, in turn, was done in such a way to provide insight into the evolution of controls over the entire nuclear age.

The overall argument of the book is that the suboptimal evolution of international nuclear controls over time can be understood primarily as a result of the intrusion of geopolitical factors, which have played the main role in shaping the nature of the international nuclear scene. These geopolitical factors constrained the overall nuclear trade control landscape and resulted in an environment in which a host of other factors, for example, commercial factors and emerging technology factors, were not adequately addressed despite the fact that non-proliferation was generally seen to be in the best interests of most states particularly as the decades went by. Put another way, the geopolitical factors present in the early nuclear age led to the creation of a non-proliferation collective action problem that proved difficult to overcome. At important junctures, key factors including the imperatives of using atomic energy for peaceful and military purposes, commercial interests, and other domestic political factors played important roles in influencing how the controls evolved. These intervening factors persisted even after the existence of a collective action problem was recognised by policymakers in the US and elsewhere in the 1970s. Indeed, a combination of vested interests and technical

DOI: 10.4324/9781003194262-7

naivety intervened to prevent the problem from being effectively addressed. This was true even after the end of the Cold War. Ultimately, it took the increasing involvement of the UN Security Council in the 2000s to utilise externally imposed regulation in an effort to universalise and complete the international nuclear control regime. While it could be argued that the UN is only as strong as its member states, the near consensus among the permanent members of the UNSC in relation to the principle of non-proliferation has allowed the UNSC to take significant steps forward, even though in many specific cases their wider geopolitical interests have limited the scope of UN actions. This includes the cases of Iran and the DPRK where Russia and China, respectively, curbed some aspects of UN action when it was deemed detrimental to their national interests. Despite this, numerous vested interests and practical enforcement challenges continued to restrain the effectiveness of controls.

The remainder of this chapter presents the analysis of the propositions of the research framework to identify the most important factors that explain the sub-optimal evolution of controls. The implications of these findings for further improving non-proliferation trade controls are then examined.

Structural factors

Structural factors according to collective action literature include factors such as how actors are linked and how benefits are shared among participants. Evidently, the structural dynamics of the Cold War were important throughout much of the research period. The findings *vis-à-vis* structural factors are covered in the following.

> Proposition: The number and type of actors involved in nuclear-related trade will affect the ability of states to cooperate on nuclear non-proliferation trade controls. Specifically, more actors of different types will make cooperation less likely.

The general pattern in the evolution of the nuclear non-proliferation trade controls has been for smaller groups of key states to take decisions on governance measures and for these then to be presented to even larger groups. This is a reflection of how international agreements are generally developed by states across all fields given the practical challenges associated with holding negotiations within large groups of states.

It is notable that a consensus was often reachable on the principle of non-proliferation trade controls between the Superpowers. This was perhaps to be expected as maintaining control on the number of nuclear weapons states was in their mutual interest. It is also notable that it was often difficult for agreement to be reached with states that sought to pursue non-aligned foreign policy lines, such as France and India. As the number of actors expanded, the challenge associated with achieving consensus generally increased, often resulting in agreement only on the 'lowest common denominator' controls.

Examples of this include the safeguards adopted alongside the NPT which European states sought to weaken so that they aligned to Euratom measures and the sanctions measures adopted by the UNSCR on Iran and North Korea.

The number of actors involved in the nuclear field increased significantly over time. Following the easing of the McMahon Act, for example, commercial companies began to become involved in nuclear matters. With the launch of the Atoms for Peace initiative, an international organisation – the IAEA – became involved in international nuclear governance. During the 1960s and 1970s, commercial organisations subsequently became involved in the provision of nuclear services and commercial firms also became heavily involved in the supply of dual-use goods. The growth in the number of actors involved was compounded by the effects of globalisation after the end of the Cold War and the spread of relevant manufacturing capabilities to further centres of control. This growth in the number and type of actors has clearly complicated efforts to overcome the trade control collective action problem. First, the number and significance of vested interests has expanded over time. This can be seen most directly in the reluctance of some states to agree controls on so-called dual-use goods. Second, it has made the implementation and enforcement of controls more difficult, allowing some states to progress their nuclear programmes. More problematically in the context of the evolution of controls, these enforcement challenges have also undermined some state's commitment to controls, thus making some states more reluctant to accept additional control measures when there have been signs other states were not acting in good faith. Several examples of this have been noted in this book. In one notable example, Henry Kissinger said that the US would go only as far as other states in the 1970s even while taking a lead in coordinating international nuclear trade controls.

> Proposition: The heterogeneity of participants will influence the ability of states to cooperate.

Despite the fact that relatively small groups were often involved in leading on trade control initiatives, the need to engage larger numbers of states in order to overcome non-proliferation challenges had the effect of limiting the effectiveness of the regime and related controls. There are various reasons for this. Broadening the number of actors involved meant bringing in actors with ideologically different views from those states that lead most non-proliferation efforts. Broadening the groups of states also brought into the fold states with an interest in acquiring nuclear weapons thereby complicating governance arrangements. India is a country that fell into both categories, using its involvement in the IAEA statute negotiations, as well as other governance forums, to frustrate and minimise the adoption of non-proliferation trade controls. This was done specifically for national gain.

It was not only states interested in acquiring nuclear weapons that acted to frustrate the development of controls. For example, Euratom states acted to limit NPT safeguards negotiations in order to strengthen Euratom's position *vis-à-vis* the IAEA in safeguards negotiations. Moreover, while the Superpowers carried substantial influence over other states in the evolution of non-proliferation trade controls, this was not sufficient to overcome all of the individual interests of states. The NPT negotiation is an example of this. It was largely the Superpowers that negotiated the core treaty. However, the US and the USSR were not able to convince other states to sign up without offering additional concessions that acted to undermine the controls sought.

> Proposition: The issue of whether benefits are subtractive or fully shared will affect the extent to which states are willing to cooperate. Specifically, states will be more likely to pursue subtractive rather than shared benefits when taking decisions about restricting supply or allowing transactions.

Several points become apparent about 'benefits', which can be loosely considered to include the shared security benefit resulting from the policy objective of non-proliferation as well as commercial or financial benefits.

To begin with, let us consider non-proliferation as a shared benefit. One important observation here is that the concept of non-proliferation has had different meanings for different actors at different points during the nuclear age. As a result, the question of precisely what 'benefit' was being sought was not always clear. For example, in the 1960s the US wished to keep its options open to transfer nuclear weapons to allies while also in parallel pursuing non-proliferation arrangements. In the 1970s, the US prioritised countering the spread of reprocessing capabilities over other non-proliferation goals. As a result, it was difficult at times for there to be a clear articulation of the benefit to participants of a shared international approach to trade controls and non-proliferation.

Beyond the collective benefit of non-proliferation, it is apparent that the pursuit of a number of other benefits affected the evolution of non-proliferation trade controls. For example, several states placed benefits such as stronger political relationships with partner countries ahead of non-proliferation. Examples of this from the book include Canadian sales to India in the 1950s, US aid to Pakistan and Iraq in the 1980s, and the US–India nuclear deal of the 2000s. Companies and individuals have also placed profit and personal status above states' commitments with thousands of illegal transactions taking place over the nuclear age. These 'subtractive benefits' have often been clearer and more tangible than the benefits of a common approach to non-proliferation. As a result, it has not always been clear that collective action on specific proliferation episodes has been in the interests of key states. An added factor here has been that the benefits of non-proliferation arguably have a longer-term payoff than, for example, the financial payoff resulting from the sale of a research reactor.

> Proposition: The ability for face-to-face communications to take place will positively affect the ability of states to cooperate on non-proliferation trade controls.

The book demonstrates that the existence or absence of forums for face-to-face meetings appears to have been significant with regard to nuclear non-proliferation trade controls. For example, the US was sceptical about Russia's insistence on the need for safeguards as part of the Atoms for Peace initiative until bilateral face-to-face talks of technical experts took place. Moreover, it seems likely that meetings of the NSG after 1977 would have resulted in a more systematic strengthening of dual-use export controls after the discovery of Pakistan's enrichment programme. Instead, the UK led an *ad hoc* and largely bilateral campaign to have states control dual-use goods during the 1980s. Moreover, meetings of the NSG in 1992 allowed the newer states to overcome commercial interests in controlling dual-use goods.

> Proposition: Information about past actions will positively influence the willingness of states to implement non-proliferation trade controls.

Throughout the nuclear age there have been countless rumours about states not living up to their commitments. In some instances, this is doubtless true. But in many instances states either did not know that a violation was occurring or that, from a strict legal perspective, alleged violations were not actual violations. Nonetheless, efforts to strengthen controls were plagued by an imperfect information picture, a problem compounded at times by breaks in forums such as the NSG, which reduced the opportunities for states to offer reassurance that rules were being followed.[1]

A key challenge in this area involved commercial confidentiality. Information on nuclear trade is often commercially sensitive meaning that information is not releasable into the public domain. While the IAEA has somewhat acted like a repository of information for certain transfers, as had been proposed in the WSG meetings of the 1950s, the IAEA's mandate prevents it from sharing this trade-related information with other states. Beyond this, however, it was perhaps the suspicion that other states might be undercutting their own commitments that posed the greatest challenge to overcoming the trade control collective action problem. Overall, the lack of information on past actions has had a significant and often negative effect on the evolution of non-proliferation trade controls.

> Proposition: How actors are linked will affect the willingness of states to cooperate.

The question of how actors in the non-proliferation regime are linked is a complex one because, as demonstrated in the book, there are several types of actors. State actors can also be linked institutionally, geographically, or through security and economic alliances. Non-proliferation by its nature requires cooperation between actors from across these divides. Ultimately, it was cooperation between the USSR and the US that brought the NPT to fruition, for example. At the same time, limitations in cooperation between the US and the USSR have exacerbated proliferation issues. It was because of the security dynamic between the US and USSR that the UNAEC failed and the Atoms for Peace initiative went forward without an effective system of control.

There are grounds to believe that the institutionalisation of relationships between states can help in the formulation of norms. This is perhaps a result of having a dedicated professional staff focused on attainment of a particular outcome. Institutionalisation of the NSG in the 1990s through regular political and technical meetings provided a mechanism for ongoing improvements to nuclear export controls over the following decade, for example. However, as the next section highlights, in relation to non-proliferation, there are signs that institutionalisation can create inertia against structural change. It is clear that IAEA safeguards could be improved, for example, but there is resistance to the IAEA taking on additional roles and responsibilities or even taking steps to optimise safeguards implementation for fear that it could result in a more discriminatory approach.[2] This point is compounded by the refusal of some states to conclude an Additional Protocol, which has some trade provisions, with the IAEA unless there is progress on disarmament. Any truly effective system of control would likely see stronger linkage between international trade control and verification mechanisms such as safeguards. Had the underpinning architecture of the non-proliferation regime been better designed this might not have been a problem. However, given the underpinning structural issues with the non-proliferation regime, this has had the effect of setting back efforts to improve non-proliferation trade controls.

Core factors

The second set of propositions derived from the collective action literature related to so-called 'core factors': reputation, trust, reciprocity, levels of cooperation, and net benefit. As the introduction recognised, there is clearly some overlap between these factors and the structural variables examined earlier.

Core factors such as norms and trust appear to have had an important role in the evolution of non-proliferation trade controls. For example, in order for cooperation to take place between the US and USSR, trust was necessary. At key points, this trust was developed through meetings of technical experts and maintained through dialogues intended to overcome ambiguities, such as in relation to the need for safeguards to be associated with the Atoms for Peace initiative.

> Proposition: The existence of trust will positively influence the willingness of states to cooperate on non-proliferation trade controls.

From the perspective of the US there was a relatively sincere effort to bring about nuclear disarmament in the 1940s, but after this point successions of officials in each Presidential administration began to believe that disarmament was not achievable. Perhaps most significant was the expression of this view in 1954, when Eisenhower's Cabinet debated to proceed with the Atoms for Peace initiative.[3] It is evident that US and Soviet proposals for disarmament became less sincere after this point. There was an evident geo-strategic rationale for the two Superpowers to be seen to pursue disarmament in order to influence diplomatic relations with non-aligned states, as well as the public narrative and propaganda related to the Cold War.

For states other than the US and the USSR, there was a mixture of geo-strategic factors that affected the evolution of the non-proliferation trade controls. For India and Pakistan, for example, there was clear geo-strategic interest in keeping open the option of acquiring nuclear weapons. Given India's major influence on the non-proliferation regime from the 1950s through the 1970s, it can be argued that these factors directly affected the positions that India took on, for example, the IAEA statute discussions.

Pakistan was driven to acquire nuclear weapons primarily as a result of its strategic security concerns *vis-à-vis* India. Pakistan faced a decision about whether to address this concern through conventional or strategic nuclear weapons. However, the Reagan administration would ultimately turn a partial blind eye to this question to gain Pakistan's support on combating the Soviet occupation of Afghanistan. However, unlike India, Pakistan was not in a position to substantially influence global nuclear governance from the 1950s to the 1970s.

Still, cooperation between the Superpowers – and indeed other states in the context of the Cold War – required some degree of trust. This trust developed through observation of the actions of the other in relation to non-proliferation. In particular, once both Superpowers had negative experiences of unrestrained nuclear transfer – China in the case of the Soviet Union and India in the case of the US – neither was inclined to assist other states in proliferating. As such, it was sufficient for the Superpowers to observe one another to satisfy themselves that the other was not proliferating nuclear weapons as a means to fight the Cold War. The overall result is that the Superpowers were able to maintain trust and cooperation on the non-proliferation issue in general, other than where this issue interacted with other aspects of the Cold War, as in the case of Iraq and Pakistan where the Superpowers placed their geo-strategic interests before their non-proliferation interests.

Trust was also necessary between the members of the various forums and regimes that designed and maintained non-proliferation trade controls. It was observed previously that the lack of meetings of the NSG from 1978 to 1991 removed a key forum with which relations between states could have been reinforced. A final point relates to states not involved in the development of controls. Throughout the nuclear age there has been suspicion that nuclear non-proliferation trade controls are somehow a tool of technical repression. While this suspicion might have lessened in recent years, with states like India now seeking to join the export control regimes, it has nonetheless had a significant role in shaping the evolution of non-proliferation trade controls. This suspicion contributed to the decision to suspend meetings of the NSG in the late 1970s, for example. The flip side of this suspicion was concern that the US might not fulfil commitments to partner countries as a result of non-proliferation considerations. Indeed, it was realised by some politicians in Washington in the late 1970s that the US was no longer viewed as a reliable nuclear supplier. There was thus concern that US policy could drive other states to indigenising capabilities so as not to be reliant on continued US cooperation.[4]

> Proposition: The existence of non-proliferation norms will positively influence the willingness of states to cooperate on non-proliferation trade controls.

The question of whether a non-proliferation norm affected the evolution of non-proliferation trade controls is an important but difficult one. In part the problem is definitional. If there is a non-proliferation norm, is it distinct from the norm in support of the non-use of nuclear weapons and disarmament? At heart, this question is about how such a norm would deal with states that have, or are thought to have, nuclear weapons. The definitional problem is compounded by the nature of the NPT, which includes in it certain states that have nuclear weapons. In accordance with the rules of the NPT, nuclear cooperation can take place with the nuclear weapons states as defined by the treaty but not with states that opted to remain outside of the NPT.

In the immediate aftermath of the use of nuclear weapons in the Second World War, there was certainly a fear about the power of atomic weapons. However, there are few signs that a norm existed then around either the non-use of nuclear weapons or the non-acquisition of such weapons. This loosely continued to be the case through the 1960s when ideas around 'selective proliferation' were present in strategic thinking about nuclear weapons – a concept that declined after the Chinese nuclear test in 1964 and the Gilpatric commission that followed.

It could be argued that the negotiation of the NPT marked the creation of a non-proliferation norm. However, there are certain challenges with this argument. In particular, the origins of the NPT as a multilateral instrument lay in an Irish disarmament resolution. Additionally, ratification of the NPT was initially quite slow, with some states such as India and France rejecting the treaty outright. It might instead be argued that it was the NSG meetings of the 1970s that led to the creation of a non-proliferation norm. The NSG did certainly achieve common ground in the recognition that it was in the interests of its participating states to work to prevent the proliferation of nuclear weapons to new states. However, the measures adopted by the NSG in the 1970s were limited. Additionally, these limitations persisted even after the discovery of Pakistan's efforts to covertly build an enrichment capability utilising illicitly acquired goods.

There are signs that a strong non-proliferation imperative emerged following the discovery of Iraq's clandestine nuclear programme in the early 1990s. Following this, the NSG resumed its meeting with a larger number of participants and extended its guidelines to cover a number of gaps that were left unaddressed in the 1970s such as control of dual-use goods. A key question therefore is what changed between the 1970s and the 1990s. Evidently, the collapse of the Soviet Union was a major factor. However, both Superpowers had cooperated on non-proliferation before this point as it was recognised that proliferation was not in the interest of either country. Another possibility is an 'emergent effect' in which the emergence of the norm was gradual, perhaps as more states signed up to the NPT, for example.

It is also important to ask: for whom there is a non-proliferation norm? NSG participation in the 1990s, despite being larger than in the 1970s, was still relatively limited. As mentioned, only 25 states attended the NSG meeting in 1993. It was not until after the adoption of UNSCR 1540 that many states in Asia, Africa, and South America began to adopt non-proliferation trade controls, although most states had previously signed the NPT. Moreover, the existence of a non-proliferation norm at the state level does not necessarily equate to individuals and companies being affected by it. Indeed, it is clear that a norm can only be effective if all actors across all levels are aware of the norm and how their actions could potentially contravene or uphold it. Given that many countries did not have in place non-proliferation control laws, it is evident that many sub-state actors were not aware of the issue or affected by the law. Indeed, there continues to be a concern to this day that there is an 'awareness gap' in relation to non-proliferation and export controls within companies and across societies as a whole.

> Proposition: Technological change including proliferation 'shocks' will negatively affect the evolution of non-proliferation trade controls.

Substantial technological development has taken place since the end of the Second World War. While the principles of atomic energy have not changed, the technological revolution that has taken place since the 1940s has resulted in new atomic processes. New types of nuclear reactor have been developed, new methods of enriching uranium have been devised, and advancing computational capabilities allow for ever greater understanding of atomic applications. Technological advancement has been driven primarily by commercial and safety-related factors, although the application of advanced computational techniques has been driven by a need to prove atomic weapons processes without testing. As a result, while the understanding of atomic energy that existed in the 1940s continues to be largely applicable today, certain enabling technologies have emerged that have profoundly shaped the nature of the proliferation challenge. The manufacturing base for dual-use items has also spread in this period, and the factors associated with globalisation – such as the increasing movement of information and people – have helped to spread relevant knowledge. The overall effect has been to introduce new potential suppliers of technology.

As previously mentioned, a key consideration in the early nuclear age was that the technologies that were the readiest for commercialisation were developed by states for strategic purposes. Perhaps the main technological evolution involved uranium enrichment using centrifuges. In the early nuclear age, enrichment was feasible only by electromagnetic diffusion routes. However, from the 1960s it began to be possible to enrich uranium via rotational centrifuge.

There are signs that the non-proliferation regime was adaptable to emerging technological risks. The URENCO governments (UK, Germany, and Netherlands) had agreed to make centrifuge information subject to classification rules in the 1960s at the request of the US, which had identified the risk that a foreigner could gain access to the programme, for example.[5] These agreed rules were inadequately enforced in URENCO's supply chain in the 1970s resulting in the technology leaking out first to Pakistan and then to other states including, as highlighted, Iran, Libya, and North Korea. Had the NSG continued meeting in the 1970s, it could perhaps have been expected that the regime would have expanded controls on enrichment-related dual-use technologies after the UK discovered Pakistan was procuring such items. After the US decided to suspend meetings of the NSG, the UK instead opted to approach only those countries capable of manufacturing the specific item – inverters – rather than take up the issue in a multilateral setting like the NSG.[6]

NSG controls were later extended to many dual-use items required in nuclear fuel cycle applications. The manufacturing base for such items continues to be limited.[7] However, the practical challenge of controlling industry-related items is significant, and several countries and the A.Q. Khan network have had success in procuring such goods despite the implementation of increasingly robust trade controls. While it is beyond the scope of this book, there remains the possibility that a new technology could emerge that undermines non-proliferation trade controls. One possibility is laser enrichment. While no state or company has thus far succeeded in mastering this technology for large-scale deployment, doing so could substantially undermine the non-proliferation regime.

Imperatives

Imperative for use of atomic energy

It was recognised during the Second World War that atomic energy could have both significant military and civil utility. As Chapter 2 illustrated, there was even discussion during the war about the need to devise methods of control to allow civil uses to be exploited without enabling further states to utilise atomic energy for military purposes.[8] In fact, the Atoms for Peace initiative was an embodiment of this sentiment as was the 'inalienable right' embodied in the NPT. The very purpose of the UNAEC was to devise and agree such a system.[9] Throughout the nuclear age, therefore, there has been an imperative to utilise atomic energy for peaceful purposes, although recognition that the duality of atomic energy means it could be misused for military purposes.

The imperative to utilise atomic energy for peaceful purposes has been important during the whole nuclear age, albeit with some variation following nuclear accidents such as the one at Chernobyl.[10] This imperative has been recognised both by states that hold nuclear technology and states that would like to exploit atomic energy. There have, however, been periods in which the interests of states to utilise atomic energy have been debated. Chapter 2 demonstrated that some members of the US Cabinet and US Congress during the Truman administration wished, and believed it was possible, to keep atomic energy purely for the US.[11] This view was countered by leading scientists, however, who demonstrated that the US could not expect to maintain a monopoly on the use of atomic energy. The outcome was that the US controlled technology through the McMahon Act, but only temporarily until an adequate system of control could be agreed.

The second instance relates to the USSR's immediate response to the US when it announced the Atoms for Peace initiative. As argued in Chapter 3 and 4, the Soviet Union was against the spread of nuclear technology at this point in part because a system of control had not then been devised.

It must also be recognised that many states did have an interest in acquiring nuclear technology for both peaceful and military purposes. Indeed, absent an effective system of control, it is argued that all states embarking on a nuclear programme are potentially 'nuclear hedgers'. This dual interest of at least some states affected the evolution of the non-proliferation regime. States such as India had an incentive to secure nuclear assistance which was free from control. As Chapter 3 demonstrated, this directly affected the negotiation of the IAEA Board of Governor's statute and the safeguards resolution, where states such as India acted to minimise controls.

The risks inherent in this approach were recognised by key states, including the UK and the US. Indeed, the US and the UK even insisted that Canada allow them to review the safeguards agreement for the CANDU reactor export to India and expressed concerns about its content. These risks were understood by certain nuclear suppliers at the time decisions were taken to enter into nuclear supply transfers, such as when Canada agreed to supply the CANDU-type reactor to India in the knowledge that it would duplicate this design indigenously and could utilise it for military purposes.[12] This drove efforts to coordinate common approaches to the problem through both the WSG and later the NSG. However, commercial and diplomatic interests made the task of coordination between the suppliers more difficult. It was not until after the revelations about Iraq in 1991 that the NSG was able to agree full-scope safeguards as a condition of supply and this loophole was addressed. A final point relates to the dual-use imperative: it is important for economic trade and development for trade in so-called dual-use items to go forward with as few impediments as possible. A challenge for authorities committed to controlling such items is how to do it in a way that minimises impact on legitimate trade which, inevitably, results in some residual proliferation risk.

Overall, therefore, the imperative of uses of atomic energy has been driven by a variety of factors that have been more or less constant across the nuclear age. This imperative has driven the provision of atomic assistance at the same time as introducing factors that acted to counter the adoption of an effective system of control.

Disarmament imperative

Interest in disarmament has significantly affected the nature and scope of the non-proliferation discourse and controls throughout the nuclear age. After the Second World War, it was understood that non-proliferation would only be possible if disarmament could be realised. This drove the creation of the UNAEC. After this effort failed, the US opted to launch the Atoms for Peace initiative with the understanding that disarmament was unlikely or impossible and that proliferation was inevitable, which it was argued is a key reason why the initiative went forward absent an effective system of control. At an important Cabinet meeting in 1954, the US expressly opted to proceed with the initiative despite knowing the limitations of controls.[13] The main factor at play here was America's geopolitical interests in the context of the Cold War which compelled Washington to proceed with the Atoms for Peace programme without effective non-proliferation trade controls.

Efforts to strengthen non-proliferation trade controls from the 1960s were then set back by the lack of agreement concerning disarmament. States such as India utilised the argument that intrusive controls could be agreed only in the context of disarmament (and not for the purposes of non-proliferation) to justify the weakening of non-proliferation trade controls. This principled argument became embedded into the NPT and has since been utilised by states such as Brazil to justify opposition to enhanced non-proliferation trade controls, including with regards to the Additional Protocol.

Non-proliferation imperative

This examination of the evolution of international nuclear trade controls demonstrates that non-proliferation has often been a secondary interest of states. In the early nuclear age, key states simply did not think that measures to prevent the spread of nuclear weapons could be effective. As a result, non-proliferation policies were not pursued. The limitations of this approach were gradually recognised and redressed. However, even though non-proliferation proved to be a topic on which the US and Soviet Union could cooperate in general terms, specific proliferation episodes were often not adequately addressed by the superpowers because of more immediate geopolitical considerations in the context of the Cold War. Non-proliferation, quite simply, has often proven not to be a short-term priority in geopolitical decision-making. Non-proliferation measures have been adopted at key junctures such as in the NPT and the NSG in the 1970s and UNSCRs in the 2000s particularly when these measures have not conflicted with other foreign policy priorities of states such as great power competition. While a substantial non-proliferation infrastructure now exists, the reality is that for much of the nuclear age, a non-proliferation imperative has been lacking.

Other factors not covered by the research framework

By applying the framework to this study of non-proliferation trade controls, it became possible to identify and understand common factors that affected their evolution over time. From this application it emerged that the framework did not fully account for all factors affecting the evolution of non-proliferation trade controls as set out in previous chapters. One issue in particular stands out and this relates to domestic political and bureaucratic factors. While these factors were accounted for to some extent in the preceding chapters, changes in the domestic policies of certain states, particularly the US, have had an important impact on the development of non-proliferation trade controls. Key points when bureaucratic factors had an important influence include the debate in the US about how to manage atomic energy, the design of the Atoms for Peace initiative; the negotiation of the IAEA statute; and changes to the domestic US political narrative between the Ford, Carter, and Nixon administrations. When conceiving Atoms for Peace in 1953, the initiative was not circulated widely within the US interagency process or to the majority of the commissioners at the AEC. In retrospect, it seems likely that a broader circulation of the proposal would have resulted in the problem being identified with it. After the initiative was launched, Eisenhower responded to Churchill that while he did not think there were security concerns with the initiative, that issue should be studied.[14] Later, in 1956, the President defended Strauss during the "soft impeachment" that followed the AEC's development of a small power research reactor. The President stated that he could not comprehend why the AEC's failure to develop such a reactor mattered.[15] In 1956, during the

IAEA statute discussions, the USAEC and State Department each pursued different minimum fallback positions, which left the UK the "ungrateful task of holding the Americans in check".[16] Central to each of these episodes was Lewis Strauss, who was chairman of the USAEC. As noted earlier, Strauss was a close confidant of Eisenhower, but not a nuclear expert and his relationship with the other atomic energy commissioners was often fraught.

In the 1970s, the differing policies of the Ford, Carter, and Reagan administrations to non-proliferation was also significant. Chapter 4 highlighted that it was not so much that these administrations placed differing levels of importance on the benefits and need for non-proliferation. Rather, the approaches taken by the administrations were dissimilar and somewhat incompatible, partly explaining why it was Washington which began to be seen as an unreliable partner in terms of the provision of civil nuclear services and assistance. It seems likely that inconsistency in one key state's policy would undermine efforts to overcome a collective action problem. Therefore, while it might be that these differing policy approaches were the result of underlying structural problems with the non-proliferation regime, it is likely that inconsistency in US policy did set back efforts to overcome the non-proliferation collective action problem, particularly because US policy prevented further meetings of the NSG after 1977.

Having now utilised the research framework to examine the evolution of nuclear trade controls over time, it is apparent that there are a complex mix of factors that have resulted in the sub-optimal evolution of non-proliferation controls. Geo-strategic factors have often been placed above non-proliferation matters and in the early nuclear age this all but prevented cooperation on international nuclear trade controls. The limitations of this approach were recognised particularly after the Chinese nuclear test in 1964 and the Indian test of 1974, but a variety of factors restrained efforts to coordinate adoption of controls including the ever-increasing number of actors involved, the imperfect information picture, and the mixed benefits of nuclear commerce and nuclear restraint. Combined with the imperatives of nuclear use and nuclear disarmament, this has meant that non-proliferation controls have evolved in a suboptimal way.

Implications of this research

This book has conceptualised non-proliferation as a collective action problem and examined the evolution of controls since the early nuclear age to the present day. In addition to providing new insight into why controls evolved in a sub-optimal way, it is argued that conceptualising non-proliferation in this way has lessons for non-proliferation practice today. This last section before the overall book conclusion offers some insights from this research for non-proliferation policy and practice in the future.

First, it is apparent that the problem of nuclear proliferation is an intractable one. Short of an entirely different system of control being introduced such as that envisioned in the 1940s, the international control framework is likely to be inadequate to prevent nuclear proliferation. There are a number of reasons for this. The ever-growing number of actors – be they states or otherwise – involved in nuclear technology increases the coordination challenge around controls. In particular, the move to 'universalise' controls, which would be necessary for an effective system, results in it becoming necessary to engage actors driven by factors other than non-proliferation. Beyond such vested interests, there are also simply communication challenges with coordinating among large numbers of states including with regards to sharing sensitive information noted in the following.

Second, continuity of meetings is necessary to sustain momentum toward controls. However, there are also good reasons to 'forum shop' and allow for the passage of time. For example, in switching discussions from the NSG to the Zangger Committee in the 1980s, the UK was able to apply pressure for more countries (and particularly Switzerland) to adopt controls. Moreover, the gap in meetings of the NSG allowed for the change in the political situation in a number of countries, including most notably France, which allowed progress on controls when such progress had appeared impossible. Thus far, the evolution of international nuclear controls has proven to operate like a ratchet in which controls largely do not regress. As such, it can be expected that controls will gradually continue to improve over time.

Third, while forum shopping and gaps between meetings can have positive effects, it is important to have forums in which to raise concerns. The decision by the UK not to put its evidence about Pakistani procurement of dual-use goods to the NSG in the late 1970s is an example of this. The decision was taken so as not to give the Soviet Union information that it could leverage for geopolitical purposes. However, the result was that there was no coordinated international discussion of controls from 1978 until the early 1980s. These were key years for Pakistan's procurement.

Fourth, while perhaps unwelcome for non-proliferation practitioners, evidence from the history of controls is that non-proliferation will often be given a lower priority than other topics deemed to be of geo-strategic importance. This is particularly apparent with regards to Pakistan's program in the 1980s. However, it is also true with regards to other episodes, including the US–India deal of the mid-2000s.

Fifth, the technicalities of the non-proliferation issue create a barrier to effective policymaking. This is exemplified in the actions of Lewis Strauss who 'failed to comprehend' the difference between types of reactor in the 1950s. However, it is also true with regards to the overemphasis on reprocessing controls in the Carter administration and the focus on centrifuge proliferation in the 1980s instead on all methods of separating uranium. There has been a tendency to focus on the hot topic of the day rather than to look comprehensively at controls.

Sixth, the lack of common ground between international nuclear trade controls and safeguards is problematic. This is manifest, for example, in the fact that the IAEA has not updated the annex of the Additional Protocol in line with changes to the NSG lists. However, it speaks to the broader tensions that exist in needing all countries, including those with ideologically different outlooks, to be engaged in international nuclear controls. This is thus an example that demonstrates the non-proliferation collective action problem continues to impair controls to this day.

Conclusion

The international nuclear non-proliferation trade control regime as it exists today is the result of several decades of evolution. It is based upon several underpinning structural elements, including international treaties, informal supplier groups, and UN Security Council decisions. These elements encompass a variety of actors including international organisations, states, and non-state actors. While progressively strengthened and broadened over the decades, it should be recognised that the nuclear trade control regime as it stands today remains imperfect. It is not yet loophole-free and it has evolved in a sub-optimal way.

The reasons for this are complex but also understandable. On the one hand, it is clear that a non-proliferation norm now exists and that states assign value to the goal of non-proliferation. On the other hand, states and non-state actors continue to take decisions that place shorter-term self-interest ahead of longer-term collective interests in this field. This, it has been argued, is a result of the existence of a non-proliferation collective action problem and is a direct result of the structure of the non-proliferation regime, which itself reflects the broader international environment. Indeed, this collective action problem, in turn was a direct result of the US decision to proceed with the Atoms for Peace initiative in the absence of an effective system of control as had been envisioned in the 1940s under the UN Atomic Energy Commission. The reason the US did this was to use the initiative as an instrument of the Cold War.

Starting from this foundation, the reasons for the sub-optimal evolution of the non-proliferation regime are readily apparent. With no rules agreed in advance, the actors involved in the provision of nuclear assistance would make decisions based upon their evolving self-interest. In the early nuclear age, such decisions were taken without the benefit of expertise on nuclear technology and without existing knowledge about how other actors would act. States would continue to be hesitant to agree to impose controls unless they could be certain that other states would not cheat. In important cases, the development of trade controls has also been hampered by the fact that the interests of key states have been in direct conflict with non-proliferation principles. This was the case with India, for example, which was involved in the IAEA statute negotiations and wanted to keep open its options to develop nuclear weapons. It was true also of European states wanting to ensure IAEA safeguards did not prejudice how Euratom would function.

States have routinely recognised and sought to overcome the collective action problem associated with proliferation over the years. This has included efforts to secure agreement between likeminded states and to increase information sharing so as to dispel rumours that could lead to distrust. Nonetheless, such efforts have been hampered by the sheer number of actors capable of providing nuclear technology. It seems unlikely that such bottom-up approaches to non-proliferation could ever fully overcome the collective action problem, and the adoption of UNSCRs can be understood as a response to this. Such resolutions are a means to impose a form of top-down 'external regulation', which is one way in which collective action problems may potentially be overcome.

Non-proliferation trade controls as an element of the non-proliferation regime have been central to maintaining international peace and security despite their flaws. Without non-proliferation trade controls it is possible – or perhaps even likely – that more states would by now possess nuclear weapons, increasing the likelihood of their use by design, accident, or miscalculation. The regime is not perfect principally because it has evolved in response to 'shocks' without addressing underpinning structural issues. The launch of the Atoms for Peace initiative absent an effective system of control created an environment in which vested interests could frustrate efforts to design and implement effective controls.

Alternatives can and indeed have been envisioned. These have included the plan for international control for atomic energy as pursued by the UN Atomic Energy Commission, and the development of a comprehensive non-proliferation regime that would build upon the types of measures contained in the Joint Comprehensive Plan of Action. In reality, however, in order to bring about either of these approaches, progress would be required on the question of disarmament which seems like a distant prospect.

In the absence of comprehensive controls, which can only be foreseen as a complement to multilateral nuclear disarmament, the collective action problem associated with the problem of nuclear proliferation will persist. As a result, it is likely that a multi-pronged approach will be taken in relation to non-proliferation trade controls. This will continue to involve continued efforts to utilise the UN Security Council and perhaps the General Assembly to secure universally binding non-proliferation arrangements. Multilateral arrangements between so-called likeminded states will also likely persist. Finally, efforts to improve national implementation of non-proliferation trade controls are also likely to continue.

Whether this patchwork approach to non-proliferation trade controls can be effective is unclear. Given the fact that measures such as the IAEA's Additional Protocol are not yet universal and that many countries have not yet adopted effective non-proliferation trade controls, it is feasible that more states could proliferate in the future. Nonetheless, conceptualising non-proliferation as a collective action problem is helpful in formulating ideas on how the effectiveness of non-proliferation trade controls could be maximised even despite foreseeable limitations in the non-proliferation control framework.

Notes

1 Although as Chapter 5 noted, the Nukam case resulted in the evolution of non-proliferation controls in Germany even through the case probably did not take place.
2 Rockwood, L., 'The IAEA's state-level concept and the law of unintended consequences'. Available online at: www.armscontrol.org/act/2014_09/Features/The-IAEAs-State-Level-Concept-and-the-Law-of-Unintended-Consequences.
3 "Summary of meeting in the White House, 16 January 1954", Ann Whitman files, Confidential File Subject Series, Box 12. DDEPL (5266).
4 Ibid., Smith, G., *Disarming diplomat.*
5 "German Classification of Centrifuge Work", 4 October 1960. S.27 Cooperation in the Diffusion Field, BSA.
6 Moberly to Alston R.J., Joint Nuclear Unit, 'Pakistan Inverters', 12 December 1978, FCO Files, BSA.
7 For example, see Stewart, I., 'Export controls at the crossroads', *Bulletin of the Atomic Scientists*, 15 October 2015.
8 Anderson to Bush, 5 August 1942, NARA, RG59 Box 56, USNARA.
9 Resolution 1/46, United Nations General Assembly, New York, 24 January 1946.
10 Chernobyl and other nuclear accidents have not been discussed in this book as such accidents do not directly relate to the question of nuclear supply. Despite such accidents, metrics such as the amount of energy generated from nuclear power over time appear relatively consistent, with installed capacity actually tending upwards. See: Outline history of nuclear energy, World Nuclear Association. Available online at: www.world-nuaclear.org/information-library/current-and-future-generation/outline-history-of-nuclear-energy.aspx (accessed 28 December 2021).
11 Minutes of a US Cabinet Meeting on the Atomic bomb, 21 September 1945, President's Secretary's Files Containers 134–139, HSTPL.
12 Atomic Energy Advisory Panel meeting, 25 July 1963, 14003-J2-3-40, LAC.
13 "Summary of meeting in the White House, 16 January 1954", Ann Whitman files, Confidential File Subject Series, Box 12. DDWPL (5266).
14 International Atomic Energy Agency, brief for 12 power meeting, safeguarding of assistance given by the International Atomic Energy Agency, FO371/123086, BNA (UK 361).
15 Discussion at the 276th Meeting of the National Security Council, 9 February 1956. Ann Whitman files, Administration Series, Box 7, DDEPL (4917).
16 "Report on the Conference on the Statute of the International Atomic Energy Agency – New York – September 20 – October 26, 1956", FCO371/123088, BSA.

Bibliography

Anderson to Bush, 5 August 1942, NARA, RG59 Box 56, USNARA.
Atomic Energy Advisory Panel meeting, 25 July 1963, 14003-J2-3-40, LAC.
Discussion at the 276th Meeting of the National Security Council, 9 February 1956. Ann Whitman files, Administration Series, Box 7, DDEPL.

"German Classification of Centrifuge Work", 4 October 1960. S.27 Cooperation in the Diffusion Field, BSA.
International Atomic Energy Agency, brief for 12 power meeting, safeguarding of assistance given by the International Atomic Energy Agency, FO371/123086, BNA.
Minutes of a US Cabinet Meeting on the Atomic bomb, 21 September 1945, President's Secretary's Files Containers 134–139, HSTPL.
Moberly to Alston R.J. Joint Nuclear Unit, 'Pakistan Inverters', 12 December 1978, FCO Files, BSA.
Outline history of nuclear energy, World Nuclear Association. Available online at: www.world-nuaclear.org/information-library/current-and-future-generation/outline-history-of-nuclear-energy.aspx (Accessed 28 December 2021).
"Report on the Conference on the Statute of the International Atomic Energy Agency – New York – September 20 – October 26, 1956", FCO371/123088, BSA.
Resolution 1/46, United Nations General Assembly, New York, 24 January 1946.
Rockwood, L. The IAEA's state-level concept and the law of unintended consequences. Available online at: www.armscontrol.org/act/2014_09/Features/The-IAEAs-State-Level-Concept-and-the-Law-of-Unintended-Consequences.
Smith, G. *Disarming diplomat: The memoirs of Ambassador Gerard C. Smith, Arms Control Negotiator*, Madison Books, 1996.
Stewart, I. Export controls at the crossroads, *Bulletin of the Atomic Scientists*, 15 October 2015.
"Summary of meeting in the White House, 16 January 1954", Ann Whitman files, Confidential File Subject Series, Box 12. DDEPL (5266).

Annexes

Annex 1: Declaration on atomic bomb by President Truman and Prime Ministers Attlee and King[1]

Washington, November 15, 1945

The President of the United States, the Prime Minister of the United Kingdom, and the Prime Minister of Canada have issued the following statement.

1 We recognize that the application of recent scientific discoveries to the methods and practice of war has placed at the disposal of mankind means of destruction hitherto unknown, against which there can be no adequate military defense, and in the employment of which no single nation can in fact have a monopoly.

2 We desire to emphasize that the responsibility for devising means to insure that the new discoveries shall be used for the benefit of mankind, instead of as a means of destruction, rests not on our nations alone but upon the whole civilized world. Nevertheless, the progress that we have made in the development and use of atomic energy demands that we take an initiative in the matter, and we have accordingly met together to consider the possibility of international action:—

   a To prevent the use of atomic energy for destructive purposes.

   b To promote the use of recent and future advances in scientific knowledge, particularly in the utilization of atomic energy, for peaceful and humanitarian ends.

3 We are aware that the only complete protection for the civilized world from the destructive use of scientific knowledge lies in the prevention of war. No system of safeguards that can be devised will of itself provide an effective guarantee against production of atomic weapons by a nation bent on aggression. Nor can we ignore the possibility of the development of other weapons, or of new methods of warfare, which may constitute as great a threat to civilization as the military use of atomic energy.

4 Representing as we do, the three countries which possess the knowledge essential to the use of atomic energy, we declare at the outset our willingness, as a first contribution, to proceed with the exchange of fundamental scientific information and the interchange of scientists and scientific literature for peaceful ends with any nation that will fully reciprocate.

5 We believe that the fruits of scientific research should be made available to all nations, and that freedom of investigation and free interchange of ideas are essential to the progress of knowledge. In pursuance of this policy, the basic scientific information essential to the development of atomic energy for peaceful purposes has already been made available to the world. It is our intention that all further information of this character that may become available from time to time shall be similarly treated. We trust that other nations will adopt the same policy, thereby creating an atmosphere of reciprocal confidence in which political agreement and cooperation will flourish.

6 We have considered the question of the disclosure of detailed information concerning the practical industrial application of atomic energy. The military exploitation of atomic energy depends, in large part, upon the same methods and processes as would be required for industrial uses.

We are not convinced that the spreading of the specialized information regarding the practical application of atomic energy, before it is possible to devise effective, reciprocal, and enforceable safeguards acceptable to all nations, would contribute to a constructive solution of the problem of the atomic bomb.

On the contrary we think it might have the opposite effect. We are, however, prepared to share, on a reciprocal basis with others of the United Nations, detailed information concerning the practical industrial application of atomic energy just as soon as effective enforceable safeguards against its use for destructive purposes can be devised.

7 In order to attain the most effective means of entirely eliminating the use of atomic energy for destructive purposes and promoting its widest use for industrial and humanitarian purposes, we are of the opinion that at the earliest practicable date a commission should be set up under the United Nations Organization to prepare recommendations for submission to the organization.

The commission should be instructed to proceed with the utmost dispatch and should be authorized to submit recommendations from time to time dealing with separate phases of its work.

In particular the commission should make specific proposals:

a For extending between all nations the exchange of basic scientific information for peaceful ends,

b For control of atomic energy to the extent necessary to insure its use only for peaceful purposes,

c For the elimination from national armaments of atomic weapons and of all other major weapons adaptable to mass destruction,

d For effective safeguards by way of inspection and other means to protect complying states against the hazards of violations and evasions.

8 The work of the commission should proceed by separate stages, the successful completion of each one of which will develop the necessary confidence of the world before the next stage is undertaken. Specifically, it is considered that the commission might well devote its attention first to the wide exchange of scientists and scientific information, and as a second stage to the development of full knowledge concerning natural resources of raw materials.

9 Faced with the terrible realities of the application of science to destruction, every nation will realize more urgently than before the overwhelming need to maintain the rule of law among nations and to banish the scourge of war from the earth This can only be brought about by giving wholehearted support to the United Nations Organization and by consolidating and extending its authority, thus creating conditions of mutual trust in which all peoples will be free to devote themselves to the arts of peace. It is our firm resolve to work without reservation to achieve these ends

The City of Washington,
The White House.
November 15, 1945.
Signed:
HARRY S. TRUMAN, President of the United States
C. R. ATTLEE, Prime Minister of the United Kingdom
W. L. MacKENZIE KING, Prime Minister of Canada

Note

1 Text from www.nuclearfiles.org/menu/key-issues/nuclear-energy/history/dec-truma-atlee-king_1945-11-15.htm (accessed 29 August 2018).

Annex 2: Atoms for Peace Speech

Address by Mr. Dwight D. Eisenhower, President of the United States of America, to the 470th Plenary Meeting of the United Nations General Assembly

Tuesday, 8 December 1953, 2:45 p.m.

General Assembly President: Mrs. Vijaya Lakshmi Pandit (India)

Madam President and Members of the General Assembly,

When Secretary General Hammarskjold's invitation to address the General Assembly reached me in Bermuda, I was just beginning a series of conferences with the prime Ministers and Foreign Ministers of the United Kingdom and France. Our subject was some of the problems that beset our world. During the remainder of the Bermuda Conference, I had constantly in mind that ahead of me lay a great honour. That honour is mine today as I stand here, privileged to address the General Assembly of the United Nations.

At the same time that I appreciate the distinction of addressing you, I have a sense of exhilaration as I look upon this Assembly. Never before in history has so much hope for so many people been gathered together in a single organization. Your deliberations and decisions during these sombre years have already realized part of those hopes.

But the great tests and the great accomplishments still lie ahead. And in the confident expectation of those accomplishments, I would use the office which, for the time being, I hold, to assure you that the Government of the United States will remain steadfast in its support of this body. This we shall do in the conviction that you will provide a great share of the wisdom, of the courage and of the faith which can bring to this world lasting peace for all nations, and happiness and well-being for all men.

Clearly, it would not be fitting for me to take this occasion to present to you a unilateral American report on Bermuda. Nevertheless, I assure you that in our deliberations on that lovely island we sought to invoke those same great concepts of universal peace and human dignity which are so clearly etched in your Charter. Neither would it be a measure of this great opportunity to recite, however hopefully, pious platitudes. I therefore decided that this occasion warranted my saying to you some of the things that have been on the minds and hearts of my legislative and executive associates, and on mine, for a great many months: thoughts I had originally planned to say primarily to the American people.

I know that the American people share my deep belief that if a danger exists in the world, it is a danger shared by all; and equally, that if hope exists in the mind of one nation, that hope should be shared by all. Finally, if there is to be advanced any proposal designed to ease even by the smallest measure the tensions of today's world, what more appropriate audience could there be than the members of the General Assembly of the United Nations.

I feel impelled to speak today in a language that in a sense is new, one which I, who have spent so much of my life in the military profession, would have preferred never to use. That new language is the language of atomic warfare.

The atomic age has moved forward at such a pace that every citizen of the world should have some comprehension, at least in comparative terms, of the extent of this development, of the utmost significance to every one of us. Clearly, if the peoples of the world are to conduct an intelligent search for peace, they must be armed with the significant facts of today's existence.

My recital of atomic danger and power is necessarily stated in United States terms, for these are the only incontrovertible facts that I know, I need hardly point out to this Assembly, however, that this subject is global, not merely national in character.

On 16 July 1945, the United States set off the world's biggest atomic explosion. Since that date in 1945, the United States of America has conducted forty-two test explosions. Atomic bombs are more than twenty-five times as powerful as the weapons with which the atomic age dawned, while hydrogen weapons are in the ranges of millions of tons of TNT equivalent.

Today, the United States stockpile of atomic weapons, which, of course, increases daily, exceeds by many times the total equivalent of the total of all bombs and all shells that came from every plane and every gun in every theatre of war in all the years of the Second World War. A single air group whether afloat or land based, can now deliver to any reachable target a destructive cargo exceeding in power all the bombs that fell on Britain in all the Second World War.

In size and variety, the development of atomic weapons has been no less remarkable. The development has been such that atomic weapons have virtually achieved conventional status within our armed services. In the United States, the Army, the Navy, the Air Force and the Marine Corps are all capable of putting this weapon to military use.

But the dread secret and the fearful engines of atomic might are not ours alone.

In the first place, the secret is possessed by our friends and allies, the United Kingdom and Canada, whose scientific genius made a tremendous contribution to our original discoveries and the designs of atomic bombs.

The secret is also known by the Soviet Union. The Soviet Union has informed us that, over recent years, it has devoted extensive resources to atomic weapons. During this period the Soviet Union has exploded a series of atomic devices, including at least one involving thermo-nuclear reactions.

If at one time the United States possessed what might have been called a monopoly of atomic power, that monopoly ceased to exist several years ago. Therefore, although our earlier start has permitted us to accumulate what is today a great quantitative advantage, the atomic realities of today comprehend two facts of even greater significance. First, the knowledge now possessed by several nations will eventually be shared by others, possibly all others.

Second, even a vast superiority in numbers of weapons, and a consequent capability of devastating retaliation, is no preventive, of itself, against the fearful material damage and toll of human lives that would be inflicted by surprise aggression.

The free world, at least dimly aware of these facts, has naturally embarked on a large programme of warning and defence systems. That programme will be accelerated and extended. But let no one think that the expenditure of vast sums for weapons and systems of defence can guarantee absolute safety for the cities and citizens of any nation. The awful arithmetic of the atomic bomb doesn't permit of any such easy solution. Even against the most powerful defence, an aggressor in possession of the effective minimum number of atomic bombs fora surprise attack could probably place a sufficient number of his bombs on the chosen targets to cause hideous damage.

Should such an atomic attack be launched against the United States, our reactions would be swift and resolute. But for me to say that the defence capabilities of the United States are such that they could inflict terrible losses upon an aggressor, for me to say that the retaliation capabilities of the United States are so great that such an aggressor's land would be laid waste, all this, while fact, is not the true expression of the purpose and the hopes of the United States.

To pause there would be to confirm the hopeless finality of a belief that two atomic colossi are doomed malevolently to eye each other indefinitely across a trembling world. To stop there would be to accept helplessly the probability of civilization destroyed, the annihilation of the irreplaceable heritage of mankind handed down to us from generation to generation, and the condemnation of mankind to begin all over again the age-old struggle upward from savagery towards decency, and right, and justice. Surely no sane member of the human race could discover victory in such desolation. Could anyone wish his name to be coupled by history with such human degradation and destruction? Occasional pages of history do record the faces of the "great destroyers", but the whole book of history reveals mankind's never-ending quest for peace and mankind's God-given capacity to build.

It is with the book of history, and not with isolated pages, that the United States will ever wish to be identified. My country wants to be constructive, not destructive. It wants agreements, not wars, among nations. It wants itself to live in freedom and in the confidence that the peoples of every other nation enjoy equally the right of choosing their own way of life.

So my country's purpose is to help us to move out of the dark chamber of horrors into the light, to find a way by which the minds of men, the hopes of men, the souls of men everywhere, can move forward towards peace and happiness and well-being.

In this quest, I know that we must not lack patience. I know that in a world divided, such as ours today, salvation cannot be attained by one dramatic act. I know that many steps will have to be taken over many months before the world can look at itself one day and truly realize that a new climate of mutually peaceful confidence is abroad in the world. But I know, above all else, that we must start to take these steps - now.

The United States and its allies, the United Kingdom and France, have over the past months tried to take some of these steps. Let no one say that we shun the conference table. On the record has long stood the request of the United States, the United Kingdom and France to negotiate with the Soviet Union the problems of a divided Germany. On that record has long stood the request of the same three nations to negotiate an Austrian peace treaty. On the same record still stands the request of the United Nations to negotiate the problems of Korea.

Most recently we have received from the Soviet Union what is in effect an expression of willingness to hold a four-Power meeting. Along with our allies, the United Kingdom and France, we were pleased to see that this note did not contain the unacceptable pre-conditions previously put forward. As you already know from our joint Bermuda communique, the United States, the United Kingdom and France have agreed promptly to meet with the Soviet Union.

The Government of the United States approaches this conference with hopeful sincerity. We will bend every effort of our minds to the single purpose of emerging from that conference with tangible results towards peace, the only true way of lessening international tension.

We never have, and never will, propose or suggest that the Soviet Union surrender what rightly belongs to it. We will never say that the peoples of the USSR are an enemy with whom we have no desire ever to deal or mingle in friendly and fruitful relationship.

On the contrary, we hope that this coming conference may initiate a relationship with the Soviet Union which will eventually bring about a freer mingling of the peoples of the East and of the West - the one sure, human way of developing the understanding required for confident and peaceful relations.

Instead of the discontent which is now settling upon Eastern Germany, occupied Austria and the countries of Eastern Europe, we seek a harmonious family of free European nations, with none a threat to the other, and least of all a threat to the peoples of the USSR. Beyond the turmoil and strife and misery of Asis, we seek peaceful opportunity for these peoples to develop their natural resources and to elevate their lot.

These are not idle words or shallow visions. Behind them lies a story of nations lately come to independence, not as a result of war, but through free grant or peaceful negotiation. There is a record already written of assistance gladly given by nations of the West to needy peoples and to those suffering the temporary effects of famine, drought and natural disaster. These are deeds of peace. They speak more loudly than promises or protestations of peaceful intent.

But I do not wish to rest either upon the reiteration of past proposals or the restatement of past deeds. The gravity of the time is such that every new avenue of peace, no matter how dimly discernible, should be explored.

There is at least one new avenue of peace which has not been well explored -an avenue now laid out by the General Assembly of the United Nations.

In its resolution of 28 November 1953 (resolution 715 (VIII)) this General Assembly suggested: "that the Disarmament Commission study the desirability of establishing a sub-committee consisting of representatives of the Powers principally involved, which should seek in private an acceptable solution and report...on such a solution to the General Assembly and to the Security Council not later than 1 September 1954".

The United States, heeding the suggestion of the General Assembly of the United Nations, is instantly prepared to meet privately with such other countries as may be "principally involved", to seek "an acceptable solution" to the atomic armaments race which overshadows not only the peace, but the very life, of the world.

We shall carry into these private or diplomatic talks a new conception. The United States would seek more than the mere reduction or elimination of atomic materials for military purposes. It is not enough to take this weapon out of the hands of the soldiers. It must be put into the hands of those who will know how to strip its military casing and adapt it to the arts of peace.

The United States knows that if the fearful trend of atomic military build-up can be reversed, this greatest of destructive forces can be developed into a great boon, for the benefit of all mankind. The United States knows that peaceful power from atomic energy is no dream of the future. The capability, already proved, is here today. Who can doubt that, if the entire body of the world's scientists and engineers had adequate amounts of fissionable material with which to test and develop their ideas, this capability would rapidly be transformed into universal, efficient and economic usage?

To hasten the day when fear of the atom will begin to disappear from the minds the people and the governments of the East and West, there are certain steps that can be taken now.

I therefore make the following proposal.

The governments principally involved, to the extent permitted by elementary prudence, should begin now and continue to make joint contributions from their stockpiles of normal uranium and fissionable materials to an international atomic energy agency. We would expect that such an agency would be set up under the aegis of the United Nations. The ratios of contributions, the procedures and other details would properly be within the scope of the "private conversations" I referred to earlier.

The United States is prepared to undertake these explorations in good faith. Any partner of the United States acting in the same good faith will find the United States a not unreasonable or ungenerous associate.

Undoubtedly, initial and early contributions to this plan would be small in quantity. However, the proposal has the great virtue that it can be undertaken without the irritations and mutual suspicions incident to any attempt to set up a completely acceptable system of world-wide inspection and control.

The atomic energy agency could be made responsible for the impounding, storage and protection of the contributed fissionable and other materials. The ingenuity of our scientists will provide special safe conditions under which such a bank of fissionable material can be made essentially immune to surprise seizure.

The more important responsibility of this atomic energy agency would be to devise methods whereby this fissionable material would be allocated to serve the peaceful pursuits of mankind. Experts would be mobilized to apply atomic energy to the needs of agriculture, medicine and other peaceful activities. A special purpose would be to provide abundant electrical energy in the power-starved areas of the world.

Thus the contributing Powers would be dedicating some of their strength to serve the needs rather than the fears of mankind.

The United States would be more than willing - it would be proud to take up with others "principally involved" the development of plans whereby such peaceful use of atomic energy would be expedited.

Of those "principally involved" the Soviet Union must, of course, be one.

I would be prepared to submit to the Congress of the United States, and with every expectation of approval, any such plan that would, first, encourage world-wide investigation into the most effective peacetime uses of fissionable material, and with the certainty that the investigators had all the material needed for the conducting of all experiments that were appropriate; second, begin to diminish the potential destructive power of the world's atomic stockpiles; third, allow all peoples of all nations to see that, in this enlightened age, the great Powers of the earth, both of the East and of the West, are interested in human aspirations first rather than in building up the armaments of war; fourth, open up a new channel for peaceful discussion and initiative at least a new approach to the many difficult problems that must be solved in both private and public conversations if the world is to shake off the inertia imposed by fear and is to make positive progress towards peace.

Against the dark background of the atomic bomb, the United States does not wish merely to present strength, but also the desire and the hope for peace. The coming months will be fraught with fateful decisions. In this Assembly, in the capitals and military headquarters of the world, in the hearts of men everywhere, be they governed or governors, may they be the decisions which will lead this world out of fear and into peace.

To the making of these fateful decisions, the United States pledges before you, and therefore before the world, its determination to help solve the fearful atomic dilemma - to devote its entire heart and mind to finding the way by which the miraculous inventiveness of man shall not be dedicated to his death, but consecrated to his life.

I again thank representatives for the great honour they have done me in inviting me to appear before them and in listening to me so graciously.

Annex 3: Bernard Baruch, Speech before the first session of the United Nations Atomic Energy Commission, Hunter College, New York, June 14, 1946

My Fellow Members of the United Nations Atomic Energy Commission, and My Fellow Citizens of the World:

We are here to make a choice between the quick and the dead.

That is our business.

Behind the black portent of the new atomic age lies a hope which, seized upon with faith, can work our salvation. If we fail, then we have damned every man to be the slave of Fear. Let us not deceive ourselves: We must elect World Peace or World Destruction.

Science has torn from nature a secret so vast in its potentialities that our minds cower from the terror it creates. Yet terror is not enough to inhibit the use of the atomic bomb. The terror created by weapons has never stopped man from employing them. For each new weapon a defense has been produced, in time. But now we face a condition in which adequate defense does not exist.

Science, which gave us this dread power, shows that it can be made a giant help to humanity, but science does not show us how to prevent its baleful use. So we have been appointed to obviate that peril by finding a meeting of the minds and the hearts of our peoples. Only in the will of mankind lies the answer.

It is to express this will and make it effective that we have been assembled. We must provide the mechanism to assure that atomic energy is used for peaceful purposes and preclude its use in war. To that end, we must provide immediate, swift, and sure punishment of those who violate the agreements that are reached by the nations. Penalization is essential if peace is to be more than a feverish interlude between wars. And, too, the United Nations can prescribe individual responsibility and punishment on the principles applied at Nuremberg by the Union of Soviet Socialist Republics, the United Kingdom, France and the United States – a formula certain to benefit the world's future.

In this crisis, we represent not only our governments but, in a larger way, we represent the peoples of the world. We must remember that the peoples do not belong to the governments but that the governments belong to the peoples. We must answer their demands; we must answer the world's longing for peace and security.

In that desire the United States shares ardently and hopefully. The search of science for the absolute weapon has reached fruition in this country. But she stands ready to proscribe and destroy this instrument – to lift its use from death to life – if the world will join in a pact to that end.

In our success lies the promise of a new life, freed from the heart-stopping fears that now beset the world. The beginning of victory for the great ideals for which millions have bled and died lies in building a workable plan. Now we approach fulfillment of the aspirations of mankind. At the end of the road lies the fairer, better, surer life we crave and mean to have.

Only by a lasting peace are liberties and democracies strengthened and deepened. War is their enemy. And it will not do to believe that any of us can escape war's devastation. Victor, vanquished, and neutrals alike are affected physically, economically and morally.

Against the degradation of war we can erect a safeguard. That is the guerdon for which we reach. Within the scope for the formula we outline here there will be found, to those who seek it, the essential elements of our purpose. Others will see only emptiness. Each of us carries his own mirror in which is reflected hope or determined desperation, courage or cowardice.

There is a famine throughout the world today. It starves men's bodies. But there is a greater famine – the hunger of men's spirit. That starvation can be cured by the conquest of fear, and the substitution of hope, from which springs faith – faith in each other, faith that we want to work together toward salvation, and determination that those who threaten the peace and safety shall be punished.

The peoples of these democracies gathered here have a particular concern with our answer, for their peoples hate war. They will have a heavy exaction to make of those who fail to provide an escape. They are not afraid of an internationalism that protects; they are unwilling to be fobbed off by mouthings about narrow sovereignty, which is today's phrase for yesterday's isolation.

The basis of a sound foreign policy, in this new age, for all the nations here gathered, is that anything that happens, no matter where or how, which menaces the peace of the world, or the economic stability, concerns each and all of us.

That roughly, may be said to be the central theme of the United Nations. It is with that thought we begin consideration of the most important subject that can engage mankind – life itself.

Let there be no quibbling about the duty and the responsibility of this group and of the governments we represent. I was moved, in the afternoon of my life, to add my effort to gain the world's quest, by the broad mandate under which we were created. The resolution of the General Assembly, passed January 24, 1946 in London reads:

Section V. Terms of References of the Commission

The Commission shall proceed with the utmost despatch and enquire into all phases of the problem, and make such recommendations from time to time with respect to them as it finds possible. In particular the Commission shall make specific proposals:

1 For extending between all nations the exchange of basic scientific information for peaceful ends;
2 For control of atomic energy to the extent necessary to ensure its use only for peaceful purposes;
3 For the elimination from national armaments of atomic weapons and of all other major weapons adaptable to mass destruction;
4 For effective safeguards by way of inspection and other means to protect complying States against the hazards of violations and evasions.

The work of the Commission should proceed by separate stages, the successful completion of each of which will develop the necessary confidence of the world before the next stage is undertaken.

Our mandate rests, in text and spirit, upon the outcome of the Conference in Moscow of Messrs Molotov of the Union of Soviet Socialist Republics, Bevin of the United Kingdom, and Byrnes of the United States of America. The three Foreign Ministers on December 27, 1945 proposed the establishment of this body.

Their action was animated by a preceding conference in Washington on November 15, 1945, when the President of the United States, associated with Mr. Attlee, Prime Minister of the United Kingdom, and Mr. Mackenzie King, Prime Minister of Canada, stated that international control of the whole field of atomic energy was immediately essential. They proposed the formation of this body. In examining that source, the Agreed Declaration, it will be found that the fathers of the concept recognized the final means of world salvation – the abolition of war. Solemnly they wrote:

> We are aware that the only complete protection for the civilized world from the destructive use of scientific knowledge lies in the prevention of war. No system of safeguards that can be devised will of itself provide an effective guarantee against production of atomic weapons by a nation bent on aggression. Nor can we ignore the possibility of the development of other weapons, or of new methods of warfare, which may constitute as great a threat to civilization as the military use of atomic energy.

Through the historical approach I have outlined, we find ourselves here to test if man can produce, through his will and faith, the miracle of peace, just as he has, through science and skill, the miracle of the atom.

The United States proposes the creation of an International Atomic Development Authority, to which should be entrusted all phases of the development and use of atomic energy, starting with the raw material and including:

1 Managerial control or ownership of all atomic-energy activities potentially dangerous to world security.

2 Power to control, inspect, and license all other atomic activities.
3 The duty of fostering the beneficial uses of atomic energy.
4 Research and development responsibilities of an affirmative character intended to put the Authority in the forefront of atomic knowledge and thus to enable it to comprehend, and therefore to detect, misuse of atomic energy. To be effective, the Authority must itself be the world's leader in the field of atomic knowledge and development and thus supplement its legal authority with the great power inherent in possession of leadership in knowledge.

I offer this as a basis for beginning our discussion.

But I think the peoples we serve would not believe – and without faith nothing counts – that a treaty, merely outlawing possession or use of the atomic bomb, constitutes effective fulfillment of the instructions to this Commission. Previous failures have been recorded in trying the method of simple renunciation, unsupported by effective guaranties of security and armament limitation. No one would have faith in that approach alone.

Now, if ever, is the time to act for the common good. Public opinion supports a world movement toward security. If I read the signs aright, the peoples want a program not composed merely of pious thoughts but of enforceable sanctions – an international law with teeth in it.

We of this nation, desirous of helping to bring peace to the world and realizing the heavy obligations upon us arising from our possession of the means of producing the bomb and from the fact that it is part of our armament, are prepared to make our full contribution toward effective control of atomic energy.

When an adequate system for control of atomic energy, including the renunciation of the bomb as a weapon, has been agreed upon and put into effective operation and condign punishments set up for violations of the rules of control which are to be stigmatized as international crimes, we propose that:

1 Manufacture of atomic bombs shall stop;
2 Existing bombs shall be disposed of pursuant to the terms of the treaty; and
3 The Authority shall be in possession of full information as to the know-how for the production of atomic energy.

Let me repeat, so as to avoid misunderstanding: My country is ready to make its full contribution toward the end we seek, subject of course to our constitutional processes and to an adequate system of control becoming fully effective, as we finally work it out.

Now as to violations: In the agreement, penalties of as serious a nature as the nations may wish and as immediate and certain in their execution as possible should be fixed for:

1 Illegal possession or use of an atomic bomb;
2 Illegal possession, or separation, of atomic material suitable for use in an atomic bomb;
3 Seizure of any plant or other property belonging to or licensed by the Authority;
4 Willful interference with the activities of the Authority;
5 Creation or operation of dangerous projects in a manner contrary to, or in the absence of, a license granted by the international control body.

It would be a deception, to which I am unwilling to lend myself, were I not to say to you and to our peoples that the matter of punishment lies at the very heart of our present security system. It might as well be admitted, here and now, that the subject goes straight to the veto power contained in the Charter of the United Nations so far as it relates to the field of atomic energy. The Charter permits penalization only by concurrence of each of the five great powers – the Union of Soviet Socialist Republics, the United Kingdom, China, France, and the United States.

I want to make very plain that I am concerned here with the veto power only as it affects this particular problem. There must be no veto to protect those who violate their solemn agreements not to develop or use atomic energy for destructive purposes.

The bomb does not wait upon debate. To delay may be to die. The time between violation and preventive action or punishment would be all too short for extended discussion as to the course to be followed.

As matters now stand several years may be necessary for another country to produce a bomb, de novo. However, once the basic information is generally known, and the Authority has established producing plants for peaceful purposes in the several countries, an illegal seizure of such a plant might permit a malevolent nation to produce a bomb in 12 months, and if preceded by secret preparation and necessary facilities perhaps even in a much shorter time. The time required – the advance warning given of the possible use of a bomb – can only be generally estimated but obviously will depend upon many factors, including the success with which the Authority has been able to introduce elements of safety in the design of its plants and the degree to which illegal and secret preparation for the military use of atomic energy will have been eliminated. Presumably no nation would think of starting a war with only one bomb.

This shows how imperative speed is in detecting and penalizing violations.

The process of prevention and penalization – a problem of profound statecraft – is, as I read it, implicit in the Moscow statement, signed by the Union of Soviet Socialist Republics, the United States and the United Kingdom a few months ago.

But before a country is ready to relinquish any winning weapons it must have more than words to reassure it. It must have a guarantee of safety, not only against the offenders in the atomic area but against the illegal users of other weapons – bacteriological, biological, gas, perhaps – why not! – against war itself.

In the elimination of war lies our solution, for only then will nations cease to compete with one another in the production and use of dread 'secret' weapons which are evaluated solely by their capacity to kill. This devilish program takes us back not merely to the Dark Ages but from cosmos to chaos. If we succeed in finding a suitable way to control atomic weapons, it is reasonable to hope that we may also preclude the use of other weapons adaptable to mass destruction. When a man learns to say 'A' he can, if he chooses, learn the rest of the alphabet too.

Let this be anchored in our minds:

Peace is never long preserved by weight of metal or by an armament race. Peace can be made tranquil and secure only by understanding and agreement fortified by sanctions. We must embrace international cooperation or international disintegration.

Science has taught us how to put the atom to work. But to make it work for good instead of for evil lies in the domain dealing with the principles of human duty. We are now facing a problem more of ethics than of physics.

The solution will require apparent sacrifice in pride and in position, but better pain as the price of peace than death as the price of war.

I now submit the following measures as representing the fundamental features of a plan which would give effect to certain of the conclusions with I have epitomized.

1 General. The Authority should set up a thorough plan for control of the field of atomic energy, through various forms of ownership, dominion, licenses, operation, inspection, research, and management by competent personnel. After this is provided for, there should be as little interference as may be with the economic plans and the present private, corporate and state relationships in the several countries involved.
2 Raw Materials. The Authority should have as one of its earliest purposes to obtain and maintain complete and accurate information on world supplies of uranium and thorium. and to bring them under its dominion. The precise pattern of control for various types of deposits of such materials will have to depend upon the geological, mining, refining and economic facts involved in different situations.

The Authority should conduct continuous surveys so that it will have the most complete knowledge of the world geology of uranium and thorium. Only after all current information on world sources of uranium and thorium is known to us all can equitable plans be made for their productions, refining, and distribution.

3 Primary Production Plants. The Authority should exercise complete managerial control of the production of fissionable materials in dangerous quantities and must own and control the product of these plants.

4 Atomic Explosives. The Authority should be given sole and exclusive right to conduct research in the field of atomic explosives. Research activities in the field of atomic explosives are essential in order that the Authority may keep in the forefront of knowledge in the field of atomic energy and fulfill the objective of preventing illicit manufacture of bombs. Only by maintaining its position as the best-informed agency will the Authority be able to determine the line between intrinsically dangerous and non-dangerous activities.
5 Strategic Distribution of Activities and Materials. The activities entrusted exclusively to the Authority because they are intrinsically dangerous to security should be distributed throughout the world. Similarly, stockpiles of raw materials and fissionable materials should not be centralized.
6 Non-Dangerous Activities. A function of the Authority should be promotion of the peacetime benefits of atomic energy.

Atomic research (except in explosives), the use of research reactors, the production of radioactive tracers by means of non-dangerous reactors, the use of such tracers, and to some extent the production of power should be open to nations and their citizens under reasonable licensing arrangements from the Authority. Denatured materials, whose use we know also requires suitable safeguards, should be furnished for such purposes by the Authority under lease or other arrangement. Denaturing seems to have been overestimated by the public as a safety measure.

7 Definition of Dangerous and Non-Dangerous Activities. Although a reasonable dividing line can be drawn between dangerous and non-dangerous activities, it is not hard and fast. Provision should, therefore, be made to assure constant re-examination of the questions and to permit revision of the dividing line as changing conditions and new discoveries may require.
8 Operations of Dangerous Activities. Any plant dealing with uranium or thorium after it once reaches the potential of dangerous use must be not only subject to the most rigorous and competent inspection by the Authority, but its actual operation shall be under the management, supervision, and control of the Authority.
9 Inspection. By assigning intrinsically dangerous activities exclusively to the Authority, the difficulties of inspection are reduced. If the Authority is the only agency which may lawfully conduct dangerous activities, then visible operation by others than the Authority will constitute an unambiguous danger signal. Inspection will also occur in connection with the licensing functions of the Authority.
10 Freedom of Access. Adequate ingress and egress for all qualified representatives of the Authority must be assured. Many of the inspection activities of the Authority should grow out of and be incidental to its other functions. Important measures of inspection will be associated with the tight control of raw materials, for this is a keystone of the plan. The continuing activities of prospecting, survey, and research in relation to

raw materials will be designed not only to serve the affirmative development functions of the Authority but also to assure that no surreptitious operations are conducted in the raw-materials field by nations or their citizens.

11 Personnel. The personnel of the Authority should be recruited on a basis of proven competence but also so far as possible on an international basis.

12 Progress by Stages. A primary step in the creation of the system of control is the setting forth, in comprehensive terms, of the functions, responsibilities, powers, and limitations of the Authority. Once a charter for the Authority has been adopted, the Authority and the system of control for which it will be responsible will require time to become fully organized and effective. The plan of control will, therefore, have to come into effect in successive stages. These should be specifically fixed in the charter or means should be otherwise set forth in the charter for transitions from one stage to another, as contemplated in the resolution of the United Nations Assembly which created this Commission.

13 Disclosures. In the deliberations of the United Nations Commission on Atomic Energy, the United States is prepared to make available the information essential to a reasonable understanding of the proposals which it advocates. Further disclosures must be dependent, in the interests of all, upon the effective ratification of the treaty. When the Authority is actually created, the United States will join the other nations in making available the further information essential to that organization for the performance of its functions. As the successive stages of international control are reached, the United States will be prepared to yield, to the extent required by each stage, national control of activities in this field to the Authority.

14 International Control. There will be questions about the extent of control to be allowed to national bodies, when the Authority is established. Purely national authorities for control and development of atomic energy should to the extent necessary for the effective operation of the Authority be subordinate to it. This is neither an endorsement nor a disapproval of the creation of national authorities. The Commission should evolve a clear demarcation of the scope of duties and responsibilities of such national authorities.

And now I end. I have submitted an outline for present discussion. Our consideration will be broadened by the criticism of the United States proposals and by the plans of the other nations, which, it is to be hoped, will be submitted at their early convenience. I and my associates of the United States Delegation will make available to each member of this body books and pamphlets, including the Acheson-Lilienthal report, recently made by the United States Department of State, and the McMahon Committee Monograph No. I entitled 'Essential Information on Atomic Energy' relating to the McMahon bill recently passed by the United States Senate, which may prove of value in assessing the situation.

All of us are consecrated to making an end of gloom and hopelessness. It will not be an easy job. The way is long and thorny, but supremely worth traveling. All of us want to stand erect, with our faces to the sun, instead of being forced to burrow into the earth, like rats.

The pattern of salvation must be worked out by all for all.

The light at the end of the tunnel is dim, but our path seems to grow brighter as we actually begin our journey. We cannot yet light the way to the end. However, we hope the suggestions of my Government will be illuminating.

Let us keep in mind the exhortation of Abraham Lincoln, whose words, uttered at a moment of shattering national peril, form a complete text for our deliberation. I quote, paraphrasing slightly:

We cannot escape history. We of this meeting will be remembered in spite of ourselves. No personal significance or insignificance can spare one or another of us. The fiery trial through which we are passing will light us down in honor or dishonor to the latest generation.

We say we are for Peace. The world will not forget that we say this. We know how to save Peace. The world knows that we do. We, even we here, hold the power and have the responsibility.

We shall nobly save, or meanly lose, the last, best hope of earth. The way is plain, peaceful, generous, just – a way which, if followed, the world will forever applaud.

My thanks for your attention.

Index

For Product Safety Concerns and Information please contact our EU
representative GPSR@taylorandfrancis.com
Taylor & Francis Verlag GmbH, Kaufingerstraße 24, 80331 München, Germany

www.ingramcontent.com/pod-product-compliance
Ingram Content Group UK Ltd.
Pitfield, Milton Keynes, MK11 3LW, UK
UKHW021248190926
475569UK00002BA/55
9781032046877